COMPANY LAW IN PAKISTAN

(Companies Act 2017)

Muhammad Azhar Ghani

THE COMPANIES ACT, 2017

PROVISIONS APPLICABLE TO CREDITORS' VOLUNTARY WINDING UP

PROVISIONS APPLICABLE TO EVERY VOLUNTARY WINDING UP

SCHEDULES, TABLES, FORMS AND GENERAL RULES

SCHEDULES

Comparative Table
Companies Act 2017 and Companies Ordinance 1984

Companies Act 2017 Sections	Companies Ord. 1984 Sections	Companies Act 2017 Sections	Companies Ord. 1984 Sections	Companies Act 2017 Sections	Companies Ord. 1984 Sections
1	1	40	36	79	80
2	2	41	29	80	78A
3	5	42	42	81	83
4	6	43	-	82	84
5	7,8	44	-	83	86
6	9,10	45	43	84	88
7	12	46	44	85	92,93
8	13	47	45	86	95
9	14	48	109	87	95
10	37	49	-	88	95A
11	38	50	41	89	96
12	39	51	110	90	99
13	40	52	46	91	100
14	15	53	48	92	101
15	47	54	49	93	102
16	30	55	50	94	104
17	31	56	51	95	105
18	32	57	52, 57	96	104
19	146	58	90, 91	97	107
20	146(3),(5)	59	108	98	111
21	142	60	89	99	112
22	143	61	89	100	121,122
23	-	62	89	101	123
24	144	63	113	102	125
25	145	64	118	103	126
26	-	65	119	104	128
27	16	66	120	105	129
28	17	67	67	106	129(3)
29	18	68	71	107	130
30	19(2)	69	72	108	131
31	19	70	73	109	132
32	21	71	74	110	133
33	22	72	-	111	134
34	23	73	75	112	135
35	34	74	76	113	137
36	26	75	77	114	138
37	27	76	77(2)-	115	139
38	28	77	78	116	140
39	35	78	79	117	141
Companies	Companies	Companies	Companies	Companies	Companies

Act 2017 Sections	Ord. 1984 Sections	Act 2017 Sections	Ord. 1984 Sections	Act 2017 Sections	Ord. 1984 Sections
118	2(21)	160	179	202	211,212
119	147	161	180	203	213
120	147(2)	162	-	204	-
121	148	163	181	205	214
122	149	164	182	206	215
123	149(2)	165	183	207	216
124	150	166	-	208	-
125	151	167	184	209	219
126	152	168	185	210	-
127	153	169	186	211	-
128	154	170	191	212	217
129	155	171	188	213	218
130	156	172	-	214	225
131	157	173	-	215	-
132	158	174	192	216	-
133	159	175	189	217	226
134	160	176	193	218	227
135	160	177	190	219	229
136	160A	178	173	220	230
137	161	179	-	221	231
138	162	180	194	222	232
139	163	181	-	223	233
140	164	182	195	224	-
141	165	183	196	225	234
142	166	184	197	226	-
143	167	185	197A	227	236
144	-	186	198	228	237
145	168	187	199	229	238
146	169	188	200	230	239
147	170	189	201	231	240
148	171	190	202	232	241
149	-	191	203	233	242
150	172	192	-	234	-
151	173	193	204	235	243
152	173	194	204A	236	244
153	187	195	204A	237	245
154	174	196	206,207	238	246
155	-	197	205	239	247
156	-	198	205(4)	240	248
157	176	199	208	241	249
158	177	200	209	242	250
159	178	201	210	243	251-
Companies	Companies	Companies	Companies	Companies	Companies

Act 2017 Sections	Ord. 1984 Sections		Act 2017 Sections	Ord. 1984 Sections		Act 2017 Sections	Ord. 1984 Sections
244	-		286	290		328	353
245	-		287	291		329	341
246	252,253		288	292		330	342
247	254		289	293		331	343
248	255		290	294		332	344
249	-		291	295		333	345
250	258		292	296		334	346
251	257		293	297		335	347
252	259		294	298		336	348
253	260		295	299		337	333
254	261		296	300		338	336
255	262		297	301		339	337
256	263		298	302		340	338
257	265		299	303		341	349
258	-		300	304		342	350
259	266		301	305		343	354
260	267		302	306		344	355
261	268		303	307		345	356
262	269		304	309		346	357
263	270		305	310		347	358
264	271		306	311		348	359
265	272		307	313		349	360
266	273		308	314		350	361
267	274		309	315		351	362
268	275		310	316		352	362(5)
269	276		311	317		353	364
270	277		312	318		354	365
271	278		313	319		355	366
272	279		314	320		356	367
273	280		315	321		357	368
274	281		316	322		358	369
275	282		317	323		359	370
276	-		318	324		360	371
277	-		319	326		361	372
278	283		320	328		362	373,374
279	284		321	329		363	375
280	285		322	-		364	377
281	286		323	339		365	378
282	287		324	330		366	379
283	288		325	340		367	380
284	-		326	351		368	381
285	289		327	352		369	382
Companies	Companies		Companies	Companies		Companies	Companies

Act 2017 Sections	Ord. 1984 Sections	Act 2017 Sections	Ord. 1984 Sections	Act 2017 Sections	Ord. 1984 Sections
370	385	412	427	454	-
371	386	413	428	455	-
372	387	414	429	456	-
373	388	415	430	457	-
374	389	416	431	458	-
375	390	417	432	459	-
376	391	418	433	460	-
377	392	419	434	461	-
378	393	420	435	462	466
379	394	421	436	463	467
380	395	422	437	464	468
381	396	423	438	465	-
382	397	424	-	466	-
383	398	425	439	467	-
384	399	426	-	468	469
385	400	427	453	469	470
386	401	428	444	470	471
387	402	429	445	471	-
388	403	430	446	472	-
389	404	431	447	473	-
390	405	432	448	474	472
391	406	433	449	475	473
392	407	434	450	476	474
393	408	435	451	477	474
394	409	436	452	478	-
395	410	437	453	479	476
396	411	438	454	480	477
397	412	439	455	481	-
398	413	440	451,455	482	476(4)
399	414	441	456	483	478
400	415	442	457	484	479
401	416	443	458	485	479(4)
402	417	444	459	486	480
403	418	445	460	487	481
404	419	446	461	488	482
405	420	447	462	489	483
406	421	448	463	490	486
407	422	449	464	491	487
408	423	450	465	492	488
409	424	451	-	493	489
410	425	452	-	494	490
411	426	453	-	495	491
Companies	Companies	Companies	Companies	Companies	Companies

Act 2017 Sections	Ord. 1984 Sections	Act 2017 Sections	Ord. 1984 Sections	Act 2017 Sections	Ord. 1984 Sections
496	492	503	499	510	506B
497	493	504	501	511	507
498	494	505	503	512	506A
499	495	506	504	513	-
500	496	507	505	514	511
501	497	508	506	515	514
502	498	509	508		

THE COMPANIES ACT, 2017
(ACT NO. XIX OF 2017)[1]

An act to reform and re-enact the law relating to companies and for matters connected therewith

WHEREAS it is expedient to reform company law with the objective of facilitating corporatization and promoting development of corporate sector, encouraging use of technology and electronic means in conduct of business and regulation thereof, regulating corporate entities for protecting interests of shareholders, creditors, other stakeholders and general public, inculcating principles of good governance and safeguarding minority interests in corporate entities and providing an alternate mechanism for expeditious resolution of corporate disputes and matters arising out of or connected therewith;[2]

It is hereby enacted as follows:-

PART I

PRELIMINARY

1. **Short title, extent and commencement.**— (1) This Act may be called the Companies Act, 2017.

(2) It extends to the whole of Pakistan.

(3) This Act shall come into force at once, except section 456 which shall come into force on such date as the Federal Government or an authority or person authorized by it may, by notification in the official Gazette, appoint.

2. **Definitions.**—(1) In this Act, unless there is anything repugnant in the subject or context,-

(1)   **"advocate"** shall have the same meaning as assigned to it in section 2 of the Legal Practitioners and Bar Councils Act, 1973 (XXXV of 1973);

(2)   **"alter"** or **"alteration"** includes making of additions or omissions without substituting or destroying main scheme of the document;[3]

---

[1] The Companies Act, 2017 was published in in the Gazette of Pakistan, Extraordinary dated 31 May 2017 at pages 181-610.

[2] 2017 CLD 587; 2016 CLD 1164;2016 GBLR 266; 2010 PTD 2064; 2009 CLD 212; 2009 PLD 1; 2008 YLR 206; 2008 CLD 85; 2006 CLD 895;2006 PTD 584; 2003 CLD 1734; 2002 CLD 978; 2002 PTD 324; 1998 PLD 15; 1998 CLC 1890; 1996 PLD 543; 1987 MLD 2511; 1986 MLD 1870; 1984 CLC 256; 1984 PLD 139; 1982 CLC 2471; 1982 CLC 2137; 1979 SCMR 62; 1972 PLD 175; 1969 PLD 474; 1951 PLD 293

[3] 2000 PLD 78; 2000 PLD 83

(3) **"articles"** mean the articles of association of a company framed in accordance with the company law or this Act;

(4) **"associated companies"** and **"associated undertakings"** mean any two or more companies or undertakings, or a company and an undertaking, interconnected with each other in the following manner, namely:—

    (a) if a person who is owner or a partner or director of a company or undertaking, or who, directly or indirectly, holds or controls shares carrying not less than twenty percent of the voting power in such company or undertaking, is also the owner or partner or director of another company or undertaking, or directly or indirectly, holds or controls shares carrying not less than twenty percent of the voting power in that company or undertaking; or

    (b) if the companies or undertakings are under common management or control or one is the subsidiary of another; or

    (c) if the undertaking is a *modaraba* managed by the company;

and a person who is the owner of or a partner or director in a company or undertaking or, who so holds or controls shares carrying not less than ten percent of the voting power in a company or undertaking, shall be deemed to be an "associated person" of every such other person and of the person who is the owner of or a partner or director in such other company or undertaking, or who so holds or controls such shares in such company or undertaking:

    Provided that—

        (i) shares shall be deemed to be owned, held or controlled by a person if they are owned, held or controlled by that person or by the spouse or minor children of the person;

        (ii) directorship of a person or persons by virtue of nomination by concerned Minister-in-Charge of the Federal Government or as the case may be, a Provincial Government or a financial institution directly or indirectly owned or controlled by such Government or National Investment Trust; or

        (iii) directorship of a person appointed as an "independent director"; or

(iv)   shares owned by the National Investment Trust or a financial institution directly or indirectly owned or controlled by the Federal Government or a Provincial Government; or shares registered in the name of a central depository, where such shares are not beneficially owned by the central depository;

shall not be taken into account for determining the status of a company, undertaking or person as an associated company, associated undertaking or associated person;

(5)   **"authorised capital"** or "nominal capital" means such capital as is authorised by the memorandum of a company to be the maximum amount of share capital of the company;

(6)   **"banking company"** means a banking company as defined in clause (c) of section 5 of the Banking Companies Ordinance, 1962 (LVII of 1962)

(7)   **"beneficial ownership of shareholders or officer of a company"** means ownership of securities beneficially owned, held or controlled by any officer or substantial shareholder directly or indirectly, either by-

(a)   him or her;

(b)   the wife or husband of an officer of a company, not being herself or himself an officer of the company;

(c)   the minor son or daughter of an officer where "son" includes step-son and "daughter" includes step-daughter; and "minor" means a person under the age of eighteen years;

(d)   in case of a company, where such officer or substantial shareholder is a shareholder, but to the extent of his proportionate shareholding in the company:

Provided that **"control"** in relation to securities means the power to exercise a controlling influence over the voting power attached thereto:

Provided further that in case the substantial shareholder is a non-natural person, only those securities will be treated beneficially owned by it, which are held in its name.

Explanation. --For the purpose of this Act **"substantial shareholder"**, in relation to a company, means a person who has an interest in shares of a company-

(a)   the nominal value of which is equal to or more than ten per cent of the issued share capital of the company; or

(b) which enables the person to exercise or control the exercise of ten per cent or more of the voting power at a general meeting of the company;

(8) **"board"**, in relation to a company, means board of directors of the company;

(9) **"body corporate"** or "corporation" includes—

(a) a company incorporated under this Act or company law; or

(b) a company incorporated outside Pakistan, or

(c) a statutory body declared as body corporate in the relevant statute,

but does not include—

(i) a co-operative society registered under any law relating to cooperative societies; or

(ii) any other entity, not being a company as defined in this Act or any other law for the time being which the concerned Minister-in-Charge of the Federal Government may, by notification, specify in this behalf;

(10) **"book and paper"** and **"book or paper"** includes books of account, cost accounting records, deeds, vouchers, writings, documents, minutes and registers maintained on paper or in electronic form;

(11) **"books of account"** includes records maintained in respect of—

(a) all sums of money received and expended by a company and matters in relation to which the receipts and expenditure take place;

(b) all sales and purchases of goods and services by the company;

(c) all assets and liabilities of the company; and

(d) items of cost in respect of production, processing, manufacturing or mining activities;

(12) **"central depository"** shall have the same meaning as assigned to it under the Securities Act, 2015 (III of 2015);

(13) **"chartered accountant"** shall have the same meaning as assigned to it under the Chartered Accountants Ordinance, 1961 (X of 1961);

(14) **"chief executive"**, in relation to a company means an individual who, subject to control and directions of the board, is entrusted with whole, or substantially whole, of the powers of management of affairs of the company and includes a director or any other person occupying the position of a chief executive, by whatever name called, and whether under a contract of service or otherwise;

(15) **"chief financial officer"** means an individual appointed to perform such functions and duties as are customarily performed by a chief financial officer;

(16) **"Commission"** shall have the same meaning as assigned to it under the Securities and Exchange Commission of Pakistan Act, 1997 (XLII of 1997);

(17) **"company"** means a company formed and registered under this Act or the company law;

(18) **"company law"** means the repealed Companies Act, 1913 (VII of 1913), Companies Ordinance, 1984(XLVII of 1984) and Companies Ordinance, 2016 (VI of 2016) and also includes this Act unless the context provides otherwise;

(19) **"company limited by guarantee"** means a company having the liability of its members limited by the memorandum to such amount as the members may respectively thereby undertake to contribute to the assets of the company in the event of its being wound up;

(20) **"company limited by shares"** means a company; having the liability of its members limited by the memorandum to the extent of amount, if any, remaining unpaid on the shares respectively held by them;

(21) **"company secretary"** means any individual appointed to perform secretarial and other duties customarily performed by a company secretary and declared as such, having such qualifications and experience, as may be specified;

(22) **"cost and management accountant"** shall have the same meaning as assigned to it under the Cost and Management Accountants Act, 1966 (XIV of 1966);

(23) **"Court"** means a Company Bench of a High Court having jurisdiction under this Act;

(24) **"debenture"** includes debenture stock, bonds, term finance certificate or any other instrument of a company evidencing a debt, whether constituting a mortgage or charge on the assets of the company or not;

(25) **"director"** includes any person occupying the position of a director, by whatever name called;

(26) **"document"** includes any information or data recorded in any legible form or through use of modern electronic devices or techniques whatsoever, including books and papers, returns, requisitions, notices, certificates, deeds, forms, registers, prospectus, communications, financial statements or statement of accounts or records maintained by financial institutions in respect of its customers;

(27) **"e-service"** means any service or means provided by the Commission for the lodging or filing of electronic documents;

(28) **"electronic document"** includes documents in any electronic form and scanned images of physical documents;

(29) **"employees' stock option"** means the option given to the directors, officers or employees of a company or of its holding company or subsidiary company or companies, if any, which gives such directors, officers or employees, the right to purchase or to subscribe for shares of the company at a price to be determined in the manner as may be specified;

(30) **"expert"** includes an engineer, a valuer, an actuary, a chartered accountant or a cost and management accountant and any other person who has the power or authority to issue a certificate in pursuance of any law for the time being in force or any other person notified as such by the Commission;

(31) **"financial institution"** includes—

   (a) any company whether incorporated within or outside Pakistan which transacts the business of banking or any associated or ancillary business in Pakistan through its branches within or outside Pakistan and includes a government savings bank, but excludes the State Bank of Pakistan;

   (b) a *modaraba* or *modaraba* management company, leasing company, investment bank, venture capital company, financing company, asset management company and credit or investment institution, corporation or company; and

   (c) any company authorised by law to carry on any similar business, as the concerned Minister-in-Charge of the Federal Government may by notification in the official Gazette, specify;

(32) **"financial period"** in relation to a company or any other body corporate, means the period (other than financial year) in respect of which any financial statements thereof are required to be made pursuant to this Act;

(33) **"financial statements"** in relation to a company, includes—

   (a) a statement of financial position as at the end of the period;

   (b) a statement of profit or loss and other comprehensive income or in the case of a company carrying on any activity not for profit, an income and expenditure statement for the period;

   (c) a statement of changes in equity for the period;

   (d) a statement of cash flows for the period;

(e) notes, comprising a summary of significant accounting policies and other explanatory information;

(f) comparative information in respect of the preceding period; and

(g) any other statement as may be prescribed;

(34) **"financial year"** in relation to a company or any other body corporate, means the period in respect of which any financial statement of the company or the body corporate, as the case may be, laid before it in general meeting, is made up, whether that period is a year or not;

(35) **"foreign company"** means any company or body corporate incorporated outside Pakistan, which—

(a) has a place of business or liaison office in Pakistan whether by itself or through an agent, physically or through electronic mode; or

(b) conducts any business activity in Pakistan in any other manner as may be specified;

(36) **"Government"** includes Federal Government or, as the case may be, Provincial governments unless otherwise expressly provided in this Act;

(37) **"holding company"**, means a company which is another company's holding company if, but only if, that other company is its subsidiary[1];

(38) **"listed company"** means a public company, body corporate or any other entity whose securities are listed on securities exchange;

(39) **"listed securities"** means securities listed on the securities exchange;

(40) **"memorandum"** means the memorandum of association of a company as originally framed or as altered from time to time in pursuance of company law or of this Act;

(41) **"*modaraba*"** and **"*modaraba company*"** shall have the same meaning as assigned to it in the Modaraba Companies and Modaraba (Floatation and Control) Ordinance, 1980 (XXXI of 1980);

(42) **"mortgage or charge"** means an interest or lien created on the property or assets of a company or any of its undertakings or both as security;

(43) **"net worth"** means the amount by which total assets exceed total liabilities;

(44) **"notification"** means a notification published in the official Gazette and the expression **"notify"** shall be construed accordingly;

(45) **"officer"** includes any director, chief executive, chief financial officer, company secretary or other authorised officer of a company;

---

[1] 2007 PTD 2422; 1996 PLD 1; 1993 CLC 1915

(46) **"ordinary resolution"** means a resolution passed by a simple majority of such members of the company entitled to vote as are present in person or by proxy or exercise the option to vote through postal ballot, as provided in the articles or as may be specified, at a general meeting;

(47) **"postal ballot"** means voting by post or through any electronic mode:

Provided that voting through postal ballot shall be subject to the provision in the articles of association of a company, save as otherwise provided in this Act;

(48) **"prescribed"** means prescribed by rules made by the Federal Government under this Act;

(49) **"private company"** means a company which, by its articles-

(a) restricts the right to transfer its shares;

(b) limits the number of its members to fifty not including persons who are in the employment of the company; and

(c) prohibits any invitation to the public to subscribe for the shares, if any, or debentures or redeemable capital of the company:

Provided that, where two or more persons hold one or more shares in a company jointly, they shall, for the purposes of this definition, be treated as a single member;

(50) **"promoter"** means a person[1]--

(a) who is named as a subscriber to the memorandum of association of a company; or

(b) who has been named as such in a prospectus; or

(c) who has control over affairs of the company, directly or indirectly whether as a shareholder, director or otherwise; or

(d) in accordance with whose advice, directions or instructions the board of the company is accustomed to act:

Provided that—

(i) nothing in sub-clause (d) shall apply to a person who is acting merely in a professional capacity; and

(ii) nothing contained in sub-clause (d) shall apply to the Commission, registrar or any authorised officer by virtue of enforcement or regulation of the provisions of this Act or any rules, regulations, instructions, directions, orders thereof;

---

[1] 2018 CLD 177

(51) **"prospectus"** shall have the same meaning as assigned to it under the Securities Act, 2015 (III of 2015);

(52) **"public company"** means a company which is not a private company;

(53) **"public interest company"** means a company which falls under the criteria as laid down in the Third Schedule to this Act or deemed to be such company under section 216;

(54) **"public sector company"** means a company, whether public or private, which is directly or indirectly controlled, beneficially owned or not less than fifty-one percent of the voting securities or voting power of which are held by the Government or any agency of the Government or a statutory body, or in respect of which the Government or any agency of the Government or a statutory body, has otherwise power to elect, nominate or appoint majority of its directors and includes a public sector association not for profit, licenced under section 42:

   Provided that nomination of directors by the Commission on the board of the securities exchange or any other entity or operation of any other law shall not make it a public sector company;

(55) **"redeemable capital"** includes sukuk and other forms of finances obtained on the basis of participation term certificate (PTC), musharika certificate, term finance certificate (TFC) or any other security or obligation not based on interest, representing an instrument or a certificate of specified denomination, called the face value or nominal value, evidencing investment of the holder in the capital of the company other than share capital, on terms and conditions of the agreement for the issue of such instrument or certificate or such other certificate or instrument as the concerned Minister-in-Charge of the Federal Government may, by notification in the official Gazette, specify for the purpose;

   Explanation.--"*sukuk*" represents redeemable investment in certificates of equal nominal value representing undivided shares in ownership of tangible assets of a particular project or specific investment activity, usufruct and services;

(56) **"register of companies"** means the register of companies maintained by the registrar on paper or in any electronic form under this Act;

(57) **"registrar"** means registrar, an additional registrar, an additional joint registrar, a joint registrar, a deputy registrar or an assistant registrar or such other officer as may be designated by the Commission, performing duties and functions under this Act;

(58) **"regulations"** means the regulations made by the Commission under this Act;

(59) **"rules"** means rules made by the Federal Government under this Act;

(60) **"scheduled bank"** shall have the same meaning as assigned to it under the State Bank of Pakistan Act, 1956 (XXXIII of 1956);

(61) **"securities"** include the securities as provided in sub-clauses (a) to (i) of clause (lii) of section 2 of the Securities Act, 2015 (III of 2015) whether listed or not;

(62) **"securities exchange"** means a public company licenced by the Commission as a securities exchange under the Securities Act, 2015 (III of 2015);

(63) **"share"** means a share in the share capital of a company;

(64) **"*Shariah* compliant company"** means a company which is conducting its business according to the principles of *Shariah*;

(65) **"single member company"** means a company which has only one member;

(66) **"special resolution"** means a resolution which has been passed by a majority of not less than three-fourths of such members of the company entitled to vote as are present in person or by proxy or vote through postal ballot at a general meeting of which not less than twenty-one days' notice specifying the intention to propose the resolution as a special resolution has been duly given:

Provided that if all the members entitled to attend and vote at any such meeting so agree, a resolution may be proposed and passed as a special resolution at a meeting of which less than twenty-one days notice has been given;

(67) **"specified"** means specified through regulations made under this Act;

(68) **"subsidiary company"** or **"subsidiary"**, in relation to any other company (that is to say the holding company), means a company in which the holding company

(a) controls the composition of the board; or

(b) exercises or controls more than one-half of its voting securities either by itself or together with one or more of its subsidiary companies[1]:

Provided that such class or classes of holding companies shall not have layers of subsidiaries beyond such numbers, as may be notified,

Explanation.--For the purposes of this clause

(i) a company shall be deemed to be a subsidiary company of the holding company even if the control referred to in sub-clause

---

[1] 2007 PTD 2422; 1996 PLD 1; 1993 CLC 1915

(ii) (a) or sub-clause (b) is of another subsidiary company of the holding company;

(iii) the composition of a company's board shall be deemed to be controlled by another company if that other company by exercise of power exercisable by it at its discretion can appoint or remove all or a majority of the directors;

(iv) the expression "**company**" includes any body corporate;

(v) "**layer**" in relation to a holding company means its subsidiary or subsidiaries;

(69) **"Table"** means Table in a Schedule to this Act;

(70) **"turnover"** means the aggregate value of sale, supply or distribution of goods or on account of services rendered, or both, net of discounts, if any, held by the company during a financial year;

(71) **"unlimited company"** means a company not having any limit on the liability of its members;

(72) **"valuer"** means a valuer registered with the Commission;

(73) **"voting right"** means the right of a member of a company to vote on any matter in a meeting of the company either present in person or through video-link or by proxy or by means of postal ballot:

Provided that attending of meeting through video-link shall be subject to such facility arranged by the company and in the manner as may be specified, save as otherwise provided in this Act; and

(74) **"wholly owned subsidiary"** a company shall be deemed to be a wholly owned subsidiary of another company or the statutory body if all its shares are owned by that other company or the statutory body.

(2) The words and expressions used and not defined in this Act but defined in the Securities Act, 2015 (III of 2015) or the Securities and Exchange Commission of Pakistan Act, 1997(XLII of 1997) or the Central Depositories Act, 1997 (XIX of 1997) shall have the meanings respectively assigned to them in those Acts.

3. **Application of Act to non-trading companies with purely provincial objects.**—(1) The powers conferred by this Act on the concerned Minister-in-Charge of the Federal Government or the Commission, in relation to companies which are not trading corporations and the objects of which are confined to a single Province, may be exercised by the Minister-in-Charge of the Provincial Government[1]:

---

[1] 2008 CLD 1353

Provided that where the licence is issued by the Provincial Government or, as the case may be, its concerned Minister-in-Charge, in exercise of the powers conferred by this section, the company shall mention this fact in all its documents.

(2) A non-trading corporation formed under sub-section (1) extending its operational activities beyond the territorial limits of its respective province shall be liable to a penalty of level 3 on the standard scale and be wound up on the application by the Commission.

4. **Act to override.**—Save as otherwise expressly provided herein--

(a) the provisions of this Act shall have effect notwithstanding anything contained in any other law or the memorandum or articles of a company or in any contract or agreement executed by it or in any resolution passed by the company in general meeting or by its directors, whether the same be registered, executed or passed, as the case may be, before or after the coming into force of the said provisions[1]; and

(b) any provision contained in the memorandum, articles, contract, agreement, arrangement or resolution aforesaid shall, to the extent to which it is repugnant to the aforesaid provisions of this Act, become, or be, void, as the case may be.

PART II

JURISDICTION OF COURT

5. **Jurisdiction of the Court and creation of Benches[2].**— (1) The Court having jurisdiction under this Act shall be the High Court having jurisdiction in the place at which the registered office of the company is situate.

(2) Notwithstanding anything contained in any other law no civil court as provided in the Code of Civil Procedure, 1908 (Act V of 1908) or any other court shall have jurisdiction to entertain any suit or proceeding in respect of any matter which the Court is empowered to determine by or under this Act.

(3) For the purposes of jurisdiction to wind up companies, the expression "registered office" means the place which has longest been the registered office of the company during the one hundred and eighty days immediately preceding the presentation of the petition for winding up.

(4) There shall be, in each High Court, one or more benches on permanent basis, each to be known as the Company Bench, to be constituted by

---

[1] 2018 CLD 1214; 2004 CLD 373; 2003 CLD 1209

[2] 2019 SLD 7; 2017 CLD 1039; 2017 CLD 1165; 2016 CLD 1077; 2013 CLD 108; 2009 MLD 1294; 2003 YLR 2150; 2002 CLD 575; 2001 CLC 1833; 2000 PLD 78; 2000 PLD 83; 1997 CLC 970; 1996 PLD 1; 1992 CLC 1658; 1982 PLD 566; 1968 PLD 381; 1968 PLD 412; 1962 PLD 176

the Chief Justice of the High Court to exercise the jurisdiction vested in the High Court under this Act:

Provided that Benches constituted under the Companies Ordinance, 1984 (XLVII of 1984), shall continue to function accordingly unless otherwise notified by the respective Chief Justice of the High Court:

Provided further that provisions of section 6 shall be effective from the date of notification by the Chief Justice of the respective High Court within one hundred and eighty days from the date of the commencement of this Act.

(5) There shall be a Registrar to be known as "Registrar of the Company Bench" duly notified by the Chief Justice of the respective High Court who shall be assisted by such other officers as may be assigned by the Chief Justice of the respective High Court.

(6) The Registrar of the Company Bench shall perform all the functions assigned to it under this Act including all ministerial and administrative business of the Company Bench such as the receipt of petitions, applications, written replies, issuance of notices, service of summons and such other functions or duties as may be prescribed under section 423.

(7) The Chief Justice of the respective High Court, if deemed appropriate, may also establish a secretariat in each Company Bench of the respective High Court in such form and manner to provide secretarial support and to perform such functions as may be prescribed under section 423.

6. **Procedure of the Court and appeal.**—(1) Notwithstanding anything contained in any other law for the time being in force all written submissions to the Court under this Act shall be filed with the Registrar of the Company Bench[1].

(2)   For the purposes of this Act, written submissions shall, *inter alia*, include[2]-

---

[1] 2019 CLD 227; 2019 SCMR 306; 2019 SLD 7; 2017 CLD 436; 2016 SCMR 213; 2016 CLD 393; 2015 CLD 569; 2015 CLD 719; 2013 CLD 114; 2012 CLD 323; 2012 PLD 15; 2011 CLD 1029; 2011 CLD 1737; 2009 PLD 367; 2009 CLD 784; 2009 CLD 1225; 2009 MLD 1294; 2008 CLD 277; 2008 PLD 707; 2008 CLD 1117; 2007 CLD 334; 2007 CLD 888; 2005 SCMR 971; 2005 SCMR 1450; 2005 CLD 558; 2005 CLD 747; 2005 CLD 976; 2005 CLD 1624; 2004 CLD 1; 2004 CLD 640; 2004 PLD 95; 2004 CLD 1037; 2003 PLD 124; 2003 CLD 211; 2003 CLD 621; 2003 CLD 1442; 2003 YLR 2150; 2002 CLD 1485; 2002 PLD 1100; 2002 CLD 1781; 2002 CLD 1747; 2002 SCMR 415; 2002 SCMR 450; 2002 CLD 1747; 2002 CLD 1485; 2001 YLR 1797; 2001 PLD 523; 2000 PLD 283; 1999 SCMR 25; 1999 PLD 1; 1999 SCMR 1850; 1998 SCMR 1533; 1998 CLC 426; 1998 PLD 332; 1997 CLC 260; 1996 PLD 1; 1996 PLD 543; 1995 PLD 41; 1995 PLD 320; 1994 CLC 403; 1993 CLC 1540; 1993 SCMR 80; 1992 SCMR 1795; 1991 PLD 467; 1989 PLD 106; 1988 CLC 206; 1988 CLC 866; 1988 MLD 395; 1988 CLC 1541; 1988 CLC 2127; 1987 PLD 569

[2] 2012 PLD 15; 1996 PLD 1

(a) a petition or application setting out a concise statement of facts, grounds and the relief claimed;

(b) a written reply with particulars of set off, if any;

(c) an affidavit of facts by the petitioner or applicant, or respondent, as the case may be, including affidavits, if required, of other persons in support of the case, duly attested by the oath commissioner, or as may be provided under the rules;

(d) any other relevant documents in possession of the petitioner or applicant or respondent, as the case may be;

(e) any application for discovery of documents or interim injunction, if required;

(f) a list of any case law along with a summary of the same on which the petitioner or applicant is placing reliance;

(g) address for effecting service, mobile number, email and fax or any other mode notified by the Court; and

(h) any other document as may be required by the Registrar of the Company Bench.

(3) Where any petition or application is filed under any provision of this Act, summons may be issued by the Registrar of the Company Bench along with a copy of the petition or application and the documents annexed therewith and the same shall be served on the respondent through the bailiff or process-server of the Court, through registered post, acknowledgement due, by courier and by publication in one English language and one Urdu language daily newspaper and, in addition, if so directed by the Court through electronic modes, and the service duly effected through any one of the modes mentioned under this sub-section shall be deemed to be valid service[1].

Explanation.—**electronic modes** means service of summons on a party or other person by electronic transmission through devices such as, facsimile, email, or in such other form or mode as may be notified by the Court.

(4) The respondent shall file a written reply and particulars of set-off, if any, as set out in sub-section (2) of this section with the concerned Registrar of the Company Bench within thirty days from the date of first service through any of the modes as laid down in sub-section (3).

(5) Where the respondent fails to file the written reply within the time prescribed in sub-section (4), a report shall be submitted by the Registrar of the Company Bench before the Court and the Court may pass necessary orders to

---

[1] 2016 CLD 393

proceed *exparte* and announce the final order on the basis of the documents available on record.

(6) The Registrar of the Company Bench, on completion of receipt of all written submissions and after ensuring that all copies of such written submissions are duly supplied to the parties as per procedure laid down by the Court, shall present the case file to the Court on a day fixed under notice to the parties, within forty-five days of the first service of notices or such extended time as may be granted by the Court.

(7) The Court after consulting the counsel of the parties shall fix a date and allocate time for hearing of the case.

(8) No adjournment shall be granted once the Court has fixed a date of hearing under sub-section (7) and it will be duty of the parties to ensure the presence of their respective counsel or in absence of the counsel make alternate arrangements:

Provided that only in exceptional circumstances beyond control of a party, the Court may grant another opportunity of hearing subject to the payment of an amount of rupees ten thousand or such higher amount as may be determined by the Court as costs to be paid to the Court.

(9) The Court shall treat affidavits, counter affidavits and other documents filed by the parties to the proceedings as evidence and decide the matter on the basis of the documents and affidavits placed before the Court, in a summary manner and pass final orders within the time stipulated in sub-section (11).

(10) In exceptional circumstances where the Court is of the view that any issue of facts requires cross examination, the Court may order attendance of the relevant deponent or deponents for the purposes of cross examination by such opposing party or parties as the Court deems fit and for the purposes of this section the affidavit filed by such deponent shall be considered as his examination-in-chief:

Provided that—

(i)   the Court may refer the matter to the Registrar of the Company Bench or any other person for recording of cross examination of the deponent who shall complete recording of cross examination within thirty days from the date of the order of the Court, or such extended time as may be allowed by the Court which shall not be more than fifteen days on payment of rupees ten thousand or such higher amount as may be determined by the Court as costs payable to the Court and to submit a report accordingly;

(ii)   all questions and answers along with any objections raised by any party shall be duly recorded in writing; and

    (iii)   the Registrar of the Company Bench shall have all the powers of the Civil Court under the Code of Civil Procedure, 1908 (V of 1908) for the purposes of execution of service and summoning of

    (iv)   deponents and conducting cross examination in accordance with the directions of the Court.

(11) The petition presented before the Court shall be decided within a period of one hundred and twenty days from the date of presentation of the case and for this purpose the Court may, if it is in the interest of justice, conduct the proceedings on a day to day basis and if the Court deems fit it may impose costs which may extend to one hundred thousand rupees per day or such higher amount as the Court may determine against any party to the proceeding causing the delay.

(12) The Court may, at any time, take notice of serious misstatements and material non-disclosure of facts by any party to the proceedings and dismiss the petition or application or close the right of defence of the respondent with costs of the proceedings and impose a fine which may extend to one hundred thousand rupees whichever is higher and pass a final order.

(13) Notwithstanding anything contained in this section, the Registrar of the Company Bench shall place any application for interim relief including any interlocutory order before the Court for adjudication immediately upon its filing.

(14) Any person aggrieved by any judgment or final order of the Court passed in its original jurisdiction under this Act may, within sixty days, file a petition for leave to appeal in the Supreme Court of Pakistan:

Provided that no appeal or petition shall lie against any interlocutory order of the Court.

(15) Save as otherwise expressly provided under this Act, the provisions of the Qanun-e-Shahadat (Order)1984 (P.O. No. X of 1984) and the Code of Civil Procedure, 1908 (Act V of 1908) shall not apply to the proceedings under this section except to such extent as the Court may determine in its discretion.

PART III

POWERS AND FUNCTIONS OF THE SECURITIES AND EXCHANGE COMMISSION OF PAKISTAN

7. Powers and functions of the Commission.— (1) The Commission shall exercise such powers and perform such functions as are conferred on it by or under this Act.

(2) The powers and functions of the Commission under this Act shall be in addition to and not in derogation to the powers and functions of the

Commission under the Securities and Exchange Commission of Pakistan Act, 1997 (XLII of 1997)[1].

8. **Reference by the Federal Government or Commission to the Court.**— (1) Without prejudice to the powers, jurisdiction and authority exercisable by the concerned Minister-in-Charge of the Federal Government or any functionary thereof or the Commission under this Act, the concerned Minister-in-Charge of the Federal Government or the Commission, as the case may be, may make a reference to the Court, on any question or matter which is considered to be of special significance requiring orders, determination or action concerning affairs of a company or class of companies or any action of any officer thereof[2].

Explanation.—In this sub-section "officer" includes an auditor, liquidator or agent of the company.

(2) Where a reference is made to the Court under sub-section (1), the Court may make such order as it may deem just and equitable under the circumstances.

PART IV

INCORPORATION OF COMPANIES AND MATTERS INCIDENTAL THERETO

9. **Obligation to register certain associations, partnerships as companies.**—(1) No association, partnership or entity consisting of more than twenty persons shall be formed for the purpose of carrying on any business that has for its object the acquisition of gain by the association, partnership or entity, or by the individual members thereof, unless it is registered as a company under this Act and any violation of this section shall be an offence punishable under this section[3].

(2)   A person guilty of an offence under this section shall be liable to a penalty not exceeding of level 1 on the standard scale and also be personally liable for all the liabilities incurred in such business.

(3)   Nothing in this section shall apply to—

(a)   any society, body or association, other than a partnership, formed or incorporated under any law for the time being in force in Pakistan; or

(b)   a joint family carrying on joint family business; or

---

[1] 2002 CLD 726; 1985 MLD 1083

[2] 2002 PLC 1655; 2002 PLD 1079; 2000 SCMR 928; 1984 PLD 170; 1984 PLD 194; PLD 1977 SC 109

[3] 2019 CLD 1; 2007 PTD 2029; 1992 PLD 230; 1983 PLD 178; 1977 PLD 109

(c) a partnership of two or more joint families where the total number of members of such families, excluding the minor members, does not exceed twenty; or

(d) a partnership formed to carry on practice as lawyers, accountants or any other profession where practice as a limited liability company

(e) is not permitted under the relevant laws or regulations for such practice.

PROVISIONS WITH RESPECT TO NAMES OF COMPANIES

10. **Prohibition of certain names.**— (1) [1]No company shall be registered by a name which contains such word or expression, as may be notified by the Commission or in the opinion of the registrar is—

(a) identical with or resemble or similar to the name of a company; or

(b) inappropriate; or

(c) undesirable; or

(d) deceptive; or

(e) designed to exploit or offend religious susceptibilities of the people; or

(f) any other ground as may be specified.

(2) Except with prior approval in writing of the Commission, no company shall be registered by a name which contains any word suggesting or calculated to suggest—

(a) the patronage of any past or present Pakistani or foreign head of state;

(b) any connection with the Federal Government or a Provincial Government or any department or authority or statutory body of any such Government;

(c) any connection with any corporation set up by or under any Federal or Provincial law;

(d) the patronage of, or any connection with, any foreign Government or any international organisation;

(e) establishing a *modaraba* management company or to float a *modaraba*; or

(f) any other business requiring licence from the Commission[2].

---

[1] 2011 CLD 193; 2011 PCrLJ 1289; 2011 CLD 1268; 2011 CLD 1192; 2010 CLD 1856; 2010 CLD 983; 2010 CLD 1856; 2009 CLD 1; 2005 CLD 808; 2005 CLD 1546; 2005 CLD 808; 2002 CLD 726
[2] 2002 CLD 726

(3) Whenever a question arises as to whether or not the name of a company is in violation of the foregoing provisions of this section, decision of the Commission shall be final[1].

(4) A person may make an application, in such form and manner and accompanied by such fee as may be specified, to the registrar for reservation of a name set out in the application for a period not exceeding sixty days[2].

(5) Where it is found that a name was reserved under sub-section (4), by furnishing false or incorrect information, such reservation shall be cancelled and in case the company has been incorporated, it shall be directed to change its name. The person making application under sub-section (4) shall be liable to a penalty not exceeding level 1 on the standard scale.

(6) If the name applied for under sub-section (4) is refused by the registrar, the aggrieved person may within thirty days of the order of refusal prefer an appeal to the Commission.

(7) An order of the Commission under sub-section (6) shall be final and shall not be called in question before any court or other authority.

11. **Rectification of name of a company.**— (1) A company which, through inadvertence or otherwise, is registered by a name in contravention of the provisions of section 10 or the name was obtained by furnishing false or incorrect information--

(a)   may, with approval of the registrar, change its name; and

(b)   shall, if the registrar so directs, within thirty days of receipt of such direction, change its name with approval of the registrar[3]:

Provided that the registrar shall, before issuing a direction for change of the name, afford the company an opportunity to make representation against the proposed direction.

(2)   If the company fails to report compliance with the direction issued under sub-section within the specified period, the registrar may enter on the register a new name for the company selected by him, being a name under which the company may be registered under this Act and issue a certificate of incorporation on change of name for the purpose of section 13.

(3)   If a company makes default in complying with the direction issued by the registrar under sub-section (1) or continue using previous name after the name has been changed by the registrar under sub-section (2), shall be liable to a penalty of level 1 on the standard scale.

---

[1] 2002 CLD 726

[2] 2002 CLD 726

[3] 2018 CLD 268; 2011 CLD 1192; 2010 CLD 983; 2005 CLD 1546; 2005 CLD 808; 2002 CLD 726

12. **Change of name by a company.**— A company may, by special resolution and with approval of the registrar signified in writing, change its name[1]:

Provided that no approval under this section shall be required where the change in the name of a company is only the addition thereto, or the omission therefrom, of the expression "(Private)" or "(SMC-Private)" or "(Guarantee) Limited" or "Limited" or "Unlimited", as the case may be, consequent upon the conversion of the status of a company in accordance with the provisions of sections 46 to 49.

13. **Registration of change of name and effect thereof.**— (1) Where a company changes its name the registrar shall enter the new name on the register in place of the former name, and shall issue a certificate of incorporation altered to meet the circumstances of the case and, on the issue of such a certificate, the change of name shall be complete[2].

(2)   Where a company changes its name it shall, for a period of ninety days from the date of issue of a certificate by the registrar under sub-section (1), continue to mention its former name along with its new name on the outside of every office or place in which its business is carried on and in every document or notice referred to in section 22.

(3)   The change of name shall not affect any rights or obligations of the company, or render defective any legal proceedings by or against the company and any legal proceedings that might have been continued or commenced against the company by its former name may be continued by or commenced against the company by its new name.

14. **Mode of forming a company.**— (1) Any--

(a)   three or more persons associated for any lawful purpose may, by subscribing their names to a memorandum of association and complying with the requirements of this Act in respect of registration, form a public company; or

(b)   two or more persons so associated may in the like manner form a private company; or

(c)   one person may form a single member company by complying with the requirements in respect of registration of a private company and such other requirement as may be specified[3]. The subscriber to the memorandum shall nominate a person who in the event of death of the sole member shall be responsible to-

---

[1] 2013 CLD 2120; 2009 CLD 839; 1992 CLC 2282; 1985 CLC 529; 1970 PLD 132; 1956 PLD 1
[2] 2015 PTD 1863; 2013 CLD 2120; 2010 CLD 135; 2009 CLD 839; 2008 CLC 7; 2008 CLD 48
[3] 2019 CLD 1; 1979 PTD 431; 1993 SCMR 287; 1991 SCMR 1447; 2004 PTD 1994; 1999 PLD 880; 2006 PTD 2639; 2015 SCMR 1494; 2015 CLD 1482; 2011 CLD 23; 2010 CLD 1856; 1984 CLC 103

(i) transfer the shares to the legal heirs of the deceased subject to succession to be determined under the Islamic law of inheritance and in case of a non-*Muslim* members, as per their respective law; and

(ii) manage the affairs of the company as a trustee, till such time the title of shares are transferred:

> Provided that where transfer by virtue of this sub-section is made to more than one legal heir, the company shall cease to be a single member company and comply with the provisions of section 47.

(2) A company formed under this section may be a company with or without limited liability, that is to say-

(a) a company limited by shares; or

(b) a company limited by guarantee; or

(c) an unlimited company.

15. **Liability for carrying on business with less than three or, in the case of a private company, two members.**—If at any time the number of members of a company is reduced, in the case of a private company other than a single member company, below two or in the case of any other company, below three and the company carries on business for more than one hundred and eighty days while the number is so reduced, every person who is a member of the company during the time that it so carries on business after those one hundred and eighty days and is cognizant of the fact that it is carrying on business with fewer than two members or three members, as the case may be, shall be severally liable for payment of whole debts of the company contracted during that time and may be sued therefor without joinder in the suit of any other member[1].

GENERAL PROVISIONS WITH RESPECT TO REGISTRATION OF MEMORANDUM AND ARTICLES

16. **Registration of memorandum and articles.**—(1) There shall be filed with the registrar an application on the specified form containing the following information and documents for incorporation of a company, namely:—

(a) a declaration on the specified form, by an authorized intermediary or by a person named in the articles as a director, of compliance with all or any of the requirements of this Act and the rules and regulations made thereunder in respect of registration and matters precedent or incidental thereto;

---

[1] 2001 PTD 3146

(b) memorandum of association of the proposed company signed by all subscribers, duly witnessed and dated;

(c) there may, in the case of a company limited by shares and there shall, in the case of a company limited by guarantee or an unlimited company, be the articles of association signed by the subscribers duly witnessed and dated; and

(d) an address for correspondence till its registered office is established and notified[1].

(2) Where the registrar is of the opinion that any document or information filed with him in connection with the incorporation of the company contains any matter contrary to law or does not otherwise comply with the requirements of law or is not complete owing to any defect, error or omission or is not properly authenticated, the registrar may either require the company to file a revised document or remove the defects or deficiencies within the specified period.

(3) Where the applicant fails under sub-section (2) to remove the deficiencies conveyed within the specified period, the registrar may refuse registration of the company.

(4) If the registrar is satisfied that all the requirements of this Act and the rules or regulations made thereunder have been complied with, he shall register the memorandum and other documents delivered to him.

(5) On registration of the memorandum of a company, the registrar shall issue a certificate that the company is incorporated.

(6) The certificate of incorporation shall state—

(a) the name and registration number of the company;

(b) the date of its incorporation;

(c) whether it is a private or a public company;

(d) whether it is a limited or unlimited company; and

(e) if it is limited, whether it is limited by shares or limited by guarantee.

(7) The certificate under sub-section (5) shall be signed by the registrar or authenticated by the registrar's official seal.

(8) The certificate under sub-section (5) shall be conclusive evidence that the requirements of this Act as to registration have been complied with and that the company is duly registered under this Act.

---

[1] 2012 CLD 675; 2012 PLD 1; 2011 CLD 23; 2010 CLD 1856; 2009 CLD 883; 2005 MLD 1165; 2005 MLD 1165; 1996 CLC 370

(9) If registration of the memorandum is refused, the subscribers of the memorandum or any one of them authorised by them in writing may, within thirty days of the order of refusal, prefer an appeal to the Commission.

(10) An order of the Commission under sub-section (9) shall be final and shall not be called in question before any court or other authority.

17. **Effect of memorandum and articles.**— (1) The memorandum and articles shall, when registered, bind the company and the members thereof to the same extent as if they respectively had been signed by each member and contained a covenant on the part of each member, his heirs and legal representatives, to observe and be bound by all the provisions of the memorandum and of the articles, subject to the provisions of this Act[1].

(2) All moneys payable by a subscriber in pursuance of his undertaking in the memorandum of association against the shares subscribed shall be a debt due from him and be payable in cash within thirty days from the date of incorporation of the company:

Provided that in case the share money is not deposited within the prescribed time, the shares shall be deemed to be cancelled and the name of that subscriber shall be removed from the register and the registrar shall give such direction to the company in each case as deemed appropriate for compliance with the provisions of the company law.

(3) The receipt of subscription money from the subscribers shall be reported by the company to the registrar on a specified form within forty-five days from the date of incorporation of the company, accompanied by a certificate by a practicing chartered accountant or a cost and management accountant verifying receipt of the money so subscribed.

(4) Any violation of this section shall be an offence liable to a penalty of level 1 on the standard scale.

18. **Effect of registration.**—The registration of the company has the following effects[2], as from the date of incorporation--

(a)   the subscribers to the memorandum, together with such other persons as may from time to time become members of the company, are a body corporate by the name stated in the certificate of incorporation;

---

[1] 1990 PLD SC 1; 2003 SCMR 132; 2005 SCMR 512; 2009 CLD 1589; 2017 CLD 587; 2012 CLD 675; 2012 PLD 1; 2005 CLD 1875; 2004 CLD 373; 1999 PLD 450; 1996 CLC 370; 1991 MLD 1225; 1982 PLD 768; 1971 PLD 564

[2] 2012 CLD 675; 2012 PLD 1; 2006 PTD 2639; 2005 SCMR 800; 2005 CLD 720; 2005 PLD 478; 2002 CLD 157; 1999 PLD 450; 1993 CLC 1565; 1992 MLD 1085; 1991 MLD 313; 1989 MLD 2968; 1984 CLC 2170; 1982 PLD 768; 1978 PLD 193; 1973 PLD 46; 1973 PLD 361; 1964 PLD 666; 1958 PLD 721; 1956 PLD 731

(b) the body corporate is capable of exercising all the functions of an incorporated company, having perpetual succession and a common seal;

(c) the status and registered office of the company are as stated in, or in connection with, the application for registration;

(d) in case of a company having share capital, the subscribers to the memorandum become holders of the initial shares; and

(e) the persons named in the articles of association as proposed directors, are deemed to have been appointed to that office.

COMMENCEMENT OF BUSINESS BY A PUBLIC COMPANY

19. **Commencement of business by a public company.**— (1) A public company shall not start its operations or exercise any borrowing powers unless—

(a) shares held subject to payment of the whole amount thereof in cash have been allotted to an amount not less in the whole than the minimum subscription and the money has been received by the company;

(b) every director of the company has paid to the company full amount on each of the shares taken or contracted to be taken by him and for which he is liable to pay in cash;

(c) no money is or may become liable to be repaid to applicants for any shares which have been offered for public subscription;

(d) there has been filed with the registrar a duly verified declaration by the chief executive or one of the directors and the secretary in the specified form that the aforesaid conditions have been complied with; and

(e) in the case of a company which has not issued a prospectus inviting the public to subscribe for its shares, there has been filed with the registrar a statement in lieu of prospectus as per the Second Schedule annexed to this Act[1].

Explanation. —"**minimum subscription**" means the amount, if any, fixed by the memorandum or articles of association as minimum subscription upon which the directors may proceed to allotment or if no amount is so fixed and specified, the whole amount of the share capital other than that issued or agreed to be issued as paid up otherwise than in cash.

(2) The registrar shall, on filing of a duly verified declaration in accordance with the provisions of sub-section (l) and after making such

---

[1] 2008 CLD 879

enquiries as he may deem fit to satisfy himself that all the requirements of this Act have been complied with in respect of the commencement of business and matters precedent and incidental thereto, accept and register all the relevant documents.

(3) The acceptance and registration of documents under sub-section (2) shall be a conclusive evidence that the company is entitled to start its operations and exercise any borrowing powers.

(4) Nothing in this section shall apply—

(a) to a company converted from private to a public;

(b) to a company limited by guarantee and not having a share capital.

20. **Consequences of non-compliance of section 19.**— (1) If any company starts its business operations or exercises borrowing powers in contravention of section 19, every officer or other person who is responsible for contravention shall without prejudice to other liabilities be liable to a penalty not exceeding level 2 on the standard scale.

(2) Any contract made by a company before the date at which it is entitled to commence business shall be provisional only and shall not be binding on the company until that date and on that date it shall become binding.

REGISTERED OFFICE AND PUBLICATION OF NAME

21. **Registered office of company.**— (1) A company shall have a registered office to which all communications and notices shall be addressed and within a period of thirty days of its incorporation, notify to the registrar in the specified manner[1].

(2) Notice of any change in situation of the registered office shall be given to the registrar in a specified form within a period of fifteen days after the date of change:

Provided that the change of registered office of a company from--

(a)   one city in a Province to another; or

(b)   a city to another in any part of Pakistan not forming part of a Province;

shall require approval of general meeting through special resolution.

(3) If a company fails to comply with the requirements of sub-section (1) or (2), the company and its every officer who is responsible for such non-compliance shall be liable to a penalty not exceeding of level 1 on the standard scale.

---

[1] 2006 CLD 810; 1968 PLD 412; 1962 PLD 176

22. **Publication of name by a company.**—[1]Every company shall—

(a)   display in a conspicuous position, in letters easily legible in English or Urdu characters its name and incorporation number outside the registered office and every office or the place in which its business is carried on;

(b)   display a certified copy of certificate of incorporation at every place of business of the company;

(c)   get its name, address of its registered office, telephone number, fax number, e-mail and website addresses, if any, printed on letter-head and all its documents, notices and other official publications; and

(d)   have its name mentioned in legible English or Urdu characters, in all bills of exchange, promissory notes, endorsements, cheques and orders for money or goods purporting to be signed by or on behalf of the company and in all bills of parcels, invoices, receipts and letters of credit of the company.

23. **Company to have common seal.**—(1) Every company shall have a common seal.

(2) A company's common seal must be a seal having the company's name engraved on it in legible form.

(3) If any of the provision of this section is contravened or an officer of a company or a person on behalf of a company uses or authorises the use of another seal that purports to be the company's common seal, shall be liable to a penalty not exceeding of level 1 on the standard scale.

24. **Penalties for non-publication of name.**—(l) If a company does not display its name in the manner provided for by this Act, it shall be liable to a penalty not exceeding level 1 on the standard scale and every officer of the company who authorises or permits the default shall be liable to the like penalty[2].

(2) If any officer of a limited company issues or authorises the issue of any bill-head, letter paper, document, notice or other official publication of the company, or signs or authorises to be signed on behalf of the company any bill of exchange, promissory note, endorsement, cheque or order for money or goods, or issues or authorises to be issued any bill of parcels, invoice, receipt or letter of credit of the company, wherein its name is not mentioned in the manner aforesaid, he shall be liable to a penalty not exceeding of level 1 on the standard scale and shall further be personally liable to the holder of any such bill of exchange, promissory note or order for money or goods, for the amount thereof unless the same is duly paid by the company.

[1] 2014 MLD 957; 2013 CLD 2202; 2011 CLD 193
[2] 2014 MLD 957; 2013 CLD 2202

25. **Publication of authorised as well as paid-up capital.**—(1) Where any notice, advertisement or other official publication of a company contains a statement of amount of authorised capital of the company, such notice, advertisement or other official publication shall also contain a statement in an equally prominent position and in equally conspicuous characters of amount of the paid up capital.

(2) Any company which makes default in complying with the requirements of sub-section and every officer of the company who is party to the default shall be liable to a penalty not exceeding of level 1 on the standard scale.

26. **Business and objects of a company.**— (1) A company may carry on or undertake any lawful business or activity and do any act or enter into any transaction being incidental and ancillary thereto which is necessary in attaining its business activities:

Provided that—

(i)   the principal line of business of the company shall be mentioned in the memorandum of association of the company which shall always commensurate with name of the company; and

(ii)   any change in the principal line of business shall be reported to the registrar within thirty days from the date of change, on the form as may be specified and registrar may give direction of change of name if it is in violation of this section.

Explanation.— "**principal line of business**" means the business in which substantial assets are held or likely to be held or substantial revenue is earned or likely to be earned by a company, whichever is higher.

(2)   A company shall not engage in a business which is—

(a)   prohibited by any law for the time being in force in Pakistan; or

(b)   restricted by any law, rules or regulations, unless necessary licence, registration, permission or approval has been obtained or compliance with any other condition has been made:

Provided nothing in sub-section (1) shall be applicable to the extent of such companies.

MEMORANDUM AND ARTICLES OF ASSOCIATION

27. **Memorandum of company limited by shares.**—In the case of a company limited by shares-

(A)   the memorandum shall state[1]—

(i)   the name of the company with the word "Limited" as last word of the name in the case of a public limited company, the parenthesis and words "(Private) Limited" as last words of the name in the case of a private limited company, and the parenthesis and words "(SMC-Private) Limited" as last words of the name in the case of a single member company;

(ii)   the Province or the part of Pakistan not forming part of a Province, as the case may be, in which the registered office of the company is to be situate;

(iii)   principal line of business:

Provided that—

(a)   the existing companies shall continue with their existing memorandum of association and the object stated at serial number 1 of the object clause shall be treated as the principal line of business;

(b)   if the object stated at serial number 1 of the object clause is not the principal line of business of the company, it shall be required to intimate to the registrar their principal line of business within such time from commencement of this Act and in the form as may be specified. A revised copy of the memorandum of association indicating therein its principal business at serial number 1 of the object clause shall also be furnished to the registrar; and

(c)   the existing companies or the companies to be formed to carry on or engage in any business which is subject to a licence or registration, permission or approval shall mention the businesses as required under the respective law and the rules and regulations made thereunder;

(iv)   an undertaking as may be specified;

(v)   that the liability of the members is limited; and

---

[1] 2019 CLD 1; 2015 CLD 1482; 2011 CLD 193; 1967 PLD 637; 1956 PLD 12

(vi) the amount of share capital with which the company proposes to be registered and the division thereof into shares of a fixed amount;

(B) no subscriber of the memorandum shall take less than one share; and

(C) each subscriber of the memorandum shall write opposite to his name the number of shares he agrees to take.

28. Memorandum of company limited by guarantee.—(1) In the case of a company limited by guarantee the memorandum shall state[1]—

(a) the name of the company with the parenthesis and words "(Guarantee) Limited" as last words of its name;

(b) the Province or the part of Pakistan not forming part of a Province, as the case may be, in which the registered office of the company is to be situate;

(c) principal line of business:

Provided that—

(i) the existing companies shall continue with their existing memorandum of association and the object stated at serial number 1 of the object clause shall be treated as the principal line of business;

(ii) if the object stated at serial number 1 of the object clause is not the principal line of business of the company, it shall be required to intimate to the registrar their principal line of business within such time from the commencement of this Act and in the form as may be specified. A revised copy of the memorandum of association indicating therein its principal business at serial number 1 of the object clause shall also be furnished to the registrar; and

(iii) the existing companies or the companies to be formed to carry on or engage in any business which is subject to a licence or registration, permission or approval shall mention the businesses as required under the respective law;

(d) an undertaking as may be specified;

(e) that the liability of the members is limited; and

(f) such amount as may be required, not exceeding a specified amount that each member undertakes to contribute to the assets of the

---

[1] 2015 CLD 1482; 2011 CLD 193; 2010 PLC(CS) 1150; 2009 CLD 1329; 2000 PLD 602; 1987 CLC 726; 1980 PLD 86

company in the event of its being wound up while he is a member or within one year afterwards for payment of the debts and liabilities of the company contracted before he ceases to be a member and of the costs, charges and expenses of winding up and for adjustment of rights of the contributories among themselves.

(2) If the company has a share capital, the memorandum shall also state the amount of share capital with which the company proposes to be registered and the division thereof into shares of a fixed amount and the number of shares taken by each subscriber.

29. **Memorandum of unlimited company.**— In the case of an unlimited company the memorandum shall state[1]—

(a)   the name of the company with the word "Unlimited" as last words of its name;

(b)   the Province or the part of Pakistan not forming part of a Province, as the case may be, in which registered office of the company is to be situate;

(c)   principal line of business:

Provided that—

(i)   the existing companies shall continue with their existing memorandum of association and the object stated at serial number 1 of the object clause shall be treated as the principal line of business;

(ii)   if the object stated at serial number 1 of the object clause is not the principal line of business of the company, it shall be required to intimate to the registrar their principal line of business within such time from the commencement of this Act and in the form as may be specified. A revised copy of the memorandum of association indicating therein its principal business at serial number 1 of the object clause shall also be furnished to the registrar; and

(iii)   the existing companies or the companies to be formed to carry on or engage in any business which is subject to a licence or registration, permission or approval shall mention the businesses as required under the respective law; and

(d)   an undertaking as may be specified;

(e)   that the liability of the members is unlimited.

---

[1] 2015 CLD 1482; 2011 CLD 193; 2009 CLD 1; 1969 PLD 278

(2) If the company has a share capital, the memorandum shall also state the amount of share capital with which the company proposes to be registered and the number of shares taken by each subscriber.

30. **Borrowing powers to be part of memorandum.**— Notwithstanding anything contained in this Act or in any other law for the time being in force or the memorandum and articles, the memorandum and articles of a company shall be deemed to include and always to have included the power to enter into any arrangement for obtaining loans, advances, finances or credit, as defined in the Banking Companies Ordinance, 1962 (LVII of 1962) and to issue

31. other securities not based on interest for raising resources from a scheduled bank, a financial institution or general public.

32. **Memorandum to be printed, signed and dated.**—The memorandum shall be[1]—

(a) printed in the manner generally acceptable;

(b) divided into paragraphs numbered consecutively;

(c) signed by each subscriber, who shall add his present name in full, his occupation and father's name or, in the case of a married woman or widow, her husband's or deceased husband's name in full, his nationality and his usual residential address and such other particulars as may be specified, in the presence of a witness who shall attest the signature and shall likewise add his particulars; and

(d) dated.

32. **Alteration of memorandum.**—(1) Subject to the provisions of this Act, a company may by special resolution alter the provisions of its memorandum so as to[2]—

(a) change the place of its registered office from.—

(i) one Province to another or from Islamabad Capital Territory and *vice versa*; or

(ii) one Province or Islamabad Capital Territory to a part of Pakistan not forming part of a Province and *vice versa*; or

(b) change its principal line of business; or

(c) adopt any business activity or any change therein which is subject to licence, registration, permission or approval under any law.

---

[1] 2015 CLD 1482; 2015 PTD 2210; 1999 CLC 106; 1996 PLD 99

[2] 2017 CLD 1411; 2017 CLD 587; 2015 SCMR 1494; 2015 CLD 323; 2013 CLD 1432;2010 CLD 1737; 2009 CLD 1; 2009 CLD 883; 2001 CLC 2019; 1991 MLD 1225; 1984 PLD 225; 1982 PLD 301; 1982 PLD 664; 1970 PLD 132; 1969 PLD 71; 1968 PLD 211; 1967 PLD 695; 1966 PLD 204; 1964 PLD 666

(2) The alteration shall not take effect until and except in so far as it is confirmed by the Commission on petition:

Provided that an alteration so as to change its principal line of business shall not require confirmation by the Commission.

(3) A copy of the order confirming the alteration duly certified by an authorised officer of the Commission shall be forwarded to the company and to the registrar within seven days from the date of the order.

(4) A copy of the memorandum of association as altered pursuant to the order under this section shall within thirty days from the date of the order be

(5) filed by the company with the registrar, who shall register the same and issue a certificate which shall be conclusive evidence that all the requirements of this Act with respect to the alteration and the confirmation thereof have been complied with and thenceforth the memorandum so filed shall be the memorandum of the company:

Provided that the Commission may by order, at any time on an application by the company, on sufficient cause shown extend the time for the filing of memorandum with the registrar under this section for such period as it thinks proper.

(5) Where the alteration involves a transfer of registered office from the jurisdiction of one company registration office to another, physical record of the company shall be transferred to the registrar concerned of the company registration office in whose jurisdiction the registered office of the company has been shifted.

(6) Where the alteration involves change in principal line of business, the company shall file the amended memorandum of association with the registrar within thirty days, which shall be recorded for the purposes of this Act.

33. **Powers of Commission when confirming alteration.**—The Commission may make an order confirming the alteration on such terms and conditions as it thinks fit and make such order as to costs as it thinks proper[1].

34. **Exercise of discretion by Commission.**—The Commission shall in exercising its discretion under sections 32 and 33 have regard to the rights and interests of the members of the company or of any class of them, as well as to the rights and interests of the creditors and may, if it thinks fit, give such directions and make such orders as it may think expedient for facilitating or carrying into effect any such arrangement[2].

35. **Effect of alteration in memorandum or articles.**— Notwithstanding anything contained in the memorandum or articles of a

---

[1] 2015 CLD 1482; 2010 CLD 1737; 2004 CLD 469; 1964 PLD 666
[2] 2017 CLD 1411; 2015 CLD 1482; 1964 PLD 666

company, no member of the company shall be bound by an alteration made in the memorandum or articles after the date on which he became a member if and so far as the alteration requires him to take or subscribe for more shares than the number held by him at the date on which the alteration is made or in any way increases his liability as at that date to contribute to the share capital of or otherwise to pay money to the company[1]:

Provided that this section shall not apply in any case where the member agrees in writing either before or after the alteration is made to be bound thereby.

ARTICLES OF ASSOCIATION

36. **Registration of articles.**—(1) There may, in the case of company limited by shares and there shall, in the case of a company limited by guarantee or an unlimited company, be registered with the memorandum, articles of association signed by the subscribers to the memorandum and setting out regulations for the company[2].

(2) Articles of association of a company limited by shares may adopt all or any of the regulations contained in Table A in the First Schedule to this Act.

(3) In the case of an unlimited company or a company limited by guarantee, the articles, if the company has a share capital, shall state the amount of share capital with which the company proposes to be registered.

(4) In the case of an unlimited company or a company limited by guarantee, if the company has no share capital, the articles shall state the number of members with which the company proposes to be registered.

(5) In the case of a company limited by shares and registered after the commencement of this Act, if articles are not registered, or, if articles are registered, in so far as the articles do not exclude or modify the regulations in Table A in the First Schedule to this Act, those regulations shall, so far as applicable, be the regulations of the company in the same manner and to the same extent as if they were contained in duly registered articles.

(6) The articles of every company shall be explicit and without ambiguity and, without prejudice to the generality of the foregoing, shall list and enumerate the voting and other rights attached to the different classes of shares and other securities, if any, issued or to be issued by it.

(7) If a company contravenes the provisions of its articles of association, the company and every officer of the company shall be liable to a penalty not exceeding of level 1 on the standard scale.

---

[1] 2016 CLD 1077; 2005 SCMR 1237; 2001 PLD 116; 2001 CLC 1267; 2000 CLC 1438; 1996 SCMR 88; 1987 PLD 512; 1987 CLC 2109; 1983 PLD 178; 1983 PLD 589; 1981 SCMR 108; 1968 PLD 412
[2] 2017 CLD 587; 2015 PTD 2210; 2015 SCMR 1494; 2008 CLD 31; 2006 PTD 1072; 2003 SCMR 132; 2003 CLD 183; 2001 PLD 37; 1999 PLD 450; 1986 MLD 1870

37. **Articles to be printed, signed and dated.**—The articles shall be[1]—

(a)   printed in the manner generally acceptable;

(b)   divided into paragraphs numbered consecutively;

(c)   signed by each subscriber, who shall add his present name in full, his occupation and father's name or, in the case of a married woman or widow, her husband's or deceased husband's name in full, his nationality and his usual residential address and such other particulars as may be specified, in the presence of a witness who shall attest the signature and shall likewise add his particulars; and

(d)   dated.

38.   **Alteration of articles.**—(1) Subject to the provisions of this Act and to the conditions contained in its memorandum, a company may, by special resolution, alter its articles and any alteration so made shall be as valid as if originally contained in the articles and be subject in like manner to alteration by special resolution[2]:

Provided that, where such alteration affects the substantive rights or liabilities of members or of a class of members, it shall be carried out only if a majority of at least three-fourths of the members or of the class of members affected by such alteration, as the case may be, exercise the option through vote personally or through proxy vote for such alteration.

(2) A copy of the articles of association as altered shall, within thirty days from the date of passing of the resolution, be filed by the company with the registrar and he shall register the same and thenceforth the articles so filed shall be the articles of the company.

39. **Copies of memorandum and articles to be given to members.**—(1) Each company shall send to every member, at his request and within fourteen days thereof, on payment of such sum, as the company may fix, a copy of the memorandum and the articles[3], if any.

(2) If a company makes default in complying with the requirements of sub-section (1), it shall be liable to a penalty not exceeding of level 1 on the standard scale.

40. **Alteration of memorandum or articles to be noted in every copy.**— (1) Where an alteration is made in the memorandum or articles of a company, every copy of the memorandum or articles issued after the date of the alteration shall conform to the memorandum or articles as so altered.

---

[1] 2015 PTD 2210

[2] 1983 PLD 589; 1956 PLD 731

[3] 2002 PTD 1889

(2) If, where any such alteration has been made, the company at any time after the date of the alteration issues any copies of the memorandum or articles which do not conform to the memorandum or articles as so altered it shall be liable to a penalty not exceeding of level 1 on the standard scale for each copy so issued and every officer of the company who is in default shall be liable to the like penalty.

41. **Form of memorandum and articles.**—The form of—

(a) memorandum of association of a company limited by shares;

(b) memorandum and articles of association of a company limited by guarantee and not having a share capital;

(c) memorandum and articles of association of a company limited by guarantee and having a share capital; and

(d) memorandum and articles of association of an unlimited company having a share capital,

shall be respectively in accordance with the forms set out in Tables B, C, D and E in the First Schedule or as near thereto as circumstances admit[1].

42. **Licencing of associations with charitable and not for profit objects.**—(1) Where it is proved to the satisfaction of the Commission that an association is to be formed as a limited company—

(a) for promoting commerce, art, science, religion, health, education, research, sports, protection of environment, social welfare, charity or any other useful object;

(b) such company—

(i) intends to apply the company's profits and other income in promoting its objects; and

(ii) prohibits the payment of dividends to the company's members; and

(c) such company's objects and activities are not and shall not, at any time, be against the laws, public order, security, sovereignty and national interests of Pakistan,

the Commission may, by licence for a period to be specified, permit the association to be registered as a public limited company, without addition of the word "Limited" or the expression "(Guarantee) Limited", to its name[2].

---

[1] 2011 CLD 23; 2006 CLD 85; 1971 PLD 550

[2] 2017 PLD 79; 2017 CLD 218; 2017 CLD 1127; 2017 CLD 1734; 2017 PLD 718; 2016 CLD 2155; 2013 CLD 2056; 2012 PLC 251; 2011 CLD 1228; 2011 PLD 276; 2011 SCMR 1709; 2011 PTD 756; 2011 CLD 1268; 2009 CLD 1; 2009 PTD 820; 2005 CLD 30; 1997 CLC 970; 1986 PTD 441; 1985 PTD 287; 1984 PTD 282; 1983 PLD 457; 1980 PLD 84; 1979 PLC 179; 1979 PLD 189

(2) A licence under sub-section (1) may be granted on such conditions and subject to such regulations as the Commission thinks fit and those conditions shall be inserted in and deemed part of the memorandum and articles, or in one of those documents.

(3) Memorandum and articles of association of a company, licenced under this section, shall be in accordance with the form set out in Table F in the First Schedule or as near thereto as circumstances admit and approved by the Commission.

(4) The association on registration under this section shall enjoy all the privileges and be subject to all the obligations of a limited company.

(5) The Commission may at any time by order in writing, revoke a licence granted under sub-section (1), with such directions as it may deem fit, on being satisfied that—

(a)   the company or its management has failed to comply with any of the terms or conditions subject to which a licence is granted; or

(b)   any of the requirements specified in sub-section (1) or any regulations made under this section are not met or complied with; or

(c)   affairs of the company are conducted in a manner prejudicial to public interest; or

(d)   the company has made a default in filing with the registrar its financial statements or annual returns for immediately preceding two consecutive financial years; or

(e)   the company has acted against the interest, sovereignty and integrity of Pakistan, the security of the State and friendly relations with foreign States; or

(f)   the number of members is reduced, below three; or

(g)   the company is—

    (i)   conceived or brought forth for, or is or has been carrying on, unlawful or fraudulent activities; or

    (ii)   run and managed by persons who fail to maintain proper and true accounts or they commit fraud, misfeasance or malfeasance in relation to the company; or

    (iii) run and managed by persons who are involved in terrorist financing or money laundering; or

    (iv)   managed by persons who refuse to act according to the requirements of the memorandum or articles or the provisions of this Act or failed to carry out the directions or decisions of the Commission or the registrar given in exercise of the powers conferred by this Act; or

    (v)   not carrying on its business or is not in operation for one year; or

(h)   it is just and equitable that the licence should be revoked:

Provided that before a licence is so revoked, the Commission shall give to the company a notice, in writing of its intention to do so, and shall afford the company an opportunity to be heard.

(6) Notwithstanding anything contained in this Act or any other law, no association shall be registered as a company with the objects as mentioned in clause (a) and the conditions provided in clause (b) of sub-section (1) without a licence granted in pursuance of this section.

43. **Effect of revocation of licence.**— (1) On revocation of licence of a company under section 42, by the Commission-

(a)   the company shall stop all its activities except the recovery of money owed to it, if any;

(b)   the company shall not solicit or receive donations from any source; and

(c)   all the assets of the company after satisfaction of all debts and liabilities shall, in the manner as may be specified, be transferred to another company licenced under section 42, preferably having similar or identical objects to those of the company, within ninety days from the revocation of the licence or such extended period as may be allowed by the Commission:

Provided that a reasonable amount to meet the expenses of voluntary winding up or making an application to the registrar for striking the name of the company off the register in terms of sub-section (3), may be retained by the company.

(2) After compliance of the requirements mentioned in sub-section (1), the board of the company shall file within fifteen days from the date of such compliance, a report to the registrar containing such information and supported with such documents as may be specified.

(3) Within thirty days of acceptance of the report by the registrar, submitted by the company under sub-section (2), the board shall initiate necessary proceedings for winding up of the company voluntarily or where it has no assets and liabilities make an application to the registrar for striking the name of the company off the register.

(4) If the company fails to comply with any of the requirements of this section within the period specified or such extended period as may be allowed

by the Commission, the Commission may, without prejudice to any other action under the law, appoint an administrator to manage affairs of the company subject to such terms and conditions as may be specified in the order and initiate necessary proceedings for winding up of the company.

(5)   The provisions of section 291, except those of sub-section (1) thereof, shall apply *mutatis mutandis* to the administrator appointed under this section.

(6) Where any assets of the company are transferred, in consequence of revocation of licence, to another company licenced under section 42, the members and officers of the first mentioned company or any of their family members shall not be eligible to hold any office in the later company for a period of five years from the date of transfer of such assets.

(7) Where the licence of a company has been revoked before the commencement of this Act and such company is not in the process of winding up, this section shall apply as if the licence was revoked immediately after the commencement of this Act.

44. **Penalty.**—If a company licenced under section 42 or any of its officers makes default in complying with any of the requirements of sections 42 and 43 or the rules or regulations or the terms or conditions to which the licence is subject or any directions contained in a revocation order, it shall without prejudice to any other action be punishable by a penalty not exceeding of level 2 on the standard scale.

45. **Provision as to companies limited by guarantee.**— (1) A company limited by guarantee may have share capital.

(2) In the case of a company limited by guarantee and not having a share capital, every provision in the memorandum or articles or in any resolution of the company purporting to give any person a right to participate in the divisible profits of the company otherwise than as a member shall be void.

(3) For the purpose of the provisions of this Act relating to the memorandum of a company limited by guarantee and of sub-section (2), every provision in the memorandum or articles, or in any resolution, of a company limited by guarantee purporting to divide the undertaking of the company into shares or interests shall be treated as a provision for a share capital, notwithstanding that the nominal amount or number of the shares or interests is not mentioned thereby.

CONVERSION OF A COMPANY OF ANY CLASS INTO A COMPANY OF OTHER CLASS AND RELATED MATTERS

46. **Conversion of public company into private company and *vice-versa*.**—(1) A public company may be converted into a private company with the prior approval of the Commission in writing by passing a special resolution

in this behalf by the public company amending its memorandum and articles of association in such a manner that they include the provisions relating to a private company in the articles and complying with all the requirements as may be specified:

Provided that in case of conversion of a listed company into a private company, the Commission shall give notice of every application made to it, to the securities exchange and shall take into consideration the representation if any, made to it by the securities exchange.

(2) On an application for change in status of a company under sub-section (1), if the Commission is satisfied that the company is entitled to be so converted, such conversion shall be allowed by an order in writing.

(3) A copy of the order, confirming the conversion under sub-section (2), duly certified by an authorised officer of the Commission shall be forwarded to the company and to the registrar within seven days from the date of the order.

(4) A copy of the memorandum and articles of association as altered pursuant to the order under sub-section (2) shall, within fifteen days from the date of the order, be filed by the company with the registrar and he shall register the same and thenceforth the memorandum and articles so filed shall be the memorandum and articles of the newly converted company.

(5) If a company, being a private company, alters its articles in such a manner that they no longer include the provisions which, under sub-section (1) of section 2, are required to be included in the articles of a company in order to constitute it a private company, the company shall—

(a)   as on the date of the alteration, cease to be a private company; and

(b)   file with the registrar a copy of the memorandum and articles of association as altered along with the special resolution.

(6) If default is made in complying with the provisions of any of the preceding sub-sections, the company and every officer of the company who is in default shall be liable to a penalty not exceeding of level 2 on the standard scale.

47.   **Conversion of status of private company into a single-member company and *vice-versa*.**—(1) A private company may be converted into a single-member company with prior approval of the Commission in writing by passing a special resolution in this behalf by the private company amending its memorandum and articles of association, in such a manner that they include the provisions relating to a single-member company in the articles and complying with all the requirements as may be specified.

(2) On an application for change in status of a company under sub-section (1), if the Commission is satisfied that the company is entitled to be so converted, such conversion shall be allowed by an order in writing.

(3) A copy of the order, confirming the conversion under sub-section (2), duly certified by an authorised officer of the Commission shall be forwarded to the company and to the registrar within seven days from the date of the order.

(4) A copy of the memorandum and articles of association as altered pursuant to the order under sub- section (2) shall, within fifteen days from the date of the order, be filed by the company with the registrar and he shall register the same and thenceforth the memorandum and articles so filed shall be the memorandum and articles of the newly converted company.

(5) If a company, being a single member company, alters its articles in such a manner that they no longer include the provisions which are required to be included in the articles of a company in order to constitute it a single member company, the company shall—

(a)   as on the date of the alteration, cease to be a single member company; and

(b)   file with the registrar a copy of the memorandum and articles of association as altered along with the special resolution.

(6) If default is made in complying with the provisions of any of the preceding sub-sections, the company, and every officer of the company who is in default, shall be liable to a penalty not exceeding of level 2 on the standard scale.

48. **Conversion of status of unlimited company as limited company and *vice-versa*.**— (1) An unlimited company may be converted into a limited company with prior approval of the Commission in writing by passing a special resolution in this behalf by the unlimited company amending its memorandum and articles of association in such a manner that they include the provisions relating to a company limited by shares in the articles and complying with all the requirements as may be specified.

(2) On an application for change in status of a company under sub-section (1), if the Commission is satisfied that the company is entitled to be so converted, such conversion shall be allowed by an order in writing.

(3) A copy of the order, confirming the conversion under sub-section (2) duly certified by an authorised officer of the Commission shall be forwarded to the company and to the registrar within seven days from the date of the order.

(4) If a company, being a limited company, alters its memorandum and articles in such a manner that they include the provisions which constitute it as a company having unlimited liability of its members, the company shall—

(a)   as on the date of the alteration, cease to be a limited company; and (b)　file with the registrar a copy of the memorandum and articles of association as altered along with the special resolution.

(5) If default is made in complying with the provisions of any of the preceding sub-sections, the company and every officer of the company who is in default shall be liable to a penalty not exceeding of level 2 on the standard scale.

49. **Conversion of a company limited by guarantee to a company limited by shares and *vice-versa*.**—(1) A company limited by guarantee may be converted into a company limited by shares with prior approval of the Commission in writing by passing a special resolution in this behalf by the company limited by guarantee amending its memorandum and articles of association in such a manner that they include the provisions relating to a company limited by shares in the articles and complying with all the requirements as may be specified.

(2) On an application for change in status of a company under sub-section (1), if the Commission is satisfied that the company is entitled to be so converted, such conversion shall be allowed by an order in writing.

(3) A copy of the order, confirming the conversion under sub-section (2) duly certified by an authorised officer of the Commission shall be forwarded to the company and to the registrar within seven days from the date of the order.

(4) A copy of the memorandum and articles of association as altered pursuant to the order under sub-section (2) shall within fifteen days from the date of the order be filed by the company with the registrar and he shall register the same and thenceforth the memorandum and articles so filed shall be the memorandum and articles of the newly converted company.

(5) If a company, being limited by shares, alters its memorandum and articles in such a manner that they include the provisions which constitute it a company limited by guarantee, the company shall—

(a)　as on the date of the alteration, cease to be a company limited by shares; and

(b)　file with the registrar a copy of the memorandum and articles of association as altered along with the special resolution.

(6) If default is made in complying with the provisions of any of the preceding sub-sections, the company and every officer of the company who is in default shall be liable to a penalty not exceeding of level 2 on the standard scale.

50. **Issue of certificate and effects of conversion.**— (1) The registrar upon registration of the memorandum and articles of association as altered by the company upon conversion under sections 46 to 49, shall issue a certificate to that effect.

(2)   The conversion of status of a company under sections 46 to 49 shall not affect

(a)   any debts, liabilities, obligations or contracts incurred or entered into, by or on behalf of the company before conversion and such debts, liabilities, obligations and contracts may be enforced in the manner as if such registration had not been done; and

(b)   any rights or obligations of the company or render defective any legal proceedings by or against the company and any legal

(c)   proceedings that might have been continued or commenced against the company before conversion may be continued or commenced upon its conversion.

51. Power of unlimited company to provide for reserve share capital on conversion of status to a limited company.—An unlimited company having a share capital may, by its resolution for registration as a limited company in pursuance of this Act, increase the nominal amount of its share capital by increasing the nominal amount of each of its shares, subject to the condition that no part of the amount by which its capital is so increased shall be capable of being called up except in the event and for the purpose of the company being wound up.

52. Consequence of default in complying with conditions constituting a company a private company.— Where the articles of a company include the provisions which, under sub-section (1) of section 2, are required to be included in the articles of a company in order to constitute it as a private company, but default is made in complying with any of those provisions, the company shall cease to be entitled to the privileges and exemptions conferred on private companies by or under this Act and this Act shall apply to the company as if it were not a private company[1]:

Provided that the Commission, on being satisfied that the failure to comply with the conditions was accidental or due to inadvertence or to some other sufficient cause or that on other ground it is just and equitable to grant relief, may, on the application of the company or any other person interested and on such terms and conditions as seem to the Commission just and expedient, make order that the company be relieved from such consequences as aforesaid.

SERVICE AND AUTHENTICATION OF DOCUMENTS

53. Service of documents on a company.— A document or information may be served on the company or any of its officers at the registered office of the company against an acknowledgement or by post or

---

[1] 2010 PTD 1861

courier service or through electronic means or in any other manner as may be specified[1].

54. **Service of documents on Commission or the registrar.**— A document or information may be served on the Commission or the registrar against an acknowledgement or by post or courier service or through electronic means or in any other manner as may be specified.

55. **Service of notice on a member.**— (1) A document or information may be served on a member at his registered address or, if he has no registered address in Pakistan, at the address supplied by him to the company for the giving of notices to him against an acknowledgement or by post or courier service or through electronic means or in any other manner as may be specified[2].

(2) Where a notice is sent by post, service of the notice shall be deemed to be effected by properly addressing, prepaying and posting a letter containing the notice and, unless the contrary is proved, to have been effected at the time at which the letter will be delivered in the ordinary course of post.

(3) A notice may be given by the company to the joint-holders of a share by giving the notice to the joint-holder named first in the register in respect of the share.

(4) A notice may, in the manner provided under sub-section (1), be given by the company to the person entitled to a share in consequence of death or insolvency of a member addressed to him by name or by the title or representatives of the deceased or assignees of the insolvent or by any like description, at the address supplied for the purpose by the person claiming to be so entitled.

56. **Authentication of documents and proceedings.**—Save as expressly provided in this Act, a document or proceeding requiring authentication by a company may be signed by an officer of the company or a representative authorized by the board.

PART V

PROSPECTUS, ALLOTMENT, ISSUE AND TRANSFER OF SHARES AND OTHER SECURITIES

57. **Prospectus.**—(1) No prospectus shall be issued by or on behalf of a company unless on or before the date of its publication, a copy thereof signed by

---

[1] 2010 CLD 254

[2] 2009 CLD 1713; 2000 CLC 477; 1999 CLC 1989; 1991 MLD 2675; 1987 CLC 726; 1968 PLD 381; 1956 PLD 731

every person who is named therein as a director or proposed director of the company has been filed with the registrar[1].

(2) In case of any contravention of this section, the company and every person who is a party to the issue, publication or circulation of the prospectus shall be liable to a penalty not exceeding of level 2 on the standard scale.

58. **Classes and kinds of share capital.**—A company having share capital shall issue only fully paid shares which may be of different kinds and classes as provided by its memorandum and articles[2]:

Provided that different rights and privileges in relation to the different kinds and classes of shares may only be conferred in such manner as may be specified.

59. **Variation of shareholders' rights.**— (1) The variation of the right of shareholders of any class shall be effected only in the manner laid down in section 38.

(2) Not less than ten percent of the class of shareholders who are aggrieved by the variation of their rights under sub-section (1) may, within thirty days of the date of the resolution varying their rights, apply to the Court for an order cancelling the resolution[3]:

Provided that the Court shall not pass such an order unless it is shown to its satisfaction that some facts which would have had a bearing on the decision of the shareholders were withheld by the company in getting the aforesaid resolution passed or, having regard to all the circumstances of the case, that the variation would unfairly prejudice the shareholders of the class represented by the applicant.

(3) An application under sub-section (2) may be made on behalf of the shareholders entitled to make it by such one or more of their number as they may authorise in writing in this behalf.

(4) The company shall, within fifteen days of the service on the company of any order made on any such application, forward a copy of the order to the registrar and, if default is made in complying with this provision, the person making the default shall be guilty of an offence under this section and be liable to a penalty not exceeding of level 1 on the standard scale.

(5) The expression "**variation**" under this section includes abrogation, revocation or enhancement.

---

[1] 2017 CLD 368; 2016 CLD 1164; 2016 CLD 2125; 2016 CLC 1561; 2013 CLD 1097; 2012 CLD 44; 2005 CLD 275

[2] 2009 CLD 1; 2000 PLD 461; 1992 CLC 2273; 1982 PLD 768; 1982 CLC 463; 1958 PLD 7

[3] 1983 CLC 162

SHARE CAPITAL AND NATURE, NUMBERING AND CERTIFICATE OF SHARES

60. **Numbering of shares.**— Every share in a company having a share capital shall be distinguished by its distinctive number:

Provided that nothing in this section shall apply to a share held by a person whose name is entered as holder of beneficial interest in such share in the records of a central depository system.

61. **Nature of shares or other securities.**—The shares or other securities of any member in a company shall be movable property transferable in the manner provided by the articles of the company[1].

62. **Shares certificate to be evidence.**— (1) A certificate, if issued in physical form under common seal of the company or under official seal, which must be facsimile of the company's common seal, or issued in book-entry form, specifying the shares held by any person or shares held in central depository system shall be *prima facie* evidence of the title of the person to such shares.

(2) Notwithstanding anything contained in the articles of a company, the manner of issue of a certificate of shares, the form of such certificate and other matters shall be such as may be specified.

SPECIAL PROVISIONS AS TO DEBENTURES

63. **Issue of debentures.**— (1) A company may issue different kinds of debentures having different classes, rights and privileges as may be specified.

(2) The rights, privileges and the procedure, for securing the issue of debentures, the form of debenture trust deed, the procedure for the debenture holders to inspect the trust deed and to obtain a copy thereof shall be such as may be specified.

64. **Payment of certain debts out of assets subject to floating charge in priority to claims under the charge.**—(1) Where either a receiver is appointed on behalf of the holders of any debentures of a company secured by a floating charge, or possession is taken by or on behalf of these debenture holders of any property comprised in or subject to the charge, then, if the company is not at the time in course of being wound up, the debts which in every winding up are under the provisions of Part-X relating to preferential payments to be paid in priority to all other debts, shall be paid forthwith out of any assets coming to the hands of the receiver or other person taking possession as aforesaid in priority to any claim for principal or interest in respect of the debentures.

(2) The periods of time mentioned in the said provisions of Part-X shall be reckoned from the date of the appointment of the receiver or of possession being taken as aforesaid, as the case may be.

---

[1] 2015 CLD 1309; 2003 SCMR 132; 2003 CLD 183; 1996 PLD 27

(3) Any payments made under sub-section (1) shall be recouped, as far as may be, out of the assets of the company available for payment of general creditors.

65. **Powers and liabilities of trustee.**—(1) The trustee nominated or appointed under the trust-deed for securing an issue of debentures shall, if so empowered by such deed, have the right to sue for all redemption monies and interest in the following cases, namely--

(a) where the issuer of the debentures as mortgagor binds himself to repay the debenture loan or pay the accrued interest thereon, or both to repay the loan and pay the interest thereon, in the manner provided on the due date;

(b) where by any cause other than the wrongful act or default of the issuer the mortgaged property is wholly or partially destroyed or the security is rendered insufficient within the meaning of section 66 of the Transfer of Property Act, 1882 (Act IV of 1882), and the trustee has given the issuer a reasonable opportunity of providing further security adequate to render the whole security sufficient and the issuer has failed to do so;

(c) where the trustee is deprived of the whole or part of the security by or in consequence of any wrongful act or default on the part of the issuer; and

(d) where the trustee is entitled to take possession of the mortgaged property and the issuer fails to deliver the same to him or to secure the possession thereof without disturbance by the issuer or any person claiming under a title superior to that of the issuer.

(2) Where a suit is brought under clause (a) or clause (b) of sub-section (1) the Court may at its discretion stay the suit and all proceedings therein notwithstanding any contract to the contrary, until the trustee has exhausted all his available remedies against the mortgaged property or what remains of it unless the trustee abandons his security and, if necessary, retransfers the mortgaged property.

(3) Notwithstanding anything contained in sub-sections (1) and (2) or any other law for the time being in force, the trustee or any person acting on his behalf shall, if so authorised by the trust-deed, sell or concur in selling, without intervention of the Court, the mortgaged property or any part thereof in default of payment according to re-payment schedule of any redemption amount or in the payment of any accrued interest on the due date by the issuer.

Explanation.— "**Issuer**" for the purpose of this section, shall mean the company issuing debentures and securing the same by mortgage of its properties or assets, or both its properties and assets, and appointing a trustee under a trust-deed.

(4) Subject to the provisions of this section, any provision contained in a trust-deed for securing an issue of debentures, or in any contract with the holders of debentures secured by a trust-deed, shall be void in so far as it would have the effect of exempting a trustee thereof from, or indemnifying him against, liability for breach of trust, where he fails to show the degree of care and diligence required of him as trustee, having regard to the provisions of the trust-deed conferring on him any power, authority or discretion.

(5)   Sub-section (4) shall not invalidate-

(a)   any release otherwise validly given in respect of any act or omission by a trustee before the giving of the release; or

(b)   any provision enabling such a release to be given-

    (i)   on the agreement thereto of a majority of not less than three-fourths in value of the debenture-holders present and voting in person or, where proxies are permitted, by proxy, at a meeting summoned for the purpose; and

    (ii)   either with respect to specific acts or omissions or on the trustee dying or ceasing to act.

(6)   Sub-section (4) shall not operate-

(a)   to invalidate any provision in force immediately before the commencement of this Act, so long as any person then entitled to the benefit of that provision or afterwards given the benefit thereof under sub-section (7) remains as trustee of the deed in question; or

(b)   to deprive any person of any exemption or right to be indemnified in respect of any act or omission by him while any such provision was in force.

(7) While any trustee of a trust-deed remains entitled to the benefit or provision saved by sub-section (6), the benefits of that provision may be given either--

(a)   to all trustees of the deed, present and future; or

(b)   to any named trustees or proposed trustees thereof;

by a resolution passed by a majority of not less than three-fourths in value of the debenture-holders present in person or, where proxies are permitted, by proxy, at a meeting called for the purpose in accordance with the provisions of the deed or, if the deed makes no provisions for calling meetings, at a meeting called for the purpose in any manner approved by the Court.

66. **Issue of securities and redeemable capital not based on interest.**— (1) A company may by public offer or, upon terms and conditions contained in an agreement in writing, issue to one or more scheduled banks, financial institutions or such other persons as are notified for the purpose by the Commission either severally, jointly or through their syndicate, any instrument in the nature of redeemable capital in any or several forms in consideration of funds, moneys or accommodations received or to be received by the company, whether in cash or in specie or against any promise, guarantee, undertaking or indemnity issued to or in favour of or for the benefit of the company.

(2) In particular and without prejudice to the generality of the forgoing provisions, the agreement referred to in sub-section (1) for redeemable capital may provide for, adopt or include, in addition to others, all or any of the following matters, namely-

(a) mode and basis of repayment by the company of the amount invested in redeemable capital within a certain period of time;

(b) arrangement for sharing of profit and loss;

(c) creation of a special reserve called the "participation reserves" by the company in the manner provided in the agreement for the issue of participatory redeemable capital in which all providers of such capital shall participate for interim and final adjustment on the maturity date in accordance with the terms and conditions of such agreements ; and

(d) in case of net loss on participatory redeemable capital on the date of maturity, the right of holders to convert the outstanding, balance of such capital or part thereof as provided in the agreement into ordinary shares of the company at the break-up price calculated in the specified manner.

(3) The terms and conditions for the issue of instruments or certificates of redeemable capital and the rights of their holders shall not be challenged or questioned by the company or any of its shareholders unless repugnant to any provision of this Act or any other law or the memorandum or articles or any resolution of the general meeting or directors of the company or any other document.

(4) The provision of this Act relating to the creation, issue, increase or decrease of the capital shall not apply to the redeemable capital.

ALLOTMENT

67. **Application for, and allotment of, shares and debentures.**—(1) No application for allotment of shares in and debentures of a company in pursuance of a prospectus shall be made for shares or debentures of less than

such nominal amount as the Commission may, from time to time, specify, either generally or in a particular case.

(2) The Commission may specify the form of an application for subscription to shares in or debentures of a company which may, among other matters, contain such declarations or verifications as it may, in the public interest, deem necessary; and such form then shall form part of the prospectus.

(3) All certificates, statements and declarations made by the applicant shall be binding on him.

(4) An application for shares in or debentures of a company which is made in pursuance of a prospectus shall be irrevocable.

(5) Whoever contravenes the provisions of sub-section (1) or sub-section (2), or makes an incorrect statement, declaration or verification in the application for allotment of shares, shall be liable to a penalty of level 2 on the standard scale.

68. **Repayment of money received for shares not allotted**.— (1) Where a company issues any invitation to the public to subscribe for its shares or other securities, the company shall refund the money in the case of the unaccepted or unsuccessful applications within the time as may be specified.

(2) If the refund required by sub-section (1) is not made within the time specified, the directors of the company shall be jointly and severally liable to repay that money with surcharge at the rate of two percent for every month or part thereof from the expiration of the fifteenth day and, in addition, shall be liable to a penalty of level 3 on the standard scale.

69. **Allotment of shares and other securities to be dealt in on securities exchange.**—

(1)   Where a prospectus, whether issued generally or not, states that application has been or will be made for permission for the shares or other securities offered thereby to be dealt in on the securities exchange, any allotment made on an application in pursuance of the prospectus shall, whenever made, be void if the permission has not been applied for before the seventh day after the first issue of the prospectus or if the permission has not been granted before the expiration of twenty-one days from the date of the closing of the subscription lists or such longer period not exceeding forty-two days as may, within the said twenty-one days, be notified to the applicants for permission by the securities exchange[1].

(2) Where the permission has not been applied for or has not been granted as aforesaid, the company shall forthwith repay without surcharge all money received from applicants in pursuance of the prospectus, and, if any such

---

[1] 1989 PTD 676

money is not repaid within eight days after the company becomes liable to repay it, the directors of the company shall be jointly and severally liable to repay that money from the expiration of the eighth day together with surcharge at the rate of two percent for every month or part thereof from the expiration of the eighth day and in addition, shall be liable to a penalty of level 3 on the standard scale.

(3) All moneys received as aforesaid shall be deposited and kept in a separate bank account in a scheduled bank so long as the company may become liable to repay it under sub-section (2); and, if default is made in complying with this sub-section, the company and every officer of the company who authorises or permits the default shall be liable to a penalty of level 2 on the standard scale.

(4) For the purposes of this section, permission shall not be deemed to be refused if it is intimated that the application for it, though not at present granted, will be given further consideration.

(5) This section shall have effect--

(a)   in relation to any shares or securities agreed to be taken by a person underwriting an offer thereof by a prospectus as if he had applied therefor in pursuance of the prospectus; and

(b)   in relation to a prospectus offering shares for sale with the following modifications, that is to say--

(i)   reference to sale shall be substituted for reference to allotment;

(ii)   the person by whom the offer is made and not the company, shall be liable under sub-section (2) to repay the money received from applicant, and reference to the company's liability under that sub-section shall be construed accordingly; and

(iii)   for the reference in sub-section (3) to the company and every officer of the company there shall be substituted a reference to any person by or through whom the offer is made and who authorises or permits the default.

70. **Return as to allotments.**— (1) Whenever a company having a share capital makes any allotment of its shares, the company shall, within forty-five days thereafter[1]-

(a)   file with the registrar a return of the allotment, stating the number and nominal amount of the shares comprised in the allotment and such particulars as may be specified, of each allottee, and the amount paid on each share; and

---

[1] 2007 CLD 334; 2005 PTD 2403; 2003 PTD 1097; 2001 PTD 1180; 1999 CLC 1989; 1991 PLD 441; 1980 PLD 401; 1968 PLD 381; 1956 PLD 731

(b)   in the case of shares allotted as paid up in cash, submit along with the return of allotment, a report from its auditor to the effect that the amount of consideration has been received in full by the company and shares have been issued to each allottee:

>   Provided that in case, the appointment of auditor is not mandatory by a company, the report for the purpose shall be obtained from a practicing chartered accountant or a cost and management accountant;

(c)   in the case of shares allotted as paid up otherwise than in cash, submit along with the return of allotment, a copy of the document evidencing the transfer of non-cash asset to the company, or a copy of the contract for technical and other services, intellectual property or other consideration, along with copy of the valuation report (verified in the specified manner) for registration in respect of which that allotment was made;

(d)   file with the registrar--

(i)   in the case of bonus shares, a return stating the number and nominal amount of such shares comprised in the allotment and the particulars of allottees together with a copy of the resolution authorising the issue of such shares;

(ii)   in the case of issue of shares at a discount, a copy of the resolution passed by the company authorising such issue and where the maximum rate of discount exceeds ten per cent, a copy of the order of the Commission permitting the issue at the higher percentage.

>   ***Explanation.***— Shares shall not be deemed to have been paid for in cash except to the extent that the company shall actually have received cash therefor at the time of, or subsequent to, the agreement to issue the shares, and where shares are issued to a person who has sold or agreed to sell property or rendered or agreed to render services to the company, or to persons nominated by him, the amount of any payment made for the property or services shall be deducted from the amount of any cash payment made for the shares and only the balance, if any, shall be treated as having been paid in cash for such shares, notwithstanding any bill of exchange or cheques or other securities for money.

(2)   If the registrar is satisfied that in the circumstances of any particular case the period of forty five days specified in sub-sections (1) for compliance with the requirements of this section is inadequate, he may extend that period as he thinks fit, and, if he does so, the provisions of sub-sections (1) shall have effect in that particular case as if for the said period of forty five days the extended period allowed by the registrar were substituted.

(3) No return of allotment shall be required to be filed for the shares taken by the subscribers to the memorandum on the formation of the company.

(4) Any violation of this section shall be an offence liable to a penalty of level 1 on the standard scale.

(5) This section shall apply *mutatis mutandis* to shares which are allotted or issued or deemed to have been issued to a scheduled bank or a financial institution in pursuance of any obligation of a company to issue shares to such scheduled bank or financial institution:

Provided that where default is made by a company in filing a return of allotment in respect of the shares referred to in this sub-section, the scheduled bank or the financial institution to whom shares have been allotted or issued or deemed to have been issued may file a return of allotment in respect of such shares with the registrar together with such documents as may be specified by the Commission in this behalf, and such return of allotment shall be deemed to have been filed by the company itself and the scheduled bank the financial institution shall be entitled to recover from the company the amount of any fee properly paid by it to the registrar in respect of the return.

CERTIFICATE OF SHARES AND OTHER SECURITIES

71. **Limitation of time for issue of certificates.**— (1) Every company shall issue certificates of shares or other securities within thirty days after the allotment of any of its shares or other securities and ensure delivery of the certificates to the person entitled thereto at his registered address[1].

(2) Any violation of this section shall be an offence liable to a penalty of level 1 on the standard scale.

72. **Issuance of shares in book-entry form.**—(1) After the commencement of this Act from a date notified by the Commission, a company having share capital, shall have shares in book-entry form only.

(2) Every existing company shall be required to replace its physical shares with book-entry form in a manner as may be specified and from the date notified by the Commission, within a period not exceeding four years from the commencement of this Act:

Provided that the Commission may notify different dates for different classes of companies:

Provided further that the Commission may, if it deems appropriate, extend the period for another two years besides the period stated herein.

(3) Nothing contained in this section shall apply to the shares of such companies or class of companies as may be notified by the Commission.

---

[1] 2012 CLD 1439; 2006 CLD 295; 2006 CLD 350; 2006 CLD 1386; 2005 PTD 2403; 1987 CLC 2079

73. **Issue of duplicate certificates.**—(1) A duplicate of a certificate of shares, or other securities, shall be issued by the company within thirty days from the date of application if the original[1]-

(a)   is proved to have been lost or destroyed, or

(b)   having been defaced or mutilated or torn is surrendered to the company.

(2) The company, after making such inquiry as to the loss, destruction, defacement or mutilation of the original, as it may deem fit to make, shall, subject to such terms and conditions, if any, as it may consider necessary, issue the duplicate:

Provided that the company may charge fee and the actual expenses incurred on such inquiry.

(3) If the company for any reasonable cause is unable to issue duplicate certificate, it shall notify this fact, along with the reasons within twenty days from the date of the application, to the applicant.

(4) Any violation of this section shall be an offence liable to a penalty of level 1 on the standard scale.

(5) If a company with intent to defraud, issues a duplicate certificate thereof, the company shall be punishable with fine which may extend to one hundred thousand rupees and every officer of the company who is in default shall be punishable with imprisonment for a term which may extend to one hundred and eighty days, or with fine which may extend to fifty thousand rupees, or with both.

TRANSFER OF SHARES AND OTHER SECURITIES

74.   **Transfer of shares and other securities.**— (1) An application for registration of transfer of shares and other transferable securities along with proper instrument of transfer duly stamped and executed by the transferor and the transferee may be made to the company either by the transferor or the transferee, and subject to the provisions of this section, the company shall within fifteen days after the application for the registration of the transfer of any such securities, complete the process[2] and—

(a)   ensure delivery of the certificates to the transferee at his registered address; and

(b)   enter in its register of members the name of the transferee:

---

[1] 2011 CLD 1211

[2] 2015 CLD 1532; 2012 CLD 1966; 2012 PTD 1883; 2012 CLD 1439; 2011 CLD 634; 2007 CLD 637; 2005 CLD 1291; 2000 CLC 4; 2000 CLC 477; 2000 CLC 1559; 1998 CLC 1157; 1997 CLC 514; 1996 PLD 27; 1994 SCMR 2284; 1993 MLD 42; 1991 MLD 203; 1989 MLD 4338; 1987 MLD 2729; 1977 PLD 814; 1971 PLD SC 61; 1954 PLD 745; 1967 PLD 144

Provided that in case of conversion of physical shares and other transferable securities into book-entry form, the company shall, within ten days after an application is made for the registration of the transfer of any shares or other securities to a central depository, register such transfer in the name of the central depository:

Provided further that nothing in this section shall apply to any transfer of shares or other securities pursuant to a transaction executed on the securities exchange.

(2) Where a transfer deed is lost, destroyed or mutilated before its lodgment, the company may on an application made by the transferee and bearing the stamp required by an instrument of transfer, register the transfer of shares or other securities if the transferee proves to the satisfaction of the board that the transfer deed duly executed has been lost, destroyed or mutilated:

Provided that before registering the transfer of shares or other securities, the company may demand such indemnity as it may think fit.

(3) All references to the shares or other securities in this section, shall in case of a company not having share capital, be deemed to be references to interest of the members in the company.

(4) Every company shall maintain at its registered office a register of transfers of shares and other securities and such register shall be open to inspection by the members and supply of copy thereof in the manner stated in section 124.

(5) Nothing in sub-section (1) shall prevent a company from registering as shareholder or other securities holder a person to whom the right to any share or security of the company has been transmitted by operation of law.

(6) Any violation of this section shall be an offence liable to a penalty of level 2 on the standard scale.

75. **Board not to refuse transfer of shares.**—The board shall not refuse to transfer any shares or securities unless the transfer deed is, for any reason, defective or invalid[1]:

Provided that the company shall within fifteen days or, where the transferee is a central depository, within five days from the date on which the instrument of transfer was lodged with it notify the defect or invalidity to the transferee who shall, after the removal of such defect or invalidity, be entitled to re-lodge the transfer deed with the company:

Provided further that the provisions of this section shall, in relation to a private company, be subject to such limitations and restrictions as may have been imposed by the articles of such company.

---

[1] 2012 CLD 710; 2011 CLD 634; 2006 CLD 1386; 1997 MLD 2155

76. **Restriction on transfer of shares by the members of a private company**.— (1) Notwithstanding anything contained in section 75, a member of a private company desirous of selling any shares held by him, shall intimate to the board of his intention through a notice.

(2) On receipt of such notice, the board shall, within a period of ten days, offer those shares for sale to the members in proportion to their existing shareholding:

Provided that a private company may transfer or sell its shares in accordance with its articles of association and agreement among the shareholders, if any, entered into prior to the commencement of this Act:

Provided further that any such agreement will be valid only if it is filed with the registrar within ninety days of the commencement of this Act.

(3)   The letter of offer for sale specifying the number of shares to which the member is entitled, price per share and specifying the time limit, within which the offer, if not accepted, be deemed as declined, shall be dispatched to the members through registered post or courier or through electronic mode.

(4)   If the whole or any part of the shares offered is declined or is not taken, the board may offer such shares to the other members in proportion to their shareholding.

(5)   If all the members decline to accept the offer or if any shares are left over, the shares may be sold to any other person as determined by the member, who initiated the offer.

(6)   For the purpose of this section, the mechanism to determine the price of shares shall be such, as may be specified.

77. **Notice of refusal to transfer.**—(1) If a company refuses to register a transfer of any shares or other securities, the company shall, within fifteen days after the date on which the instrument of transfer was lodged with the company, send to the transferee notice of the refusal indicating reasons for such refusal[1]:

Provided that failure of the company to give notice of refusal after the expiry of the period mentioned in this section or section 75, shall be deemed refusal of transfer.

(2) Any violation of this section shall be an offence liable to a penalty of level 2 on the standard scale.

---

[1] 2017 CLD 1237; 2012 CLD 710; 2011 CLD 634

78. Transfer to successor-in-interest.—The shares or other securities of a deceased member shall be transferred on application duly supported by succession certificate or by lawful award, as the case may be, in favour of the successors to the extent of their interests and their names shall be entered in the register of members[1].

79. Transfer to nominee of a deceased member.—(1) Notwithstanding anything contained in any other law for the time being in force or in any disposition by a member of a company of his interest represented by the shares held by him as a member of the company, a person may on acquiring interest in a company as member, represented by shares, at any time after acquisition of such interest deposit with the company a nomination conferring on a person the right to protect the interest of the legal heirs in the shares of the deceased in the event of his death, as a trustee and to facilitate the transfer of shares to the legal heirs of the deceased subject to succession to be determined under the Islamic law of inheritance and in case of a non-*Muslim* members, as per their respective law[2].

(2) The person nominated under this section shall, after the death of the member, be deemed as a member of company till the shares are transferred to the legal heirs and if the deceased was a director of the company, not being a listed company, the nominee shall also act as director of the company to protect the interest of the legal heirs.

(3) The person to be nominated under this section shall not be a person other than the relatives of the member, namely, a spouse, father, mother, brother, sister and son or daughter.

(4) The nomination as aforesaid, shall in no way prejudice the right of the member making the nomination to transfer, dispose of or otherwise deal in the shares owned by him during his lifetime and, shall have effect in respect of the shares owned by the said member on the day of his death.

80. Appeal against refusal for registration of transfer.—(1) The transferor or transferee, or the person who gives intimation of the transmission by operation of law, as the case may be, aggrieved by the refusal of transfer under section 75 to 79 may appeal to the Commission within a period of sixty days of the date of refusal.

(2) The Commission shall, provide opportunity of hearing to the parties concerned and may, by an order in writing, direct that the transfer or transmission should be registered by the company and the company shall give effect to the decision within fifteen days of the receipt of the order.

---

[1] 2013 CLD 1229; 2011 CLD 634; 2010 CLD 1234
[2] 2009 CLD 1; 1989 PTD 676

(3) The Commission may, in its aforesaid order, give such incidental and consequential directions as to the payment of costs or otherwise as it deems fit.

(4) If default is made in giving effect to the order of the Commission within the period specified in sub-section (2), every director and officer of the company shall be liable to a penalty of level 3 on the standard scale.

COMMISSION, DISCOUNT AND PREMIUM

81. **Application of premium received on issue of shares.**— (1) If a company issues shares at a premium, whether for cash or otherwise, a sum equal to the aggregate amount or the value of the premiums on those shares must be transferred to an account, called "the share premium account"[1].

(2)   Where, on issuing shares, a company has transferred a sum to the share premium account, it may use that sum to write off--

(a)   the preliminary expenses of the company;

(b)   the expenses of, or the commission paid or discount allowed on, any issue of shares of the company; and

(c)   in providing for the premium payable on the redemption of any redeemable preference shares of the company[2].

(3)   The company may also use the share premium account to issue bonus shares to its members.

82. **Power to issue shares at a discount.**—(1) Subject to the provisions of this section, it shall be lawful for a company to issue shares in the company at a discount[3]:

Provided that--

(a)   the issue of shares at a discount must be authorised by special resolution passed in the general meeting of the company;

(b)   the resolution must specify the number of shares to be issued, rate of discount, not exceeding the limits permissible under this section and price per share proposed to be issued;

(c)   in case of listed companies discount shall only be allowed if the market price is lower than the par value of the shares for a continuous period of past ninety trading days immediately preceding the date of announcement by the board; and

(d)   the issue of shares at discount must be sanctioned by the Commission:

---

[1] 2006 CLD 556
[2] 1988 MLD 666; 1988 MLD 678
[3] 2017 CLD 1395; 2011 CLD 1783

Provided further that approval of the Commission shall not be required by a listed company for issuing shares at a discount if the discounted price is not less than ninety percent of the par value;

(e)　no such resolution for issuance of shares at discount shall be sanctioned by the Commission if the offer price per share, specified in the resolution, is less than-

　(i)　in case of listed companies, ninety percent of volume weighted average daily closing price of shares for ninety days prior to the announcement of discount issue; or

　(ii)　in case of other than listed companies, the breakup value per share based on assets (revalued not later than 3 years) or per share value based on discounted cash flow:

Provided that the calculation arrived at, for the purpose of sub-clause (i) or (ii) of clause (e) above, shall be certified by the statutory auditor;

(f)　directors and sponsors of listed companies shall be required to subscribe their portion of proposed issue at volume weighted average daily closing price of shares for ninety days prior to the announcement of discount issue;

(g)　not less than three years have elapsed since the date on which the company was entitled to commence business;

(h)　the share at a discount must be issued within sixty days after the date on which the issue is sanctioned by the Commission or within such extended time as the Commission may allow.

(2) Where a company has passed a special resolution authorising the issue of shares at a discount, it shall apply to the Commission where applicable, for an order sanctioning the issue. The Commission on such application may, if, having regard to all the circumstances of the case, thinks proper so to do, make an order sanctioning the issue of shares at discount subject to such terms and conditions as it deems fit.

(3) Issue of shares at a discount shall not be deemed to be reduction of capital.

(4) Every prospectus relating to the issue of shares, and every statement of financial position issued by the company subsequent to the issue of shares, shall contain particulars of the discount allowed on the issue of the shares.

(5) Any violation of this section shall be an offence liable to a penalty of level 3 on the standard scale.

83. **Further issue of capital.**—(1) Where the directors decide to increase share capital of the company by issue of further share capital, such shares shall be offered[1]:

(a)   to persons who, at the date of the offer, are members of the company in proportion to the existing shares held by sending a letter of offer subject to the following conditions, namely-

   (i)   the shares so offered shall be strictly in proportion to the shares already held in respective kinds and classes;

   (ii)   the letter of offer shall state the number of shares offered and limiting a time not being less than fifteen days and not exceeding thirty days from the date of the offer within which the offer, if not accepted, shall be deemed to have been declined;

   (iii) in the case of a listed company any member, not interested to subscribe, may exercise the right to renounce the shares offered to him in favour of any other person, before the date of expiry stated in the letter of offer; and

   (iv)   if the whole or any part of the shares offered under this section is declined or is not subscribed, the directors may allot such shares in such manner as they may deem fit within a period of thirty days from the close of the offer as provided under sub-clause (ii) above or within such extended time not exceeding thirty day with the approval of the Commission:

       Provided that a public company may reserve a certain percentage of further issue for its employees under "Employees Stock Option Scheme" to be approved by the Commission in accordance with the procedure and on such conditions as may be specified.

(b)   subject to approval of the Commission, to any person, in the case of public company on the basis of a special resolution either for cash or for a consideration other than cash:

Provided that the value of non-cash asset, service, intellectual property shall be determined by a valuer registered by the Commission.

(2) The letter of offer referred to in sub-clause (ii) of clause (a) of sub-section (1) duly signed by at least two directors shall be dispatched through

---

[1] 2018 CLD 285; 2017 CLD 587; 2017 CLD 1395; 2017 CLD 1477; 2016 CLD 1283; 2015 CLD 569; 2015 CLD 1978; 2014 CLD 961; 2013 CLD 397; 2012 CLD 1394; 2011 CLD 1783; 2010 CLD 426; 2010 CLD 942; 2009 CLD 1593; 2009 CLD 1602;2008 CLD 879; 2006 CLD 627; 2006 CLD 635; 2006 CLD 1016; 2006 CLD 1470; 2006 CLD 1577; 2005 CLD 430; 2004 CLD 123; 2003 CLD 463; 2003 CLC 695; 2003 CLD 1393; 2002 CLD 325; 1987 CLC 2047; 1973 PLD 387

registered post or courier or through electronic mode to all the existing members, ensuring that it reaches the members before the commencement of period for the acceptance of offer.

(3) A copy of the letter of offer, referred to in sub-section (2) shall, simultaneously with the dispatch to the members, be sent to the registrar.

(4) Notwithstanding anything contained in this section, where loan has been obtained from any Government by a public sector company, and if that Government considers it necessary in the public interest so to do, it may, by order, direct that such loan or any part thereof shall be converted into shares in that company, on such terms and conditions as appear to the Government to be just and reasonable in the circumstances of the case even if the terms of such loan does do not include the option for such conversion.

(5) In determining the terms and conditions of conversion under sub-section (4), the Government shall have due regard to the financial position of the public sector company, the terms of the rate of interest payable thereon and such other matters as it may consider necessary.

(6) Notwithstanding anything contained in this Act or any other law for the time being in force or the memorandum and articles, where the authorised capital of a company is fully subscribed, or the un-subscribed capital is insufficient, the same shall be deemed to have been increased to the extent necessary for issue of shares to the Government, a scheduled bank or financial institution in pursuance of any obligation of the company to issue shares to such scheduled bank or financial institution.

(7) In case shares are allotted in terms of sub-section (6), the company shall be required to file the notice of increase in share capital along with the fee prescribed for such increase with the registrar within the period prescribed under this Act:

Provided that where default is made by a company in complying with the requirement of filing a notice of increase in the authorised capital under this Act as well as the fee to be deposited on the authorised capital as deemed to have been increased, the Government, scheduled bank or the financial institution to whom shares have been issued may file notice of such increase with the registrar and such notice shall be deemed to have been filed by the company itself and the Government, scheduled bank or financial institution shall be entitled to recover from the company the amount of any fee paid by it to the registrar in respect of such increase.

(8) Any violation of this section shall be an offence liable to a penalty of level 2 on the standard scale.

INVITATION OF DEPOSITS

84. **Prohibition on acceptance of deposits from public.**— (1) On and after the commencement of this Act, no company shall invite, accept or renew deposits from the public[1]:

Provided that nothing in this sub-section shall apply to a banking company and such other company or class of companies or such deposits as the Commission may, notify in this behalf.

Explanation.—For the purposes of this section, "deposit" means any deposit of money with, and includes any amount borrowed by, a company, but shall not include a loan raised by issue of debentures or a loan obtained from a banking company or financial institution or an advance against sale of goods or provision of services in the ordinary course of business.

(2) Where a company accepts or invites, or allows or causes any other person to accept or invite on its behalf, any deposit, the company shall be punishable--

(a) where such contravention relates to the acceptance of any deposit, with penalty which shall not be less than the amount of the deposit so accepted; and

(b) where such contravention relates to the invitation for any deposit, shall be liable to a penalty of level 3 on the standard scale.

(3) In addition to the fine on the company under sub-section (2), every officer of the company which is in default shall be punishable with imprisonment for a term which may extend to two years and shall also be liable to fine which may extend to five million rupees.

85. **Power of company to alter its share capital.**— (1) A company having share capital may, if so authorised by its articles, alter the conditions of its memorandum through a special resolution[2], so as to-

(a) increase its authorised capital by such amount as it thinks expedient;

(b) consolidate and divide the whole or any part of its share capital into shares of larger amount than its existing shares;

(c) sub-divide its shares, or any of them, into shares of smaller amount than is fixed by the memorandum:

(d) cancel shares which, at the date of the passing of the resolution in that behalf, have not been taken or agreed to be taken by any

---

[1] 2009 CLD 1; 2008 CLD 563; 2000 PTD 507

[2] 2017 CLD 587; 2016 CLD 902; 2014 CLD 961; 2010 CLD 942; 2010 CLD 1802; 2006 CLD 1364; 2003 CLD 463

person, and diminish the amount of its share capital by the amount of the share so cancelled:

Provided that, in the event of consolidation or sub-division of shares, the rights attaching to the new shares shall be strictly proportional to the rights attached to the previous shares so consolidated or sub-divided:

Provided further that, where any shares issued are of a class which is the same as that of shares previously issued, the rights attaching to the new shares shall be the same as those attached to the shares previously held.

(2)   The new shares issued by a company shall rank *pari passu* with the existing shares of the class to which the new shares belong in all matters, including the right to such bonus or right issue and dividend as may be declared by the company subsequent to the date of issue of such new shares.

(3) A cancellation of shares in pursuance of sub-section (1) shall not be deemed to be a reduction of share capital within the meaning of this Act.

(4) The company shall file with the registrar notice of the exercise of any power referred to in sub-section (1) within fifteen days from the exercise thereof.

(5) Any violation of this section shall be an offence liable to a penalty of level 1 on the standard scale.

86.   **Prohibition of purchase by company or giving of loans by it for purchase of its shares.** (1) No company having a share capital, other than a listed company shall have power to buy its own shares[1].

(2)   No public company or a private company being subsidiary of a public company shall give financial assistance whether directly or indirectly for the purpose of, or in connection with, a purchase or subscription made or to be made, by any person of any shares in the company or in its holding company.

(3)   Nothing in sub-section (2) shall apply to

(a)   the lending of money by a banking company in the ordinary course of its business;

(b)   the provision by a company of money in accordance with any scheme approved by company through special resolution and in accordance with such requirements as may be specified, for the purchase of, or subscription for shares in the company or its holding company, if the purchase of, or the subscription for, the

---

[1] 2009 CLD 1; 1991 MLD 1225

shares held by a trust for the benefit of the employees or such shares held by the employee of the company;

(c) the provision or securing an advance to any of its employees, including a chief executive who, before his appointment as such, was not a director of the company, but excluding all directors of the company, for purchase of shares of the company or of its subsidiary or holding company.

(4) Any violation of this section shall be an offence liable to a penalty of level 1 on the standard scale.

87. Subsidiary company not to hold shares in its holding company. — (1) No company shall, either by itself or through its nominees, hold any shares in its holding company and no holding company shall allot or transfer its shares to any of its subsidiary companies and any such allotment or transfer of shares of a company to its subsidiary company shall be void:

Provided that a subsidiary shall not be barred-

(a) from acting as a trustee unless its holding company is beneficially interested under the trust; and

(b) from dealing in shares of its holding company in the ordinary course of its business, on behalf of its clients only subject to non-provision of any financial assistance where such subsidiary carries on a bona fide business of brokerage:

Provided further that a subsidiary dealing in shares of its holding company in the ordinary course of its brokerage business, shall not exercise the voting rights attached to such shares:

Provided also that the provisions of this section shall not be applicable where such shares are held by a company by operation of law.

(2) Any violation of this section shall be an offence liable to a penalty of level 2 on the standard scale.

88. Power of a company to purchase its own shares.— (1) Notwithstanding anything contained in this Act or any other law, for the time being in force, or the memorandum and articles, a listed company may, subject to the provisions of this section and the regulations specified in this behalf, purchase its own shares.

(2) The shares purchased by the company may, in accordance with the provisions of this section and the regulations, either be cancelled or held as treasury shares.

(3) The shares held by the company as treasury shares shall, as long as they are so held, in addition to any other conditions as may be specified, be subject to the following conditions, namely--

(a) the voting rights of these shares shall remain suspended; and

(b) no cash dividend shall be paid and no other distribution, whether in cash or otherwise of the company's assets, including any distribution of assets to members on a winding up shall be made to the company in respect of these shares:

Provided that nothing in this sub-section shall prevent-

(a) an allotment of shares as fully paid bonus shares in respect of the treasury shares; and

(b) the payment of any amount payable on the redemption of the treasury shares, if they are redeemable.

(4) The board shall recommend to the members purchase of the shares. The decision of the board shall clearly specify the number of shares proposed to be purchased, purpose of the purchase i.e. cancellation or holding the shares as treasury shares, the purchase price, period within which the purchase shall be made, source of funds, justification for the purchase and effect on the financial position of the company.

(5)   The purchase of shares shall be made only under authority of a special resolution.

(6)   The purchase of shares shall be made within a period as specified in the regulations.

(7) The proposal of the board to purchase shares shall, on conclusion of the board's meeting, be communicated to the Commission and to the securities exchange on which shares of the company are listed.

(8)   The purchase of shares shall always be made in cash and shall be out of the distributable profits or reserves specifically maintained for the purpose.

(9) The purchase of shares shall be made either through a tender offer or through the securities exchange as may be specified.

(10)   The company may dispose of the treasury shares in a manner as may be specified.

(11) Where a purchase of shares has been made under this section, the company shall maintain a register of shares so purchased and enter therein the following particulars, namely--

(a) number of shares purchased;
(b) consideration paid for the shares purchased;

(c) mode of the purchase;

(d) the date of cancellation or re-issuance of such shares;

(e) number of bonus shares issued in respect of treasury shares; and

(f) number and amount of treasury shares redeemed, if redeemable.

(12) Any violation of this section shall be an offence liable to a penalty of level 3 on the standard scale and shall also be individually and severally liable for any or all losses or damages arising out of such contravention.

REDUCTION OF SHARE CAPITAL

89. **Reduction of share capital.—** Subject to confirmation by the Court a company limited by shares, if so authorised by its articles, may by special resolution reduce its share capital in any way[1], namely—

(a) cancel any paid-up share capital which is lost or un-represented by available assets;

(b) pay off any paid-up share capital which is in excess of the needs of the company.

90. **Objection by creditors and settlement of list of objecting creditors.—** (1) Where the proposed reduction of share capital involves the payment to any shareholder of any paid-up share capital, and in any other case if the Court so directs, every creditor of the company who is entitled to any debt or claim, shall be entitled to object to the reduction[2].

(2) The Court shall settle a list of creditors so entitled to object, and for that purpose shall ascertain, as far as possible without requiring an application from any creditor, the names of those creditors and the nature and amount of their debts or claims, and may publish notices fixing a period within which creditors not entered on the list are to claim to be so entered or are to be excluded from the right of objecting to the reduction.

91. **Power to dispense with consent of creditor on security being given for his debt.—** Where a creditor entered on the list of creditors whose debt or claim is not discharged or determined does not consent to the reduction, the Court may, if it thinks fit, dispense with the consent of that creditor, on the company securing payment of his debt or claim by appropriating as the Court may direct, the following amount, that is to say-

---

[1] 2019 CLD 1493; 2018 CLD 889; 2018 CLD 1493; 2014 CLD 1516; 2013 CLD 1432; 2013 CLD 2156; 2010 CLD 135; 2010 CLD 1802; 2008 CLD 487; 1999 CLC 1989; 1999 CLC 1603; 1991 PLD 441; 1989 MLD 3075; 1988 MLD 1408; 1976 PLD 850; 1968 PLD 381; 1956 PLD 731
[2] 1985 MLD 578

(a)   if the company admits the full amount of his debt or claim, or, though not admitting it, is willing to provide for it, then the full amount of the debt or claim; and

(b)   if the company does not admit or is not willing to provide for the full amount of the debt or claim, or if the amount is contingent or not ascertained, then an amount fixed by the Court after the like inquiry, and adjudication as if the company were being wound up by the Court.

92.   **Order confirming reduction.—** If the Court is satisfied with respect to every creditor of the company who under this Act is entitled to object to the reduction that either his consent to the reduction has been obtained or his debt or claim has been discharged or has been determined or has been secured, the Court may make an order confirming the reduction on such terms and conditions as it thinks fit[1].

93.   **Registration of order of reduction.—**(1) The registrar on the filing with him of a certified copy of order of the Court confirming the reduction of the share capital of the company, shall register the same[2].

(2) A resolution for reducing share capital as confirmed by an order of the Court registered under sub-section (1) shall take effect on such registration and not before.

(3) The registrar shall certify under his hand the registration of the order and his certificate shall be conclusive evidence that all the requirements of this Act with respect to reduction of share capital have been complied with, and that the share capital of the company is such as is stated in the order.

94.   **Liability of members in respect of reduced shares.—**(1) A member of the company, past or present, shall not be liable in respect of any share to any call or contribution exceeding in amount the difference, if any, between the amount paid, or, as the case may be, the received amount, if any, which is to be deemed to have been paid, on the share and the amount of the share as fixed by the order[3]:

Provided that, if any creditor, entitled in respect of any debt or claim to object to the reduction of share capital, is, by reason of his ignorance of the proceedings for reduction, or of their nature and effect with respect to his claim not entered on the list of creditors, and, after the reduction, the company is unable, within the meaning of the provisions of this Act with respect to winding up by the Court, to pay the amount of his debt or claim, then--

---

[1] 2019 CLD 1493; 2018 CLD 889; 2018 CLD 1493; 2014 CLD 1516; 2013 CLD 2156
[2] 2019 CLD 1493; 2018 CLD 1493
[3] 1992 CLC 2273; 1982 PLD 94

(a) every person who was a member of the company at the date of the registration of the order for reduction shall be liable to contribute for the payment of that debt, or claim an amount not exceeding the amount which he would have been liable to contribute if the company had commenced to be wound up on the day before that registration; and

(b) if the company is wound up, the Court on the application of any such creditor and proof of his ignorance as aforesaid, may, if it thinks fit, settle accordingly a list of persons so liable to contribute, and make and enforce calls and orders on the contributories settled on the list as if they were ordinary contributories in a winding up.

(2) Nothing in this section shall effect the rights of the contributories among themselves.

95. **Penalty on concealment of name of creditor.**—If any officer of the company conceals the name of any creditor entitled to object to the reduction, or willfully misrepresents the nature or amount of the debt or claim of any creditor, or if any officer of the company abets any such concealment or misrepresentation as aforesaid, every such officer shall be punishable with imprisonment for a term which may extend to one year, or with fine which may extend to five million rupees, or with both.

96. **Publication of reasons for reduction.**— In the case of reduction of share capital, the Court may require the company to publish in the manner specified by the Court the reasons for reduction, or such other information in regard thereto as the Court may think expedient with a view to giving proper information to the public, and, if the Court thinks fit, the causes which led to the reduction.

97. **Increase and reduction of share capital in case of a company limited by guarantee having a share capital.**—A company limited by guarantee may, if it has a share capital and is so authorised by its articles, increase or reduce its share capital in the same manner and on the same conditions subject to which a company limited by shares may increase or reduce its share capital under the provisions of this Act.

UNLIMITED LIABILITY OF DIRECTORS

98. **Limited company may have directors with unlimited liability.**— (1) In a limited company, the liability of the directors or of any director may, if so provided by the memorandum, be unlimited[1].

(2) In a limited company in which the liability of any director is unlimited, the directors of the company, if any, and the member who proposes a

---

[1] 2013 CLD 1280; 2011 CLD 1171; 2001 YLR 526; 2000 CLC 287; 1993 CLC 1222; 1984 CLC 2761; 1961 PLD 6

person for election or appointment to the office of director, shall add to that proposal a statement that the liability of the person holding that office will be unlimited and the promoters and officers of the company, or one of them shall, before that person accepts the office or acts therein, give him notice in writing that his liability will be unlimited.

(3) Any violation of this section shall be an offence liable to a penalty of level 1 on the standard scale and shall also be liable for any damage which the person so elected or appointed may sustain from the default, but the liability of the person elected or appointed shall not be affected by the default.

99. Special resolution of limited company making liability of directors unlimited.— A limited company, if so authorised by its articles, may, by special resolution, alter its memorandum so as to render unlimited the liability of its directors or of any director:

Provided that an alteration of the memorandum making the liability of any of the directors unlimited shall not apply, without his consent, to a director who was holding the office from before the date of the alteration, until the expiry of the term for which he was holding office on that date[1].

PART VI

REGISTRATION OF MORTGAGES, CHARGES, ETC.

100. Requirement to register a mortgage or charge.— (1) A company that creates a mortgage or charge to which this section applies must file the specified particulars of the mortgage or charge, together with a copy of the instrument, if any, verified in the specified manner, by which the mortgage or charge is created or evidenced, with the registrar for registration within a period of thirty days beginning with the day after the date of its creation[2]:

Provided that--

(a) in the case of a mortgage or charge created out of Pakistan comprising solely property situated outside Pakistan, thirty days after the date on which the instrument or copy could, in due course of post, and if dispatched with due diligence, have been received in Pakistan shall be substituted for thirty days after the date of the creation of the mortgage or charge as the time within which the particulars and instrument or copy are to be filed with the registrar; and

---

[1] 2013 CLD 1280

[2] 2006 CLD 227; 2004 CLD 449; 2004 CLD 1490; 2000 PLD 323; 1999 PLD 1; 1996 PLD 99; 1996 PLD 601; 1996 PLD 633; 1993 MLD 94; 1992 SCMR 1731; 1991 MLD 124; 1991 CLC 415; 1990 PLD 763; 1990 PLD 768; 1989 PLD 539; 1989 CLC 1743; 1987 MLD 307

(b)   in case the mortgage or charge is created in Pakistan but comprises property outside Pakistan, a copy of the instrument creating or purporting to create the mortgage or charge verified in the specified manner may be filed for registration notwithstanding that further proceedings may be necessary to make the mortgage or charge valid or effectual according to the law of the country in which the property is situate:

Provided further that any subsequent registration of a mortgage or charge shall not prejudice any right acquired in respect of any property before the mortgage or charge is actually registered.

(2)   This section applies to the following charges--

(a)   a mortgage or charge on any immovable property wherever situate, or any interest therein; or

(b)   a mortgage or charge for the purposes of securing any issue of debentures;

(c)   a mortgage or charge on book debts of the company;

(d)   a floating charge on the undertaking or property of the company, including stock-in-trade; or

(e)   a charge on a ship or aircraft, or any share in a ship or aircraft;

(f)   a charge on goodwill or on any intellectual property;

(g)   a mortgage or charge or pledge, on any movable property of the company;

(h)   a mortgage or charge or other interest, based on agreement for the issue of any instrument in the nature of redeemable capital; or

(i)   a mortgage or charge or other interest, based on conditional sale agreement, namely, lease financing, hire-purchase, sale and lease back, and retention of title, for acquisition of machinery, equipment or other goods:

Provided that where a negotiable instrument has been given to secure the payment of any book debts of a company, the deposit of the instrument for the purpose of securing an advance to the company shall not for the purpose of this sub-section be treated as a mortgage or charge on those book debts.

Explanation. For the purposes of this Act "**charge**" includes mortgage or pledge.

(3) The registrar shall, on registration of a mortgage or charge under sub-section (1) issue a certificate of registration under his signatures or authenticated by his official seal in such form and in such manner as may be specified.

(4) The provisions of this section relating to registration shall apply to a company acquiring any property subject to a mortgage or charge.

(5) Notwithstanding anything contained in any other law for the time being in force, no mortgage or charge created by a company shall be taken into account by the liquidator or any other creditor unless it is duly registered under sub-section (1) and a certificate of registration of such charge is given by the registrar under sub-section (3).

(6) Nothing in sub-section (5) shall prejudice any contract or obligation for repayment of the money thereby secured.

(7) Where any mortgage or charge on any property or assets of a company or any of its undertakings is registered under this section, any person acquiring such property, assets, undertakings or part thereof or any share or interest therein shall be deemed to have notice of the mortgage or charge from the date of such registration.

101. **Particulars in case of series of debentures entitling holders** *pari passu*.— Where a series of debentures containing, or giving by reference to any other instrument, any charge to the benefit of which the debenture-holders of that series are entitled *pari passu* is created by a company, it shall be sufficient for the purposes of section 100 if there are filed with the registrar within thirty days after the execution of the deed containing the charge or, if there is no such deed, after the execution of any debentures of the series, the following particulars, namely-

(a)   the total amount secured by the whole series;

(b)   the dates of the resolutions authorising the issue of the series and the date of the covering deed, if any, by which the security is created or defined;

(c)   a general description of the property charged; and

(d)   the names of the trustees, if any, for the debenture-holders;

together with a copy of the deed verified in the specified manner containing the charge:

Provided that, where more than one issue is made of debentures in the series, there shall be filed with the registrar for entry in the register particulars of the date and amount of each issue, but an omission to do this shall not affect the validity of the debentures issued.

102. **Register of charges to be kept by registrar.**— (1) The registrar shall, in respect of every company, keep a register containing particulars of the charges registered under this Part in such form and in such manner as may be specified.

(2) A register kept in pursuance of this section shall be open to inspection by a person on payment of such fees as may be prescribed.

103. **Index to register of mortgages and charges.**—The registrar shall keep a chronological index, in the form, containing such particulars, as may be specified, of the mortgages or charges registered with him under the company law.

104. **Endorsement of certificate of registration on debenture or certificate of debenture stock.**—The company shall cause a copy of every certificate of registration given under section 100 to be endorsed on every debenture or certificate of debenture stock which is issued by the company and the payment of which is secured by the mortgage or charge so registered:

Provided that in case the certificate of debenture or debenture stock is issued in the book-entry form, appropriate disclosure in pursuance of this section shall be made in the manner as may be specified:

Provided further that nothing in this section shall be construed as requiring a company to cause a certificate of registration of any mortgage or charge so given, to be endorsed on any debenture or certificate of debenture stock which has been issued by the company before the mortgage or charge was created.

105. **Duty of company and right of interested party as regards registration.**— (1) It shall be the duty of a company to file with the registrar for registration the specified particulars of every mortgage or charge created by the company and of the issue of debentures of a series, requiring registration under section 100, but registration of any such mortgage or charge may be effected on the application of any person interested therein.

(2) Where the registration is affected on the application of some person other than the company, that person shall be entitled to recover from the company the amount of any fees properly paid by him to the registrar on the registration.

106. **Modification in the particulars of mortgage or charge.**— Whenever the terms or conditions or extent or operation of any mortgage or charge registered under this Part are modified, it shall be the duty of the company to send to the registrar the particulars of such modification together with a copy of the instrument evidencing such modification verified in the specified manner, and the provisions of this Part as to registration of mortgage or charge shall apply to such modification of the mortgage or charge as aforesaid.

107. **Copy of instrument creating mortgage or charge to be kept at registered office.**— Every company shall cause a copy of every instrument creating any mortgage or charge requiring registration under this Part and of

every instrument evidencing modification of the terms or conditions thereof, to be kept at the registered office of the company.

108.   **Rectification of register of mortgages.**—(1) The Commission on being satisfied that—

(a)   the omission to file with the registrar the particulars of any mortgage or charge or any modification therein within the time required by section 100 or 101, as the case may be; or

(b)   the omission or mis-statement of any particular with respect to any such mortgage or charge;

was accidental or due to inadvertence or to some other sufficient cause, or is not of a nature to prejudice the position of creditors or shareholders of the company, or that on other grounds it is just and equitable to grant relief, may, on the application of the company or any person interested and, on such terms and conditions as seem to the Commission just and expedient, order that the time for filing the required particulars be extended, or, as the case may be, that the omission or mis-statement be rectified, and may make such order as to the costs of the application as it thinks fit[1].

(2) A copy of the order passed under this section duly certified by the Commission or its authorised officer shall be forwarded to the concerned registrar within seven days from the date of the order.

(3) Where the Commission extends the time for the registration of a mortgage or charge, the order shall not prejudice any rights acquired in respect of the property concerned prior to the time when the mortgage or charge is actually registered.

109.   **Company to report satisfaction of charge.**— (1) A company shall give intimation to the registrar in the manner specified, of the payment or satisfaction, in full, of any mortgage or charge created by it and registered under this Part, within a period of thirty days from the date of such payment or satisfaction[2].

(2) The registrar shall, on receipt of intimation under sub-section (1), cause a notice to be sent to the holder of the mortgage or charge calling upon him to show cause within such time not exceeding fourteen days, as may be specified in such notice, as to why payment or satisfaction in full shall not be recorded as intimated to the registrar, and if no cause is shown, by such holder of the mortgage or charge, the registrar shall accept the memorandum of satisfaction and make an entry in the register of charges kept by him under section 102:

---

[1] 2006 CLD 476; 1993 CLC 1398; 1989 MLD 555; 1989 PLD 539
[2] 2006 CLD 476; 1993 CLC 1398

Provided that the notice referred to in this sub-section shall not be required if a no objection certificate on behalf of the holder of the mortgage or charge is furnished, along-with the intimation to be submitted under sub-section (1).

(3) If any cause is shown, the registrar shall record a note to that effect in the register of charges and shall inform the company.

(4) Nothing in this section shall be deemed to affect the powers of the registrar to make an entry in the register of charges under section 102 or otherwise than on receipt of an intimation from the company.

(5) If a company fails to file the particulars of satisfaction of mortgage or charge within the period specified under this section, the required particulars may be submitted with the additional fee, as may be specified and imposing the penalty as specified in this Part.

110. **Power of registrar to make entries of satisfaction and release in absence of intimation from company.**—The registrar may, on evidence being given to his satisfaction with respect to any registered charge-

(a)   that the debt for which the charge was given has been paid or satisfied in whole or in part; or

(b)   that part of the property or undertaking charged has been released from the charge or has ceased to form part of the company's property or undertaking;

enter in the register of charges a memorandum of satisfaction in whole or in part, or of the fact that part of the property or undertaking has been released from the charge or has ceased to form part of the company's property or undertaking, as the case may be, and inform the parties concerned, notwithstanding the fact that no intimation has been received by him from the company.

111. **Punishment for contravention.**—Any violation of this Part shall be an offence liable to a penalty of level 1 on the standard scale[1].

112. **Company's register of mortgages and charges.**—(1) Every company shall maintain a register of mortgages and charges requiring registration under this Part, in such form and in such manner as may be specified and any violation under this section shall be an offence punishable under this Act[2].

(2) The register of charges maintained under this section and the copies of instrument creating any mortgage and charge or modification thereof, kept in pursuance of this part shall be open to inspection of-

---

[1] 1991 CLC 415; 1987 MLD 307
[2] 1992 PLD 295

(a) any member or creditor of the company without fee; and

(b) any other person on payment of such fee as may be fixed by the company for each inspection.

(3) The refusal of inspection of the said copies or the register shall be an offence under this section and any person guilty of an offence under this section shall be liable to a penalty of level 1 on the standard scale, and every officer of the company who knowingly authorises or permits the refusal shall incur the like penalty, and in addition to the above penalty, the registrar may by order compel an immediate inspection of the copies or register.

(4) If any officer of the company authorises or permits the omission of any entry required to be made in pursuance of sub-section (1), shall be liable to a penalty of level 1 on the standard scale.

RECEIVERS AND MANAGERS

113. **Registration of appointment of receiver or manager.**— (1) Where in order to ensure enforcement of security of a company's property, a person obtains an order for the appointment of a receiver or manager, or appoints such a receiver or manager under any powers contained in any instrument, he shall within seven days of the order or of the appointment under the powers contained in the instrument, file a notice of the fact with the registrar[1].

(2) Where a person appointed as a receiver or manager under this section ceases to act as such, the person who had obtained the order or appointed such a receiver or manager pursuant to the powers contained in any instrument shall on ceasing of the receiver or manager, give the registrar a notice to that effect within seven days.

(3) The registrar shall enter the fact of which he is given notice under this section in the register of mortgages and charges.

(4) Any violation of sub-sections (1) and (2) shall be an offence liable to a penalty of level 1 on the standard scale.

114. **Filing of accounts of receiver or manager.**— (1) Every receiver of the property of a company who has been appointed under the powers contained in any instrument, and who has taken possession, shall within thirty days of expiry of every one hundred and eighty days while he remains in possession, and also within thirty days on ceasing to act as receiver, file with the registrar an abstract in the form specified of his receipts and payments during the period to which the abstract relates, and shall also, within fifteen days of ceasing to act as receiver, file with the registrar notice to that effect, and the registrar shall enter the notice in the register of mortgages and charges.

---

[1] 2014 PLD 1

(2) Where a receiver of the property of a company has been appointed, every invoice, order for goods, or business letter issued by or on behalf of the company or the receiver of the company, being a document on or in which the name of the company appears, shall contain a statement that a receiver has been appointed.

(3) The provisions of sub-sections (1) and (2) shall apply to any person appointed to manage the property of a company under any powers contained in an instrument in the same manner as they apply to a receiver so appointed.

(4) Any contravention or default of this section by the receiver, or person appointed to manage the property of the company referred to sub-section (3), shall be an offence liable to a penalty of level 1 on the standard scale.

115. **Disqualification for appointment as receiver or manager.**— The following shall not be appointed as a receiver or manager of the company's property, namely-

(a) a minor;

(b) a person who is of unsound mind and stands so declared by a competent court;

(c) a body corporate;

(d) a director of the company;

(e) an un-discharged insolvent unless he is granted leave by the court by which he has been adjudged an insolvent; or

(f) a person disqualified by a Court from being concerned with or taking part in the management of the company in any other way, unless he is granted leave by the Court.

116. **Application to Court.**—(1) A receiver or manager of the company's property appointed under the powers contained in any instrument may apply to the Court for directions in relation to any particular matter arising in connection with the performance of his functions, and on any such application the Court may give such direction, or may make such order declaring the rights of persons before the Court, or otherwise, as the Court thinks just[1].

(2) A receiver or manager of the company's property appointed as aforesaid shall, to the same extent as if he had been appointed by order of a Court be personally liable on any contract entered into by him in the performance of his functions, except in so far as the contract otherwise provides, and entitled in respect of that liability to indemnity out of the assets; but nothing in this sub-section shall be deemed to limit any right to indemnity which he would have apart from this sub-section, or to limit his liability on contracts

---

[1] 2008 CLD 810; 2000 PLD 83; 1986 MLD 1870

entered into without authority or to confer any right to indemnity in respect of that liability.

117. **Power of Court to fix remuneration of receiver or manager.**— (1) The Court may, on an application made to it by the receiver or manager of the property, by order fix the amount to be paid by way of remuneration to any person who, under the power contained in an instrument, has been appointed as receiver or manager of the company's property:

Provided that the amount of remuneration shall not exceed such limits as may be specified.

(2) The power of the Court under sub-section (1) shall, where no previous order has been made with respect thereto-

   (a)   extend to fixing the remuneration for any period before the making of the order or the application therefore;

   (b)   be exercisable notwithstanding that the receiver or manager had died or ceased to act before the making of the order or the application therefore; and

   (c)   where the receiver or manager has been paid or has retained for his remuneration for any period before the making of the order any

   (d)   amount in excess of that so fixed for that period, extend to requiring him or his representative to account for the excess or such part thereof as may be specified in the order:

Provided that the power conferred by clause (c) shall not be exercised as respects any period before the making of the application or the order unless in the opinion of the Court there are special circumstances making it proper for the power to be so exercised.

(3) The Court may from time to time, on an application made either by the liquidator or by the receiver or manager, or by the registrar, vary or amend an order made under sub-section and issue directions to the receiver respecting his duties and functions or any other matter as it may deem expedient:

Provided that an order made under sub-section (1) shall not be varied so as to increase the amount of remuneration payable to any person.

PART VII

MANAGEMENT AND ADMINISTRATION

118. **Members of a company.**—The subscribers to the memorandum of association are deemed to have agreed to become members of the company and become members on its registration and every other person-

   (a)   to whom is allotted, or who becomes the holder of any class or kind of shares; or

    (b)   in relation to a company not having a share capital, any person who has agreed to become a member of the company;

and whose names are entered; in the register of members, are members of the company[1].

REGISTER AND INDEX OF MEMBERS

119. **Register of members**.— (1) Every company shall keep a register of its members and any contravention or default in complying with requirement of this section shall be an offence punishable under this Act[2].

(2) There must be entered in the register such particulars of each member as may be specified.

(3) In the case of joint holders of shares or stock in a company, the company's register of members shall state the names of each joint holder. In other respects joint holders shall be regarded for the purposes of this Part as a single member and the address of the person named first shall be entered in the register;

(4) A person guilty of an offence under this section shall be liable to a penalty of level 1 on the standard scale.

120. **Index of members.**—(1) Every company having more than fifty members shall keep an index of the names of the members of the company, unless the register of members is in such a form as to constitute in itself an index.

(2) The company shall make any necessary alteration in the index within fourteen days after the date on which any alteration is made in the register of members.

(3) The index shall contain, in respect of each member, a sufficient indication to enable the account of that member in the register to be readily found.

(4) A person guilty of an offence under this section shall be liable to a penalty of level 1 on the standard scale.

121. **Trust not to be entered on register**.— No notice of any trust, expressed, implied or constructive, shall be entered on the register of members of a company, or be receivable by the registrar[3].

---

[1] 1982 CLC 2198; 1981 PTD 49; 1979 PLD 723; 1970 PLD 155; 1962 PLD 176

[2] 2017 CLD 1249; 1989 CLC 2103; 1983 PLD 1; PLJ 1979 SC 13; 1979 PLD 723; 1973 PLD 491; 1970 PLD 155

[3] 2010 CLD 1675; 2007 CLD 1484; 1982 PLD 768

122. **Register of debenture-holders**.—(1) Every company shall keep a register of its debenture-holders and any contravention or default in complying with requirement of this section shall be an offence punishable under this Act.

(2) There must be entered in the register such particulars of each debenture-holder as may be specified.

(3) This section shall not apply with respect to debentures which, *ex facie*, are payable to the bearer thereof.

(4) A person guilty of an offence under this section shall be liable to a penalty of level 1 on the standard scale.

123. **Index of debenture-holders.**—(1) Every company having more than fifty debenture-holders shall keep an index of the names of the debenture-holders of the company, unless the register of debenture-holders is in such a form as to constitute in itself an index and any contravention or default in complying with requirement of this section shall be an offence punishable under this Act.

(2) The company shall make any necessary alteration in the index within fourteen days after the date on which any alteration is made in the register of debenture-holders.

(3) The index shall contain, in respect of each debenture-holder, a sufficient indication to enable the account of that debenture-holder in the register to be readily found.

(4) A person guilty of an offence under this section shall be liable to a penalty of level 1 on the standard scale.

124. **Rights to inspect and require copies.**— (1) The registers and the index referred to in sections 119, 120, 122 and 123 shall, be open to the inspection of members or debentures-holders during business hours, subject to such reasonable restrictions, as the company may impose, so that not less than two hours in each day be allowed.

(2) Inspection by any member or debenture-holder of the company shall be without charge, and in the case of any other person on payment of such fee as may be fixed by the company for each inspection.

(3) Any person may require a certified copy of register and index or any part thereof, on payment of such fee as may be fixed by the company.

(4) The certified copies requested under this section shall be issued within a period of seven days, exclusive of the days on which the transfer book of the company is closed.

(5) A person seeking to exercise either of the rights conferred by this section must make a request to the company to that effect.

(6)   The request must contain the following information--

(a)   in the case of an individual, his name and address;

(b)   in the case of an organisation, its name and address and also of the authorised person; and

(c)   the purpose for which the information is to be used.

(7) Any refusal of inspection required under sub-section (1), or if any copy required under sub-section (3) is not issued within the specified period shall be an offence and any person guilty of an offence under this section shall be liable to a penalty of level 1 on the standard scale; and the registrar may by an order compel an immediate inspection of the register and index or direct that copies required shall be sent to the persons requiring them.

125. **Power to close register.** —(1) A company may, on giving not less than seven days' previous notice close its register of members, or the part of it relating to members holding shares of any class, for any period or periods not exceeding in the whole thirty days in each year[1]:

Provided that the Commission may, on the application of the company extend the period mentioned in sub-section (1), for a further period of fifteen days.

(2) In the case of listed company, notice for the purposes of sub-section (1), must be given by advertisement in English and Urdu languages at least in one issue each of a daily newspaper of respective language having wide circulation.

(3) The provision of this section shall also apply for the purpose of closure of register of debenture-holders of a company.

(4) Any contravention or default in complying with requirement of this section shall be an offence liable to a penalty of level 2 on the standard scale.

126.   **Power of Court to rectify register.**— (1) If—

(a)   the name of any person is fraudulently or without sufficient cause entered in or omitted from the register of members or register of debenture-holders of a company; or

(b)   default is made or unnecessary delay takes place in entering on the register of members or register of debenture-holders the fact of the person having become or ceased to be a member or debenture-holder;

---

[1] 1996 MLD 1943

the person aggrieved, or any member or debenture-holder of the company, or the company, may apply to the Court for rectification of the register[1].

(2) The Court may either refuse the application or may order rectification of the register on payment by the company of any damages sustained by any party aggrieved, and may make such order as to costs as it in its discretion thinks fit.

(3) On any application under sub-section (1) the Court may decide any question relating to the title of any person who is a party to the application to have his name entered in or omitted from the register, whether the question arises between members or debenture-holders or alleged members or debenture-holders, or between members or alleged members, or debenture-holders or alleged debenture-holders, on the one hand and the company on the other hand; and generally may decide any question which it is necessary or expedient to decide for rectification of the register.

(4) Where the Court has passed an order under sub-section (3) that *prima facie* entry in or omission from, the register of members or the register of debenture-holders the name or other particulars of any person, was made fraudulently or without sufficient cause, the Court may send a reference for adjudication of offence under section 127 to the court as provided under section 482.

127.   **Punishment for fraudulent entries in and omission from register.**— Anyone who fraudulently or without sufficient cause enters in, or omits from the register of members or the register of debenture-holders the name or other particulars of any person, shall be punishable with imprisonment for a term which may extend to three years or with fine which may extend to one million rupees, or with both.

128.   **Notice to registrar of rectification of register.**— When it makes an order for rectification of the register of members in respect of a company which is required by this Act to file a list of its members with the registrar, the Court shall cause a copy of the order to be forwarded to the company and shall,

---

[1] 2018 CLD 383; 2017 CLD 1165; 2017 CLD 1477; 2016 CLD 393; 2016 CLD 1283; 2016 CLD 2325; 2016 SCMR 213; 2015 CLD 569; 2015 CLD 719; 2015 CLD 1532; 2015 CLD 1978; 2013 CLD 1229; 2012 CLD 710; 2010 CLD 232; 2009 CLD 1043; 2008 CLD 697; 2008 CLD 707; 2008 CLD 1117; 2007 CLD 334; 2007 CLD 637; 2007 CLD 1484; 2006 CLD 960; 2005 CLD 30; 2005 CLD 747; 2005 CLD 1291; 2005 CLD 1875; 2004 CLD 1100; 2004 CLC 373; 2003 CLD 201; 2003 CLD 293; 2003 CLD 1429; 2003 YLR 2150; 2003 CLD 1442; 2003 PLJ 1660; 2001 PLD 523; 1998 CLC 1157; 1998 PLJ 1017; 1997 CLC 1075; 1997 CLC 1921; 1997 MLD 2155; 1992 PLD 181; 1992 PLD 210; 1991 MLD 203; 1990 CLC 456; 1989 MLD 4338; 1988 PLD 501; 1988 CLC 1541; 1988 MLD 395; 1987 PLD 1; 1987 PLD 569; 1987 CLC 726; 1987 CLC 2079; 1987 CLC 1943; 1986 CLC 2519; 1986 CLC 2560; 1985 CLC 1239; 1983 PLD 1; 1983 PLD 176; 1982 SCMR 582; 1982 PLD 634; 1982 CLC 463; 1981 PLD 90; 1977 PLD 83; 1975 PLD 1339; 1973 PLD 49; 1973 PLD 491; 1971 PLD 252; 1964 PLD 31

by its order, direct the company to file notice of the rectification with the registrar within fifteen days from the receipt of the order.

129. **Register to be evidence.**— The registers referred to in sections 119 and 122 shall be *prima facie* evidence of any matter which by this Act is directed or authorised to be inserted therein[1].

130. **Annual return.**—(1) Every company having a share capital shall, once in each year, prepare and file with the registrar an annual return containing the particulars in a specified form as on the date of the annual general meeting or, where no such meeting is held or if held is not concluded, on the last day of the calendar year[2].

(2) A company not having a share capital shall in each year prepare and file with the registrar a return containing the particulars in a specified form as on the date of the annual general meeting or, where no such meeting is held or if held is not concluded, on the last day of the calendar year.

(3) The return referred to in sub-section (1) or sub-section (2) shall be filed with the registrar within thirty days from the date of the annual general meeting held in the year or, when no such meeting is held or if held is not concluded, from the last day of the calendar year to which it relates:

Provided that, in the case of a listed company, the registrar may for special reasons extend the period of filing of such return by a period not exceeding fifteen days.

(4) All the particulars required to be submitted under sub-section (1) and sub-section (2) shall have been previously entered in one or more registers kept by the company for the purpose.

(5) Nothing in this section shall apply to a company, in case there is no change of particulars in the last annual return filed with the registrar:

Provided that a company, other than a single member company or a private company having paid up capital of not more than three million rupees, shall inform the registrar in a specified manner that there is no change of particulars in the last annual return filed with the registrar.

(6) Any contravention or default in complying with requirement of this section shall be an offence liable-

     (a)   in case of a listed company, to a penalty of level 2 on the standard scale[3]; and

---

[1] 2012 PTD 1883; 2012 CLD 1966; 1997 CLC 1220; 1979 PLD 723; 1972 PLD 552

[2] 2012 PTD 1883; 2002 CLD 325; 2012 CLD 1966; 2007 CLD 1019; 2003 PTD 2689; 2003 PTD 1903; 2002 CLD 325; 1997 CLC 1220

[3] 2017 CLD 1039

(b)   in case of any other company, to a penalty of level 1 on the standard scale.

MEETINGS AND PROCEEDINGS

131. **Statutory meeting of company.**—(1) Every public company having a share capital shall, within a period of one hundred and eighty days from the date at which the company is entitled to commence business or within nine months from the date of its incorporation whichever is earlier, hold a general meeting of the members of the company, to be called the "statutory meeting"[1]:

Provided that in case first annual general meeting of a company is decided to be held earlier, no statutory meeting shall be required.

(2) The notice of a statutory meeting shall be sent to the members at least twenty-one days before the date fixed for the meeting along with a copy of statutory report.

(3) The statutory report shall state-

(a)   the total number of shares allotted, distinguishing shares allotted other than in cash, and stating the consideration for which they have been allotted;

(b)   the total amount of cash received by the company in respect of all the shares allotted;

(c)   an abstract of the receipts of the company and of the payments made there out up to a date within fifteen days of the date of the report, exhibiting under distinctive headings the receipts of the company from shares and debentures and other sources, the payments made there out, and particulars concerning the balance remaining in hand, and an account or estimate of the preliminary expenses of the company showing separately any commission or discount paid or to be paid on the issue or sale of shares or debentures;

(d)   the names, addresses and occupations of the directors, chief executive, secretary, auditors and legal advisers of the company and the changes, if any, which have occurred since the date of the incorporation;

(e)   the particulars of any contract the modification of which is to be submitted to the meeting for its approval, together with the particulars of the modification or proposed modification;

---

[1] 2017 CLD 1039; 2002 CLD 1164; 2001 CLC 2019; 1988 CLC 1347

(f)   the extent to which underwriting contracts, if any, have been carried out and the extent to which such contracts have not been carried out, together with the reasons for their not having been carried out; and

(g)   the particulars of any commission or brokerage paid or to be paid in connection with the issue or sale of shares to any director, chief executive, secretary or officer or to a private company of which he is a director;

and certified by the chief executive and at least one director of the company, and in case of a listed company also by the chief financial officer.

(4) The statutory report shall also contain a brief account of the state of the company's affairs since its incorporation and the business plan, including any change or proposed change affecting the interest of shareholders and business prospects of the company.

(5) The statutory report shall, so far as it relates to the shares allotted by the company, the cash received in respect of such shares and to the receipts and payments of the company, be accompanied by a report of the auditors of the company as to the correctness of such allotment, receipt of cash, receipts and payments.

(6) The directors shall cause a copy of the statutory report, along-with report of the auditors as aforesaid, to be delivered to the registrar for registration forthwith after sending the report to the members of the company.

(7) The directors shall cause a list showing the names, occupations, nationality and addresses of the members of the company, and the number of shares held by them respectively, to be produced at the commencement of the meeting and to remain open and accessible to any member of the company during the continuance of the meeting.

(8) The members of the company present at the meeting shall be at liberty to discuss any matter relating to the formation of the company or arising out of the statutory report, whether previous notice has been given or not, but no resolution of which notice has not been given in accordance with the articles may be passed.

(9) The meeting may adjourn from time to time, and at any adjourned meeting any resolution of which notice has been given in accordance with the articles, either before or after the original meeting, may be passed, and an adjourned meeting shall have the same powers as an original meeting.

(10) The provisions of this section shall not apply to a public company which converts itself from a private company after one year of incorporation.

(11) Any contravention or default in complying with requirement of this section shall be an offence liable--

(a) in case of a listed company, to a penalty of level 2 on the standard scale; and

(b) in case of any other company, to a penalty of level 1 on the standard scale.

132. **Annual general meeting.**—(1) Every company, shall hold, an annual general meeting within sixteen months from the date of its incorporation and thereafter once in every calendar year within a period of one hundred and twenty days following the close of its financial year[1]:

Provided that, in the case of a listed company, the Commission, and, in any other case, the registrar, may for any special reason extend the time within which any annual general meeting, shall be held by a period not exceeding thirty days.

(2) An annual general meeting shall, in the case of a listed company, be held in the town in which the registered office of the company is situate or in a nearest city:

Provided that at least seven days prior to the date of meeting, on the demand of members residing in a city who hold at least ten percent of the total paid up capital or such other percentage as may be specified, a listed company must provide the facility of video- link to such members enabling them to participate in its annual general meeting.

(3) The notice of an annual general meeting shall be sent to the members and every person who is entitled to receive notice of general meetings at least twenty-one days before the date fixed for the meeting:

Provided that in the case of a listed company, such notice shall be sent to the Commission, in addition to its being dispatched in the normal course to members and the notice shall also be published in English and Urdu languages at least in one issue each of a daily newspaper of respective language having nationwide circulation.

---

[1] 2018 CLD 44; 2017 CLD 656; 2017 CLD 839; 2017 CLD 1191; 2017 CLD 1237; 2017 CLD 1704; 2017 CLD 1728; 2013 CLD 1466; 2011 CLD 4; 2011 CLD 624; 2011 CLD 645; 2011 CLD 1647; 2010 CLD 66; 2010 CLD 69; 2010 CLD 193; 2010 CLD 386; 2010 CLD 1214; 2010 CLD 1044; 2010 CLD 1268; 2009 CLD 883; 2009 CLD 1577; 2009 CLD 1633; 2007 CLD 297;2007 CLD 566; 2007 CLD 605; 2007 CLD 1125; 2007 CLD 1116; 2006 CLD 334; 2006 CLD 378; 2006 CLD 533; 2006 CLD 542; 2006 CLD 660; 2006 CLD 729; 2006 CLD 1188; 2006 CLD 1295; 2006 CLD 1357; 2006 CLD 1455; 2005 CLD 1071; 2005 CLD 1137; 2005 CLD 1153; 2002 CLD 1314; 2002 CLD 188; 2002 CLD 325; 2002 CLD 1309; 2001 CLC 2019; 2000 MLD 1880; 1997 PLD 432; 1996 MLD 1943; 1991 CLC 313; 1987 CLC 726; 1987 MLD 1110; 1987 MLD 3039; 1987 CLC 2351; 1981 CLC 1051; 1980 PLD 401; 1979 CLC 267; 1978 PLD 1098; 1977 PLD 1367; 1974 PLD 362; 1970 PLD 155; 1970 PLD 521; 1969 PLD 251; 1969 PLD 615; 1957 PLD 83

Company law

1. Registration of a company and provision of its formation

sections. 4, 10 to 15, 16-18, 19 - 26, 27-35, 365
46-56, 57-59

Share capital

60 - 62, 67-70, 71-73, 74-75, 76, 80, 84-88

89-97,

Directors

98-99, 153- 171, 172-185, 197-198

Meetings & Proceedings

131-152

Accounts of companies & Audit
220-239, 246-253

Dividends
240-245

(4) Nothing in this section shall apply to a single member company.

(5) Any contravention or default in complying with requirement of this section shall be an offence liable--

(a)   in case of a listed company, to a penalty of level 2 on the standard scale; and

(b)   in case of any other company, to a penalty of level 1 on the standard scale.

133.   **Calling of extra-ordinary general meeting.**-(1) All general meetings of a company, other than the annual general meeting referred to in section 132 and the statutory meeting mentioned in section 131, shall be called extraordinary general meetings[1].

(2) The board may at any time call an extra-ordinary general meeting of the company to consider any matter which requires the approval of the company in a general meeting.

(3) The board shall, at the requisition made by the members--

(a)   in case of a company having share capital, representing not less than one-tenth of the total voting power as on the date of deposit of requisition; and

(b)   in case of a company not having share capital, not less than one-tenth of the total members;

forthwith proceed to call an extra-ordinary general meeting.

(4) The requisition shall state the objects of the meeting, be signed by the requisitionists and deposited at the registered office of the company.

(5) If the board does not proceed within twenty-one days from the date of the requisition being so deposited to cause a meeting to be called, the requisitionists, may themselves call the meeting, but in either case any meeting so called shall be held within ninety days from the date of the deposit of the requisition.

(6) Any meeting called under sub-section (5) by the requisitionists shall be called in the same manner, as nearly as possible, as that in which meetings are to be called by board.

(7) Any reasonable expenses incurred by the requisitionists in calling a meeting under sub-section (5) shall be reimbursed to the requisitionists by the company and the sums so paid shall be deducted from any fee or other

---

[1] 2017 CLD 1737; 2015 CLD 107; 2002 CLD 1314; 2001 CLC 2019; 2000 CLC 477; 1999 CLC 1989; 1991 CLC 313; 1990 PTCL 1098; 1982 PLD 664; 1981 CLC 1051; 1978 PLD 1098; 1977 PLD 902; 1977 PLD 1367; 1970 PLD 521; 1970 PLD 155; 1969 PLD 615; 1967 PLD 496

remuneration payable to such of the directors who were in default in calling the meeting.

(8) Notice of an extraordinary general meeting shall be served to the members in the manner provided for in section 55:

Provided that in case of a company other than listed, if all the members entitled to attend and vote at any extraordinary general meeting so agree, a meeting may be held at a shorter notice.

(9) Any contravention or default in complying with requirement of this section shall be an offence liable--

    (a)   in case of a listed company, to a penalty of level 2 on the standard scale; and

    (b)   in case of any other company, to a penalty of level 1 on the standard scale.

134. **Provisions as to meetings and votes.**—(1) The following provisions shall apply to the general meetings of a company or meetings of a class of members of the company[1], namely:

    (a)   notice of the meeting specifying the place and the day and hour of the meeting along with a statement of the business to be transacted at the meeting shall be given-

        (i)   to every member or class of the members of the company as the case may be;

        (ii)   to every director;

        (iii)   to any person who is entitled to a share in consequence of the death or bankruptcy of a member, if the company has been notified of his entitlement;

        (iv)   to the auditors of the company;

        in the manner in which notices are required to be served by section 55, but the accidental omission to give notice to, or the non-receipt of notice by, any member shall not invalidate the proceedings at any meeting;

    (b)   in case of a listed company, if certain members who hold ten percent of the total paid up capital or such other percentage as may be specified, reside in a city, it shall be mentioned in the notice that

[1] 2018 CLD 111; 2018 CLD 229; 2018 CLD 889; 2017 CLD 587; 2016 CLD 1697; 2013 CLD 1953; 2012 CLD 691; 2012 CLD 1895; 2011 CLD 1149; 2009 CLD 56; 2009 CLD 1197; 2009 CLD 1582; 2009 CLD 1713; 2007 CLD 1271; 2006 CLD 283; 2006 CLD 317; 2004 CLD 1; 2002 CLD 17; 2002 CLD 1314; 2002 SCMR 510; 2001 PLD 230; 1998 PLD 295; 1997 PLD 432; 1997 CLC 1873; 1995 PLD 264; 1991 MLD 2675; 1991 PLD 441; 1988 MLD 1408; 1988 CLC 1347; 1987 MLD 2729

(c)   such members, may demand the company to provide them the facility of video-link for attending the meeting.

(2)   For the purposes of sub-section (1), in the case of an annual general meeting, all the businesses to be transacted shall be deemed special, other than--

(a)   the consideration of financial statements and the reports of the board and auditors;

(b)   the declaration of any dividend;

(c)   the election and appointment of directors in place of those retiring; and

(d)   the appointment of the auditors and fixation of their remuneration.

(3) Where any special business is to be transacted at a general meeting, there shall be annexed to the notice of the meeting a statement setting out all material facts concerning such business, including, in particular, the nature and extent of the interest, if any, therein of every director, whether directly or indirectly, and, where any item of business consists of the according of an approval to any document by the meeting, the time when and the place where the document may be inspected, shall be specified in the statement.

(4) Members of a company may participate in the meeting personally, through video-link or by proxy.

(5) The chairman of the board, if any, shall preside as chairman at every general meeting of the company, but if there is no such chairman, or if at any meeting he is not present within fifteen minutes after the time appointed for holding the meeting, or is unwilling to act as chairman, any one of the directors present may be elected to be chairman, and if none of the directors is present or is unwilling to act as chairman the members present shall choose one of their member to be the chairman.

(6) In the case of a company having a share capital, every member shall have votes proportionate to the paid-up value of the shares or other securities carrying voting rights held by him according to the entitlement of the class of such shares or securities, as the case may be:

Provided that, at the time of voting, fractional votes shall not be taken into account.

(7) No member holding shares or other securities carrying voting rights shall be debarred from casting his vote, nor shall anything contained in the articles have the effect of so debarring him.

(8) In the case of a company limited by guarantee and having no share capital, every member thereof shall have one vote.

(9) On a poll, votes may be given either personally or through video-link or by proxy or through postal ballot in a manner and subject to the conditions as may be specified.

(10) Notwithstanding anything contained in this Act, the Commission shall have the power to notify any business requiring the approval of the members shall only be transacted through postal ballot for any company or class of companies.

(11) All the requirements of this Act regarding calling of, holding and approval in general meeting, board meeting and election of directors in case of a single member company, shall be deemed complied with; if the decision is recorded in the relevant minutes book and signed by the sole member or sole director as the case may be.

(12) Any contravention or default in complying with requirement of this section shall be an offence liable-

<blockquote>

(a)   in case of a listed company, to a penalty of level 3 on the standard scale; and

(b)   in case of any other company, to a penalty of level 2 on the standard scale.

</blockquote>

135. **Quorum of general meeting**.—(1) The quorum of a general meeting shall be--

<blockquote>

(a)   in the case of a public listed company, unless the articles provide for a larger number, not less than ten members present personally, or through video-link who represent not less than twenty-five percent of the total voting power, either of their own account or as proxies;

(b)   in the case of any other company having share capital, unless the articles provide for a larger number, two members present personally, or through video-link who represent not less than

(c)   twenty-five percent of the total voting power, either of their own account or as proxies;

(d)   in the case of a company not having share capital, as provided in the articles:

> Provided that, if within half an hour from the time appointed for the meeting a quorum is not present, the meeting, if called upon the requisition of members, shall be dissolved; in any other case, it shall stand adjourned to the same day in the next week at the same time and place, and, if at the adjourned meeting a quorum is not present within half an hour from the time appointed for the meeting, the members present personally or through video-link

</blockquote>

being not less than two shall be a quorum, unless the articles provide otherwise[1].

(2) Any contravention or default in complying with requirement of this section shall be an offence liable-

(a) in case of a listed company, to a penalty of level 2 on the standard scale; and

(b) in case of any other company, to a penalty of level 1 on the standard scale.

136. **Power of the Court to declare the proceedings of a general meeting invalid.**— The Court may, on a petition, by members having not less than ten percent of the voting power in the company, that the proceedings of a general meeting be declared invalid by reason of a material defect or omission in the notice or irregularity in the proceedings of the meeting, which prevented members from using effectively their rights, declare such proceedings or part thereof invalid and direct holding of a fresh general meeting[2]:

Provided that the petition shall be made within thirty days of the impugned meeting.

137. **Proxies.**—(1) A member of a company entitled to attend and vote at a meeting of the company may appoint another person as his proxy to exercise all or any of his rights to attend, speak and vote at a meeting[3]:

Provided that-

(a) unless the articles of a company otherwise provide, this sub-section shall not apply in the case of a company not having a share capital;

(b) a member shall not be entitled to appoint more than one proxy to attend any one meeting;

(c) if any member appoints more than one proxy for any one meeting and more than one instruments of proxy are deposited with the company, all such instruments of proxy shall be rendered invalid; and

(d) a proxy must be a member unless the articles of the company permit appointment of a non-member as proxy.

---

[1] 2009 CLD 541

[2] 2017 CLD 436; 2017 CLD 587; 2016 CLD 1049; 2015 CLD 323; 2013 CLD 1953; 2009 CLD 1713; 2004 CLD 373

[3] 2004 CLD 373; 2005 CLD 747; 2001 CLC 2019; 2000 CLC 477; 1997 PLD 432; 1996 MLD 1943; 1995 PLD 264; 1992 PLD 181; 1992 CLC 1658; 1987 CLC 726; 1968 PLD 381

(2) Subject to the provisions of sub-section (1), every notice of a meeting of a company shall prominently set out the member's right to appoint a proxy and the right of such proxy to attend, speak and vote in the place of the member at the meeting and every such notice shall be accompanied by a proxy form.

(3) The instrument appointing a proxy shall-

(a) be in writing; and

(b) be signed by the appointer or his attorney duly authorised in writing, or if the appointer is a body corporate, be under its seal or be signed by an officer or an attorney duly authorised by it.

(4) An instrument appointing a proxy, if in the form set out in Regulation 43 of Table A in the First Schedule shall not be questioned on the ground that it fails to comply with any special requirements specified for such instruments by the articles.

(5) The proxies must be lodged with the company not later than forty-eight hours before the time for holding a meeting and any provision to the contrary in the company's articles shall be void.

(6) In calculating the period mentioned in sub-section (5), no account shall be taken of any part of the day that is not a working day.

(7) The members or their proxies shall be entitled to do any or all the following things in a general meeting, namely-

(a) subject to the provisions of section 143, demand a poll on any question; and

(b) on a question before the meeting in which poll is demanded, to abstain from voting or not to exercise their full voting rights;

and any provision to the contrary in the articles shall be void.

(8) Every member entitled to vote at a meeting of the company shall be entitled to inspect during the business hours of the company all proxies lodged with the company.

(9) The provisions of this section shall apply *mutatis mutandis* to the meeting of a particular class of members as they apply to a general meeting of all the members.

(10) Failure to issue notices in time or issuing notices with material defect or omission or any other contravention of this section which has the effect of preventing participation or use of full rights by a member or his proxy shall make the company and its every officer who is a party to the default or contravention liable to-

(a) a penalty of level 2 on the standard scale if the default relates to a listed company; and

(b) to a penalty of level 1 on the standard scale if the default relates to any other company.

138. **Representation of body corporate or corporation at meetings.**—(1) A body corporate or corporation (whether or not a company within the meaning of this Act) which is a member of another company may, by resolution of its board or other governing body authorise an individual to act as its representative at any meeting of that other company, and the individual so authorised shall be entitled to exercise the same powers on behalf of the corporation which he represents[1].

(2) A body corporate or corporation (whether or not a company within the meaning of this Act) which is a creditor of another company may, by resolution of its board or other governing body authorise an individual to act as its representative at any meeting of the creditors of that other company held in pursuance of this Act or any other meeting to which it is entitled to attend in pursuance of the provisions contained in any instrument and the person so authorised shall be entitled to exercise the same powers on behalf of the corporation which he represents.

139. **Representation of Federal Government at meetings of companies.**—(1) The concerned Minister-in-Charge of the Federal Government, or as the case may be, a Provincial Government, as the case may be, if a member of a company, may appoint such individual as it thinks fit to act as its representative at any meeting of the company or at any meeting of any class of members of the company.

(2) An individual appointed to act as aforesaid shall, for the purpose of this Act, be deemed to be a member of such a company and shall be entitled to exercise the same rights and powers, including the right to appoint proxy, as the concerned Minister-in-Charge of the Federal Government or as the case may be, the Provincial Government, as the case may be, may exercise as a member of the company.

140. **Notice of resolution.**—(1) The notice of a general meeting of a company shall state the general nature of each business proposed to be considered and dealt with at a meeting, and in case of special resolution, accompanied by the draft resolution[2].

(2) The members having not less than ten percent voting power in the company may give notice of a resolution and such resolution together with the supporting statement, if any, which they propose to be considered at the meeting, shall be forwarded so as to reach the company--

---

[1] 2011 CLD 1029; 2001 CLC 2019
[2] 2001 CLC 2019; 1988 PTCL 401

(a)   in the case of a meeting requisitioned by the members, together with the requisition for the meeting;

(b)   in any other case, at least ten days before the meeting; and the company shall forthwith circulate such resolution to all the members.

(3) Any contravention or default in complying with requirement of this section shall be an offence liable--

(a)   in case of a listed company, to a penalty of level 2 on the standard scale; and

(b)   in case of any other company, to a penalty of level 1 on the standard scale.

141.   **Voting to be by show of hands in first instance.**—At any general meeting, a resolution put to the vote of the meeting shall, unless a poll is demanded, be decided on a show of hands[1].

142.   **Declaration by chairman on a show of hands.**-(1) On a vote on a resolution at a meeting on a show of hands, a declaration by the chairman that the resolution--

(a)   has or has not been passed; or

(b)   passed unanimously or by a particular majority;

is conclusive evidence of that fact without proof of the number or proportion of the votes recorded in favour of or against the resolution.

(2) An entry in respect of such a declaration in minutes of the meeting recorded in accordance with section 151 is also conclusive evidence of that fact without such proof.

143.   **Demand for poll.**—(1) Before or on the declaration of the result of the voting on any resolution on a show of hands, a poll may be ordered to be taken by the chairman of the meeting of his own motion, and shall be ordered to be taken by him on a demand made in that behalf by the members present in person or through video-link or by proxy, where allowed, and having not less than one-tenth of the total voting power.

(2)   The demand for a poll may be withdrawn at any time by the members who made the demand.

144. **Poll through secret ballot**.— Notwithstanding anything contained in this Act, when a poll is demanded on any resolution, it may be ordered to be taken by the chairman of the meeting by secret ballot of his own motion, and shall be ordered to be taken by him on a demand made in that behalf by the

---

[1] 2005 CLD 1875; 1997 CLC 1943

members present in person, through video-link or by proxy, where allowed, and having not less than one-tenth of the total voting power.

145. **Time of taking poll.**—(1) A poll demanded on the election of a chairman or on a question of adjournment shall be taken forthwith and a poll demanded on any other question shall be taken at such time, not more than fourteen days from the day on which it is demanded, as the chairman of the meeting may direct.

(2) When a poll is taken, the chairman or his nominee and a representative of the members demanding the poll shall scrutinize the votes given on the poll and the result shall be announced by the chairman.

(3) Subject to the provisions of this Act, the chairman shall have power to regulate the manner in which a poll shall be taken.

(4) The result of the poll shall be deemed to be the decision of the meeting on the resolution on which the poll was taken.

146. **Resolutions passed at adjourned meeting.**—Where a resolution is passed at an adjourned meeting of—

(a)   a company;

(b)   the holders of any class of shares in a company;

(c)   the board; or

(d)   the creditors of a company;

the resolution shall, for all purposes, be treated as having been passed on the date on which it was in fact passed, and shall not be deemed to have been passed on any earlier date.

147. **Power of Commission to call meetings.**—(1) If default is made in holding the statutory meeting, annual general meeting or any extraordinary general meeting in accordance with sections 131, 132 or 133, as the case may be, the Commission may, notwithstanding anything contained in this Act or in the articles of the company, either of its own motion or on the application of any director or member of the company, call, or direct the calling of, the said meeting of the company in such manner as the Commission may think fit, and give such ancillary or consequential directions as the Commission thinks expedient in relation to the calling, holding and conducting of the meeting and preparation of any document required with respect to the meeting[1].

---

[1] 2017 CLD 1039; 2017 CLD 1237; 2016 GBLR 266; 2013 CLD 1466; 2011 CLD 645; 2009 CLD 883; 2007 CLD 297; 2006 CLD 542; 2006 CLD 1092; 1998 PLD 332; 1991 CLC 313; 1990 PTCL 1098; 1990 PLJ 180; 1987 CLC 1943

Explanation. The directions that may be given under sub-section (1) may include a direction that one member of the company present in person or by proxy shall be deemed to constitute a meeting.

(2) Any meeting called, held and conducted in accordance with any such direction shall, for all purposes, be deemed to be a meeting of the company duly called, held and conducted, and all expenses incurred in connection thereto shall be paid by the company unless the Commission directs the same to be recovered from any officer of the company which he is hereby authorised to do.

148. **Punishment for default in complying with provisions of section 147.--** If any person makes default in holding a meeting of the company in accordance with section 147 or in complying with any directions of the Commission, shall be liable to a penalty of level 3 on the standard scale[1].

149. **Passing of resolution by the members through circulation.-** (1) Except for the businesses specified under sub-section (2) of section 134 to be conducted in the annual general meeting, the members of a private company or a public unlisted company (having not more than fifty members), may pass a resolution (ordinary or special) by circulation signed by all the members for the time being entitled to receive notice of a meeting.

(2) Any resolution passed under sub-section (1), shall be as valid and effectual as if it had been passed at a general meeting of the company duly convened and held.

(3) A resolution shall not be deemed to have been duly passed, unless the resolution has been circulated, together with the necessary papers, if any, to all the members.

(4) A members' agreement to a written resolution, passed by circulation, once signified, may not be revoked.

(5) A resolution under sub-section (1) shall be noted at subsequent meeting of the members and made part of the minutes of such meeting.

150. **Filing of resolution.-** (1) Every special resolution passed by a company shall, within fifteen days from the passing thereof, be filed with the registrar duly authenticated by a director or secretary of the company[2].

(2) Where articles have been registered, a copy of every special resolution for the time being in force shall be embodied in or annexed to every copy of the articles issued after the date of the resolution.

---

[1] 2017 CLD 1249; 2013 CLD 1466; 2011 CLD 645; 2009 CLD 883; 2007 CLD 297; 2006 CLD 1092; 1991 CLC 313; 1990 PTCL 1098
[2] 1968 PLD 412; 1956 PLD 731

(3) A copy of every special resolution shall be forwarded to any member at his request on payment of such fee not exceeding the amount as the company may determine.

(4) Any contravention or default in complying with requirement of this section shall be an offence liable to a penalty of level 1 on the standard scale.

151. **Records of resolutions and meetings.-**(1) Every company shall keep records of--

(a)   copies of all resolutions of members passed otherwise than at general meetings; and

(b)   minutes of all proceedings of general meetings along with the names of participants, to be entered in properly maintained books[1];

(2) Minutes recorded in accordance with sub-section (1), if purporting to be authenticated by the chairman of the meeting or by the chairman of the next meeting, shall be the evidence of the proceedings at the meeting.

(3) Until the contrary is proved, every general meeting of the company in respect of the proceedings whereof minutes have been so made shall be deemed to have been duly called, held and conducted.

(4) The records must be kept at the registered office of the company from the date of the resolution, meeting or decision simultaneously in physical and electronic form and it shall be preserved for at least twenty years in physical form and permanently in electronic form.

(5) Any contravention or default in complying with requirement of this section shall be an offence liable to a penalty of level 1 on the standard scale.

152. **Inspection of records of resolutions and meetings.-** (1) The books containing the minutes of proceedings of the general meetings shall be open to inspection by members without charge during business hours, subject to such reasonable restrictions as the company may by its articles or in general meeting impose so that not less than two hours in each day be allowed for inspection.

(2) Any member shall at any time after seven days from the meeting be entitled to be furnished, within seven days after he has made a request in that behalf to the company, with a certified copy of the minutes of any general meeting at such charge not exceeding the amount as may be fixed by the company.

(3) If any inspection required under sub-section (1) is refused, or if any copy required under sub-section (2) is not furnished within the time specified therein, the person guilty of an offence shall be liable to a penalty of level 1 on

---

[1] 2017 PTD 201; 2017 CLD 1249; 2016 CLD 2233; 2011 CLD 599; 2000 CLC 477; 1993 CLC 66; 1991 MLD 2675; 1987 MLD 2729

(4) the standard scale, and the registrar may direct immediate inspection or supply of copy, as the case may be.

APPOINTMENT AND REMOVAL OF DIRECTORS

153. **Ineligibility of certain persons to become director.-** A person shall not be eligible for appointment as a director of a company, if he[1] —

(a)   is a minor;

(b)   is of unsound mind;

(c)   has applied to be adjudicated as an insolvent and his application is pending;

(d)   is an undischarged insolvent;

(e)   has been convicted by a court of law for an offence involving moral turpitude;

(f)   has been debarred from holding such office under any provision of this Act;

(g)   is lacking fiduciary behaviour and a declaration to this effect has been made by the Court under section 212 at any time during the preceding five years;

(h)   does not hold National Tax Number as per the provisions of Income Tax Ordinance, 2001 (XLIX of 2001):

Provided that the Commission may grant exemption from the requirement of this clause as may be notified.

(i)   is not a member:

Provided that clause (i) shall not apply in the case of, –

(i)   a person representing a member which is not a natural person;

(ii)   a whole-time director who is an employee of the company;

(iii)   a chief executive; or

(iv)   a person representing a creditor or other special interests by virtue of contractual arrangements;

(j)   has been declared by a court of competent jurisdiction as defaulter in repayment of loan to a financial institution;

(k)   is engaged in the business of brokerage, or is a spouse of such person or is a sponsor, director or officer of a corporate brokerage house:

---

[1] 2019 SCMR 1; 2018 CLD 149; 2015 CLD 345; 2007 CLD 165; 1999 CLC 1989; 1982 CLC 2198

Provided that clauses (j) and (k) shall be applicable only in case of listed companies.

154. **Minimum number of directors of a company.**-(1) Notwithstanding anything contained in any other law for the time being in force[1]-

(a)   a single member company shall have at least one director;

(b)   every other private company shall have not less than two directors;

(c)   a public company other than a listed company shall have not less than three directors; and

(d)   a listed company shall have not less than seven directors:

Provided that public interest companies shall be required to have female representation on their board as may be specified by the Commission.

(2)   Only a natural person shall be a director.

155. **Number of directorships.**--(1) No person shall, after the commencement of this Act, hold office as a director, including as an alternate director at the same time in more than such number of companies as may be specified:

Provided that this limit shall not include the directorships in a listed subsidiary.

(2) A person holding the position of director in more than seven companies on the commencement of this Act shall ensure the compliance of this section within one year of such commencement.

(3) Any casual vacancy on the board of a listed company shall be filled up by the directors at the earliest but not later than ninety days from the date, the vacancy occurred.

156. **Compliance with the Code of Corporate Governance.**--The Commission may provide for framework to ensure good corporate governance practices, compliance and matters incidental and axillary for companies or class of companies in a manner as may be specified[2].

157. **First directors and their term.**-(1) The number of directors and the names of the first directors shall be determined by the subscribers of the

---

[1] 2016 CLD 176; 2015 CLD 345; 2007 CLD 1735; 1991 MLD 2675

[2] 1982 CLC 2198

memorandum and their particulars specified under section 197 shall be submitted along with the documents for the incorporation of the company[1].

(2) The number of first directors may be increased by appointing additional directors by the members in a general meeting. The first directors shall hold office until the election of directors in the first annual general meeting of the company.

158.   **Retirement of first and subsequent directors.** (1) All directors of the company

(a)   on the date of first annual general meeting; or

(b)   in case of subsequent directors on expiry of term of office of directors mentioned in section 161,

shall stand retired from office and the directors so retiring shall continue to perform their functions until their successors are elected[2].

(2) The directors so continuing to perform their functions shall take immediate steps to hold the election of directors and in case of any impediment report such circumstances to the registrar within forty-five days before the due date of the annual general meeting or extra ordinary general meeting, as the case may be, in which elections are to be held:

Provided that the holding of annual general meeting or extra ordinary general meeting, as the case may be, shall not be delayed for more than ninety days from the due date of the meeting or such extended time as may be allowed by the registrar, for reasons to be recorded, only in case of exceptional circumstances beyond the control of the directors, or in compliance of any order of the court.

(3) The registrar, may on expiry of period as provided in sub-section (2), either-

(a)   on its own motion; or

(b)   on the representation of the members holding not less than one tenth of the total voting powers in a company having share capital; or

(c)   on the representation of the members holding not less than one tenth of the total members of the company not having share capital of the company,

---

[1] 1991 MLD 2675; 1991 PLJ 399

[2] 2017 CLD 1035; 2015 CLD 107; 2013 CLD 2056; 2007 CLD 574; 2007 CLD 1722; 2006 CLD 347; 1997 PLD 432; 1996 MLD 1943

directs the company to hold annual general meeting or extra ordinary general meeting for the election of directors on such date and time as may be specified in the order.

(4) Any officer of the company or any other person who fails to comply with the direction given under sub-section (3) shall be guilty of an offence liable to a fine of level 2 on the standard scale.

159. **Procedure for election of directors.-**(1) Subject to the provision of section 154, the existing directors of a company shall fix the number of directors to be elected in the general meeting, not later than thirty-five days before convening of such meeting and the number of directors so fixed shall not be changed except with the prior approval of the general meeting in which election is to be held[1].

(2) The notice of the meeting at which directors are proposed to be elected shall among other matters, expressly state--

(a) the number of directors fixed under sub-section (1); and

(b) the names of the retiring directors.

(3) Any member who seeks to contest an election to the office of director shall, whether he is a retiring director or otherwise, file with the company, not later than fourteen days before the date of the meeting at which elections are to be held, a notice of his intention to offer himself for election as a director:

Provided that any such person may, at any time before the holding of election, withdraw such notice.

(4) All notices received by the company in pursuance of sub-section (3) shall be transmitted to the members not later than seven days before the date of the meeting, in the same manner as provided under this Act for sending of a notice of general meeting. In the case of a listed company such notice shall be published in English and Urdu languages at least in one issue each of a daily newspaper of respective language having wide circulation.

(5) The directors of a company having a share capital shall, unless the number of persons who offer themselves to be elected is not more than the number of directors fixed under sub-section (1), be elected by the members of the company in general meeting in the following manner, namely-

(a) a member shall have such number of votes as is equal to the product of the number of voting shares or securities held by him and the number of directors to be elected;

---

[1] 2018 CLD 80; 2018 CLC 1376; 2009 CLD 883; 2006 CLD 326; 2006 CLD 418; 2006 PTD 2639; 2005 SCMR 318; 2005 CLD 224; 2004 CLD 373; 2002 SCMR 250; 2000 CLC 477; 2000 PLD 283; 1999 CLC 926; 1999 CLC 1989; 1996 MLD 1943; 1993 SCMR 468; 1993 PLD 473; 1991 CLC 589; 1991 MLD 2675; 1987 CLC 726; 1983 PLD 457; 1983 PLD 693; 1977 SCMR 220; 1971 PLD 585

(b)   a member may give all his votes to a single candidate or divide them between more than one of the candidates in such manner as he may choose; and

(c)   the candidate who gets the highest number of votes shall be declared elected as director and then the candidate who gets the next highest number of votes shall be so declared and so on until the total number of directors to be elected has been so elected.

(6) The directors of a company limited by guarantee and not having share capital shall be elected by members of the company in general meeting in the manner as provided in articles of association of the company.

160.   **Powers of the Court to declare election of directors invalid.-** The Court may, on the application of members holding ten percent of the voting power in the company, made within thirty days of the date of election, declare election of all directors or any one or more of them invalid if it is satisfied that there has been material irregularity in the holding of the elections and matters incidental or relating thereto[1].

161.   **Term of office of directors.-** (1) A director elected under sections 159 or 162 shall hold office for a period of three years unless he earlier resigns, vacates office due to fresh election required under section 162 as the case may be, becomes disqualified from being a director or otherwise ceases to hold office[2]:

Provided that the term of office of directors of a company limited by guarantee and not having share capital may be a period of less than three years as provided in the articles of association of a company.

(2) Any casual vacancy occurring among the directors may be filled up by the directors and the person so appointed shall hold office for the remainder of the term of the director in whose place he is appointed.

162.   **Fresh election of directors.--** (1) Notwithstanding anything contained in this Act, a member having acquired, after the election of directors, the requisite shareholding to get him elected as a director on the board of a company not being a listed company, may require the company to hold fresh election of directors in accordance with the procedure laid down in section 159:

Provided that the number of directors fixed in the preceding election shall not be decreased;

---

[1] 2017 CLD 436; 2009 CLD 1; 2006 CLD 326; 2004 CLD 373; 2000 CLC 477; 2000 MLD 1880; 1999 CLC 1989; 1999 CLC 926; 1991 MLD 2675

[2] 2018 CLC 1376; 2018 CLD 80; 2017 CLD 1039; 2017 PLC(CS)N 55; 2017 CLD 1035; 2017 CLD 1039; 2017 CLD 1237; 2016 CLD 204; 2006 CLD 347; 2002 CLD 1309; 1996 MLD 1943

Provided further that a listed company for the purpose of fresh election of directors under this section shall follow such procedure as may be specified by the Commission.

(2) The board shall upon receipt of requisition under sub-section (1), as soon as practicable but not later than thirty days from the receipt of such requisition, proceed to hold fresh election of directors of the company.

163. **Removal of directors.-**A company may by resolution in general meeting remove a director appointed under sections 157, 161 or section 162 or elected in the manner provided for in section 159:

Provided that a resolution for removing a director shall not be deemed to have been passed if the number of votes cast against it is equal to, or exceeds--

(a)   the total number of votes for the time being computed in the manner laid down in sub-section (5) of section 159 divided by the number of directors for the time being, if the resolution relates to removal of a director appointed under sections 157, 161 or section 162 or where the directors were elected unopposed; or

(b)   the minimum number of votes that were cast for the election of a director at the immediately preceding election of directors, if the resolution relates to removal of a director elected in the manner provided in sub-section (5) of section 159[1].

164. **Nominee directors.-**(1) In addition to the directors elected or deemed to have been elected by shareholders, a company may have directors nominated by the company's creditors or other special interests by virtue of contractual arrangements.

(2) A body corporate or corporation owned or controlled by the Federal Government or as the case may be, a Provincial Government may also have directors nominated on the board to whom such corporation or company has extended credit facilities.

165.   **Certain provisions not to apply to directors representing special interests.-** (1)[2]Nothing in sections 158, 159,161, 162 or 163 shall apply to--

(a)   directors nominated by a body corporate or company or any other entity owned or controlled, whether directly or indirectly, by the Federal Government or as the case may be, a Provincial Government on the board of the company in which such body corporate or company or entity has made investment;

---

[1] 2018 CLC 1376; 2018 CLD 80; 2012 CLD 1402

[2] 2018 CLC 1376; 2018 CLD 80; 2016 CLD 134; 2016 LHC 666; 108 TAX 281; 2014 CLD 664;
2014 CLD 004, 2014 PLD 575; 2006 PTD 2639; 1997 CLC 783

(b)   directors nominated by virtue of investment made by the Federal Government or as the case may be, a Provincial Government or the Commission on the board; or

(c)   directors nominated by foreign equity holders on the board or any other body corporate set up under a regional co-operation or other co-operation arrangement approved by the Federal Government.

(2) For the purpose of nominating directors referred to in clause (a), (b) and (c), the number of votes computed in the manner laid down in sub-section (5) of section 159 as are proportionate to the number of votes required to elect the director if they had offered themselves for election, shall stand excluded from the total number of votes available to the nominating body at an election of directors, which may be proportionate to their voting power required to elect directors at an election of directors of a company.

(3) A director nominated under sub-section (1) shall hold office during the pleasure of the nominating body.

166.   **Manner of selection of independent directors and maintenance of databank of independent directors.-** (1) An independent director to be appointed under any law, rules, regulations or code, shall be selected from a data bank containing names, addresses and qualifications of persons who are eligible and willing to act as independent directors, maintained by any institute, body or association, as may be notified by the Commission, having expertise in creation and maintenance of such data bank and post on their website for the use by the company making the appointment of such directors:

Provided that responsibility of exercising due diligence before selecting a person from the data bank referred to above, as an independent director shall lie with the company or the Government, as the case may be, making such appointment.

(2) For the purpose of this section, an independent director means a director who is not connected or does not have any other relationship, whether pecuniary or otherwise, with the company, its associated companies, subsidiaries, holding company or directors; and he can be reasonably perceived as being able to exercise independent business judgment without being subservient to any form of conflict of interest:

Provided that without prejudice to the generality of this sub-section no director shall be considered independent if one or more of the following circumstances exist--

(a)   he has been an employee of the company, any of its subsidiaries or holding company within the last three years;

(b)   he is or has been the chief executive officer of subsidiaries, associated company, associated undertaking or holding company in the last three years;

(c)   he has, or has had within the last three years, a material business relationship with the company either directly, or indirectly as a

(d)   partner, major shareholder or director of a body that has such a relationship with the company.

   Explanation: The major shareholder means a person who, individually or in concert with his family or as part of a group, holds 10% or more shares having voting rights in the paid-up capital of the company;

(d)   he has received remuneration in the three years preceding his/her appointment as a director or receives additional remuneration, excluding retirement benefits from the company apart from a director's fee or has participated in the company's stock option or a performance-related pay scheme;

(e)   he is a close relative of the company's promoters, directors or major shareholders:

   Explanation: **"close relative"** means spouse(s), lineal ascendants and descendants and siblings;

(f)   he holds cross-directorships or has significant links with other directors through involvement in other companies or bodies not being the associations licenced under section 42;

(g)   he has served on the board for more than three consecutive terms from the date of his first appointment, and for more than two consecutive terms in case of a public sector company, provided that such person shall be deemed "independent director" after a lapse of one term;

(h)   a person nominated as a director under sections 164 and 165:

   Provided further that for determining the independence of directors for the purpose of sub-clauses (a), (b) and (c) in respect of public sector companies, the time period shall be taken as two years instead of three years. Further, an independent director in case of a public sector company shall not be in the service of Pakistan or of any statutory body or anybody or institution owned or controlled by the Government.

(3) The independent director of a listed company shall be elected in the same manner as other directors are elected in terms of section 159 and the statement of material facts annexed to the notice of the general meeting called

(4) for the purpose shall indicate the justification for choosing the appointee for appointment as independent director.

(5) No individual shall be selected for the data bank referred to in sub-section (1) without his consent in writing.

(6) The manner and procedure of selection of independent directors on the databank who fulfill the qualifications and other requirements shall be specified by the Commission.

(7) The requirements of sub-section (1)--

(a) shall be deemed relaxed till such time a notification is issued by the Commission; and

(b) may be relaxed by the Commission on an application made by the company supported with the sufficient justification or the practical difficulty, as the case may be.

167. **Consent to act as director to be filed with company**–(1)No person shall be appointed or nominated as a director or chief executive of a company or represent as holding such office, nor shall any person describe or name any other person as a director or proposed director or chief executive or proposed chief executive of any company, unless such person or such other individual has given his consent in writing to the company for such appointment or nomination[1].

(2) The consent given to the company under sub-section (1) shall be filed with the registrar within fifteen days thereof.

168. **Validity of acts of directors.--** The acts of a person acting as a director are valid notwithstanding that it is afterwards discovered that there was a defect in his appointment; or he was disqualified from holding office; or he had ceased to hold such office[2]:

Provided that, as soon as any such defect has come to notice, the director shall not exercise the right of his office till the defect has been removed.

169. **Penalties.--**Whoever contravenes or fails to comply with any of the provisions of sections 154 to 168 or is a party to the contravention of the said provisions shall be liable to a penalty of level 2 on the standard scale and may also be debarred by the authority which imposes the penalty from becoming or continuing a director of the company for a period not exceeding three years[3].

---

[1] 2006 CLD 326; 2006 CLD 418; 1990 MLD 348

[2] 2015 CLD 345; 1990 PLD 198

[3] 2017 CLD 1035; 2017 CLD 1249; 2016 CLD 204; 2015 CLD 345; 2007 CLD 574; 2006 CLD 326; 2006 CLD 347; 2006 CLD 418; 1990 MLD 348; 1987 PLD 569

170. **Restriction on director's remuneration.--** (l) The remuneration of a director for performing extra services, including the holding of the office of chairman, shall be determined by the board or the company in general meeting, as the case may be, in accordance with the provisions in the company's articles[1].

(2) The remuneration to be paid to any director for attending the meetings of the board or a committee of directors shall not exceed the scale approved by the company or the board, as the case may be, in accordance with the provisions of the articles:

171.   **Vacation of office by the directors.-**(1) A director shall *ipso facto* cease to hold office if[2]—

(a)   he becomes ineligible to be appointed as a director on any one or more of the grounds enumerated in section 153;

(b)   he absents himself from three consecutive meetings of the board without seeking leave of absence;

(c)   he or any firm of which he is a partner or any private company of which he is a director--

   (i)   without the sanction of the company in general meeting accepts or holds any office of profit under the company other than that of chief executive or a legal or technical adviser; or

   (ii)   accepts a loan or guarantee from the company in contravention of section 182;

(2) Nothing contained in sub-section (l) shall be deemed to preclude a company from providing by its articles that the office of director shall be vacated on any grounds additional to those specified in that sub-section.

DISQUALIFICATION OF DIRECTORS BY THE COMMISSION

172. **Disqualification orders.-**(1) In any of the circumstances stated hereunder, the Commission may pass a disqualification order against a person to hold the office of a director of a company for a period up to five years beginning from the date of order--

(a)   conviction of an offence in connection with the promotion, formation, management or liquidation of a company, or with the receivership or management of a company's property;

(b)   persistent default in relation to provisions of this Act requiring any return, account or other document to be filed with, delivered or sent, or notice of any matter to be given, to the Commission or the registrar;

---

[1] 1977 PLD 814
[2] 2015 CLD 345; 2010 CLD 408; 2010 CLD 1531

(c) a person has been a director of a company which became insolvent at any time (while he was a director or subsequently):

Provided that order against any such person shall not be made after the end of the period of two years beginning with the day on which the company of which that person is or has been a director became insolvent;

(d) the business of the company in which he is or has been a director, has conducted to defraud its creditors, members or any other persons or for a fraudulent or unlawful purpose, or in a manner oppressive of any of its members or that the company was formed for any fraudulent or unlawful purpose; or

(e) the person concerned in the formation of the company or the management of its affairs have in connection therewith been guilty of fraud, misfeasance, breach of trust or other misconduct towards the company or towards any of its member; or

(f) the affairs of the company of which he is a director have been conducted in a manner which has deprived the shareholders thereof of a reasonable return; or

(g) the person has been convicted of allotment of shares of a company for inadequate consideration; or

(h) the person is involved in illegal deposit taking; or

(i) the person has been convicted of financial irregularities or malpractices in a company; or

(j) the company of which he is a director has acted against the interests of the sovereignty and integrity of Pakistan, the security of the State, friendly relations with foreign States; or

(k) the company of which he is a director refuses to act according to the requirements of the memorandum or articles or the provisions of this Act or fail to carry out the directions of the Commission given in the exercise of powers under this Act; or

(l) the person is convicted of insider trading or market manipulation practices; or

(m) the person has entered into a plea bargain arrangement with the National Accountability Bureau or any other regulatory body;

(n) the person has been declared a defaulter by the securities exchange;

(o) that it is expedient in the public interest so to do.

(2) Where a disqualification order is made against a person who is already subject to such an order, the periods specified in those orders shall run concurrently.

(3) An order under this section may be made by the Commission on its own motion or upon a complaint made in this regard.

(4) Before making an order the Commission shall afford the person concerned an opportunity of representation and of being heard.

(5) Any order made by the Commission under this section shall be without prejudice to the powers of the Commission to take such further action as it deems fit with regard to the person concerned.

173. **Personal liability for company's debts where person acts while disqualified.**(1) A person shall be personally responsible for all the relevant debts of a company if at any time--

(a)   in contravention of a disqualification order under section 172, he is involved in the management of the company, or

(b)   as a person who is involved in the management of the company, he acts on instructions given without the leave of the Commission by a person whom he knows at that time to be the subject of a disqualification order:

Provided that where the decision is taken in the board, the disqualified director shall be personally responsible to the extent of proportionate amount of liability so incurred.

(2) Where a person is personally responsible under this section for the relevant debts of a company, he is jointly and severally liable in respect of those debts with the company and any other person who, whether under this section or otherwise, is so liable.

(3) For the purposes of this section, the relevant debts of a company are-

(a)   in relation to a person who is personally responsible under paragraph (a) of sub-section (1), such debts and other liabilities of the company as are incurred at a time when that person was involved in the management of the company; and

(b)   in relation to a person who is personally responsible under paragraph (b) of that sub-section, such debts and other liabilities of the company as are incurred at a time when that person was acting on instructions given as mentioned in that paragraph.

(4) For the purposes of this section, company means a public interest company and a person shall be deemed involved in the management of the

company, if he is a director or concerned, whether directly or indirectly or takes part in the management of such company.

174. **Prohibition on assignment of office by directors.--**(1) A director of any company shall not assign his office to any other person and any such appointment shall be void *ab-initio*.

(2) Notwithstanding anything contained in sub-section (1), the appointment by a director, with the approval of the board, of an alternate or substitute director to act for him during his absence from Pakistan of not less than ninety days, shall not be deemed to be an assignment of office.

(3) The alternate director appointed under sub-section (2) shall *ipso facto* vacate office if and when the director appointing him returns to Pakistan.

175. **Penalty for unqualified person acting as director.--**If a person who is not qualified to be a director or chief executive or who has otherwise vacated the office of director or chief executive describes or represents himself or acts as a director or chief executive, or allows or causes himself to be described as such, shall be liable to a penalty of level 1 on the standard scale[1].

176. **Proceedings of the board.--** (1) The quorum for a meeting of board of a listed company shall not be less than one-third of number of directors or four, whichever is greater and the participation of the directors by video conferencing or by other audio visual means shall also be counted for the purposes of quorum under this sub-section[2]:

Provided that if at any time, there are not enough directors to form a quorum to fill a casual vacancy, all the remaining directors shall be deemed to constitute a quorum for this limited purpose.

(2) The quorum for a meeting of the board of other than listed company shall be as provided in the articles.

(3) The board of a public company shall meet at least once in each quarter of a year.

(4) If a meeting of the board is conducted in the absence of a quorum or a meeting of board is not held as required by sub-section (3), the chairman of the directors and the directors shall be liable--

    (a)   if the default relates to a listed company, to a penalty of level 2 on the standard scale; and

    (b)   if the default relates to any other company, to a penalty of level 1 on the standard scale.

---

[1] 2018 CLD 149; 2015 CLD 345; 2010 CLD 408; 1987 PLD 569
[2] 2017 CLD 1249; 2017 CLD 759; 2009 CLD 1602

177. **Ineligibility of bankrupt to act as director.-** If any person being an undischarged insolvent acts as chief executive or director of a company, he shall be liable to imprisonment for a term not exceeding two years or to a fine not exceeding one hundred thousand rupees, or to both.

178. **Records of resolutions and meetings of board.-**(1) Every company shall keep records comprising[1]--

(a)   all resolutions of the board passed by circulation; and

(b)   minutes of all proceedings of board meetings or committee of directors along with the names of participants, to be entered in properly maintained books.

(2) Minutes recorded in accordance with sub-section (1), if purporting to be authenticated by the chairman of the meeting or by the chairman of the next meeting, shall be the evidence of the proceedings at the meeting.

(3) Until the contrary is proved, every meeting of board or committee of directors in respect of the proceedings whereof minutes have been so made shall be deemed to have been duly called, held and conducted.

(4) A copy of the draft minutes of meeting of board shall be furnished to every director within fourteen days of the date of meeting.

(5) The records must be kept at the registered office of the company from the date of the resolution, meeting or decision simultaneously in physical and electronic form and it shall be preserved for at least ten years in physical form and permanently in electronic form.

(6) Any contravention or default in complying with requirement of this section shall be an offence liable to a penalty of level 1 on the standard scale.

179. **Passing of resolution by the directors through circulation.-** (1) A resolution in writing signed by all the directors or the committee of directors for the time being entitled to receive notice of a meeting of the directors or committee of directors shall be as valid and effectual as if it had been passed at a meeting of the directors or the committee of directors duly convened and held.

(2) A resolution shall not be deemed to have been duly passed, unless the resolution has been circulated, together with the necessary papers, if any, to all the directors.

(3) A resolution under sub-section (1) shall be noted at a subsequent meeting of the board or the committee thereof, as the case may be, and made part of the minutes of such meeting.

(4) A directors' agreement to a written resolution, passed by circulation, once signified, may not be revoked.

---

[1] 1968 PLD 412; 1960 PLD 609; 1956 PLD 731

180. **Liabilities of directors and officers.--** Any provision, whether contained in the articles of a company or in any contract with a company or otherwise, for exempting any officer or auditor of the company, from, or indemnifying him against, any liability which by virtue of any law would otherwise attach to him in respect of any negligence, default, breach of duty or breach of trust of which he may be guilty in relation to the company, shall be void except as otherwise specified for[1]:

(a)   provisions of insurance undertaken by a company on behalf of such officers of the company; or

(b)   qualifying third party indemnify provisions undertaken by a company on behalf of such officers of the company:

Provided that, notwithstanding anything contained in this section, a company may, in pursuance of any such provision as aforesaid, indemnify any such director, chief executive, officer against any liability incurred by him in defending any proceedings, whether civil or criminal, in which judgment is given in his favour or in which he is acquitted, or in connection with any application under section 493 in which relief is granted to him.

181. **Protection to independent and non-executive directors.—** (1) Notwithstanding anything contained in this Act—

(a)   an independent director; and

(b)   a non-executive director;

shall be held liable, only in respect of such acts of omission or commission by a listed company or a public sector company which had occurred with his knowledge, attributable through board processes, and with his consent or connivance or where he had not acted diligently.

(2) For the purpose of this section a non-executive director means, a person on the board of the company who-

(a)   is not from among the executive management team and may or may not be independent;

(b)   is expected to lend an outside viewpoint to the board of a company;

(c)   does not undertake to devote his whole working time to the company and not involve in managing the affairs of the company;

(d)   is not a beneficial owner of the company or any of its associated companies or undertakings;

(e)   does not draw any remuneration from the company except the meeting fee.

---

[1] 2016 CLD 792; 2016 CLD 840; 2016 CLD 1021; 2016 CLD 1073; 1992 MLD 142; 1986 MLD 1870

182. **Loans to directors: requirement of members' approval.-**(1) A company shall not--

(a)   make a loan to a director of the company or of its holding company; or to any of his relatives;

(b)   give a guarantee or provide security in connection with a loan made by any person to such a director; or to any of his relatives;

unless the transaction has been approved by a resolution of the members of the company[1]:

Provided that in case of a listed company, approval of the Commission shall also be required before sanctioning of any such loan.

Explanation.--For the purpose of this section "relative" in relation to a director means his spouse and minor children.

(2) Nothing contained in sub-section (1) shall apply to a company which in the ordinary course of its business provides loans or gives guarantees or securities for the due repayment of any loan.

(3) Every person who is a party to any contravention of this section, including in particular any person to whom the loan is made or who has taken the loan in respect of which the guarantee is given or the security is provided, shall be punishable with fine which may extend to one million rupees or with simple imprisonment for a term which may extend to one year.

(4) All persons who are parties to any contravention of sub-section (1) shall be liable, jointly and severally, to the lending company for the repayment of the loan or for making good the sum with markup not less than the borrowing cost of the lending company which the lending company may have been called upon to pay by virtue of the guarantee given or the security provided by such company.

(5) Sub-section (1) shall apply to any transaction represented by a book-debt which was from its inception in the nature of a loan or an advance.

183. **Powers of board.**—(1) The business of a company shall be managed by the board, who may exercise all such powers of the company as are not by this Act, or by the articles, or by a special resolution, required to be exercised by the company in general meeting[2].

---

[1] 2013 CLD 28; 2012 CLD 1065; 2010 CLD 1210; 2009 CLD 1; 2009 CLD 1106; 2008 CLD 746; 2006 CLD 684; 1988 PLD 1

[2] 2019 CLD 355; 2018 CLD 111; 2017 CLD 587; 2017 CLD 759; 2017 CLD 1142; 2017 PTD 201; 2016 CLD 17; 2016 CLD 176; 2016 CLD 739; 2016 CLD 792; 2016 CLD 840; 2016 CLC 878; 2016 CLD 1021;2016 CLD 1073; 2015 CLD 345; 2014 CLD 1715; 2013 CLD 28; 2012 PLD 52; 2012 CLD 298; 2012 CLD 1065; 2012 CLD 2019; 2011 CLD 1783; 2011 CLD 1430; 2011 CLD 1425; 2011 PLD 586; 2010 CLD 169; 2010 CLD 211; 2010 CLD 286; 2010 CLD 355; 2010 CLD 1210; 2009 CLD 65; 2009 CLC 291; 2009 CLD 390; 2009 CLD 548; 2009 CLD 1502, 2009 CLD 1687; 2008 CLD 746;

(2) The board shall exercise the following powers on behalf of the company, and shall do so by means of a resolution passed at their meeting, namely:-

(a)   to issue shares;

(b)   to issue debentures or any instrument in the nature of redeemable capital;

(c)   to borrow moneys otherwise than on debentures;

(d)   to invest the funds of the company;

(e)   to make loans;

(f)   to authorise a director or the firm of which he is a partner or any partner of such firm or a private company of which he is a member or director to enter into any contract with the company for making sale, purchase or supply of goods or rendering services with the company;

(g)   to approve financial statements;

(h)   to approve bonus to employees;

(i)   to incur capital expenditure on any single item or dispose of a fixed asset in accordance with the limits as may be specified:

Provided that the acceptance by a banking company in the ordinary course of its business of deposit of money from the public repayable on demand or otherwise and withdrawable by cheque, draft, order or otherwise, or placing of moneys on deposit by a banking company with another banking company such conditions as the board may prescribe, shall not be deemed to be a borrowing of money or, as the case may be, a making of loan by a banking company with the meaning of this section;

(j)   to undertake obligations under leasing contracts exceeding such amount as may be notified;

(k)   to declare interim dividend; and

(l)   having regard to such amount as may be determined to be material (as construed in Generally Accepted Accounting Principles) by the board--

(i)   to write off bad debts, advances and receivables;

(ii)   to write off inventories and other assets of the company; and

---

2008 CLD 1300; 2007 CLD 1038; 2007 CLD 1251; 2005 CLD 1208; 2002 CLD 557; 2000 PLD 414; 2000 PLD 602; 1992 MLD 142; 1991 CLC 589; 1986 MLD 1870

> (iii)   to determine the terms of and the circumstances in which a law suit may be compromised and a claim or right in favour of a company may be released, extinguished or relinquished.

(m)   to take over a company or acquire a controlling or substantial stake in another company;

(n)   any other matter which may be specified.

(3) The board of a company shall not except with the consent of the general meeting either specifically or by way of an authorisation, do any of the following things[1], namely.--

(a)   sell, lease or otherwise dispose of the undertakings or a sizeable part thereof unless the main business of the company comprises of such selling or leasing; and

> *Explanation*.—For the purposes of this clause-

> (i)   **"undertaking"** shall mean an undertaking in which the investment of the company exceeds twenty percent of its net worth as per the audited financial statements of the preceding financial year or an undertaking which generates twenty percent of the total income of the company during the previous financial year;

> (ii)   the expression **"sizeable part"** in any financial year shall mean twenty five percent or more of the value of the assets in that class as per the audited financial statements of the preceding financial year;

(b)   sell or otherwise dispose of the subsidiary of the company;

(c)   remit, give any relief or give extension of time for the repayment of any debt outstanding against any person specified in sub-section (1) of section 182.

(4) Nothing contained in sub-section (3) shall entitle a listed company to sell or otherwise dispose of the undertaking, which results in or may lead to closure of business operation or winding up of the company, without there being a viable alternate business plan duly authenticated by the board.

(5) Any resolution passed under sub-section (3) if not implemented within one year from the date of passing shall stand lapsed.

(6) Any contravention or default in complying with requirement of this section shall be an offence liable to a penalty of level 2 on the standard scale and shall be individually and severally liable for losses or damages arising out of such action.

---

[1] 2018 CLC 1602; 2012 CLD 1065; 2010 CLD 1210; 2009 CLD 1106; 2009 CLD 1; 2008 CLD 746

184. **Prohibition regarding making of political contributions.**-(1) Notwithstanding anything contained in this Act, a company shall not contribute any amount or allow utilization of its assets—

    (a)   to any political party; or

    (b)   for any political purpose to any individual or body.

    (2)   If a company contravenes the provisions of sub-section (1), then--

    (a)   the company shall be liable to a penalty of level 2 on the standard scale; and

    (b)   every director and officer of the company who is in default shall be punishable with imprisonment of either description for a term which may extend to two years and shall also be liable to a fine of one million rupees.

185. **Prohibition regarding distribution of gifts.**-(1) Notwithstanding anything contained in this Act, a company shall not distribute gifts in any form to its members in its meeting.

    (2) Any contravention or default in complying with requirement of this section shall be an offence liable to a penalty of level 1 on the standard scale.

CHIEF EXECUTIVE

186. **Appointment of first chief executive**.- (1) Every company shall have a chief executive appointed in the manner provided in this section and section 187[1].

(2) The name of first chief executive shall be determined by the subscribers of the memorandum and his particulars specified under section 197 shall be submitted along with the documents for the incorporation of the company.

(3) The first chief executive shall, unless he earlier resigns or otherwise ceases to hold office, hold office up to the first annual general meeting of the company or, if a shorter period is fixed by the subscribers at the time of his appointment, for such period.

(4) Notwithstanding anything contained in this section, the Government shall have the power to nominate chief executive of a public sector company in such manner as may be specified.

187. **Appointment of subsequent chief executive.**- (1) Within fourteen days from the date of election of directors under section 159 or the office of the chief executive falling vacant, as the case may be, the board shall appoint any person, including an elected director, to be the chief executive, but

---

[1] 2010 CLD 1234

such appointment shall not be for a period exceeding three years from the date of appointment[1]:

Provided that the chief executive appointed against a casual vacancy shall hold office till the directors elected in the next election appoint a chief executive.

(2) On the expiry of his term of office under section 186 or sub-section (1) of this section, a chief executive shall be eligible for reappointment.

(3) The chief executive retiring under section 186 or this section shall continue to perform his functions until his successor is appointed, unless non-appointment of his successor is due to any fault on his part or his office is expressly terminated.

(4) Notwithstanding anything contained in this section, the Government shall have the power to nominate chief executive of a company where majority of directors is nominated by the Government, in such manner as may be specified[2].

188. **Terms of appointment of chief executive.--**(1) Save as provided in sub-section (2), the terms and conditions of appointment of a chief executive shall be determined by the board or the company in general meeting in accordance with the provisions in the company's articles[3].

(2) The terms and conditions of appointment of a chief executive nominated under section 186 or 187 shall be determined by the Government, in such manner as may be specified.

(3) The chief executive shall if he is not already a director of the company, be deemed to be its director and be entitled to all the rights and privileges, and subject to all the liabilities, of that office.

189. **Restriction on appointment of chief executive.--** No person who is ineligible to become a director of a company under section 153 or disqualified under sections 171 or 172 shall be appointed or continue as the chief executive of any company.

190. **Removal of chief executive.--**(1) The board by resolution passed by not less than three-fourths of the total number of directors for the time being, or the company by a special resolution, may remove a chief executive before the expiration of his term of office notwithstanding anything contained in the articles or in any agreement between the company and such chief executive[4].

[1] 2019 PLC(CS) 300; 2017 PLC(CS) 55; 2017 PLC(CS) 1393; 2002 CLD 1309
[2] 2019 PLC 300
[3] 2002 CLD 1309
[4] 2019 PLC(CS) 300, 1985 MLD 1195

(2) Notwithstanding anything contained in this section, the Government or an authority or a person authorized by it shall have the power to remove chief executive of a company where more than seventy-five percent of the voting rights are held by the Government.

191. Chief executive not to engage in business competing with company's business.-- (1) A chief executive of a public company shall not directly or indirectly engage in any business which is of the same nature as and directly competes with the business carried on by the company of which he is the chief executive or by a subsidiary of such company[1].

Explanation.--A business shall be deemed to be carried on indirectly by the chief executive if the same is carried on by his spouse or any of his minor children.

(2) Every person who is appointed as chief executive of a public company shall forthwith on such appointment disclose to the company in writing the nature of such business and his interest therein.

192. Chairman in a listed company.-- (1) The board of a listed company shall within fourteen days from the date of election of directors, appoint a chairman from among the non-executive directors who shall hold office for a period of three years unless he earlier resigns, becomes ineligible or disqualified under any provision of this Act or removed by the directors.

(2) The board shall clearly define the respective roles and responsibilities of the chairman and chief executive:

Provided that the Commission may specify the classes of companies for which the chairman and chief executive shall not be the same individual.

(3) The chairman shall be responsible for leadership of the board and ensure that the board plays an effective role in fulfilling its responsibilities.

(4) Every financial statements circulated under section 223 of this Act shall contain a review report by the chairman on the overall performance of the board and effectiveness of the role played by the board in achieving the company's objectives.

193. Penalty.--Any contravention or default in complying with requirements of sections 186 to 192 shall be an offence liable to a penalty of level 2 on the standard scale and may also be debarred by the authority which imposes the penalty from becoming a director or chief executive of a company for a period not exceeding five years.

194. Public company required to have secretary.--A public company must have a company secretary; possessing such qualification as may be specified.

---

[1] 2003 CLD 1209

195. **Listed company to have share registrar.--** Every listed company shall have an independent share registrar possessing such qualifications and performing such functions as may be specified.

196. **Bar on appointment of sole purchase, sales agents.--**(1) No company whether incorporated in Pakistan or outside Pakistan which is carrying on business in Pakistan shall, without the approval of the Commission, appoint any sole purchase, sale or distribution agent:

Provided that this sub-section shall not apply to a sole purchase, sale or distribution agent appointed by a company incorporated, outside Pakistan, unless the major portion of the business of such company is conducted in Pakistan.

(2) Whoever contravenes any of the provisions of this section shall be punished with imprisonment for a term which may extend to two years, or with fine which may extend to one hundred thousand rupees, or with both; and, if the person guilty of the offence is a company or other body corporate, every director, chief executive, or other officer, agent or partner thereof shall, unless he proves that the offence was committed without his knowledge or that he exercised all due diligence to prevent its commission, be deemed to be guilty of the offence.

REGISTER OF DIRECTORS AND OTHER OFFICERS

197. **Register of directors, officers.--** (1) Every company shall keep at its registered office a register of its directors and officers, including the chief executive, company secretary, chief financial officer, auditors and legal adviser, containing with respect to each of them such particulars as may be specified[1].

(2) Every person referred to in sub-section (1) shall, within a period of ten days of his appointment or any change therein, as the case may be, furnish to the company the particulars specified under sub-section (1).

(3) Every company shall, within a period of fifteen days from the date of appointment of any person referred in sub-section (1) or any change among them, or in any of their particulars, file with the registrar a return in the specified form:

Provided that this sub-section shall not apply to the first appointment made at the time of incorporation of the company.

(4) Any contravention or default in complying with requirement of sub-section (1) or sub-section (3) shall be an offence liable to a penalty of level 1 on the standard scale.

---

[1] 2018 CLD 383; 2008 CLD 522; 2007 CLD 1019; 2006 PTD 2639; 2005 CLD 1029; 2002 CLD 325; 2002 CLD 1164; 1987 PLD 569; 1987 MLD 2511

(5) If the name of any person is fraudulently or without sufficient cause entered in or omitted from the register of directors of a company the person aggrieved or the company, may apply to the Court for rectification of the register of directors.

(6) The Court may either refuse the application or may order rectification of the register on such terms and conditions as it may deem fit and may make order as to costs.

(7) Where the Court has passed and order under sub-section (6) that *prima facie* entry in or omission from, the register of directors the name or other particulars of any person, was made fraudulently or without sufficient cause, the Court may send a reference for adjudication of offence under sub-section (8) to the court as provided in section.

(8) Anyone who fraudulently or without sufficient cause enters in, or omits from the register of directors the name or other particulars of any person, shall be punishable with imprisonment for a term which may extend to three years or with fine which may extend to one million rupees, or with both.

(9) When it makes an order for rectification of the register of directors in respect of a company, the Court shall cause a copy of the order to be forwarded to the company and shall, by its order, direct the company to file notice of the rectification with the registrar within fifteen days from the receipt of the order.

198.   **Rights to inspect.--** (1) The register kept under section 197 shall, be open to the inspection of any member of the company and of any other person during business hours, subject to such reasonable restrictions, as the company may impose by its articles or in general meeting, so that not less than two hours in each day are allowed.

(2) Inspection by any member of the company shall be without charge, and in the case of any other person on payment of such fee as may be fixed by the company for each inspection.

(3) A person seeking to exercise the rights conferred by this section must make a request to the company to that effect.

(4) The request must contain the following information--

(a)   in the case of an individual, his name and address;

(b)   in the case of an organisation, its name and address and also of the authorised person; and

(c)   the purpose for which the information is to be used.

(5) In the case any inspection is refused, the registrar on application made by the person to whom inspection has been refused and upon notice to the company, may by order direct an immediate inspection of the register.

(6) Any contravention or default in complying with requirements of this section shall be an offence shall be liable to a penalty of level 1 on the standard scale.

MISCELLANEOUS PROVISIONS REGARDING INVESTMENTS, CONTRACTS OFFICERS AND SHAREHOLDINGS, TRADING AND INTERESTS

199. **Investments in associated companies and undertaking**.--(1) A company shall not make any investment in any of its associated companies or associated undertakings except under the authority of a special resolution which shall indicate the nature, period, amount of investment and terms and conditions attached thereto[1].

Explanation: The term "investment" shall include equity, loans, advances, guarantees, by whatever name called, except for the amount due as normal trade credit, where the terms and conditions of trade transaction(s) carried out on arms-length and in accordance with the trade policy of the company.

(2) The company shall not invest in its associated company or associated undertaking by way of loans or advances except in accordance with an agreement in writing and such agreement shall *inter-alia* include the terms and conditions specifying the nature, purpose, period of the loan, rate of return, fees or commission, repayment schedule for principal and return, penalty clause in case of default or late repayments and security, if any, for the loan in accordance with the approval of the members in the general meeting:

Provided that the return on such investment shall not be less than the borrowing cost of the investing company or the rate as may be specified by the Commission whichever is higher and shall be recovered on regular basis in accordance with the terms of the agreement, failing which the directors shall be personally liable to make the payment:

Provided further that the directors of the investing company shall certify that the investment is made after due diligence and financial health of the borrowing company is such that it has the ability to repay the loan as per the agreement.

---

[1] 2019 CLD 508; 2017 CLD 169; 2016 CLD 1077; 2016 CLD 1697; 2016 CLD 1713; 2015 CLD 1098; 2014 CLD 449; 2013 CLD 220; 2013 CLD 1179; 2013 CLD 1300; 2013 CLD 1385; 2012 CLD 691; 2012 CLD 741; 2012 CLD 1408; 2012 CLD 1430; 2012 CLD 2019; 2012 CLD 1835; 2011 CLD 614; 2011 CLD 1149; 2010 CLD 36; 2010 CLD 75; 2010 CLD 169; 2010 CLD 286; 2010 CLD 355; 2010 CLD 408; 2010 CLD 415; 2010 CLD 1071; 2010 CLD 1096; 2010 CLD 1210; 2010 CLD 1690; 2010 CLD 1729; 2009 CLD 56; 2009 CLD 65; 2009 CLD 1106; 2009 CLD 1191; 2009 CLD 1636; 2008 CLD 17; 2008 CLD 252; 2008 CLD 436; 2008 CLD 746; 2008 CLD 786; 2008 CLD 825; 2008 CLD 809; 2007 CLD 370; 2007 CLD 557;2007 CLD 983; 2007 CLD 1060; 2007 CLD 1291; 2007 CLD 1491; 2006 CLD 458; 2006 CLD 997; 2006 CLD 1055; 2003 CLD 131; 2003 CLD 293; 2002 CLD 1150; 1998 PLD 1; 1995 PLD 264; 1993 MLD 42

(3)   The Commission may--

(a)   by notification in the official Gazette, specify the class of companies or undertakings to which the restriction provided in sub-section (1) shall not apply; and

(b)   through regulations, specify such disclosure requirements, conditions and restrictions on the nature, period, amount of investment and terms and conditions attached thereto, and other ancillary matters.

(4)   An increase in the amount or any change in the nature of investment or the terms and conditions attached thereto shall be made only under the authority of a special resolution.

(5) Every company shall maintain and keep at its registered office a register of investments in associated companies and undertakings containing such particulars as may be specified.

(6) Any contravention or default in complying with requirements of this section shall be an offence liable to a penalty of level 3 on the standard scale and in addition, shall jointly and severally reimburse to the company any loss sustained by the company in consequence of an investment which was made without complying with the requirements of this section.

200. **Investments of company to be held in its own name.**--(1) All investments made by a company on its own behalf shall be made and held by it in its own name[1]:

Provided that the company may hold any shares in its subsidiary company in the name of any nominee of the company, if it is necessary to do so, to ensure that the number of members of the subsidiary company is not reduced below the statutory limit.

(2) Where the company has a right to appoint or get elected any person as a director of any other company and a nominee of the company in exercise of such right has been so appointed or elected, the shares in such other company of an amount not exceeding the nominal value of the qualification shares which are required to be held by a director thereof, may be registered or held by such company jointly in its own name and in the name of such person or nominee, or in the name of such person or nominee alone.

(3) Nothing in this section shall be deemed to prevent a company from depositing with, or transferring to, or holding, or registering in the name of a central depository any shares or securities.

---

[1] 2015 CLD 345; 2012 CLD 1895; 2010 CLD 963; 2010 CLD 1115; 2010 CLD 1531; 2000 PLD 461

(4) Where, in pursuance of proviso to sub-section (1) or provisions of sub-sections (2) or (3), any shares or securities in which investments have been made by a company are not held by it in its own name, the company shall forthwith enter in a register maintained by it for the purpose at its registered office the nature, value and such other particulars as may be necessary fully to identify such shares or securities.

(5) The register maintained under sub-section (4) shall, be open to the inspection of members without charge, and to any other person on payment of such fees as the company may specify in this behalf during business hours, subject to such reasonable restrictions, as the company may impose, so that not less than two hours in each day be allowed.

(6) Any member may require a certified copy of register or any part thereof, on payment of such fee as may be fixed by the company.

(7) The certified copies requested under this section shall be issued within a period of seven days.

(8) A member seeking to exercise either of the rights conferred by sub-sections (5) or (6) must make a request to the company to that effect.

(9) If a company contravenes the provisions of sub-section (1), the company shall be punishable with fine which may extend to five million rupees and every officer of the company who is in default shall be punishable with imprisonment for a term which may extend to two years or with fine which may extend to one million rupees, or with both.

(10) Any contravention or default in complying with requirements of sub-sections (4), (5) or (6), shall be an offence liable to a penalty of level 1 on the standard scale; and the registrar may by an order compel an immediate inspection of the register or direct that copies required shall be sent to the persons requiring them.

201. **Method of contracting.--**(1) A contract or other enforceable obligation may be entered into by a company as follows[1]:

(a)   an obligation which, if entered into by a natural person, will, by law, be required to be by deed or otherwise in writing, may be entered into on behalf of the company in writing signed under the name of the company by a director, attorney or any other person duly authorised by the board and may affix common seal of the company;

(b)   an obligation which, if entered into by a natural person, is not, by law, required to be in writing, may be entered into on behalf of the

---

[1] 2003 YLR 1000

(c)   company in writing or orally by a person acting under the company's express or implied authority.

(2) All contracts made according to sub-section (1) shall be effectual in law and shall bind the company and its successors and all other parties thereto, their heirs, or legal representatives as the case may be.

202. Execution of bills of exchange, promissory notes and deeds.-- (1) A bill of exchange or promissory note shall be deemed to have been made, drawn, accepted or endorsed on behalf of a company if made, drawn, accepted or endorsed in the name of, or on behalf of or on account of, the company by any person acting under its authority, express or implied[1].

(2) A company may, by writing, authorise any person, either generally or in respect of any specified matters, as its attorney to execute deeds on its behalf in any place either in or outside Pakistan.

(3) A deed signed by such an attorney on behalf of the company and under his seal shall bind the company and have the effect as if it was made by the company itself.

203. Company to have official seal for use abroad.- (1) A company that has a common seal may have an official seal for use outside Pakistan.

(2) The official seal must be a facsimile of the company's common seal, with the addition on its face of the name of every territory where it is to be used.

(3) The official seal when duly affixed to a document has the same effect as the company's common seal.

(4) A company having such an official seal may, by writing under its common seal, authorise any person appointed for the purpose in any territory not situate in Pakistan to affix the same to any deed or other document to which the company is party in that territory.

(5) The authority of any such agent shall, as between the company and any person dealing with the agent, continue during the period, if any, mentioned in the instrument conferring the authority, or if no period is mentioned therein, then until notice of the revocation or determination of the agent's authority has been given to the person dealing with him.

(6) The person affixing any such official seal shall, by writing under his hand, on the deed or other document to which the seal is affixed, certify the date and place of affixing the same.

(7) A deed or other document to which an official seal is duly affixed shall bind the company as if it had been sealed with the common seal of the company.

---

[1] 2009 CLD 390; 2009 CLC 291; 2001 SCMR 1578

204. **Duties of directors.**--(1) Subject to the provisions of this Act, a director of a company shall act in accordance with the articles of the company[1].

(2) A director of a company shall act in good faith in order to promote the objects of the company for the benefit of its members as a whole, and in the best interests of the company, its employees the shareholders the community and for the protection of environment.

(3) A director of a company shall discharge his duties with due and reasonable care, skill and diligence and shall exercise independent judgment.

(4) A director of a company shall not involve in a situation in which he may have a direct or indirect interest that conflicts, or possibly may conflict, with the interest of the company.

(5) A director of a company shall not achieve or attempt to achieve any undue gain or advantage either to himself or to his relatives, partners, or associates and if such director is found guilty of making any undue gain, he shall be liable to pay an amount equal to that gain to the company.

(6) A director of a company shall not assign his office and any assignment so made shall be void.

(7) In addition to the preceding sub-sections, the Commission may provide for the extent of duties and the role of directors as may be specified.

(8) Any breach of duty, default or negligence by a director in contravention of the articles of the company or any of its policy or decision of the board may be ratified by the company through a special resolution and the Commission may impose any restriction as may be specified.

(9) Without prejudice to any other action that may be taken under this Act or any other law, any contravention or default in complying with requirements of this section shall be an offence liable to a penalty of level 1 on the standard scale.

205. **Disclosure of interest by director.**--(1) Every director of a company who is in any way, whether directly or indirectly, concerned or interested in any contract or arrangement entered into, or to be entered into, by or on behalf of the company shall disclose the nature of his concern or interest at a meeting of the board[2]:

Provided that a director shall be deemed also to be interested or concerned if any of his relatives, is so interested or concerned.

Explanation. For the purpose of this section "**director's relatives**", are--

(a)   the director's spouse;

---

[1] 2019 SCMR 1
[2] 2017 CLD 759, 2016 CLD 17; 2013 CLD 357; 2012 CLD 1588; 2010 CLD 408; 1995 PLD 264

(b)   the director's children, including the step children;

(c)   the director's parents;

(2)   The disclosure required to be made by a director under sub-section (1) shall be made-

(a)   in the case of a contract or arrangement to be entered into, at the meeting of the board at which the question of entering into the contract or arrangement is first taken into consideration or, if the director was not, on the date of that meeting, concerned or interested in the contract or arrangement, at the first meeting of the board held after he becomes so concerned or interested; and

(b)   in the case of any other contract or arrangement, at the first meeting of the board held after the director becomes concerned or interested in the contract or arrangement.

(3) For the purposes of sub-sections (1) and (2), a general notice given to the board to the effect that a director is a director or a member of a specified body corporate or a partner of a specified firm and is to be regarded as concerned or interested in any contract or arrangement which may, after the date of the notice, be entered into with that body corporate or firm, shall be deemed to be a sufficient disclosure of concern or interest in relation to any contract or arrangement so made.

(4) Any such general notice shall expire at the end of the financial year in which it is given, but may be renewed for further period of one financial year at a time, by a fresh notice given in the last month of the financial year in which it would otherwise expire.

(5) No such general notice, and no renewal thereof, shall be of effect unless either it is given at a meeting of the board, or the director concerned takes reasonable steps to ensure that it is brought up and read at the first meeting of the board after it is given.

(6) Any contravention or default in complying with requirements of sub-sections (1) or (2), shall be an offence liable to a penalty of level 1 on the standard scale.

206. **Interest of officers.**--(1) Save as provided in section 205 in respect of directors, no other officer of a company who is in any way, directly or indirectly, concerned or interested in any proposed contract or arrangement with the company shall, unless he discloses the nature and extent of his interest in the transaction and obtains the prior approval of the board, enter into any such contract or arrangement[1].

---

[1] 2012 CLD 1588; 2010 CLD 408; 1995 PLD 264

(2) Any contravention or default in complying with requirement under this section shall be an offence liable to a penalty of level 1 on the standard scale.

207. **Interested director not to participate or vote in proceedings of board.--** (1) No director of a company shall, as a director, take any part in the discussion of, or vote on, any contract or arrangement entered into, or to be entered into, by or on behalf of the company, if he is in any way, whether directly or indirectly, concerned or interested in the contract or arrangement, nor shall his presence count for the purpose of forming a quorum at the time of any such discussion or vote; and if he does vote, his vote shall be void[1]:

Provided that a director of a listed company who has a material personal interest in a matter that is being considered at a board meeting shall not be present while that matter is being considered.

(2) If majority of the directors are interested in, any contract or arrangement entered into, or to be entered into, by or on behalf of the company, the matter shall be laid before the general meeting for approval.

(3)   Sub-section (1) shall not apply to--

(a)   a private company which is neither a subsidiary nor a holding company of a public company;

(b)   any contract of indemnity or insurance coverage executed by the company in favour of interested director against any loss which he may suffer or incur by reason of becoming or being a surety for the company or while undertaking any transaction on behalf of the company:

        Provided that for the purpose of clause (b), a company shall only insure the liability of interested director where such liability arises out of a transaction validly approved by the board or the members of the company as the case may be:

(4) Any contravention or default in complying with requirements under this section shall be an offence liable to a penalty of level 1 on the standard scale.

208. **Related party transactions.--** (1) A company may enter into any contract or arrangement with a related party only in accordance with the policy approved by the board, subject to such conditions as may be specified, with respect to-

(a)   sale, purchase or supply of any goods or materials;

(b)   selling or otherwise disposing of, or buying, property of any kind;

---

[1] 2017 CLD 759; 2013 CLD 357; 2012 CLD 1588; 2010 CLD 408; 1995 PLD 264

(c)   leasing of property of any kind;

(d)   availing or rendering of any services;

(e)   appointment of any agent for purchase or sale of goods, materials, services or property; and

(f)   such related party's appointment to any office or place of profit in the company, its subsidiary company or associated company:

Provided that where majority of the directors are interested in any of the above transactions, the matter shall be placed before the general meeting for approval as special resolution:

Provided also that nothing in this sub-section shall apply to any transactions entered into by the company in its ordinary course of business on an arm's length basis.

Explanation.— In this sub-section-

(a)   the expression "**office of profit**" means any office--

(i)   where such office is held by a director, if the director holding it receives from the company anything by way of remuneration over and above the remuneration to which he is entitled as director, by way of salary, fee, commission, perquisites, any rent-free accommodation, or otherwise;

(ii)   where such office is held by an individual other than a director or by any firm, private company or other body corporate, if the individual, firm, private company or body corporate holding it receives from the company anything by way of remuneration,

(iii)   salary, fee, commission, perquisites, any rent-free accommodation, or otherwise;

(b)   the expression "**arm's length transaction**" means a transaction which is subject to such terms and conditions as may be specified.

(c)   the expression "**related party**" includes--

(i)   a director or his relative:

(ii)   a key managerial personnel or his relative;

(iii)   a firm, in which a director, manager or his relative is a partner;

(iv)   a private company in which a director or manager is a member or director;

(v)   a public company in which a director or manager is a director or holds along with his relatives, any shares of its paid up share capital;

(vi)   any body corporate whose chief executive or manager is accustomed to act in accordance with the advice, directions or instructions of a director or manager;

(vii) any person on whose advice, directions or instructions a director or manager is accustomed to act:

Provided that nothing in sub-clauses (*vi*) and (*vii*) shall apply to the advice, directions or instructions given in a professional capacity;

(viii) any company which is—

(A)   a holding, subsidiary or an associated company of such company; or
(B)   a subsidiary of a holding company to which it is also a subsidiary;

(*xi*) such other person as may be specified;

Explanation.— For the purpose of this section "**relative**" means spouse, siblings and lineal ascendants and descendants of a person.

(2) Every contract or arrangement entered into under sub-section (1) shall be referred to in the board's report to the shareholders along-with the justification for entering into such contract or arrangement.

(3) The Commission may specify the record to be maintained by the company with regards to transactions undertaken with the related party.

(4) Where any contract or arrangement is entered into by a director or any other employee, without obtaining the consent of the board or approval by a special resolution in the general meeting under sub-section (1) and if it is not ratified by the board or, as the case may be, by the shareholders at a meeting within ninety days from the date on which such contract or arrangement was entered into, such contract or arrangement shall be voidable at the option of the board and if the contract or arrangement is with a related party to any director, or is authorised by any other director, the directors concerned shall indemnify the company against any loss incurred by it.

(5) Without prejudice to anything contained in sub-section (4), it shall be open to the company to proceed against a director or any employee who had entered into such contract or arrangement in contravention of the provisions of

(6) this section for recovery of any loss sustained by it as a result of such contract or arrangement.

(7) Any director or any other employee of a company, who had entered into or authorised the contract or arrangement in violation of the provisions of this section shall be liable--

(a)   in case of listed company, be punishable with imprisonment for a term which may extend to three years or with fine which shall not be less than five million rupees, or with both; and

(b)   in case of any other company, to a penalty of level 2 on the standard scale.

209.   **Register of contracts or arrangements in which directors are interested.--** (1) Every company shall keep one or more registers giving separately the particulars of all contracts or arrangements, in such manner and containing such particulars as may be specified by the Commission.

(2) Every director shall, within a period of thirty days of his appointment, or relinquishment of his office, as the case may be, disclose to the company the particulars relating to his concern or interest in the other associations which are required to be included in the register under sub-section (1) or such other information relating to himself as may be specified.

(3) The register referred to in sub-section (1) shall be kept at the registered office of the company and it shall be open for inspection at such office during business hours and extracts may be taken therefrom, and copies thereof as may be required by any member of the company shall be furnished by the company to such extent, in such manner, and on payment of such fees as may be specified.

(4) The register to be kept under this section shall also be produced at the commencement of every annual general meeting of the company and shall remain open and accessible during the continuance of the meeting to any person having the right to attend the meeting.

(5) Nothing contained in sub-section (1) shall apply to any contract or arrangement--

(a)   for the sale, purchase or supply of any goods, materials or services if the value of such goods and materials or the cost of such services does not exceed five hundred thousand rupees in the aggregate in any year; or

(b)   by a banking company for the collection of bills in the ordinary course of its business.

(6) Any contravention or default in complying with requirements under this section shall be an offence liable to a penalty of level 1 on the standard scale.

210. **Contract of employment with directors.--** (1) Every company shall keep at its registered office--

    (a)   where a contract of service with a director is in writing, a copy of the contract; or

    (b)   where such a contract is not in writing, a written memorandum setting out its terms.

(2) The copies of the contract or the memorandum kept under sub-section (1) shall be open to inspection by any member of the company without payment of fee.

(3) Any contravention or default in complying with requirement under this section shall be an offence liable to a penalty of level 1 on the standard scale.

(4) The provisions of this section shall not apply to a private company.

211. **Restriction on non-cash transactions involving directors.--** (1) No company shall enter into an arrangement by which—

    (a)   a director of the company or its holding, subsidiary or associated company or a person connected with him acquires or is to acquire assets for consideration other than cash, from the company; or

    (b)   the company acquires or is to acquire assets for consideration other than cash, from such director or person so connected;

unless prior approval for such arrangement is accorded by a resolution of the company in general meeting and if the director or connected person is a director

of its holding company, approval under this sub-section shall also be required to be obtained by passing a resolution in general meeting of the holding company.

(2) The notice for approval of the resolution by the company or holding company in general meeting under sub-section (1) shall include the particulars of the arrangement along-with the value of the assets involved in such arrangement duly calculated by a registered valuer.

(3) Any arrangement entered into by a company or its holding company in contravention of the provisions of this section shall be voidable at the instance of the company unless—

    (a)   the restitution of any money or other consideration which is the subject-matter of the arrangement is no longer possible and the

(b)   company has been indemnified by any other person for any loss or damage caused to it; or

(c)   any rights are acquired *bona fide* for value and without notice of the contravention of the provisions of this section by any other person.

(4)   The company shall ensure that all cash transactions with its directors are conducted only through banking channels.

212.   **Declaring a director to be lacking fiduciary behaviour.**--The Court may declare a director to be lacking fiduciary behaviour if he contravenes the provisions of section 205 or sub-section (1) of section 206 or sections 207 or 208[1]:

Provided that before making a declaration the Court shall afford the director concerned an opportunity of showing cause against the proposed action.

213.   **Disclosure to members of directors' interest in contract appointing chief executive or secretary.--** (1) Every director of a company who is in any way, whether directly or indirectly, concerned or interested, in any appointment or contract for the appointment of a chief executive, whole-time director or secretary of the company shall disclose the nature of his interest or concern at a meeting of the board in which such appointment or contract is to be approved and the interested director shall not participate or vote in the proceedings of the board[2].

(2) All contracts entered into by a company for the appointment of a chief executive, whole-time director or secretary shall be kept at the registered office of the company.

(3) Every contract required to be kept under sub-section (2) must be open to inspection by any member of the company without charge.

(4) Any member of the company is entitled, on request and on payment of such fee as may be fixed by the company, to be provided with a copy of any such contract. The copy must be provided within seven days after the request is received by the company.

(5) Any contravention or default in complying with requirements under this section shall be an offence liable to a penalty of level 1 on the standard scale.

214.   **Contracts by agents of company in which company is undisclosed principal.**— Every officer or other agent of a company, other than a private company, not being the subsidiary company of a public company, who enters into a contract for or on behalf of the company in which contract the

[1] 2012 CLD 1588; 2010 CLD 408; 1995 PLD 264; 1983 CLC 162
[2] 2017 CLD 767; 2017 CLD 767; 2010 CLD 1190; 2006 CLD 1060

company is an undisclosed principal shall, at the time of entering into the contract, make a memorandum in writing of the terms of contract, and specify therein the person with whom it has been made.

(2) Every such officer or other agent shall forthwith deliver the memorandum aforesaid to the company and its directors which shall be laid before next meeting of the board.

(3) If any such officer or other agent makes default in complying with the requirements of this section--

(a)   the contract shall, at the option of the company, be void as against the company; and

(b)   such officer or other agent shall be liable to a penalty of level 1 on the standard scale.

215. **Liability for undesired activities of the shareholders.**--(1)A member of a company shall act in good faith while exercising its powers as a shareholder at the general meetings and shall not conduct themselves in a manner that is considered disruptive to proceedings of the meeting.

(2) Without prejudice to his rights under this Act, a member of the company shall not exert influence or approach the management directly for decisions which may lead to create hurdle in the smooth functioning of management.

(3) Any shareholder who fails to conduct in the manner provided in this section and as specified by the Commission shall be guilty of an offence under this section and shall be liable to a penalty not exceeding of level 1 on the standard scale.

216. **Company deemed to be a public interest company in certain circumstances.**--(1) Notwithstanding anything contained in this Act, a company shall be deemed to be a company with public interest as envisaged in the Third Schedule.

(2) Upon being deemed as a company with public interest, the company shall be required to comply with such disclosure and reporting requirements as may be specified by the Commission.

(3) The Commission may as specified, after giving an opportunity of hearing to a company or class of companies, by an order in writing exempt such company from the requirements of this section if the Commission determines that such exemption is in the interest of the public:

Provided that such order shall be posted on the official website of the Commission.

217. **Securities and deposits.--**(1) Save as provided in section 84, no company or any of its officers or agents shall receive or utilise any money received as security or deposit, except in accordance with a contract in writing[1].

(2) The money so received shall be kept in a special account maintained by a company with a scheduled bank.

(3) This section shall not apply where the money received is in the nature of an advance payment for goods to be delivered or sold to an agent, dealer or sub-agent in accordance with a contract in writing.

218. **Employees' provident funds, contributory retirement funds and securities.--** (1) All moneys or securities deposited with a company by its employees in pursuance of their contracts of service with the company shall be kept or deposited by the company within fifteen days from the date of deposit in a special account to be opened by the company for the purpose in a scheduled bank or in the National Saving Schemes, and no portion thereof shall be utilized by the company except for the breach of the contract of service on the part of the employee as provided in the contract and after notice to the employee concerned[2].

(2) Where a provident fund, contributory pension fund or any other contributory retirement fund has been constituted by a company for its employees or any class of its employees, all moneys contributed to such fund, whether by the company or by the employees or by both, or received or accruing by way of interest, profit or otherwise from the date of contribution, receipt or accrual, as the case may be, shall either--

    (a)   be deposited--

        (i)   in a National Savings Scheme;

        (ii)   in a special account to be opened by the company for the purpose in a scheduled bank; or

        (iii)   where the company itself is a scheduled bank, in a special account to be opened by the company for the purpose either in itself or in any other scheduled bank; or

    (b)   be invested in--

        (i)   Government securities; or

        (ii)   bonds, redeemable capital, debt securities or instruments issued by a statutory body, units of collective investment schemes registered as notified entities with the Commission,

---

[1] 2014 CLD 430; 2010 CLD 1716; 2009 CLD 76; 2007 CLD 1504

[2] 2016 CLD 2077; 2014 CLD 862; 2013 CLD 108; 2013 CLD 1710; 2012 CLD 1423; 2011 CLD 1141; 2010 CLD 60; 2010 CLD 1725; 2009 CLD 61; 2009 CLD 76; 2009 CLD 951; 2008 CLD 266; 2008 CLD 731; 2008 CLD 803; 2007 CLD 93; 2006 CLD 1376; 2006 CLD 454; 2005 CLD 350

    (iii)   and in listed securities including shares of companies, bonds, redeemable capital, debt securities and equity securities, subject to the conditions as may be specified.

(3) Where a trust has been created by a company with respect to any provident fund or a contributory pension fund or any contributory retirement fund referred to in sub-section (2), the company shall be bound to collect the contribution of the employees concerned and pay such contributions as well as its own contributions, if any, to the trustees within fifteen days from the date of collection, and thereupon, the obligations laid on the company by that sub-section shall devolve on the trustees and shall be discharged by them instead of the company.

(4) The trustees of provident fund, contributory pension or retirement fund shall have appropriate representation from the members of the funds.

219. **Penalty for contravention of section 217 or 218.--** Any contravention or default in complying with requirements of sections 217 or 218 shall be an offence liable to a penalty of level 1 on the standard scale and shall also be liable to pay the loss suffered by the depositor of security or the employee, on account of such contravention[1].

ACCOUNTS OF COMPANIES

220. **Books of account, to be kept by company.--**(1) Every company shall prepare and keep at its registered office books of account and other relevant books and papers and financial statements for every financial year which give a true and fair view of the state of the affairs of the company, including that of its branch office or offices, if any[2]:

Provided that in the case of a company engaged in production, processing, manufacturing or mining activities, such particulars relating to utilisation of material or labour or the other inputs or items of cost as may be specified, shall also be maintained:

Provided further that all or any of the books of account aforesaid and other relevant papers may be kept at such other place in Pakistan as the board may decide and where such a decision is taken, the company shall, within seven days thereof, file with the registrar a notice in writing giving the full address of that other place.

---

[1] 2016 CLD 2077; 2014 CLD 430; 2014 CLD 862; 2013 CLD 108; 2013 CLD 1710; 2012 CLD 1423; 2010 CLD 60; 2010 CLD 1725; 2010 CLD 1716; 2009 CLD 61; 2009 CLD 76; 2009 CLD 951; 2008 CLD 266; 2008 CLD 731; 2008 CLD 803; 2007 CLD 93; 2007 CLD 1504; 2006 CLD 1376; 2005 CLD 350

[2] 2016 CLD 1604; 2014 CLD 873; 2014 SCMR 1376; 2012 CLD 323; 2012 PLD 15; 2009 CLD 1687; 2005 CLD 463; 2002 CLD 669; 2002 CLD 1487; 2002 SCMR 450; 2001 CLS 2019; 1996 CLC 1863; 1991 PCrLJ 831; 1987 CLC 726

(2) Where a company has a branch office in Pakistan or outside Pakistan, it shall be deemed to have complied with the provisions of sub-section (1), if proper books of account relating to the transactions effected at the branch office are kept at that office and proper summarized returns are sent periodically by the branch office to the company at its registered office or the other place referred to in sub-section (1).

(3) The books of account and other books and papers maintained by the company within Pakistan shall be open for inspection at the registered office of the company or at such other place in Pakistan by any director during business hours, and in the case of financial information, if any, maintained outside the country, copies of such financial information shall be maintained and produced for inspection by any director.

(4) Where an inspection is made under sub-section (3), the officers and other employees of the company shall give to the director making such inspection all assistance in connection with the inspection which the company is reasonably expected to give.

(5) The books of account of every company relating to a period of not less than ten financial years immediately preceding a financial year, or where the company had been in existence for a period less than ten years, in respect of all the preceding years together with the vouchers relevant to any entry in such books of account shall be kept in good order.

(6) If a company fails to comply with any of the requirements of this section, every director, including chief executive and chief financial officer, of the company who has by his act or omission been the cause of such default shall--

(a)   in respect of a listed company, be punishable with imprisonment for a term which may extend to two year and with fine which shall not be less than five hundred thousand rupees nor more than five million rupees, and with a further fine which may extend to ten thousand rupees for every day after the first during which the default continues; and

(b)   in respect of any other company, be punishable with imprisonment for a term which may extend to one year and with fine which may extend to one hundred thousand rupees.

(7) The provisions of this section except those of sub-section (5), shall apply *mutatis mutandis* to the books of account which a liquidator is required to maintain and keep[1].

---

[1] 2012 PLD 15

221. **Inspection of books of account by the Commission.**-- (1) The books of account and books and papers of every company shall be open to inspection by any officer authorised by the Commission in this behalf if, for reasons to be recorded in writing, the Commission considers it necessary so to do[1].

(2) It shall be the duty of every director, officer or other employee of the company to produce to the person making inspection under sub-section (1) all such books of account and books and papers of the company in his custody or under his control, and to furnish him with any such statement, information or explanation relating to the affairs of the company, as the said person may require of him within such time and at such place as he may specify.

(3) It shall also be the duty of every director, officer or other employee of the company to give to the person making inspection under this section all assistance and facilitation in connection with the inspection which the company may be reasonably expected to give.

(4)   The officer making the inspection under this section may, during the course of inspection--

(a)   make or cause to be made copies of books of account and other books and papers; or

(b)   place or cause to be placed by marks of identification thereon in token of the inspection having been made;

(c)   take possession of such documents and retain them for thirty days if there are reasonable grounds for believing that they are evidence of the commission of an offence.

(5) Where an inspection of the books of account and books and papers of the company has been conducted under this section, by an officer authorised by the Commission, such officer shall make a report to the Commission.

(6) Any officer authorised to make an inspection under this section shall have all the powers that the Commission has under this Act in relation to the making of inquiries.

222. **Default in compliance with provisions of section 221.**--(1) If default is made in complying with the provisions of section 221, every person who is in default shall be punishable with imprisonment for a term which may extend to one hundred and eighty days and with fine which may extend to one hundred thousand rupees[2].

---

[1] 2018 CLD 111; 2018 CLD 229; 2017 CLD 1371; 2016 CLD 1604; 2016 CLD 2293; 2015 CLD 385; 2014 CLD 263; 2014 CLD 1509; 2012 CLD 923; 2010 CLD 1240; 2010 CLD 1733; 2009 CLD 931; 2009 CLD 1106; 2006 CLD 627; 1989 MLD 3909
[2] 2014 CLD 263; 2002 CLD 1309

(2) Where a director or any other officer of a company has been convicted of an offence under this section, he shall, on and from the date on which he is so convicted, be deemed to have vacated his office as such and, on such vacation of office, shall be disqualified for holding such office in any company, for a period of three years.

223. **Financial Statements.**--(1) The board of every company must lay before the company in annual general meeting its financial statements for the period, in the case of first such statements since the incorporation of the company and in any other case since the preceding financial statements, made up to the date of close of financial year adopted by the company[1].

(2) The financial statements must be laid within a period of one hundred and twenty days following the close of financial year of a company:

Provided that, in the case of a listed company the Commission, and in any other case the registrar, may, for any special reason, extend the period for a term not exceeding thirty days.

(3) Subject to the provision of sub-section (2), the first financial statement must be laid at some date not later than sixteen months after the date of incorporation of the company and subsequently once at least in every calendar year.

(4) The period to which the statements aforesaid relate, not being the first, shall not exceed one year except where special permission of the registrar has been obtained.

(5) The financial statement shall be audited by the auditor of the company, in the manner hereinafter provided, and the auditor's report shall be attached thereto:

Provided that nothing in this sub-section shall apply to a private company having the paid up capital not exceeding one million rupees or such higher amount of paid up capital as may be notified by the Commission.

(6) Every company shall send in the form and manner specified audited financial statements together with the auditors' report, directors' report and in the case of a listed company the chairman's review report to every member of the company and every person who is entitled to receive notice of general meeting, either by post or electronically at least twenty-one days before the date of meeting at which it is to be laid before the members of the company, and shall keep a copy at the registered office of the company for the inspection of the members.

---

[1] 2017 CLD 990; 2016 CLD 1697; 2011 CLD 1647; 2011 CLD 4; 2010 YLR 3294; 2009 CLD 1577; 2008 CLD 627; 2006 CLD 533; 2006 CLD 542; 2006 CLD 667; 2005 CLD 747; 2005 CLD 1153; 2002 CLD 1487; 2002 SCMR 450; 1999 MLD 2609; 1997 PLD 432; 1996 CLC 1863; 1989 CLC 2103

(7) A listed company shall, simultaneously with the dispatch of the financial statements together with the reports referred to in sub-section (6), send by post three copies and electronically a copy of such financial statements together with said reports to each of the Commission, registrar and the securities exchange and shall also post on the company's website:

Provided that the reports shall be made available on the website of the Company for a time period as may be specified.

(8) The provisions of sub-section (6) of section 220 shall apply to any person who is a party to the default in complying with any of the provisions of this section.

(9) This section shall not apply to a single member company except to the extent as provided in sub-section (5).

224. **Classification of Companies.--** For the purpose of this Act, the companies may be classified in such categories as may be specified in the Third Schedule.

225. **Contents of Financial Statements.--**(1) The financial statements shall give a true and fair view of the state of affairs of the company, comply with the financial reporting standards notified by the Commission and shall be prepared in accordance with the requirements contained in the Third Schedule for different class or classes of companies[1]:

Provided that for the purpose of preparation of financial statements and related accounting treatment of associated companies shall be in accordance with financial reporting standards or such other standards as may be notified by the Commission:

Provided further that, except to the extent, otherwise notified in the official Gazette by the Commission, this sub-section shall not apply to an insurance or banking company or to any other class of companies for which the requirements of financial statements are specified in the law regulating such class of companies[2].

(2) The Commission may, of its own motion or upon application by a company, modify, in relation to that company, the requirements of the relevant Schedule for the purpose of adapting it to the circumstances of a company.

(3) The Commission shall have power from time to time to grant exemption to any company or any class of companies if it is in the public

---

[1] 2014 CLD 588; 2014 CLD 873; 2014 SCMR 1376; 2012 PTD 1385; 2012 PTD 1942; 2012 CLD 323; 2012 PLD 15; 2006 CLD 381; 2006 CLD 533; 2006 CLD 542; 2004 PTD 1135; 2002 PTD 324; 1999 MLD 2609; 1992 CLC 1668; 1992 PLC 622

[2] 2010 CLD 1271; 2010 CLD 1303; 2010 CLD 1377; 2010 CLD 1410; 2010 CLD 1454; 2010 CLD 1586; 2009 CLD 525

interest so to do, from compliance with all or any of the requirements of the relevant Schedule.

(4) Notwithstanding anything in this Act any company that intends to make unreserved compliance of IFRS issued by the IASB shall be permitted to do so.

Explanation.-- The expression "IFRS" means International Financial Reporting Standards and the expression "IASB" means International Accounting Standards Board.

(5) The provisions of sub-section (6) of section 220 shall apply to any person who is a party to the default in complying with any of the provisions of this section[1].

226. **Duty to prepare directors' report and statement of compliance.--**(1) The board shall prepare a directors' report for each financial year of the company:

Provided that nothing in this sub-section shall apply to a private company, not being a subsidiary of public company, having the paid up capital not exceeding three million rupees.

(2) The Commission may by general or special order, direct such class or classes of companies to prepare a statement of compliance.

(3) The board of a holding company, required to prepare consolidated financial statements under section 228, shall in its report to the members as provided in section 227, include information on matters specified in sub-section (2) of section 227 with respect to the consolidated financial statements.

(4) The directors in their report shall give greater emphasis to the matters that are significant to the undertakings included in the consolidation.

(5) Any contravention or default in complying with requirements of this section shall be an offence liable to a penalty of level 1 on the standard scale.

227. **Contents of directors' report and statement of compliance.--** (1) The directors shall make out and attach to the financial statements, a report with respect to the state of the company's affairs and a fair review of its business, the amount (if any), that the directors recommend should be paid by way of dividend and the amount (if any), they propose to carry to the Reserve Fund, General Reserve or Reserve Account[2].

(2) In the case of a public company or a private company which is a subsidiary of a public company, the directors report, in addition to the matters specified in sub-section (1) must state--

---

[1] 2012 PLD 15
[2] 2017 CLD 1019; 2016 CLD 176; 2012 CLD 691

(a)   the names of the persons who, at any time during the financial year, were directors of the company;

(b)   the principal activities and the development and performance of the company's business during the financial year;

(c)   a description of the principal risks and uncertainties facing the company;

(d)   any changes that have occurred during the financial year concerning the nature of the business of the company or of its subsidiaries, or any other company in which the company has interest;

(e)   the information and explanation in regard to any contents of modification in the auditor's report;

(f)   information about the pattern of holding of the shares in the form specified;

(g)   the name and country of origin of the holding company, if such company is a foreign company;

(h)   the earning per share;

(i)   the reasons for loss if incurred during the year and future prospects of profit, if any;

(j)   information about defaults in payment of any debts and reasons thereof;

(k)   comments in respect of adequacy internal financial controls;

(l)   any material changes and commitments affecting the financial position of the company which have occurred between the end of the financial year of the company to which the financial statement relates and the date of the report; and

(m)   any other information as may be specified.

(3) In the case of a listed company, the business review must, to the extent necessary for understanding the development, performance or position of the company's business, include--

(a)   the main trends and factors likely to affect the future development, performance and position of the company's business;

(b)   the impact of the company's business on the environment;

(c)   the activities undertaken by the company with regard to corporate social responsibility during the year; and

(d)   directors' responsibility in respect of adequacy of internal financial controls as may be specified.

(4) The board shall make out and attach to the financial statement such statement of compliance as may be specified.

(5) The directors' report and statement of compliance must be approved by the board and signed by the chief executive and a director of the company.

(6) Whoever contravenes any of the provisions of this section shall--

(a)   in respect of a listed company, be punishable with imprisonment for a term which may extend to two years and with fine may extend to five hundred thousand rupees and with a further fine which may extend to ten thousand rupees for every day after the first during which the default continues; and

(b)   in respect of any other company, be punishable with imprisonment for a term which may extend to one year and with fine which may extend to one hundred thousand rupees.

228. **Consolidated financial statements.--** (1) There shall be attached to the financial statements of a holding company having a subsidiary or subsidiaries, at the end of the financial year at which the holding company's financial statements are made out, consolidated financial statements of the group presented as those of a single enterprise and such consolidated financial statements shall comply with the disclosure requirements of the relevant Schedule and financial reporting standards notified by the Commission[1]:

Provided that nothing in this sub-section shall apply to a private company and its subsidiary, where none of the holding and subsidiary company has the paid up capital exceeding one million rupees.

(2) Where the financial year of a subsidiary precedes the day on which the holding company's financial year ends by more than ninety days, such subsidiary shall make an interim closing, on the day on which the holding company's financial year ends, and prepare financial statements for consolidation purposes.

(3) Every auditor of a holding company appointed under section 246 shall also report, in the specified form, on consolidated financial statements and exercise all such rights and duties as are vested in him under sections 248 and 249 respectively.

(4) There shall be disclosed in the consolidated financial statements any note or saving contained in such accounts to call attention to a matter which, apart from the note or saving, would properly have been referred to in such a qualification, in so far the matter which is the subject of the qualification or note is not covered by the holding company's own accounts and is material from the point of view of its members.

---

[1] 2017 CLD 1112; 2011 CLD 1249; 2006 CLD 667

(5) Every consolidated financial statement shall be signed by the same persons by whom the individual financial statements of the holding company are required to be signed, under section 232.

(6) All provisions of sections 223, 233, 234, 235 and 236 shall apply to a holding company required to prepare consolidated financial statements under this section as if for the word "company" appearing in these sections, the words "holding company" were substituted.

(7) The Commission may, on an application of a holding company, direct that the provisions of this section shall not apply to such extent as may be specified in the direction.

(8) Any contravention or default in complying with requirements of this section shall be an offence liable to a penalty of level 2 on the standard scale.

229. **Financial year of holding company and subsidiary.--**(1) The board of a holding company shall ensure that, except where in their opinion there are good reasons against it, its financial year and each of its subsidiaries coincides.

(2) The Commission may, on an application of a holding company or a subsidiary of the holding company, extend the financial year of any such company for the purpose of sub-section (1).

(3) While granting any extension under sub-section (2), the Commission may grant such other relaxations as may be incidental or ancillary thereto.

230. **Rights of holding company's representatives and members.--**(1) A holding company may, by resolution, authorise representatives named in the resolution to inspect the books of account kept by any of its subsidiaries; and the books of account of any such subsidiary shall be open to inspection by those representatives at any time during business hours.

(2) The rights conferred by section 256 upon members of a company may be exercised, in respect of any subsidiary, by members of the holding company as if they also were members of the subsidiary.

231. **Financial Statements of *modaraba* company to include *modaraba* accounts.-**(1) There must be attached to the financial statements of a *modaraba* company, the annual accounts and other reports circulated in pursuance of the provisions of section 14 of the Modaraba Companies and Modaraba (Floatation and Control) Ordinance, 1980 (XXXI of 1980), made out-

(a)   as at the end of the financial year of the *modaraba* where such financial year coincides with the financial year of the *modaraba* company; and

(b)   as at the end of the financial year of the *modaraba* last before that of the *modaraba* company, where the financial year of the *modaraba* does not coincide with that of the *modaraba* company.

(2) The provisions of sub-section (8) of section 228 shall apply to any person who is a party to the default in complying with any of the provisions of this section.

232. Approval and authentication of Financial Statements.-- (1) The financial statements, including consolidated financial statement, if any, must be approved by the board of the company and signed on behalf of the board by the chief executive and at least one director of the company, and in case of a listed company also by the chief financial officer[1]:

Provided that when the chief executive is for the time being not available in Pakistan, then the financial statements may be signed by at least two directors:

Provided further that in case of a private company having a paid up capital not exceeding one million rupees, the financial statements shall also be accompanied by an affidavit executed by the chief executive if the accounts are signed by him or by any of the directors if the accounts has been signed by two directors, as the case may be, that the financial statements have been approved by the board.

(2) The financial statements of a single member company shall be signed by one director.

(3) Any contravention or default in complying with requirements of this section shall be an offence liable to a penalty of level 1 on the standard scale.

233. Copy of Financial Statements to be forwarded to the registrar.-- (1) Without prejudice to the provisions of sub-section (5) of section 223, after the audited financial statements have been laid before the company at the annual general meeting and duly adopted, a copy of such financial statements together with reports and documents required to be annexed to the same, duly signed in the manner provided by sections 226, 232 and 251, shall be filed by the company with the registrar within thirty days from the date of such meeting in case of a listed company and within fifteen days in case of any other company[2].

(2) If the general meeting before which the financial statement is laid does not adopt the same or defers consideration thereof or is adjourned, a statement of that fact and of the reasons therefor shall be annexed to the said financial statements required to be filed with the registrar.

---

[1] 2005 PTD 504

[2] 2017 CLD 581; 2017 CLD 767; 2017 CLD 1019; 2016 CLD 1814; 2016 CLD 2155; 2016 CLD 2265; 2016 CLD 2318; 1999 MLD 2609

(3) Nothing in this section shall apply to a private company having the paid up capital not exceeding ten million rupees or such higher amount of paid up capitals as may be notified by the Commission.

(4) Any contravention or default in complying with requirements of this section shall be an offence liable--

(a)   in case of a listed company, to a penalty of level 2 on the standard scale; and

(b)   in case of any other company, to a penalty of level 1 on the standard scale.

234. **Filing of unaudited financial statements.--** (1) A private company, not being a subsidiary of public company, having the paid up capital not exceeding one million rupees or such other amount of paid up capital as may be notified by the Commission, shall file the duly authenticated financial statements, whether audited or not, with the registrar within thirty days from the holding of such meeting.

(2) Any contravention or default in complying with requirement of this section shall be an offence liable to a penalty of level 1 on the standard scale.

235. **Right of member of a company to copies of the Financial Statements and the auditor's report.--** (1)Any member of the company is entitled, on request and on payment of such fee as may be fixed by the company to be provided with a copy of any financial statement. The copy must be provided within seven days after the request is received by the company.

(2) Any contravention or default in complying with requirement of this section shall be an offence liable to a penalty of level 1 on the standard scale.

236. **Penalty for improper issue, circulation or publication of Financial Statements.--**If any copy of financial statements is issued, circulated or published without there being annexed or attached thereto, as the case may be, a copy each of (i) any component of financial statements, reports, or statements referred therein, (ii) the auditors' report, (iii) review reports on the statement of compliance, (iv) the directors' report and (v) the statements of compliance, the company, and every officer of the company who is in default shall be liable to a penalty of level 1 on the standard scale[1].

---

[1] 2017 CLD 1019; 2016 CLD 2265; 2016 CLD 1814; 2014 CLD 299; 2010 CLD 34; 2010 CLD 1035; 2008 CLD 627

237. **Quarterly financial statements of listed companies.--** (1) Every listed company shall prepare the quarterly financial information[1] within the period of-

(a) thirty days of the close of first and third quarters of its year of accounts; and

(b) sixty days of the close of its second quarter of its year of accounts:

Provided that the cumulative figures for the half year, presented in the second quarter accounts shall be subjected to a limited scope review by the statutory auditors of the company in such manner and according to such terms and conditions as may be determined by the Institute of Chartered Accountants of Pakistan and approved by the Commission.

Provided further that the Commission may, upon an application by the company, extend the period of filing in case of accounts of first quarter for a period not exceeding thirty days, if the company was allowed extension in terms of sections 223.

(2) The quarterly financial statements shall be posted on the company's website for the information of its members and also be transmitted electronically to the Commission, securities exchange and with the registrar within the period specified under sub-section (1):

Provided that a copy of the quarterly financial statements shall be dispatched in physical form if so requested by any member without any fee:

Provided further that the Commission may specify the time period for which the quarterly financial statements shall be made available on the website of the company.

(3) The provisions of section 232 shall be applicable to the quarterly financial statements.

(4) If a company fails to comply with any of the requirements of this section, every director, including chief executive and chief financial officer of the company who has by his act or omission been the cause of such default shall be liable to a penalty of level 2 on the standard scale.

---

[1] 2018 CLD 1031; 2017 CLD 1191; 2017 CLD 1715; 2013 CLD 82; 2013 CLD 287; 2013 CLD 327; 2011 CLD 4; 2011 CLD 1425; 2011 CLD 1536; 2011 1546; 2010 CLD 34; 2010 CLD 53; 2010 CLD 72; 2010 CLD 386; 2010 CLD 1218; 2010 CLD 1237; 2010 CLD 1722; 2009 CLD 1154; 2009 CLD 1577; 2009 CLD 1607; 2009 CLD 1609; 2009 CLD 1633; 2008 CLD 627; 2007 CLD 566; 2007 CLD 599; 2007 CLD 621; 2007 CLD 630; 2007 CLD 1080; 2007 CLD 1088; 2007 CLD 1277; 2006 CLD 323; 2006 CLD 427; 2006 CLD 480; 2006 CLD 533; 2006 CLD 694; 2006 CLD 756; 2006 CLD 1034; 2006 CLD 1063; 2006 CLD 1157; 2006 CLD 1334; 2006 CLD 1343; 2006 CLD 1366; 2006 CLD 1482; 2005 CLD 1071; 2005 CLD 1153; 2004 PTD 1104; 1990 MLD 620

238. **Power of Commission to require submission of additional statements of accounts and reports.--** (1) Notwithstanding anything contained in any other provision of this Act the Commission may, by general or special order, require companies generally, or any class of companies or any particular company, to prepare and send to the members, the Commission, the registrar, the securities exchange and any other person such periodical statements of accounts, information or other reports, in such form and manner and within such time, as may be specified in the order[1].

(2) Any contravention or default in complying with requirement of this section shall be an offence liable to a penalty of level 3 on the standard scale.

239. **Rights of debenture-holders to obtain copies of financial statements.--**(1) The holders of debentures, including the trustees for holders of debentures, of a company shall be entitled to have copies of financial statements of the company and other reports on payment of such fee as may be fixed by the company.

(2) Any contravention or default in complying with requirements of this section shall be an offence liable to a penalty of level 1 on the standard scale.

DIVIDENDS AND MANNER AND TIME OF PAYMENT THEREOF

240. **Certain restrictions on declaration of dividend.--**(1) The company in general meeting may declare dividends; but no dividend shall exceed the amount recommended by the board[2].

(2) No dividend shall be declared or paid by a company for any financial year out of the profits of the company made from the sale or disposal of any immovable property or assets of a capital nature comprised in the undertaking or any of the undertaking of the company, unless the business of the company consists, whether wholly or partly, of selling and purchasing any such property or assets, except after such profits are set off or adjusted against losses arising from the sale of any such immovable property or assets of a capital nature:

Provided that no dividend shall be declared or paid out of unrealized gain on investment property credited to profit and loss account.

241. **Dividend to be paid only out of profits.--** Any dividend may be paid by a company either in cash or in kind only out of its profits[3].

Explanation.-- The payment of dividend in kind shall only be in the form of shares of listed company held by the distributing company.

---

[1] 2012 CLD 68; 2012 CLD 977; 2008 CLD 126; 2008 CLD 796; 2007 CLD 1271; 2005 CLD 1071; 2005 CLD 1137; 2005 CLD 1153

[2] 2005 PTD 504; 2002 CLD 1519

[3] 2017 CLD 587; 2004 CLD 640; 2000 PTD 507; 1999 MLD 108

242. **Dividend not to be paid except to registered shareholders.--** Any dividend declared by a company must be paid to its registered shareholders or to their order within such period and in such manner as may be specified:

Provided that any dividend payable in cash may be paid by cheque or warrant or in any electronic mode to the shareholders entitled to the payment of the dividend, as per their direction:

Provided further that in case of a listed company, any dividend payable in cash shall only be paid through electronic mode directly into the bank account designated by the entitled shareholders.

243. **Directors not to withhold declared dividend.--**(1) When a dividend has been declared, it shall not be lawful for the directors of the company to withhold or defer its payment and the chief executive of the company shall be responsible to make the payment in the manner provided in section 242[1].

Explanation.-- Dividend shall be deemed to have been declared on the date of the general meeting in case of a dividend declared or approved in the general meeting and on the date of commencement of closing of share transfer for purposes of determination of entitlement of dividend in the case of an interim dividend and where register of members is not closed for such purpose, on the date on which such dividend is approved by the board.

(2) Where a dividend has been declared by a company but is not paid within the period specified under section 242, the chief executive of the company shall be punishable with imprisonment for a term which may extend to two years and with fine which may extend to five million rupees:

Provided that no offence shall be deemed to have been committed within the meaning of the foregoing provisions in the following cases, namely—

(a)   where the dividend could not be paid by reason of the operation of any law;

(b)   where a shareholder has given directions to the company regarding the payment of the dividend and those directions cannot be complied with;

(c)   where there is a dispute regarding the right to receive the dividend;

(d)   where the dividend has been lawfully adjusted by the company against any sum due to it from the shareholder; or

(e)   where, for any other reason, the failure to pay the dividend or to post the warrant within the period aforesaid was not due to any default on the part of the company; and

---

[1] 2010 PTD 755; 2005 PTD 504; 2004 CLD 640

the Commission has, on an application of the company on the specified form made within forty-five days from the date of declaration of the dividend, and after providing an opportunity to the shareholder or person who may seem to be entitled to receive the dividend of making representation against the proposed action, permitted the company to withhold or defer payment as may be ordered by the Commission.

(3) Notwithstanding anything contained in sub-section (2), a company may withhold the payment of dividend of a member where the member has not provided the complete information or documents as specified by the Commission.

(4) Chief executive convicted under sub-section (2) shall from the day of the conviction cease to hold the office of chief executive of the company and shall not, for a period of five years from that day, be eligible to be the chief executive or a director of that company or any other company.

244. **Unclaimed shares, *modaraba* certificates and dividend to vest with the Federal Government.**(1) Notwithstanding anything to the contrary contained in this Act or any other law--

    (i)   where shares of a company or *modaraba* certificates of a *Modaraba* have been issued; or

    (ii)   where dividend has been declared by a company or *Modaraba*;

        which remain unclaimed or unpaid for a period of three years from the date it is due and payable, or

    (iii)   any other instrument or amount which remain unclaimed or unpaid, having such nature and for such period as may be specified;

the company shall give ninety days notices to the shareholders or certificate holders or the owner, as the case may be, to file claim, in the following manner--

    (a)   by a registered post acknowledgement due on his last known address; and

    (b)   after expiry of notice period as provided under clause (a), final notice in the specified form shall be published in two daily newspapers of which one will be in Urdu and one in English having wide circulation.

Explanation.-- For the purpose of this section "shares" or "*modaraba*" certificates include unclaimed or undelivered bonus shares or *modaraba* certificates and "company" includes a "*modaraba* company".

(2) If no claim is made before the company by the shareholder, certificate holder or the owner, as the case may be, the company shall after ninety days from the date of publication of notice under clause (b) of sub-section (1) shall--

(a)   in case of sum of money, deposit any unclaimed or unpaid amount to the credit of the Federal Government; and

(b)   in case of shares or *modaraba* certificates or other instrument, report and deliver to the Commission such shares or *modaraba* certificates or other instrument and the Commission shall sell such shares or *modaraba* certificates or other instrument, as the case may be, in the manner and within such period as may be specified and deposit the proceeds to the credit of Federal Government:

   Provided that where the company has deposited the unclaimed or unpaid amount or delivered the shares or *modaraba* certificates or other instrument with the Commission for credit of the Federal Government, the company shall preserve and continue to preserve all original record pertaining to the deposited unclaimed or unpaid amount and the shares or *modaraba* certificates or other instrument and provide copies of the relevant record to the Commission until it is informed by the Commission in writing that they need not to be preserved any longer.

(3) Notwithstanding anything contained in any law or procedure for the time being in force, the unclaimed or unpaid amount as well as the proceeds from the sale of shares or *modaraba* certificates or any other instrument or any benefit accrued thereon, as the case may be, shall be maintained in a profit bearing account with the State Bank of Pakistan or National Bank of Pakistan to be called "Companies Unclaimed Instruments and Dividend and Insurance Benefits and Investors Education Account" as may be notified by the concerned Minister-in-Charge of the Federal Government and shall be deemed to be part of public accounts and interest profit accumulated thereon shall be credited on quarterly basis to the Fund established under section 245 of this Act.

(4) Any person claiming to be entitled to any money paid into "Companies Unclaimed Instruments and Dividend and Insurance Benefits and Investors Education Account" may in pursuance of this section apply to the Commission in such manner along with such documents as may be specified for payment thereof, and the Commission after necessary verification from the company concerned forward to the bank as notified under sub-section (3) to make the payment to entitled person of the sum equivalent to his unclaimed or unpaid dividend or amount of proceeds:

Provided that the payment to the claimant shall be made within a period of thirty days from the date of verification by the company.

(5) A person shall be entitled to receive the shares or *modaraba* certificates or any other instrument as delivered to the Commission by the company, making a claim under this Act before the sale of such unclaimed shares or *modaraba* certificates or the instrument, is effected by the Commission.

(6) A person making a claim under this section shall be entitled to the proceeds of the sale of the shares or *modaraba* certificates or the instrument less any deduction for expenses of sale.

(7) Payment to the claimant pursuant to sub-section (4) and a receipt given by the bank in this respect shall be a good discharge to the Commission and the bank.

(8) Where any dispute regarding unclaimed shares, *modaraba* certificates, the instrument or dividend arises or is pending adjudication before the competent authority or Court, the Commission shall process the claim in accordance with the decision of such authority or Court.

(9) No claim whatsoever shall be entertained after the period of ten years from the credit of any amount to the account of the Federal Government to be maintained under this section.

(10) Every company within thirty days of the close of each financial year shall submit to the Commission a return of all unclaimed shares, *modaraba* certificates, the instruments or dividend in its books in the manner as may be specified by the Commission.

(11) Whoever contravenes the provisions of this section shall be punishable with a penalty of level 3 on the standard scale.

(12) The account to be maintained under sub-section (3) shall be available on the direction of Minister-in-Charge to serve as a collateral in order to facilitate the provision of credit facility to the clearing house to address any systemic risk in the capital market:

Provided that powers under this sub-section shall be exercised only in case where in opinion of the Commission the resources of the clearing house are or likely to be insufficient for timely settlement of trades executed at the securities and future exchanges.

245. **Establishment of Investor Education and Awareness Fund.--** (1) There is hereby established a fund to be called Investor Education and Awareness Fund (hereinafter in this section referred to as "Fund") to be managed and controlled by the Commission as may be prescribed through rules.

(2) The Fund shall be credited with--

(a) the interest/profit earned on the "Companies Unclaimed Instruments and Dividend and Insurance Benefits and Investors Education Account";

(b)   forfeited amounts under sub-section (7) of section 87 of the Securities Act, 2015;

(c)   grants or donations given by the Federal Government, Provincial Governments, companies, or any other institution or person for the purposes of the Fund;

(d)   the interest or other income received out of the investments made from the Fund;

(e)   the amount realised in terms of fourth proviso of section 341 or fourth proviso of sub-section (4) of section 372; and

(f)   such other amounts as may be prescribed.

(3)   The Fund shall be utilized for--

(a)   the promotion of investor education and awareness in such manner as may be prescribed;

(b)   without prejudice to the generality of the object of sub-clause (a) of sub-section (3), the Fund may be used for the following purposes, namely--

    (i)   educational activities including seminars, training, research and publications aimed at investors;

    (ii)   awareness programs including through media – print, electronic, social media, aimed at investors;

    (iii)   funding investor education and awareness activities approved by the Commission; and

    (iv)   to meet the administrative expenses of the Fund.

    Explanation.— "**Investors**" means investor in securities, insurance policyholders and customers of non-bank finance companies and *Modarabas.*

(4) The Commission shall, by notification in the official Gazette, constitute an advisory committee with such members as may be prescribed, for recommending investor education and awareness activities that may be undertaken directly by the Commission or through any other agency, for utilization of the Fund for the purposes referred to in sub-section (3).

(5) The accounts of the Fund shall be audited by auditors appointed by the Commission who shall be a firm of chartered accountants. The Commission shall ensure maintenance of proper and separate accounts and other relevant records in relation to the Fund giving therein the details of all receipts to, and, expenditure from, the Fund and other relevant particulars.

(6) The Commission may invest the moneys of the Fund in such manner as set out in section 20 of the Trusts Act, 1882 (II of 1882).

AUDIT

246. **Appointment, removal and fee of auditors.--**(1) The first auditor or auditors of a company shall be appointed by the board within ninety days of the date of incorporation of the company; and the auditor or auditors so appointed shall retire on the conclusion of the first annual general meeting[1].

(2) Subject to the provisions of sub-section (3), the subsequent auditor or auditors shall be appointed by the company in the annual general meeting on the recommendation of the board after obtaining consent of the proposed auditors, a notice shall be given to the members with the notice of general meeting. The auditor or auditors so appointed shall retire on the conclusion of the next annual general meeting.

(3) A member or members having not less than ten percent shareholding of the company shall also be entitled to propose any auditor or auditors for appointment whose consent has been obtained by him and a notice in this regard has been given to the company not less than seven days before the date of the annual general meeting. The company shall forthwith send a copy of such notice to the retiring auditor and shall also be posted on its website.

(4) Where an auditor, other than the retiring auditor is proposed to be appointed, the retiring auditor shall have a right to make a representation in writing to the company at least two days before the date of general meeting. Such representation shall be read out at the meeting before taking up the agenda for appointment of the auditor:

Provided that where such representation is made, it shall be mandatory for the auditor or a person authorized by him in writing to attend the general meeting in person.

(5) The auditor or auditors appointed by the board or the members in an annual general meeting may be removed through a special resolution.

(6) Any casual vacancy of an auditor shall be filled by the board within thirty days from the date thereof. Any auditor appointed to fill in any casual vacancy shall hold office until the conclusion of the next annual general meeting:

Provided that where the auditors are removed during their tenure, the board shall appoint the auditors with prior approval of the Commission.

(7)   If the company, fails to appoint--

(a)   the first auditors within a period of ninety days of the date of incorporation of the company;

(b)   the auditors at an annual general meeting; or

---

[1] 2013 CLD 1810; 2007 CLD 1498; 2006 CLD 399; 2006 CLD 381; 2006 CLD 431; 2006 CLD 588; 2005 CLD 454; 2004 CLD 1433; 2002 CLD 325; 2002 PTD 3091; 2002 CLD 1309

(c)   an auditor in the office to fill up a casual vacancy within thirty days after the occurrence of the vacancy; and

(d)   if the appointed auditors are unwilling to act as auditors of the company;

the Commission may, of its own motion or on an application made to it by the company or any of its members direct to make good the default within such time as may be specified in the order. In case the company fails to report compliance within the period so specified, the Commission shall appoint auditors of the company who shall hold office till conclusion of the next annual general meeting:

(8) The remuneration of the auditors of a company shall be fixed--

(a)   by the company in the general meeting;

(b)   by the board or by the Commission, if the auditors are appointed by the board or the Commission, as the case may be.

(9) Every company shall, within fourteen days from the date of any appointment of an auditor, send to the registrar intimation thereof, together with the consent in writing of the auditor concerned.

247. **Qualification and disqualification of auditors.--**(1) A person shall not be qualified for appointment as an auditor[1]

(a)   in the case of a public company or a private company which is subsidiary of a public company or a private company having paid up capital of three million rupees or more unless such person is a chartered accountant having valid certificate of practice from the Institute of Chartered Accountants of Pakistan or a firm of chartered accountants; and

(b)   in the case of a company other than specified in clause (a), unless such person, is a chartered accountant or cost and management accountant having valid certificate of practice from the respective institute or a firm of chartered accountants or cost and management accountants, having such criteria as may be specified:

Provided that for the purpose of clause (a) and (b), a firm whereof majority of practicing partners are qualified for appointment shall be appointed by its firm name to be auditors of the company.

(2)   Where a partnership firm is appointed as auditor of a company, only the partners who meet the qualification requirements as provided in sub-section (1), shall be authorized to act and sign on behalf of the firm.

---

[1] 2016 CLD 2188; 2013 CLD 1810; 2009 CLD 212; 2008 CLD 17; 2006 CLD 298; 2005 CLD 454; 2004 CLD 1433; 2003 CLD 1734

(3)   None of the following persons shall be appointed as auditor of a company, namely-

(a)   a person who is, or at any time during the preceding three years was, a director, other officer or employee of the company;

(b)   a person who is a partner of , or in the employment of, a director, officer or employee of the company;

(c)   the spouse of a director of the company;

(d)   a person who is indebted to the company other than in the ordinary course of business of such entities;

(e)   a person who has given a guarantee or provided any security in connection with the indebtedness of any third person to the company other than in the ordinary course of business of such entities;

(f)   a person or a firm who, whether directly or indirectly, has business relationship with the company other than in the ordinary course of business of such entities;

(g)   a person who has been convicted by a court of an offence involving fraud and a period of ten years has not elapsed from the date of such conviction;

(h)   a body corporate;

(i)   a person who is not eligible to act as auditor under the code of ethics as adopted by the Institute of Chartered Accountants of Pakistan and the Institute of Cost and Management Accountants of Pakistan; and

(j)   a person or his spouse or minor children, or in case of a firm, all partners of such firm who hold any shares of an audit client or any of its associated companies:

Provided that if such a person holds shares prior to his appointment as auditor, whether as an individual or a partner in a firm the fact shall be disclosed on his appointment as auditor and such person shall disinvest such shares within ninety days of such appointment.

Explanation. Reference in this section to an "**officer**" or "**employee**" shall be construed as not including reference to an auditor.

(4)   For the purposes of clause (d) of sub-section (3) a person who owes--

(a)   a sum of money not exceeding one million rupees to a credit card issuer; or

(b) a sum to a utility company in the form of unpaid dues for a period not exceeding ninety days;

shall not be deemed to be indebted to the company.

(5) A person shall also not be qualified for appointment as auditor of a company if he is, by virtue of the provisions of sub-section (3), disqualified for appointment as auditor of any other company which is that company's subsidiary or holding company or a subsidiary of that holding company.

(6) If, after his appointment, an auditor becomes subject to any of the disqualifications specified in this section, he shall be deemed to have vacated his office as auditor with effect from the date on which he becomes so disqualified.

(7) A person who, not being qualified to be an auditor of a company, or being or having become subject to any disqualification to act as such, acts as auditor of a company shall be liable to a penalty of level 2 on the standard scale.

(8) The appointment as auditor of a company of an unqualified person, or of a person who is subject to any disqualifications to act as such, shall be void, and, where such an appointment is made by a company, the Commission may appoint a qualified person in place of the auditor appointed by the company.

RIGHTS AND DUTIES OF AUDITOR

248. **Auditors' right to information.--**(1) An auditor of a company has a right--[1]

(a) of access at all times to the company's books, accounts and vouchers (in whatever form they are held); and

(b) of access to such copies of, an extracts from, the books and accounts of the branch as have been transmitted to the principal office of the company;

(c) to require any of the following persons to provide him with such information or explanations as he thinks necessary for the performance of his duties as auditor--

    (i) any director, officer or employee of the company;

    (ii) any person holding or accountable for any of the company's books, accounts or vouchers;

    (iii) any subsidiary undertaking of the company; and

    (iv) any officer, employee or auditor of any such subsidiary undertaking of the company or any person holding or

---

[1] 2018 CLD 952; 2016 CLD 72; 2016 CLD 1734; 2016 CLD 2276; 2015 CLD 503; 2014 CLD 330; 2014 CLD 406; 2009 CLD 564; 2009 CLD 735; 2009 CLD 1615; 2007 CLD 1439

(v)   accountable for any books, accounts or vouchers of any such subsidiary undertaking of the company.

(2) If any officer of a company refuses or fails, without lawful justification, the onus whereof shall lie on him, to allow any auditor access to any books and papers in his custody or power, or to give any such information possessed by him as and when required, or otherwise hinders, obstructs or delays an auditor in the performance of his duties or the exercise of his powers or fails to give notice of any general meeting to the auditor or provides false or incorrect information, he shall be liable to penalty as provided under section 252.

249. **Duties of auditor.--** (1) A company's auditor shall conduct the audit and prepare his report in compliance with the requirements of International Standards on Auditing as adopted by the Institute of Chartered Accountants of Pakistan.

(2) A company's auditor must carry out such examination to enable him to form an opinion as to--

(a)   whether adequate accounting records have been kept by the company and returns adequate for their audit have been received from branches not visited by him; and

(b)   whether the company's financial statements are in agreement with the accounting records and returns.

(3) The auditor shall make out a report to the members of the company on the accounts and books of accounts of the company and on every financial statements and on every other document forming part of such statements including notes, statements or schedules appended thereto, which are to be laid before the company in general meeting and the report shall state--

(a)   whether or not they have obtained all the information and explanations which to the best of their knowledge and belief were necessary for the purposes of the audit and if not, the details thereof and the effect of such information on the financial statements;

(b)   whether or not in their opinion proper books of accounts as required by this Act have been kept by the company;

(c)   whether or not in their opinion the statement of financial position and profit and loss account and other comprehensive income or the income and expenditure account and the cash flows have been drawn up in conformity with the requirements of accounting and reporting standards as notified under this Act and are in agreement with the books of accounts and returns;

(d)   whether or not in their opinion and to the best of their information and according to the explanations given to them, the said accounts give the information required by this Act in the manner so required and give a true and fair view--

(i)   in the case of the statement of financial position, of the state of affairs of the company as at the end of the financial year;

(ii)   in the case of the profit and loss account and other comprehensive income or the income and expenditure account, of the profit or loss and other comprehensive income or surplus or deficit, as the case may be, for its financial year; and

(iii) in the case of statement of cash flows, of the generation and utilisation of the cash and cash equivalents of the company for its financial year;

(e)   whether or not in their opinion--

(i)   investments made, expenditure incurred and guarantees extended, during the year, were for the purpose of company's business; and

(ii)   zakat deductible at source under the Zakat and Usher Ordinance, 1980 (XVIII of 1980), was deducted by the company and deposited in the Central Zakat Fund established under section 7 of that Act.

Explanation.-- Where the auditor's report contains a reference to any other report, statement or remarks which they have made on the financial statements examined by them, such statement or remarks shall be annexed to the auditor's report and shall be deemed to be a part of the auditor's report.

(4) Where any of the matters referred to in sub-section (2) or (3) is answered in the negative or with a qualification, the report shall state the reason for such answer along with the factual position to the best of the auditor's information.

(5) The Commission may, by general or special order, direct that, in the case of all companies generally or such class or description of companies as may be specified in the order, the auditor's report shall also include a statement of such additional matters as may be so specified.

(6) The auditor shall express unmodified or modified opinion in his report in compliance with the requirements of International Standards on Auditing as adopted by the Institute of Chartered Accountants of Pakistan.

(7) The Commission may by general or special order, direct, that the statement of compliance as contained in sub-section (4) of section 227 of this

Act, shall be reviewed by the auditor who shall issue a review report to the members on the format specified by the Commission.

(8) The auditor of a company shall be entitled to attend any general meeting of the company, and to receive all notices of, and any communications relating to, any general meeting which any member of the company is entitled to receive, and to be heard at any general meeting which he attends on any part of the business which concerns him as auditor:

Provided that, in the case of a listed company, the auditor or a person authorised by him in writing shall be present in the general meeting in which the financial statements and the auditor's report are to be considered.

250. **Audit of cost accounts.--** (1)Where any company or class of companies is required under first proviso of sub-section (1) of section 220 to include in its books of account the particulars referred to therein, the Commission may direct that an audit of cost accounts of the company shall be conducted in such manner and with such stipulations as may be specified in the order by an auditor who is a chartered accountant within the meaning of the Chartered Accountants Ordinance, 1961 (X of 1961), or a cost and management accountant within the meaning of the Cost and Management Accountants Act, 1966 (XIV of 1966); and such auditor shall have the same powers, duties and liabilities as an auditor of a company and such other powers, duties and liabilities as may be specified[1].

(2) The audit of cost accounts of the company under sub-section (1) shall be directed by the Commission subject to the recommendation of the regulatory authority supervising the business of relevant sector or any entity of the sector.

251. **Signature of auditor's report.--**(1) The auditor's report must state the name of the auditor, engagement partner, be signed, dated and indicate the place at which it is signed[2].

(2) Where the auditor is an individual, the report must be signed by him.

(3) Where the auditor is a firm, the report must be signed by the partnership firm with the name of the engagement partner.

252. **Penalty for non-compliance with provisions by companies.--** Any contravention or default in complying with requirements of sections 246, 247, 248 and 250 shall be an offence liable to a penalty of level 3 on the standard scale[3].

253. **Penalty for non-compliance with provisions by auditors.--**(1) If any auditor's report or review report is made, or any document of the company

---

[1] 2009 CLD 90; 2009 CLD 564
[2] 2002 CLD 1164; 2002 CLD 1835
[3] 2018 CLD 197; 2013 CLD 1810; 2009 CLD 90; 2006 CLD 298

is signed or authenticated otherwise than in conformity with the requirements of section 131, sections 249 and 251 or is otherwise untrue or fails to bring out material facts about the affairs of the company or matters to which it purports to relate, the auditor concerned and the person, if any, other than the auditor who signs the report or signs or authenticates the document, and in the case of a firm all partners of the firm, shall be liable to a penalty of level 2 on the standard scale[1].

(2) If the auditor's report to which sub-section (1) applies is made with the intent to profit such auditor or any other person or to put another person to a disadvantage or loss or for a material consideration, the auditor shall, in addition to the penalty provided by that sub-section, be punishable with imprisonment for a term which may extend to two years and with penalty which may extend to one million rupees.

POWER OF REGISTRAR TO CALL FOR INFORMATION

254.   **Power of registrar to call for information or explanation.**--(1) Where on a scrutiny of any document filed by a company or on any information received by him under this Act, or any notice, advertisement, other communication, or otherwise, the registrar is of opinion that any information, explanation or document is necessary with respect to any matter, he may, by a written notice, call upon the company and any of its present or past directors, officers or auditors to furnish such information or explanation in writing, or such document, within thirty days[2]:

Provided that a director, officer or auditor who ceased to hold office more than six years before the date of the notice of the registrar shall not be compelled to furnish information or explanation or document under this sub-section.

(2) On receipt of the notice under sub-section (1) it shall be the duty of the company and all persons who are or have been directors, officers or auditors of the company to furnish such information, explanation or documents as required.

(3) If no information or explanation is furnished within the time specified or if the information or explanation furnished is, in the opinion of the registrar, inadequate, the registrar may if he deems fit, by written order, call on the company and any such person as is referred to in sub-section (1) or (2) to

---

[1] 2018 CLD 952; 2017 CLD 822; 2017 CLD 1049; 2016 CLD 1734; 2016 CLD 2276; 2015 CLD 503; 2014 CLD 406; 2014 CLD 330; 2013 CLD 1319; 2013 CLD 1810; 2007 CLD 1439
[2] 2016 CLD 1544; 2010 CLD 1234; 2009 CLD 1106

produce before him for his inspection such books and papers as he considers necessary within such time as he may specify in the order; and it shall be the duty of the company and of such persons to produce such books and papers.

(4) If the company or any such person as is referred to in sub-section (1), (2) or (3) refuses or makes default in furnishing any such information or in producing any such books or papers--

(a) the company shall be liable to a penalty of level 2 on the standard scale; and

(b) every officer of the company who authorises or permits, or is a party to, the default shall be punishable with imprisonment of either description for a term which may extend to two years, and shall also be liable to fine which may extend to one million rupees and the court trying the offence may, make an order directing the company to produce such books or papers as in its opinion may reasonably be required by the registrar.

(5) On receipt of such information or explanation or production of any books and papers, the registrar may annex the same or any copy thereof or extract therefrom to the original document submitted to him; and any document so annexed shall be subject to the provisions as to inspection and the taking of extracts and furnishing of copies to which the original document is subject.

(6) If the information or explanation or book or papers required by the registrar under sub-section (1) is not furnished within the specified time, or if after perusal of such information or explanation or books or papers the registrar is of opinion that the document in question or the information or explanation or book or paper discloses an unsatisfactory state of affairs, or that it does not disclose a full and fair statement of the matter to which it purports to relate, the registrar shall without prejudice to any other provisions, and whether or not action under sub-section (3) or sub-section (4) has been taken, report in writing the circumstances of the case to the Commission.

255. **Seizure of documents by registrar, inspector or investigation officer.-** (1) Notwithstanding anything contained in Code of Criminal Procedure, 1898(Act V of 1898) or any other law including Banking Companies Ordinance (Act LVII of 1962) the registrar, inspector or investigation officer, as the case may be, upon information in his possession or otherwise or during investigation, has reasons to believe that documents, books and papers or anything relating to any company or any chief executive or officer of such company or any associate of such person or is useful or relevant to any proceedings or investigation under this Act which is required or may be destroyed, mutilated, altered, falsified or secreted, the registrar, inspector, or investigation officer after obtaining prior permission of the Commission, signed by one Commissioner, without warrants, enter such place and cause a search to

be made at any time freeze, seize or take possession of and retain any document, object, article, material, thing, account books, movable or immovable property or cause any account, property or thing to be maintained in specific manner[1].

(2) For the purposes of sub-section (1), the registrar may, after he has obtained the permission from the Commission under that sub-section (1), may also authorise any officer subordinate to him, not inferior in rank to an assistant registrar to enter, with such assistance as may be required, the place where he has reasons to believe that any of the items referred in sub-section (1) are kept;

(a)   to search that place; and

(b)   to seize any of the items referred in sub-section (1) as he considers necessary.

(3) The registrar shall return the items seized under this section as soon as may be and in any case not later than thirty day after such seizure, to the company or, as the case may be, to the chief executive or any other person from whose custody or power they were seized:

Provided that the Commission may, after providing to the company an opportunity to show cause against the order proposed to be made by it, allow the registrar to retain the items seized for a further period not exceeding thirty days:

Provided further that the registrar may, before returning items as aforesaid, take copies of, or extracts from them or put such marks of identification thereon as he considers necessary.

(4) Where, the registrar, inspector or investigation officer, as the case may be, has apprehension that any person or occupants of any place to be searched may create hindrance, resist search, or such document or thing is not known to be in the possession of any person, or where general search is required for the purposes of any proceedings, inspection or investigation under this Act, or any person will not or would not produce any document or thing as required by the registrar, inspector or investigation officer in any proceedings, inspection or investigation under this Act, a search-warrants from the concerned Magistrate may be obtained.

(5) The registrar, inspector or investigation officer after obtaining warrant under sub-section (4) may conduct search of such person and enter any place and seize any property, material, document or thing required under this Act or is associated with commission of any offence under this Act or administered legislation and Magistrate while issuing orders under this section may also direct local police, authority or any agency to provide necessary assistance to such person.

---

[1] 1987 CLC 2079

(6) The registrar, inspector or investigation officer executing the warrants shall comply and proceed in manner provided in the Code of Criminal Procedure 1898(Act V of 1898) including sections 102, 48 and 52:

Provided that any proceeding under this section shall not be vitiated or called into question for non–observance of any requirement of Section 103 of the Code and shall be admissible in the Court of law.

(7) Notwithstanding anything contained in sub section (3) in case of seizure of any property, material or thing by the investigation officer, in relation to any offense under this Act or administered legislation or scheduled offences, may retain any property, material, document or thing seized under sub section (1) or (5) which is a case property and produce the same as and when required during the trial in accordance with law.

(8) Where the Commission has reason to believe that proceeds of crime of any offence under this Act or administered legislation, it may pass an order to freeze account, securities and any other moveable property or part or parts thereof for not more than thirty days.

(9) Any person aggrieved of the seizure, freezing or retention by the investigation officer may approach the Court and obtain order for release of such accounts, securities, movable or immovable property, things or material seized or retained, after expiry of thirty days of such seizure or freezing order by the inspector or investigator under sub-sections (1), (5) or (8), if it can satisfy the Court that such property, accounts, securities, material or thing is not associated with any offence under this Act or any administered legislation and Court while passing order of release may impose such restriction and condition as deemed necessary.

Explanation I.--For the purposes of sub-section (8) the expression "Court" means the Company Bench of the High Court having jurisdiction where registered office is situated, in case of company or any connected person and in all other case, it will be the Company Bench of the High Court having territorial jurisdiction over area where the search has been conducted under this section.

Explanation II.-- For the purposes of this Act, the expression "administrated legislation" shall have the same meaning as provided in clause (aa) of sub-section (1) of section 2 of the Securities and Exchange Commission of Pakistan Act, 1997 (XLII of 1997).

INVESTIGATION AND RELATED MATTERS

256. **Investigation into affairs of company**.-- (1) Where the Commission is of the opinion, that it is necessary to investigate into the affairs of a company[1]--

(a)   on the application of the members holding not less than one tenth of the total voting power in a company having share capital;

(b)   on the application of not less than one tenth of the total members of a company not having share capital;

(c)   on the receipt of a report under sub-section (5) of section 221 or on the report by the registrar under sub-section (6) of section 254;

it may order an investigation into the affairs of the company and appoint one or more persons as inspectors to investigate into the affairs of the company and to report thereon in such manner as the Commission may direct:

Provided that before making an order of investigation, the Commission shall give the company an opportunity of being heard.

(2) While appointing an inspector under sub-section (1), the Commission may define the scope of the investigation, the period to which it is to extend or any other matter connected or incidental to the investigation.

(3) An application by members of a company under clause (a) or (b) of sub-section (1) shall be supported by such evidence as the Commission may require for the purpose of showing that the applicants have good reason for requiring the investigation.

(4) The Commission may, before appointing an inspector, require the applicants to give such security for payment of the costs of the investigation as the Commission may specify.

257. **Investigation of company's affairs in other cases.**--(1)Without prejudice to its power under section 256, the Commission[2]—

(a)   shall appoint one or more competent persons as inspectors to investigate the affairs of a company and to report thereon in such manner as the Commission may direct, if—

(i)   the company, by a special resolution, or

(ii)   the Court[1], by order,

---

[1] 2017 CLD 1371; 2016 CLD 393; 2016 SCMR 213; 2016 CLD 1544; 2016 CLD 2118; 2014 CLD 52; 2014 CLD 467; 2014 CLD 1509; 2014 PLD 1; 2013 CLD 1263; 2002 CLD 1714; 2000 MLD 1880; 1996 CLC 516

[2] 2018 CLD 898; 2016 CLD 393; 2016 CLD 2118; 2016 CLD 1544; 2016 SCMR 213; 2016 CLD 393; 2015 CLD 719; 2015 CLD 1691; 2013 CLD 1421; 2011 CLD 1485; 2010 PLD 946; 2003 CLD 621; 2003 PLD 124; 2000 MLD 1880; 1996 CLC 516; 1995 PLD 320

declares that the affairs of the company ought to be investigated; and

   (b)   may appoint one or more competent persons as inspectors to investigate the affairs of a company and to report thereon in such manner as the Commission may direct if in its opinion there are circumstances suggesting—

      (i)   that the business of the company is being or has been conducted with intent to defraud its creditors, members or any other person or for a fraudulent or unlawful purpose, or in a manner oppressive of any of its members or that the company was formed for any fraudulent or unlawful purpose; or

      (ii)   that persons concerned in the formation of the company or the management of its affairs have in connection therewith been guilty of fraud, misfeasance, breach of trust or other misconduct towards the company or towards any of its members or have been carrying on unauthorised business; or

      (iii) that the affairs of the company have been so conducted or managed as to deprive the members thereof of a reasonable return; or

      (iv)   that the members of the company have not been given all the information with respect to its affairs which they might reasonably expect; or

      (v)   that any shares of the company have been allotted for inadequate consideration; or

      (vi)   that the affairs or the company are not being managed in accordance with sound business principles or prudent commercial practices; or

      (vii) that the financial position of the company is such as to endanger its solvency:

            Provided that, before making an order under clause (b), the Commission shall give the company an opportunity of being heard.

   (2) While appointing an inspector under sub-section (1), the Commission may define the scope of the investigation, whether as respects the matters or the period to which it is to extend or otherwise.

   258. **Serious Fraud Investigation.—** (1) Notwithstanding anything contained in sections 256 and 257, the Commission may authorize any one or more of its officers or appoint such number of professionals from amongst the

---

[1] 1996 PLD 543

persons of ability, integrity and having experience in the fields of corporate affairs, accountancy, taxation, forensic audit, capital market, banking, information technology, law or such other fields as may be notified, as an inspector or investigation officer to investigate such serious nature of offences relating to a company as provided in Sixth Schedule.

(2) The persons appointed as inspectors or investigation officer under sub-section (1) shall have all powers of investigation officer under this Act, the Securities and Exchange Commission of Pakistan Act, 1997 (XLII of 1997) and Code of Criminal Procedure, 1898 (Act V of 1898), *mutatis mutandis* and shall report in such manner as the Commission may direct.

(3) Where no procedure is provided in this Act or Securities and Exchange Commission of Pakistan Act, 1997 (XLII of 1997) the investigation officer shall comply with the relevant provisions of Code of Criminal Procedure, 1898 (Act V of 1898).

(4) Notwithstanding anything contained in this Act or any other law, the Commission may, if it is satisfied that the matter is of public importance or it is in the interest of public at large, request the concerned Minister-in-Charge of the Federal Government to form a Joint Investigation Team to be headed by a senior level officer of the Commission, not below the rank of additional director, and may include any person mentioned in sub section (1) along with Gazetted officer of any Federal law enforcement agency, bureau or authority for providing assistance in investigating the offence under this section and the direction of the concerned Minister-in-Charge of the Federal Government under this section shall be binding and any person who fails to comply with such directions, shall be guilty of an offence punishable with simple imprisonment of thirty days or fine up to one hundred thousand rupees by the Court:

Provided that nothing in this section shall be in derogation to or affect any proceedings under powers of the Commission to send reference under section 41B of the Securities and Exchange Commission of Pakistan Act, 1997 (XLII of 1997).

(5) Upon completion of investigation, the Joint Investigation Team shall, through the Special Public Prosecutor, submit a report before the Court as mentioned in section 483 of this Act:

Provided that notwithstanding anything contained in the Qanun-e-Shahadat(Order), 1984 (P.O. No. X of 1984) or any other law, such report shall be admissible as an evidence in the Court.

(6) While trying any offence under this Act, the Court may also try any other offence, in which an accused may be charged under any other law, at the same trial if the offence is connected with such other offence.

(7) Where, in the course of any trial under this Act, it is found that the accused person has committed any other offence in addition to any offences connected with the scheduled offences, the Court may convict an accused for such other offence and pass any sentence under this Act or any other law:

Provided that where such offence is tried by any special court having jurisdiction, higher or equal to the Court of Session, joint trial will be conducted by such special court of all the offences and convict an accused accordingly under the process provided in the special law.

259. **Inspector to be a Court for certain purposes.**--(1) Notwithstanding anything contained in any other law for the time being in force, the Commission may either on its own motion or on the basis of any information received, is of the view that any offence has been committed under this Act or any person is engaged in any fraud, misfeasance, misconduct or any other activity prejudice to the public interest shall have all the powers as provided under the Securities and Exchange Commission of Pakistan Act, 1997(XLII of 1997).

(2) A person appointed as inspector under sections 256, 257 and 258 shall, for the purposes of his investigation, have the same powers as are vested in a Court under the Code of Civil Procedure, 1908 (Act V of 1908), while trying a suit, in respect of the following matters, namely--

(a) enforcing the attendance of persons and examining them on oath or affirmation;

(b) compelling the discovery and production of books and papers and any material objects; and

(c) issuing commissions for the examination of witnesses;

and every proceeding before such person shall be deemed to be "judicial proceeding" within the meaning of sections 193 and 228 of the Pakistan Penal Code, 1860 (Act XLV of 1860).

(3) Any contravention of or non-compliance with any orders, directions or requirement of the inspector exercising powers of a Court under sub-section (1) shall, in all respects, entail the same liabilities, consequences and penalties as are provided for such contravention, non-compliance or default under the Code of Civil Procedure, 1908 (Act V of 1908) and Pakistan Penal Code, 1860 (Act XLV of 1860).

260. **Power of inspectors to carry investigation into affairs of associated companies.**-If an inspector appointed under sections 256, 257 or 258 to investigate the affairs of a company considers it necessary for reasons to be recorded in writing, he may probe after seeking prior approval of the Commission, the affairs of any other associated company or associated

undertaking which is, or has been associated and also from the chief executive of any such company:

Provided that the Commission shall not grant approval under this section without providing opportunity of being heard to the associated company or associated undertaking or the chief executive, as the case may be.

261.   **Duty of officers to assist the inspector.**-(1) It shall be the duty of all officers and other employees and agents of the company and all persons who have dealings with the company to give to the inspector all assistance in connection with the investigation.

(2)   Any such person who makes default in complying with the provisions of sub-section shall, without prejudice to any other liability, be punishable in respect of each offence with imprisonment of either description for a term which may extend to two years and shall also be liable to a fine which may extend to one million rupees.

(3)   In this section--

(a)   the expression "agents", in relation to any company, body corporate or person, includes the bankers, legal advisers and auditors of the company;

(b)   the expression "officer", in relation to any company or body corporate, include any trustee for the debenture-holders of such company or body corporate; and

(c)   any reference to officers and other employees and agents shall be construed as a reference to past as well as present officers and other employees and agents, as the case may be.

262.   **Inspector's report.**--(1) The inspector may, and if so directed by the Commission shall, make an interim report, and on the conclusion of the investigation a final report to the Commission[1].

(2) The Commission--

(a)   shall forward a copy of any report made by the inspector to the company at its registered office with such directions as the Commission thinks fit;

(b)   may, if it thinks fit, furnish a copy thereof, on request and on payment of the specified fee, to any person-

(i)   who is a member of the company or other body corporate or is interested in the affairs of the company;

(ii)   whose interests as a creditor of the company or other body corporate appear to the Commission to be affected;

---

[1] 2014 CLD 467

(c)   shall, when the inspectors are appointed under clause (a) or clause (b) of section 256, furnish, at the request of the applicants for the investigation, a copy of the report to them;

(d)   shall, where the inspector are appointed under section 257 in pursuance of an order of the Court, furnish a copy of the report to the Court;

(e)   may forward a copy of the report to the registrar with such directions as it may deem fit; and

(f)   may also cause the report or any part thereof to be posted on its website.

263.   **Prosecution.--**(1) If, from any report made under section 262, it appears to the Commission that any person has, in relation to the company or in relation to any other body corporate, whose affairs have been investigated by virtue of sections 256, 257 and 258, been guilty of any offense for which he is criminally liable, the Commission may, prosecute such person for the offence, and it shall be the duty of all officers and other employees and agents of the company or body corporate, as the case may be, other than the accused in the proceedings, to give the Commission or any person nominated by it in this behalf all assistance in connection with the prosecution which they are reasonably able to give[1].

(2) Sub-section (3) of section 261 shall apply for the purpose of this section as it applies for the purposes of that section.

264.   **Power of Commission to initiate action against management.--**(1) If from any report made under section 262, the Commission is of the opinion that[2]--

(a)   the business of the company is being or has been conducted with intent to defraud its creditors, members or any other persons or for a fraudulent or unlawful purpose, or in a manner oppressive of any of its members or that the company was formed for any fraudulent or unlawful purpose; or

(b)   the person concerned in the formation of the company or the management of its affairs have in connection therewith been guilty of fraud, misfeasance, breach of trust or other misconduct towards the company or towards any of its member or have been carrying on unauthorized business; or

(c)   the affairs of the company have been so conducted or managed as to deprive the shareholders thereof of a reasonable return; or

[1] 1994 SCMR 2281
[2] 2002 CLD 1714

(d)   that the members of the company have not been given all the information with respect to its affairs which they might reasonably expect; or

(e)   any shares of the company have been allotted for inadequate consideration; or

(f)   the affairs of the company are not being managed in accordance with sound business principles or prudent commercial practices; or

(g)   the financial position of the company is such as to endanger its solvency;

the Commission may apply to the Court and the Court may, after taking such evidence as it may consider necessary, by an order--

(i)   remove from office any director including the chief executive or other officer of the company; or

(ii)   direct that the directors of the company shall carry out such changes in the management or in the accounting policies of the company as may be specified in the order; or

(iii)   notwithstanding anything contained in this Act or any other law for the time being in force, direct the company to call a meeting of its members to consider such matters as may be specified in the order and to take appropriate remedial actions; or

(iv)   direct that any existing contract which is to the detriment of the company or its members or is intended to or does benefit any officer or director shall be annulled or modified to the extent specified in the order:

Provided that no such order shall be made so as to have effect from any date preceding the date of the order:

Provided further that any director, including a chief executive or other officer who is removed from office under clause (i), unless the Court specified a lesser period, shall not be a director, chief executive or officer of any company for a period of five years from the date of his removal.

(2) No order under this section shall be made unless the director or other officer likely to be affected by such order has been given an opportunity of being heard.

(3) The action taken under sub-section (1) shall be in addition to and not in substitution of any other action or remedy provided in any other law for the time being in force.

265. **Effect of Court's order.--** On the issue of the Court's order under section 264 removing from office any director, including chief executive or other officer, such director or other officer shall be deemed to have vacated his office[1] and—

(a) if the Court's order has removed a director, the casual vacancy in the office of director shall be filled in accordance with the relevant provisions of section 161 of this Act; and

(b) if the Court's order has removed from office a chief executive, the board shall appoint another person to be the chief executive; and

(c) if the Court's order has removed from office all the directors including the chief executive, a general meeting of the company shall be called forthwith for electing new directors.

266. **No compensation to be payable for annulment or modification of contract.--**Notwithstanding anything contained in any other law for the time being in force, and except as ordered by the Court for special reasons to be recorded in writing, no director, chief executive or other officer of the company shall be entitled to be paid any compensation for annulment or modification of a contract to which he is a party or of which he is a beneficiary, if such contract is annulled or modified by an order issued by the Court under section 264.

267. **No right to compensation for loss of office. -–** No person shall be entitled to or be paid any compensation or damages for the loss of office by reason of an order issued under section 264.

POWERS OF COURT HEARING APPLICATION

268. **Application for winding up of company or an order under section 286.--** If any company or other body corporate the affairs of which have been investigated by inspectors is liable to be wound up under this Act, and it appears to the Commission from any report made under section 262 that it is expedient so to do by reason of any such circumstances as are referred to in sub-clause (i) or sub-clause (ii) or sub-clause (iii) or sub-clause (iv) or sub-clause (vii) of clause (b) of sub-section (1) of section 257, the Commission may, unless the company or other body corporate is already being wound up by the Court cause to be presented to the Court by the registrar or any person authorised by the Commission in this behalf[2]--

(a) a petition for the winding up of the company or body corporate, on the ground that it is just and equitable that it should be wound up;

(b) an application for an order under section 286; or

(c) both a petition and an application as aforesaid.

---

[1] 1987 CLC 2079
[2] 2001 CLC 2019

269.   **Proceedings for recovery of damages or property.--** (1) If from any report referred to in sub-section (1) of section 262 it appears to the Commission that proceedings ought, in the public interest, to be brought by the company or any body corporate whose affairs have been investigated in pursuance of section 260--

(a)   for the recovery of damages in respect of any fraud, misfeasance, breach of trust or other misconduct in connection with the promotion or formation, or the management of the affairs, of such company or body corporate; or

(b)   for the recovery of any property of such company or body corporate which has been misapplied or wrongfully retained;

the Commission may itself bring proceedings for that purpose in the name of such company or body corporate.

(2) The Commission shall be indemnified by such company or body corporate against any costs or expenses incurred by it in, or in connection with, any proceedings brought by virtue of sub-section (1) and the Court or other authority before which proceedings are brought shall pass an order accordingly.

270.   **Expenses of investigation.--** (1) When an investigation is ordered to be made under section 256 or 257 or 258, the expenses of and incidental to the investigation shall in the first instance be defrayed by the Commission; but the following persons shall, to the extent mentioned below, be liable to reimburse the Commission in respect of such expenses, namely[1]-

(a)   any person who is convicted on a prosecution instituted in pursuance of section 263 or is ordered to pay damages or restore any property as a result of proceedings under section 269 may in the same proceedings be ordered to pay the said expenses to such extent as may be specified by the Commission or the Court convicting such person or ordering him to pay such damages or restore such property, as the case may be;

(b)   any company or body corporate in whose name proceedings are brought as aforesaid shall be liable, to the extent of the amount or value of any sums or property recovered by it as a result of the proceedings;

(c)   where the investigation was ordered by the Commission under clause (c) of sub-section (1) of section 256 or 257 or 258, the company or body corporate whose affairs are ordered to be investigated, shall be liable; and

---

[1] 2009 CLD 1577

(d) where the investigation was ordered under section 256 on an application of the members, the members making the application and the company or body corporate dealt with by the report shall be liable to such extent, if any, as the Commission may direct.

(2) The amount of expenses which any company, body corporate or person is liable under this section to reimburse to the Commission shall be recoverable from that company, body corporate or person as provided under section 486.

(3) For the purposes of this section, any costs or expenses incurred by the Commission in or in connection with proceeding brought by the Commission under section 269 shall be treated as expenses of the investigation giving rise to the proceedings.

(4) Any liability to reimburse the Commission imposed by clauses (a) and (b) of sub-section (1) shall, subject to satisfaction of the right of the Commission to reimbursement, be a liability also to indemnify all persons against liability under clause (c) of that sub-section.

(5) Any such liability imposed by clause (a) of sub-section (1) shall, subject as aforesaid, be a liability also to indemnify all persons against liability under clause (b) of that sub-section.

(6) Any person liable under clause (a) or clause (b) or clause (c) of sub-section (1) shall be entitled to contribute from any other person liable under the same clause according to the amount of their respective liabilities thereunder.

(7) In so far as the expenses to be defrayed by the Commission under this section are not recovered thereunder, they shall be borne by the Commission.

271.   **Inspector's report to be evidence.--** A copy of any report of any inspector or inspectors appointed under sections 256, 257 or 258 authenticated in such manner, if any, as may be specified, shall be admissible in any legal proceedings as evidence of the opinion of the inspector or inspectors in relation to any matter contained in the report.

272.   **Imposition of restrictions on shares and debentures and prohibition of transfer of shares or debentures in certain cases.--** (1) Where it appears to the Commission in connection with any investigation that there is good reason to find out the relevant facts about any shares, whether issued or to be issued, and the Commission is of the opinion that such facts cannot be found out unless the restrictions specified in sub-section (2) are imposed, the Commission may, by order, direct that the shares shall be subject to the restrictions imposed by sub-section (2) for such period not exceeding one year as may be specified in the order[1]:

---

[1] 2006 CLD 1204; 2003 CLD 463

Provided that, before making an order under this sub-section, the Commission shall provide an opportunity of showing cause against the proposed action to the company and the persons likely to be affected by the restriction.

(2) So long as any shares are directed to be subject to the restrictions imposed by this sub-section--

(a)   any transfer of those shares shall be void;

(b)   where those shares are to be issued, they shall not be issued; and any issue thereof or any transfer of the right to be issued therewith, shall be void;

(c)   no voting right shall be exercisable in respect of those shares;

(d)   no further shares shall be issued in right of those shares or in pursuance of any offer made to the holder thereof; and any issue of such shares or any transfer of the right to be issued therewith, shall be void;

(e)   except in a liquidation, no payment shall be made of any sums due from the company on those shares, whether in respect of dividend, capital or otherwise; and

(f)   no change other than a change by operation of law shall be made in the directors or the chief executive.

(3) Where a transfer of shares in a company has taken place and as a result thereof a change in the directors of the company is likely to take place and the Commission is of opinion that any such change will be prejudicial to the public interest, the Commission may, by order, direct, that--

(a)   the voting rights in respect of those shares shall not be exercisable for such period not exceeding one year as may be specified in the order; and

(b)   no resolution passed or action taken to effect a change in the directors before the date of the order shall have effect unless confirmed by the Commission.

(4) Where the Commission has reasonable ground to believe that a transfer of shares in a company is likely to take place as a result of which a change in the directors of the company will follow and the Commission is of opinion that any such change will be prejudicial to the public interest, the Commission may, by order, prohibit any transfer of shares in the company during such period not exceeding one year as may be specified in the order.

(5) The Commission may, by order, at any time, vary or rescind any order made by it under sub-section (1) or sub-section (3) or sub-section (4).

(6) Where the Commission makes an order under sub-section (1) or sub-section (3) or sub-section (4) or sub-section (5) or refuses to rescind any such order, any person aggrieved thereby may apply to the Court and the Court may, if it thinks fit, by order, vacate any such order of the Commission:

Provided that no order, whether interim or final shall be made by the Court without giving the Commission an opportunity of being heard.

(7) Any order of the Commission rescinding an order under sub-section (1), or any order of the Court vacating any such order, which is expressed to be made with a view to permitting a transfer of any shares, may continue the restrictions mentioned in clauses (d) and (e) of sub-section (2), either in whole or in part, so far as they relate to any right acquired, or offer made, before the transfer.

(8) Any order made by the Commission under sub-section (5) shall be served on the company within fourteen days of the making of the order.

(9)   Any person who--

(a)   exercises or purports to exercise any right to dispose of any shares or of any right to be issued with any such shares, when to his knowledge he is not entitled to do so by reason of any of the restrictions applicable to the case under sub-section (1); or

(b)   votes in respect of any shares, whether as holder or proxy, or appoints a proxy to vote in respect thereof, when to his knowledge he is not entitled to do so by reason of any of the restrictions applicable to the case under sub-section (2) or by reason of any order made under sub-section (3); or

(c)   transfers any shares in contravention of any order made under sub-section (4); or

(d)   being the holder of any shares in respect of which an order under sub- section (2) or sub-section (3) has been made, fails to give notice of the fact of their being subject to any such order to any person whom he does not know to be aware of that fact but whom he knows to be otherwise entitled to vote in respect of those shares, whether as holder or a proxy;

shall be punishable with imprisonment for a term which may extend to one year, or with fine which may extend to one million rupees, or with both.

(10) Any contravention or default in complying with requirements of sub-section (2) shall be an offence liable to a penalty of level 2 on the standard scale.

(11) A prosecution shall not be instituted under this section except by or with the consent of the Commission.

(12) This section shall also apply in relation to debentures as it applies in relation to shares.

273. **Saving for legal advisers and bankers.**--Nothing in sections 256 to 263 shall require the disclosure to the registrar or to the Commission or to an inspector appointed by the Commission-

(a)   by a legal adviser, of any privileged communication made to him in that capacity, except as respects the name and address of his client; or

(b)   by the bankers of any company, body corporate, or other person, referred to in the sections aforesaid, as such bankers, of any information as to be the affairs of any of their customers other than such company, body corporate, or person.

274. **Enquiries and investigation not to be affected by winding up.--** An inspection, enquiry or investigation may be initiated or proceeded with under sections 221, 254, 255, 256, 257 and 260 and any consequential action taken in accordance with any provisions of this Act notwithstanding that--

(a)   the company has passed a resolution for winding up;

(b)   a petition has been submitted to the Court for winding up of the company; or

(c)   any other civil or criminal proceedings have been initiated against the company or its officers under any provision of this Act.

275. **Application of sections 254 to 274 to liquidators and foreign companies.--**The provisions of sections 254 to 274 shall apply *mutatis mutandis* to companies in the course of winding up, their liquidators and foreign companies[1].

PART VIII

MEDIATION, ARBITRATION, ARRANGEMENTS AND RECONSTRUCTION

276. **Mediation and Conciliation Panel.--** (1) Any of the parties to the proceedings may, by mutual consent, at any time during the proceedings before the Commission or the Appellate Bench, apply to the Commission or the Appellate Bench, as the case may be, in such form along with such fees as may be specified, for referring the matter pertaining to such proceedings to the Mediation and Conciliation Panel and the Commission or the Appellate Bench, as the case may be, shall appoint one or more individuals from the panel referred to in sub-section (2).

---

[1] 2012 PLD 15; 2012 CLD 944; 2012 CLD 589; 2007 CLD 949; 2006 CLD 308; 2006 CLD 311

(2) The Commission shall maintain a panel to be called as the Mediation and Conciliation Panel consisting of individuals having such qualifications as may be specified for mediation between the parties during the pendency of any proceedings before the Commission or the Appellate Bench under this Act.

(3) The fee and other terms and conditions of individuals of the Mediation and Conciliation Panel shall be such as may be specified.

(4) The Mediation and Conciliation Panel shall follow such procedure as and dispose of the matter referred to it within a period of ninety days from the date of such reference and forward its recommendations to the Commission or the Appellate Bench, as the case may be.

277. **Resolution of disputes through mediation.--** A company, its management or its members or creditors may by written consent, directly refer a dispute, claim or controversy arising between them or between the members or directors inter-se, for resolution, to any individuals enlisted on the mediation and conciliation panel maintained by the Commission before taking recourse to formal dispute resolution.

278. **Power for companies to refer matter to arbitration**.-- (1) A company may by written agreement refer any existing or future difference between itself and any other company or person to arbitration, in accordance with the Arbitration Act, 1940 (X of 1940)[1].

(2) Companies, parties to the arbitration, may delegate to the arbitrator power to settle any term or to determine any matter capable of being lawfully settled or determined by the companies themselves, or by the board or other managing body.

(3) The provisions of the Arbitration Act, 1940 (X of 1940), shall apply to all arbitrations between companies and persons in pursuance of this Act.

---

[1] 2009 CLD 390; 2009 MLD 1294; 2009 CLC 291; 2009 CLD 390; 1970 PLD 184

279.   **Compromise with creditors and members.**-- (1) Where a compromise or arrangement is proposed between a company and its creditors or any class of them, or between the company and its members or any class of them, the Commission may, on the application of the company or of any creditor or member of the company or, in the case of a company being wound up, of the liquidator, order a meeting of the creditors or class of creditors, or of the members of the company or class of members, as the case may be, to be called, held and conducted in such manner as the Commission directs[1].

(2) If a majority in number representing three-fourths in value of the creditors or class of creditors, or members, as the case may be, present and voting either in person or, where proxies are allowed, by proxy at the meeting, agree to any compromise or arrangement, the compromise or arrangement shall, if sanctioned by the Commission be binding on the company, all its creditors, all the members, the liquidators and the contributories of the company, as the case may be:

Provided that no order sanctioning any compromise or arrangement shall be made by the Commission unless the Commission is satisfied that the company or any other person by whom an application has been made under sub-section (1) has disclosed to the Commission, by affidavit or otherwise, all material facts relating to the company, such as the financial position of the company, the auditor's report on the latest accounts of the company, the pendency of any investigation proceedings in relation to the company and the like.

(3) A copy of the order under sub-section (2) sanctioning the compromise or arrangement duly certified by an authorised officer of the Commission shall be forwarded to the registrar within seven days from the date of the order.

---

[1] 2018 CLD 15; 2018 CLD 33; 2018 CLD 389; 2018 CLD 572; 2018 CLD 716; 2018 CLD 737; 2016 CLD 828; 2018 CLD 838; 2017 CLD 1468; 2016 CLD 902; 2016 CLD 1572; 2016 CLD 2185; 2016 CLD 2271; 2015 CLD 1274; 2015 CLD 2010; 2015 PLD 632; 2015 CLD 1119; 2015 PCrLJ 1240; 2014 CLD 26; 2014 PLD 38; 2014 CLD 961; 2014 CLD 1068; 2013 CLD 7; 2013 CLD 68; 2013 CLD 397; 2012 CLD 582; 2012 CLD 645; 2011 CLD 10; 2011 CLD 944; 2011 PTD 845; 2011 CLD 1216; 2010 CLD 26; 2010 CLD 753; 2010 CLD 1337; 2010 CLD 1802; 2009 CLD 82; 2009 CLD 102; 2009 CLD 880; 2009 CLD 1120; 2009 CLD 1172; 2008 CLD 1646; 2007 PTD 1885; 2007 CLD 900; 2007 CLD 1047; 2006 CLD 769; 2006 CLD 895; 2006 CLD 976; 2005 CLD 36; 2005 CLD 93; 2005 CLD 713; 2005 CLD 1191; 2005 CLD 1818; 2004 CLD 1; 2004 CLD 343; 2003 CLD 463; 2003 PLD 646; 2003 CLD 1209; 2003 PTD 1285; 2003 CLD 1713; 2003 CLD 1634; 2002 CLD 171; 2002 CLD 872; 2002 CLD 1314; 2002 CLD 1338; 2002 CLD 1352; 2002 CLD 1361; 2002 PTCL 218; 2002 CLD 1392; 2002 CLD 1747; 2001 CLC 1890; 2001 PLD 5; 2001 PLD 230; 1999 CLC 1037; 1998 PLD 295; 1997 PLD 230; 1997 CLC 1873; 1991 MLD 841; 1991 CLC 523; 1989 MLD 1861; 1989 CLC 818; 1987 MLD 2518; 1985 PTD 510; 1985 MLD 1467; 1984 PLD 225; 1983 CLC 1424; 1982 PLD 566; 1980 PTD 423; 1976 PLD 850; 1957 PLD 554; 1949 PLD 242

(4) A copy of the order under sub-section (2) shall be annexed to every copy of the memorandum of the company issued after the order has been made or in the case of a company not having a memorandum to every copy so issued of the instrument constituting or defining the constitution of the company.

(5) The Court may, at any time after an application has been made to the Commission under this section, stay the commencement or continuation of any suit or proceeding until final disposal of the application.

(6) In this section the expression "company" means any company liable to be wound up under this Act and the expression "arrangement" includes a re-organisation of the share-capital of the company by the consolidation of shares of different classes or by the division of shares into shares of different classes or by both those methods, and for the purposes of this section unsecured creditors who may have filed suits or obtained decrees shall be deemed to be of the same class as other unsecured creditors.

(7) Any contravention or default in complying with requirements of sub-section (4) shall be an offence liable to a penalty of level 1 on the standard scale.

280. **Power of Commission to enforce compromises and arrangements.--** (1) Where the Commission makes an order under section 279 sanctioning a compromise or an arrangement in respect of a company, it may, at the time of making such order or at any time thereafter, give such directions in regard to any matter or make such modifications in the compromise or arrangement as it may consider necessary for the proper working of the compromise or arrangement[1].

(2) If the Commission is satisfied that a compromise or arrangement sanctioned under section 279 cannot be worked satisfactorily with or without modification, it may, initiate proceedings for the winding up of the company.

281. **Information as to compromises or arrangements with creditors and members.--** (1) Where a meeting of creditors or any class of creditors, or of members or any class of members, is called under section 279[2]--

---

[1] 2018 CLD 15; 2018 CLD 33; 2018 CLD 389; 2018 CLD 572; 2017 CLD 1468; 2016 CLD 828; 2016 CLD 1572; 2016 CLD 2185; 2015 CLD 2010; 2014 CLD 26; 2014 PLD 38; 2012 CLD 582; 2010 CLD 753; 2009 CLD 102; 2009 CLD 82; 2009 CLD 1172; 2007 CLD 900; 2007 CLD 1047; 2007 PTD 1885; 2006 CLD 769; 2005 CLD 713; 2005 CLD 1818; 2004 CLD 1; 2003 CLD 1209; 2003 CLD 1634; 2003 CLD 1713; 2003 PTD 1285; 2002 CLD 171; 2002 CLD 1352; 2002 CLD 1361; 2002 CLD 1392; 2001 CLC 1890; 2001 PLD 230

[2] 2018 CLD 15; 2018 CLD 33; 2018 CLD 389; 2018 CLD 572; 2017 CLD 1468; 2016 CLD 828; 2016 CLD 2185; 2016 CLD 2271; 2015 CLD 2010; 2014 PLD 38; 2014 CLD 26; 2012 CLD 582; 2012 CLD 645; 2010 CLD 753; 2009 CLD 82; 2009 CLD 102; 2009 CLD 1172; 2007 CLD 900; 2007 PTD 1885; 2007 CLD 1047; 2006 CLD 769; 2005 CLD 1818; 2004 CLD 1; 2003 CLD 1209; 2003 CLD 1634; 2003 PTD 1285; 2002 CLD 171; 2002 CLD 1314; 2002 CLD 1352; 2002 CLD 1361; 2002 CLD 1392; 2001 CLC 1890; 2001 PLD 230

(a)   with every notice calling the meeting which is sent to a creditor or member, there shall be sent also a statement setting forth the terms of the compromise or arrangement and explaining its effect; and in particular, stating any material interest of the directors including the chief executive of the company, whether in their capacity as such or as members or creditors of the company or otherwise, and the effect on those interests, of the compromise or arrangement if, and in so far as, it is different from the effect on the like interest of other persons; and

(b)   in every notice calling the meeting which is given by advertisement, there shall be included either such a statement as aforesaid or a notification of the place at which and the manner in which creditors or members entitled to attend the meeting may obtain copies of such a statement as aforesaid.

(2) Where the compromise or arrangement affects the rights of debenture-holders of the company, the said statement shall give the like information and explanation as respects the trustees of any deed for securing the issue of the debentures as it is required to give as respects the company's directors.

(3) Where a notice given by advertisement includes a notification that copies of a statement setting forth the terms of the compromise or arrangement proposed and explaining its effect can be obtained by creditors or members entitled to attend the meeting, every creditor or member so entitled shall, on

(4) making an application in the manner indicated by the notice, be furnished by the company, free of charge, with a copy of the statement.

(5) Any contravention or default in complying with requirements of this section shall be an offence liable to a penalty of level 1 on the standard scale; and for the purpose of this sub-section any liquidator of the company and trustee of a deed for securing the issue of debentures of the company shall be deemed to be an officer of the company:

Provided that a person shall not be under this sub-section if he shows that the default was due to the refusal of any other person, being a director, including chief executive or trustee for debenture-holder, to supply the necessary particulars as to his material interests.

(5) Every director, including chief executive of the company and every trustee for debenture-holders of the company, shall give notice to the company of such matters relating to himself as may be necessary for the purposes of this section and on the request of the company shall provide such further information as may be necessary for the purposes of this section; and, if he fails to do so within the time allowed by the company, he shall be liable to a penalty of level 1 on the standard scale.

282. **Powers of Commission to facilitate reconstruction or amalgamation of companies.**—(1) Where an application is made to the Commission under section 279 to sanction a compromise or arrangement and it is shown that--

    (a)   the compromise or arrangement is proposed for the purposes of, or in connection with, a scheme for the reconstruction of any company or companies, or the amalgamation of any two or more companies or division of a company into one or more companies;

    (b)   under the scheme the whole or any part of the undertaking or property or liabilities of any company concerned in the scheme ("a transferor company") is to be transferred to another company ("the transferee company") or is proposed to be divided among and transferred to two or more companies; and

    (c)   a copy of the scheme drawn up by the applicants has been filed with the registrar;

the Commission may order a meeting of the creditors or class of creditors or the members or class of members, as the case may be, to be called, held and conducted in such manner as the Commission may direct[1].

(2) Where an order has been made by the Commission under sub-section (1), merging companies or the company in respect of which a division is proposed, shall also be required to circulate the following for the meeting so ordered by the Commission, namely:—

    (a)   the draft of the proposed terms of the scheme drawn up and adopted by the board of each of the applicant companies;

    (b)   confirmation that a copy of the draft scheme has been filed with the registrar;

    (c)   a report adopted by the board of the applicant companies explaining effect of compromise on each class of members, laying out in particular the share swap ratio, specifying any special valuation difficulties;

---

[1] 2018 CLD 15; 2018 CLD 33; 2018 CLD 389; 2018 CLD 572; 2018 CLD 838; 2017 CLD 1468; 2016 CLD 828; 2016 CLD 902; 2016 CLD 2185; 2016 CLD 2271; 2015 CLD 2010; 2015 PLD 632; 2015 1119; 2014 CLD 26; 2014 PLD 38; 2014 CLD 961; 2013 CLD 7; 2013 CLD 68; 2013 CLD 397; 2012 CLD 582; 2011 PTD 845; 2011 CLD 10; 2011 CLD 944; 2011 CLD 1216; 2010 CLD 26; 2010 CLD 753; 2010 CLD 1337; 2010 CLD 1802; 2009 CLD 82; 2009 CLD 102; 2009 CLD 880; 2009 CLD 1120; 2009 CLD 1172; 2008 PTD 1646; 2007 CLD 900; 2007 CLD 1047; 2007 PTD 1885; 2006 CLD 769; 2006 CLD 1364; 2005 CLD 93; 2005 CLD 1818; 2004 CLD 1; 2003 PTD 1285; 2003 CLD 1209; 2003 CLD 1713; 2003 CLD 2634; 2002 CLD 171; 2002 CLD 872; 2002 CLD 1314; 2002 CLD 1338; 2002 CLD 1352; 2002 CLD 1361; 2002 CLD 1747; 2002 CLD 1392; 2001 PLD 230; 2001 PLD 5; 1999 CLC 1037; 1998 PLD 295; 1997 CLC 1873; 1997 PLD 230; 1991 CLC 523; 1989 CLC 818; 1989 CLC 1323; 1986 MLD 1317; 1986 PLD 297

(d)   the report of the expert with regard to valuation, if any;

(e)   a supplementary audited financial statements if the last annual accounts of any of the applicant company relate to a financial year ending more than one hundred and eighty days before the first meeting of the company summoned for the purposes of approving the scheme.

(3) The Commission may, either by an order, sanction the compromise or arrangement or by a subsequent order, make provision for all or any of the following matters--

(a)   the transfer to the transferee company of the whole or any part of the undertaking and of the property or liabilities of any transferor company;

(b)   the allotment or appropriation by the transferee company of any shares, debentures, policies or other like interests in that company which under the compromise or arrangement are to be allotted or appropriated by that company to or for any person;

(c)   the continuation by or against the transferee company of any legal proceedings pending by or against any transferor company;

(d)   the dissolution, without winding up, of any transferor company;

(e)   the provision to be made for any persons who, within such time and in such manner as the Commission directs, dissent from the compromise or arrangement;

(f)   such incidental, consequential and supplemental matters as are necessary to secure that the reconstruction, amalgamation or bifurcation is fully and effectively carried out.

(4)   If an order under this section provides for the transfer of property or liabilities--

(a)   the property, by virtue of the order stands transferred to, and vests in, the transferee company, and

(b)   the liabilities, by virtue of the order, stand transferred to and become liabilities of that company.

(5) Notwithstanding anything contained in the Stamp Act, 1899 (II of 1899) or any other law for the time being in force, no stamp duty shall be payable on transfer to the transferee company of the whole or any part of the undertaking and of the property of any transferor company as a result of sanctioning by the Commission, any compromise or arrangement under this Part:

Provided that this sub-section (5) shall, in respect of the companies having registered office within the jurisdiction of–

(a)   the Islamabad Capital Territory, be applicable at once; and

(b)   the Provinces, be applicable upon notification or legislation by the respective Provincial Governments.

(6) The property (if the order so directs) vests freed from any charge that is by virtue of the compromise or arrangement to cease to have effect.

(7) A copy of the order passed by the Commission under this section sanctioning the reconstruction, the amalgamation or division, duly certified by an authorised officer of the Commission shall be forwarded to the registrar within seven days from the date of the order.

(8) In this section "**property**" includes property, rights and powers of every description; and "liabilities" includes duties.

(9) In this section the expression "**transferee company**" does not include any company other than a company within the meaning of this Act, and the expression "**transferor company**" includes any body corporate, whether a company within the meaning of this Act or not.

283. **Notice to be given to registrar for applications under section 279 and 282.** The Commission shall give notice of every application made to it under sections 279 to 282 to the registrar and shall take into consideration the representation if any, made to it by the registrar before passing any order under any of these sections[1].

284. **Amalgamation of wholly owned subsidiaries in holding company.**(1) A company and one or more other companies that is or that are directly or indirectly wholly owned by it, may amalgamate and continue as one company (being the company first referred to) without complying with sections 279 to 282[2], if--

(a)   the scheme of amalgamation is approved by the board of each amalgamating company; and

(b)   each resolution provides that-

(i)   the shares of each transferor company, other than the transferee company, will be cancelled without payment or other consideration; and

---

[1] 2018 CLD 33; 2018 CLD 572; 2016 CLD 828; 2016 CLD 2185; 2015 CLD 2010; 2013 CLD 108; 2013 CLD 397; 2012 CLD 582; 2010 CLD 753; 2009 CLD 102; 2009 CLD 82; 2009 CLD 1172; 2008 PTD 1646; 2007 CLD 900; 2007 CLD 1047; 2007 PTD 1885; 2006 CLD 976; 2006 CLD 769; 2006 CLD 1364; 2003 PTD 1285; 2002 CLD 872; 2002 CLD 1314; 2002 CLD 1352; 2002 CLD 1392; 2001 CLC 1890

[2] 2018 CLD 838

    (ii)   the board is satisfied that the transferee company will be able to pay its debts as they fall due during the period of one year immediately after the date on which the amalgamation is to become effective and a declaration verified by an affidavit to the effect will be filed with the registrar; and

    (iii) the person or persons named in the resolution will be the director or directors of the transferee company.

(2) Two or more companies, each of which is directly or indirectly wholly owned by the same person, may amalgamate and continue as one company without complying with section 279 or section 282 if--

    (a)   the scheme of amalgamation is approved by a resolution of the board of each amalgamating company; and

    (b)   each resolution provides that--

        (i)   the shares of all the transferor companies will be cancelled without payment or other consideration; and

        (ii)   the board is satisfied that the transferee company will be able to pay its debts as they fall due during the period of one year immediately after the date on which the amalgamation is to become effective and a declaration verified by an affidavit to the effect will be filed with the registrar; and

        (iii) the person or persons named in the resolution will be the director or directors of the transferee company.

(3) The board of each amalgamating company must, not less than twenty days before the amalgamation is proposed to take effect, give written notice of the proposed amalgamation to every secured creditor of the company.

(4) The resolutions approving an amalgamation under this section, taken together, shall be deemed to constitute an amalgamation proposal that has been approved.

(5) The transferee company shall file a copy of the scheme so approved in the manner as may be specified, with the registrar where the registered office of the company is situated.

(6) Any contravention or default in complying with requirements of this section shall be an offence liable to a penalty of level 2 on the standard scale.

285. **Power to acquire shares of members dissenting from scheme or contract.**--(1) Where a scheme or contract involving the transfer of shares or any class of shares in any company (in this section referred to as "the transferor company") to another company (in this section referred to as "transferee company") has, within one hundred and twenty days after the making of the offer in that behalf by the transferee company, been approved by the holders of

not less than nine-tenths in value of the shares whose transfer is involved (other than shares already held at the date of the offer by, or by a nominee for, the transferee company or its subsidiary), the transferee company may, at any time within sixty days after the expiry of the said one hundred and twenty days, give notice in the specified manner to any dissenting shareholder that it desires to acquire his shares; when such a notice is given the transferee company, shall, unless, on an application made by the dissenting shareholder within thirty days from the date on which the notice was given, the Commission thinks fit to order otherwise, be entitled and bound to acquire those shares on the terms on which, under the scheme or contract, the shares of the approving shareholders are to be transferred to the transferee company[1]:

Provided that, where shares in the transferor company of the same class as the shares whose transfer is involved are already held as aforesaid by the transferee company to a value greater than one-tenths of the aggregate of the value of all the shares in the company of such class, the foregoing provisions of this sub-section shall not apply, unless--

(a) the transferee company offers the same terms to all holders of the shares of that class (other than those already held as aforesaid) whose transfer is involved; and

(b) the holders who approve the scheme or contract, besides holding not less than nine-tenths in value of the shares (other than those already held as aforesaid) whose transfer is involved, are not less than three-fourths in number of the holders of those shares.

(2) Where, in pursuance of any such scheme or contract as aforesaid, shares, or shares of any class, in a company are transferred to another company or its nominee, and those shares together with any other shares or any other shares of the same class, as the case may be, in the first mentioned company held at the date of the transfer by, or by a nominee for, the transferee company or its subsidiary comprise nine-tenth in value of the shares, or shares of that class, as the case may be, in the first-mentioned company, then--

(a) the transferee company shall, within thirty days from the date of the transfer (unless on a previous transfer in pursuance of the scheme or contract it has already complied with this requirement), give notice of that fact in the specified manner to the holders of the remaining shares or of the remaining shares of that class, as the case may be, who have not assented to the scheme or contract; and

(b) any such holder may, within ninety days from the giving of the notice to him, require the transferee company to acquire the shares in question;

---

[1] 2018 CLD 838; 2005 CLD 36

and where a shareholder gives notice under clause (b) with respect to any shares, the transferee company shall be entitled and bound to acquire those shares on the terms on which, under the scheme or contract, the shares of the approving shareholders were transferred to it, or on such other terms as may be agreed, or as the Commission on the application of either the transferee company or the shareholders thinks fit to order.

(3) Where a notice has been given by the transferee company under sub-section (1) and the Commission has not, on an application made by the dissenting shareholder, made an order to the contrary, the transferee company shall, on the expiration of thirty days from the date on which the notice has been given or, if an application to the Commission by the dissenting shareholder is then pending, after that application has been disposed of, transmit a copy of the notice to the transferor company together with an instrument of transfer executed on behalf of the shareholder by any person appointed by the transferee company and on its own behalf by the transferee company and pay or transfer to the transferor company the amount or other consideration representing the price payable by the transferee company for the shares which, by virtue of this section, that company is entitled to acquire; and the transferor company shall--

(a)   thereupon register the transferee company as the holders of those shares; and

(b)   within thirty days of the date of such registration, inform the dissenting shareholders of the fact of such registration and of the receipt of the amount or other consideration representing the price payable to them by the transferee company:

Provided that an instrument of transfer shall not be required for any share for which a share warrant is for the time being outstanding.

(4) Any sums received by the transferor company under this section shall forthwith be paid into a separate bank account to be opened in a scheduled bank and any such sum and any other consideration so received shall be held by that company in trust for the several persons entitled to the shares in respect of which the said sums or other consideration were or was respectively received.

(5) The following provisions shall apply in relation to every offer of a scheme or contract involving the transfer of shares or any class of shares in the transferor company to the transferee company, namely--

(a)   every such offer or every circular containing such offer or every recommendation to the members of the transferor company by its board to accept such offer shall be accompanied by such information as may be specified;

(b)   every such offer shall contain a statement by or on behalf of the transferee company disclosing the steps it has taken to ensure that necessary cash will be available;

(c)   every circular containing or recommending acceptance of, such offer shall be presented to the registrar for registration and no such circular shall be issued until it is so registered;

(d)   the registrar may refuse to register any such circular which does not contain the information required to be given under clause (a) or which sets out such information in a manner likely to give a misleading, erroneous or false impression; and

(e)   an appeal shall lie to the Commission against an order of the registrar refusing to register any such circular.

(6) The Commission or any party may make a reference to the Court, on any matter including but not limited to the determination of liabilities of the company or incidental thereto as provided under sections 279 to 285, for necessary orders.

(7) Whoever issues a circular referred to in clause (c) of sub-section (5) which has not been registered shall be punishable to a penalty of level 1 on the standard scale.

(8) Notwithstanding anything contained in sections 279 to 283 and 285, the powers of the Commission shall be exercised by the Court for such companies or class of companies or having such capital, as may be notified by the concerned Minister-in-Charge of the Federal Government.

PART IX

PREVENTION OF OPPRESSION AND MISMANAGEMENT

286.   **Application to Court.**--(1) If any member or members holding not less than ten percent of the issued share capital of a company, or a creditor or creditors having interest equivalent in amount to not less than ten percent of the paid up capital of the company, complains, or complain, or the Commission or registrar is of the opinion, that the affairs of the company are being conducted, or are likely to be conducted, in an unlawful or fraudulent manner, or in a manner not provided for in its memorandum, or in a manner oppressive to the members or any of the members or the creditors or any of the creditors or are being conducted in a manner that is unfairly prejudicial to the public interest, such member or members or, the creditor or creditors, as the case may be, the

Commission or registrar may make an application to the Court by petition for an order under this section[1].

(2)   If, on any such petition, the Court is of opinion--

(a)   that the company's affairs are being conducted, or are likely to be conducted, as aforesaid; and

(b)   that to wind-up the company will unfairly prejudice the members or creditors;

the Court may, with a view to bringing to an end the matters complained of, make such order as it thinks fit, whether for regulating the conduct of the company's affairs in future, or for the purchase of the shares of any members of the company by other members of the company or by the company and, in the case of purchase by the company, for, the reduction accordingly of the company's capital, or otherwise.

(3) Where an order under this section makes any alteration in, or addition to, a company's memorandum or articles, then, notwithstanding anything in any other provision of this Act, the company shall not have power without the leave of the Court to make any further alteration in or addition to the memorandum or articles inconsistent with the provisions of the order; and the alterations or additions made by the order shall be of the same effect as if duly made by resolution of the company and the provisions of this Act shall apply to the memorandum or articles as so modified accordingly.

(4) A copy of any order under this section altering or adding to, or giving leave to alter or add to, a company's memorandum or articles shall, within fourteen days after the making thereof, be delivered by the company to the registrar for registration; and if the company makes default in complying with this sub-section, the company and every officer of the company who is in default shall be liable to a penalty of level 1 on the standard scale.

(5) The provisions of this section shall not prejudice the right of any person to any other remedy or action.

---

[1] 2019 CLD 355; 2018 CLD 1237; 2018 CLC 1676; 2017 CLD 587; 2017 CLD 696; 2017 CLD 1395; 2017 CLD 1442; 2017 LHC 2616; 2016 GBLR 266; 2016 CLD 1604; 2016 CLD 970; 2016 CLD 1283; 2015 CLD 719; 2015 CLD 1351; 2014 CLD 1683; 2013 CLD 114; 2013 CLD 1263; 2011 PLD 177; 2011 CLD 496; 2011 CLD 1018; 2011 CLD 1485; 2010 CLD 963; 2010 CLD 1737; 2009 CLD 497; 2009 CLD 1043; 2008 CLD 837; 2007 CLD 1614; 2006 CLD 967; 2006 CLD 1204; 2005 CLD 430; 2005 CLD 463; 2005 CLD 636; 2005 CLD 747; 2005 CLD 1670; 2004 CLD 640; 2004 CLD 1100; 2003 CLD 201; 2003 CLD 815; 2002 CLD 188; 2002 CLD 307; 2002 CLD 325; 2002 MLD 829; 2002 CLD 512; 2001 PLD 181; 2001 MLD 1708; 2000 CLC 364; 2000 CLC 477; 2000 PLD 83; 1998 CLC 1109; 1997 PLD 376; 1997 CLC 734; 1997 CLC 970; 1997 CLC 1075; 1997 CLC 1220; 1997 CLC 1921; 1996 PLD 543; 1996 CLC 1863; 1995 PLD 264; 1994 PLD 358; 1994 CLC 403; 1994 CLC 1763; 1994 CLC 2197; 1993 PLD 322; 1993 CLC 1413; 1993 CLC 1915; 1992 PLD 210; 1992 MLD 668; 1991 CLC 589; 1991 MLD 124; 1990 PLD 198; 1989 MLD 4338; 1988 PLD 1; 1988 PLD 446; 1987 CLC 577; 1987 CLC 1943; 1987 CLC 2079; 1987 CLC 2263

287. **Powers of Court under section 286.--** Without prejudice to the generality of the powers of the Court under section 286, an order under that section may provide for[1]--

    (a)   the termination, setting aside or modification of any agreement, however arrived at between the company and any director, including the chief executive or other officer, upon such terms and conditions as may, in the opinion of the Court be just and equitable in all the circumstances;

    (b)   setting aside of any transfer, delivery of goods, payment, execution or other transactions not relating to property made or done by or against the company within ninety days before the date of the application which would, if made or done by or against an individual, be deemed in his insolvency to be a fraudulent preference; and

    (c)   any other matter, including a change in management, for which in the opinion of the Court it is just and equitable that provision should be made.

288. **Interim order.--** Pending the making by it of a final order under section 286 the Court may, on the application of any party to the proceedings, make such interim order as it thinks fit for regulating the conduct of the company's affairs, upon such terms and conditions as appear to it to be just and equitable[2].

289. **Claim for damages inadmissible.--** Where an order of the Court made under section 286 terminates, sets aside, or modifies an arrangement, the order shall not give rise to any claim whatever against the company by any person for damages or for compensation for loss of office or in any other respect, either in pursuance of the agreement or otherwise[3].

290. **Application of certain sections to proceedings under this Part.-** In relation to an application under section 286, sections 395 to 400 shall *mutatis mutandis* apply as they apply in respect of winding up[4].

291. **Management by Administrator.--** (1) If at any time a creditor or creditors having interest equivalent in amount not less than sixty percent of the paid up capital of a company, represents or represent to the Commission that--

---

[1] 2019 CLD 355; 2017 LHC 2616; 2017 CLD 696; 2014 CLD 1683; 2013 CLD 114; 2005 CLD 747; 2003 CLD 815; 2002 CLD 307; 2000 PLD 83; 1994 PLD 358; 1989 MLD 4338; 1987 CLC 1943

[2] 2017 LHC 2616; 2002 CLD 307; 1996 PLD 543; 2016 CLD 970; 2013 CLD 114; 2013 CLD 1263; 2006 CLD 967; 2005 CLD 747; 2005 CLD 463; 2002 CLD 307; 2001 PLC 645; 2000 PLD 461; 1998 CLC 695; 1996 PLD 543; 1996 CLC 1926; 1994 PLD 358

[3] 2005 CLD 463; 1994 PLD 358

[4] 2005 CLD 463; 1994 PLD 358

(a)   the affairs or business of the company are or is being or have or has been conducted or managed in a manner likely to be prejudicial to the interest of the company, its members or creditors, or any director of the company or person concerned with the management of the company is or has been guilty of breach of trust, mis-feasance or other misconduct towards the company or towards any of its members or creditors or director;

(b)   the affairs or business of the company are or is being or have or has been conducted or managed with intent to defraud its members or creditors or any other person or for a fraudulent or unlawful purpose, or in a manner oppressive of any of such persons or for purposes as aforesaid; or

(c)   the affairs of the company have been so conducted or managed as to deprive the members thereof of a reasonable return; or

(d)   any industrial project or unit to be set up or belonging to the company has not been completed or has not commenced operations or has not been operating smoothly or its production or performance has so deteriorated that--

   (i)   the market value of its shares as quoted on the securities exchange or the net worth of its share has fallen by more than seventy-five per cent of its par value; or

   (ii)   debt equity ratio has deteriorated beyond 9:1; or

   (iii) current ratio has deteriorated beyond 5:1; or

(e)   any industrial unit owned by the company is not in operation for over a period of two years or has been in operation intermittently or partially during the preceding two years; or

(f)   the accumulated losses of the company exceed sixty percent of its paid up capital,

and request the Commission to take action under this section, the Commission may, after giving the company an opportunity of being heard, without prejudice to any other action that may be taken under this Act or any other law, by order in writing, appoint an Administrator, hereinafter referred to as the Administrator, within sixty days of the date of receipt of the representation, from a panel maintained by it on the recommendation of the State Bank of Pakistan to manage the affairs of the company subject to such terms and conditions as may be specified in the order:

Provided that the Commission may, if it considers it necessary so to do, for reasons to be recorded, or on the application of the creditors on whose representation it proposes to appoint the Administrator, and after giving a notice to the State Bank of Pakistan, appoint a person whose name does not appear on the panel maintained for the purpose to be the Administrator.

Explanation.--For the purposes of clause(c), the members shall be deemed to have been deprived of a reasonable return if, having regard to enterprises similarly placed, the company is unable to, or does not, declare any or adequate dividend for a period of three consecutive years.

(2)   The Administrator shall receive such remuneration as the Commission may determine.

(3) On and from the date of appointment of the Administrator, the management of the affairs of the company shall vest in him, and he shall exercise all the powers of the board or other persons in whom the management vested and all such directors and persons shall stand divested of that management and powers and shall cease to function or hold office.

(4) Where it appears to the Administrator that any purchase or sales agency contract has been entered into, or any employment given, patently to benefit any director or other person in whom the management vested or his nominees and to the detriment of the interest of the general members, the Administrator may, with the previous approval in writing of the Commission, terminate such contract or employment.

(5) No person shall be entitled to, or be paid, any compensation or damages for termination of any office, contract or employment under sub-section (3) or sub-section (4).

(6) If at any time it appears to the Commission that the purpose of the order appointing the Administrator has been fulfilled, it may permit the company to appoint directors and, on the appointment of directors, the Administrator shall cease to hold office.

(7) Save as provided in sub-section (8), no suit, prosecution or other legal proceeding shall lie against the Administrator for anything which is in good faith done or intended to be done by him in pursuance of this section or of any rules or regulations made thereunder.

(8) Any person aggrieved by an order of the Commission under sub-section (1) or sub-section (10), or of the Administrator under sub-section (4) may, within sixty days from the date of the order, appeal against such order to the concerned Minister-in-Charge of the Federal Government.

(9) If any person fails to deliver to the Administrator any property, records or documents relating to the company or does not furnish any information required by him or in any way obstructs the Administrator in the management, of the affairs of the company or acts for or represents the company in any way, the Commission may by order in writing, direct that such person shall be liable to a penalty of level 3 on the standard scale.

(10) The Commission may issue such directions to the Administrator as to his powers and duties as it deems desirable in the circumstances of the case, and the Administrator may apply to the Commission at any time for instructions as to the manner in which he shall conduct the management of the company or in relation to any matter arising in the course of such management.

(11) Any order or decision or direction of the Commission made in pursuance of this section shall be final and shall not be called in question in any Court.

(12) The Commission may, make regulations to carry out the purposes of this section.

(13) The provisions of this section shall have effect notwithstanding anything contained in any other provision of this Act or any other law or contract, or in the memorandum or articles of a company.

292. **Rehabilitation of sick public sector companies.--**(1) The provisions of this section shall apply to a public sector company which is facing financial or operational problems and is declared as a sick company by the concerned Minister-in-Charge of the Federal Government.

(2) After a company is declared as a sick company under sub-section (1), any institution, authority, committee or person authorised by the concerned Minister-in-Charge of the Federal Government in this behalf may draw up a plan for the rehabilitation, reconstruction and reorganisation of such company, hereafter in this section referred to as the rehabilitation plan.

(3) Without prejudice to the generality of the foregoing provision, the rehabilitation plan, may, in addition to any other matter, provide for all or any of the following--

(a) reduction of capital so as to provide for all or any of the matters referred to in section 89 or reconstruction, compromise, amalgamation and other arrangements so as to provide for all or any of the matters referred to in section 279 or section 282 or section 285;

(b) alteration of share capital and variation in the rights and obligations of shareholders or any class of shareholders;

(c) alteration of loan structure, debt rescheduling or conversion into shares carrying special rights or other relief and modification in the

(d) terms and conditions in respect of outstanding debts and liabilities of the company or any part of such loan, debts or liabilities or variation in the rights of the creditors or any class of them including any security pertaining thereto;

(e) acquisition or transfer of shares of the company on the specified terms and conditions;

(f) issue of further capital including shares carrying special rights and obligations relating to voting powers, dividend, redemption or treatment on winding up;

(g) removal and appointment of directors (including the chief executive) or other officers of the company;

(h) amendment, modification or cancellation of any existing contract; or

(i) alteration of the memorandum or articles or changes in the accounting policy and procedure.

(4) The rehabilitation plan shall be submitted for approval to the concerned Minister-in-Charge of the Federal Government which shall, unless it otherwise decides for reasons to be recorded, cause it to be published in the official Gazette for ascertaining the views of the shareholders, creditors and other persons concerned within a specified period.

(5) Before approving the rehabilitation plan, the concerned Minister-in-Charge of the Federal Government shall take into consideration the views relating thereto received from any quarter within the specified period.

(6) On the approval of the rehabilitation plan by the concerned Minister-in-Charge of the Federal Government, its provisions, with such modification as may be directed by the concerned Minister-in-Charge of the Federal Government, shall become final and take effect and be implemented and shall be valid, binding and enforceable in all respects notwithstanding anything in this Act or any other law or the memorandum or articles of the company or in any agreement or document executed by it or in any resolution passed by the company in general meeting or by its board, whether the same be registered, adopted, executed or passed, as the case may be, before or after the commencement of this Act.

(7) Any provision contained in the memorandum, articles, agreements, documents or resolutions as aforesaid shall, to the extent to which it is repugnant to the provisions of this Act or the rehabilitation plan, become void.

(8) No compensation or damages shall be payable to any one for any matter or arrangement provided for in, or action taken in pursuance of, the rehabilitation plan.

(9) The concerned Minister-in-Charge of the Federal Government may vary or rescind rehabilitation plan from time to time and issue such directions as to its implementation and matters ancillary thereto as it may deem expedient.

(10) The concerned Minister-in-Charge of the Federal Government or any authority or other person authorised by the concerned Minister-in-Charge of

the Federal Government in this behalf shall supervise the implementation of the rehabilitation plan and may issue such directions to the parties concerned as may be deemed necessary by such Government, authority or person, as the case may be.

(11) Whosoever fails to give effect, to carry out or implement the rehabilitation plan or any matter provided for therein or any direction issued under sub-section (10), shall be liable to imprisonment of either description for a term which may extend to three years and fine not exceeding five million rupees and, in case of a continuing failure, to a further fine not exceeding ten thousand rupees for every day after the first during which the failure or default continues.

(12) Until a rehabilitation plan has been approved by the concerned Minister-in-Charge of the Federal Government and is in operation, the provisions of this section shall not prejudice or affect the power or rights of a company or its shareholders or creditors to enter into, arrive at or make any compromise, arrangement or settlement in any manner authorised by this Act or any other law for the time being in force.

(13) The rehabilitation plan approved by the concerned Minister-in-Charge of the Federal Government and any modification thereof shall, unless otherwise directed by it, be published in the official Gazette and a copy thereof shall be forwarded by the concerned Minister-in-Charge of the Federal Government to the registrar who shall register and keep the same with the documents of the company.

(14) The Federal Government may, by notification in the official Gazette, make rules to carry out the purposes of this section.

(15) This section is in addition to and not in derogation of any other law regarding rehabilitation of any entity.

PART X

WINDING UP

PRELIMINARY

293. **Modes of winding up.**(1) The winding up of a company may be either[1]—

(a)   by the Court or

(b)   voluntary; or

(c)   subject to the supervision of the Court.

---

[1] 2012 CLD 1276; 2009 CLD 1662; 2007 PTD 1885; 2006 CLD 1347; 2000 SCMR 456; 1985 PLD 193; 1985 CLC 1223; 1983 SCMR 31

(2) Save as otherwise expressly provided, the provisions of this Act with respect to winding up shall apply to the winding up of a company in any of the modes specified in sub-section (1).

294. **Liability as contributories of present and past members.**—(1) In the event of a company being wound up, every present and past member shall, subject to the provisions of section 295, be liable to contribute to the assets of the company to an amount sufficient for payment of its debts and liabilities and the costs, charges and expenses of the winding up, and for the adjustment of the rights of the contributories among themselves[1], with the following qualifications, that is to say--

(a) a past member shall not be liable to contribute if he has ceased to be member for one year or upwards before the commencement of the winding up;

(b) a past member shall not be liable to contribute in respect of any debt or liability of the company contracted after he ceased to be a member;

(c) a past member shall not be liable to contribute unless it appears to the Court that the present members are unable to satisfy the contributions required to be made by them in pursuance of this Act;

(d) in the case of a company limited by shares, no contribution shall be required from any past or present member exceeding the amount, if any, unpaid on the shares in respect of which he is liable as such member;

(e) in the case of a company limited by guarantee, no contribution shall, subject to the provisions of sub-section (2), be required from any past or present member exceeding the amount undertaken to be contributed by him to the assets of the company in the event of its being wound up;

(f) nothing in this Act shall invalidate any provision contained in any policy of insurance or other contract whereby the liability of individual members on the policy or contract is restricted, or whereby the funds of the company are alone made liable in respect of the policy or contract; and

(g) a sum due to any past or present member of a company in his character as such, by way of dividends, profits or otherwise, shall

---

[1] 1985 PLD 193

(h)   not be deemed to be a debt of the company payable to that member in a case of competition between himself and any other creditor not being a member of the company, but any such sum may be taken into account for the purpose of the final adjustments of the rights of the contributories among themselves.

(2) In the winding up of a company limited by guarantee which has a share capital, every member of the company shall be liable, in addition to the amount undertaken to be contributed by him to the assets of the company in the event of its being wound up, to contribute to the extent of any sum unpaid on any shares held by him, as if the company were a company limited by shares.

295. **Liability of directors whose liability is unlimited.--** In the winding up of a limited company any director, whether past or present, whose liability is, in pursuance of this Act, unlimited, shall, in addition to his ability, if any, to contribute as an ordinary member, be liable to make a further contribution as if he were, at the commencement of the winding up, a member of an unlimited company[1]:

Provided that--

(a)   a past director shall not be liable to make such further contribution if he has ceased to hold office for a year or upwards before the commencement of the winding up;

(b)   a past director shall not be liable to make such further contribution in respect of any debtor liability of the company contracted after he ceased to hold office;

subject to the articles, a director shall not be liable to make such further contribution unless the Court deems it necessary to require that contribution in order to satisfy the debts and liabilities of the company, and the costs, charges and expenses of the winding up.

296. **Liability of Contributory having fully paid share.---.** A person holding fully paid-up shares in a company shall be considered as a contributory but shall have no liabilities of a contributory under this Act while retaining rights of such a contributory[2].

Explanation.— The term "**contributory**" means a person liable to contribute towards the assets of the company in the event of its being wound up.

297. **Nature of liability of contributory.--** The liability of a contributory shall create a debt accruing due from him at the time when his

[1] 1985 PLD 193; 1960 PLD 308

[2] 1985 PLD 193; 1984 PLD 541

liability commenced, but payable at the time specified in calls made on him for enforcing the liability[1].

298. **Contributories in case of death of member.--** If a contributory dies, whether before or after being placed on the list of contributories of a company[2]:

    (a)   his legal representatives shall be liable, in due course of administration, to contribute to the assets of the company in discharge of his liability, and shall be contributories accordingly; and

    (b)   if the legal representatives make default in paying any money ordered to be paid by them, proceedings may be initiated for administering the property of the deceased contributory, and of compelling payment of the money due, out of assets of the deceased.

299. **Contributory in case of insolvency of member.--** If a contributory is adjudged insolvent whether before or after he has been placed on the list of contributories of a company, then—

    (a)   his assignees in insolvency shall represent him for all the purposes of the winding up, and shall be contributories accordingly, and may be called on to admit to proof against the estate of the insolvent, or otherwise to allow to be paid out of his assets in due course of law, any money due from the insolvent in respect of his liability to contribute to the assets of the company; and

    (b)   there may be proved against the estate of the insolvent the estimated value of his liability to further calls as well as calls already made[3].

300. **Contributories in case of winding up of a body corporate which is a member.--** If a body corporate which is a contributory is ordered to be wound up, whether before or after it has been placed on the list of contributories of a company--

    (a)   the liquidator of the body corporate shall represent it for all purposes of the winding up of the company and shall be a contributory accordingly, and may be called on to admit to proof against the assets of the body corporate, or otherwise to allow to be paid out of its assets in due course of law, any money due from the body corporate in respect of its liability to contribute to the assets of the company; and

---

[1] 1985 PLD 193
[2] 1985 PLD 193
[3] 1985 PLD 193

(b) there may be proved against the assets of the body corporate the estimated value of its liability to future calls as well as calls already made.

WINDING UP BY COURT

301. **Circumstances in which a company may be wound up by Court.** A company may be wound up by the Court[1]--

(a) if the company has, by special resolution, resolved that the company be wound up by the Court; or

(b) if default is made in delivering the statutory report to the registrar or in holding the statutory meeting; or

(c) if default is made in holding any two consecutive annual general meetings[2]; or

(d) if the company has made a default in filing with the registrar its financial statements or annual returns for immediately preceding two consecutive financial years; or

(e) if the number of members is reduced, in the case of public company, below three and in the case of a private company below two; or

(f) if the company is unable to pay its debts; or

(g) if the company is—

(i) conceived or brought forth for, or is or has been carrying on, unlawful or fraudulent activities[3]; or

---

[1] 2019 SCMR 365; 2019 CLD 301; 2018 CLD 1478; 2018 SCMR 1860; 2017 CLD 1039; 2017 LHC 2616; 2016 CLD 52; 2016 CLD 393; 2015 CLD 203; 2013 CLD 818; 2013 CLD 1229; 2013 CLD 1735; 2010 PLD 23; 2010 CLD 180; 2008 CLD 411; 2006 CLD 776; 2006 CLD 852; 2005 CLD 151; 2005 CLD 897; 2005 CLD 1026; 2005 CLD 1291; 2004 CLD 1272; 2003 CLD 515; 2003 PLD 149; 2002 CLD 309; 2002 CLD 575; 2002 CLD 602; 2002 CLD 1048; 2002 PLD 1100; 2002 PLD 1111; 2002 CLD 1794; 2002 CLD 1781; 2002 SCMR 450; 2001 PTD 3146; 2000 PTCL 711; 2000 PLD 78; 2000 PLD 323; 1997 SCMR 1874; 1996 PLD 543; 1994 CLC 2202; 1989 CLC 1167; 1989 PLD 435; 1989 MLD 2963; 1988 SCMR 1717; 1988 CLC 866; 1988 SCMR 1027; 1988 MLD 301; 1988 MLD 1533; 1987 CLC 1876; 1987 CLC 2047; 1987 CLC 2263; 1986 CLC 2933; 1986 PLD 409; 1986 SCMR 1126; 1986 MLD 2983; 1986 SCMR 1612; 1986 MLD 2762; 1985 CLC 1239; 1985 PLD 193; 1984 CLC 3008; 1984 PLD 133; 1984 PLD 541; 1983 CLC 600; 1983 PLD 45; 1983 SCMR 31; 1982 CLC 1689; 1982 CLC 2137; 1982 PLD 94; 1982 PLD 103; 1982 CLC 1749; 1980 PLD 69; 1980 PLD 401; 1977 PLD 787; 1977 PLD 902; 1974 SCMR 15; 1973 PLD 60; 1973 PLD 326; 1973 PLD 491; 1972 PLD 376; 1971 PLD 598; 1970 SCMR 184; 1970 PLD 539; 1970 PLD 229; 1969 PLD 194; 1967 PLD 44; 1967 PLD 156; 1967 PLD 637; 1965 PLD 221; 1962 PLD 71; 1956 PLD 266; 1956 PLD 731; 1956 PLD 925

[2] 2008 CLD 465

[3] 2019 SCMR 365

    (ii)   carrying on business prohibited by any law for the time being in force in Pakistan; or restricted by any law, rules or regulations for the time being in force in Pakistan[1]; or

    (iii)   conducting its business in a manner oppressive to the minority members or persons concerned with the formation or promotion of the company; or

    (iv)   run and managed by persons who fail to maintain proper and true accounts, or commit fraud, misfeasance or malfeasance in relation to the company[2]; or

    (v)   managed by persons who refuse to act according to the requirements of the memorandum or articles or the provisions of this Act or failed to carry out the directions or decisions of the Commission or the registrar given in the exercise of powers under this Act[3]; or

(h)   if, being a listed company, it ceases to be such company; or

(i)   if the Court is of opinion that it is just and equitable that the company should be wound up; or

(j)   if a company ceases to have a member; or

(k)   if the sole business of the company is the licensed activity and it ceases to operate consequent upon revocation of a licence granted by the Commission or any other licencing authority; or

(l)   if a licence granted under section 42 to a company has been revoked or such a company has failed to comply with any of the provisions of section 43 or where a company licenced under section 42 is being wound up voluntarily and its liquidator has failed to complete the winding up proceedings within a period of one year from the date of commencement of its winding up; or

(m)   if a listed company suspends its business for a whole year[4].

Explanation I.-- The promotion or the carrying on of any scheme or business, howsoever described--

    (a)   whereby, in return for a deposit or contribution, whether periodically or otherwise, of a sum of money in cash or by means of coupons, certificates, tickets or other documents, payment, at future date or dates of money or grant of property, right or benefit, directly or indirectly, and whether with or without any other right

---

[1] 2019 SCMR 365
[2] 2019 SCMR 365
[3] 2019 SCMR 365
[4] 2002 CLD 166

(b)   or benefit, determined by chance or lottery or any other like manner, is assured or promised; or

(c)   raising unauthorised deposits from the general public, indulging in referral marketing, multi-level marketing (MLM), Pyramid and Ponzi Schemes, locally or internationally, directly or indirectly; or

(d)   any other business activity notified by the Commission to be against public policy or a moral hazard;

shall be deemed to be an unlawful activity.

Explanation II.--"Minority members" means members together holding not less than ten percent of the equity share capital of the company.

302. **Company when deemed unable to pay its debts.--** (1) A company shall be deemed to be unable to pay its debts[1]--

(a)   if a creditor, by assignment or otherwise, to whom the company is indebted in a sum exceeding one hundred thousand rupees, then due, has served on the company, by causing the same to be delivered by registered post or otherwise, at its registered office, a demand under his hand requiring the company to pay the sum so due and the company has for thirty days thereafter neglected to pay the sum, or to secure or compound for it to the reasonable satisfaction of the creditor[2]; or

(b)   if execution or other process issued on a decree or order of any Court or any other competent authority in favour of a creditor of the company is returned unsatisfied in whole or in part; or

(c)   if it is proved to the satisfaction of the Court that the company is unable to pay its debts, and, in determining whether a company is unable to pay its debts, the Court shall take into account the contingent and prospective liabilities of the company.

(2) The demand referred to in clause (a) of sub-section (1) shall be deemed to have been duly given under the hand of the creditor if it is signed by an agent or legal adviser duly authorised on his behalf.

303.   **Transfer of proceedings to other Courts.--** Where the Court makes an order for winding up a company under this Act, it may, if it thinks fit, direct all subsequent proceedings to be held in any other High Court, with the consent of such court and thereupon, for the purposes of the winding up of the

---

[1] 2019 CLD 301; 2018 SCMR 1860; 2016 CLD 52; 1994 CLC 2202; 2004 CLD 449; 2001 PTD 3146; 1989 PLD 435; 1989 MLD 2963; 1986 PLD 409; 1986 MLD 2762; 1986 SCMR 1126; 1985 PLD 193; 1984 PLD 133; 1983 CLC 600; 1983 SCMR 31; 1982 CLC 1749; 1982 PLD 103; 1982 CLC 1689; 1977 PLD 787; 1973 PLD 326; 1970 PLD 235; 1969 PLD 194; 1967 PLD 156
[2] 2002 SCMR 450; 2000 PLD 323

company, such Court shall be deemed to be the "Court" within the meaning of this Act and shall have all the powers and jurisdiction of the Court thereunder[1].

PETITION FOR WINDING UP

304.   **Provisions as to applications for winding up.--** An application to the Court for the winding up of a company shall be by petition presented, subject to the provisions of this section, either by the company, or by any creditor or creditors (including any contingent or prospective creditor or creditors), or by any contributory or contributories, or by all or any of the aforesaid parties, together or separately or by the registrar, or by the Commission or by a person authorised by the Commission in that behalf[2]:

Provided that--

(a)   a contributory shall not be entitled to present a petition for winding up a company unless-

(i)   either the number of members is reduced, in the case of a private company, below two, or, in the case of public company, below three; and

(ii)   the shares in respect of which he is a contributory or some of them either were originally allotted to him or have been held by him, and registered in his name, for at least one hundred and eighty days during the eighteen months before the commencement of the winding up, or have or devolved on him through the death of a former holder;

(b)   the registrar shall not be entitled to present a petition for the winding up of a company unless the previous sanction of the Commission has been obtained to the presentation of the petition[3]:

Provided that no such sanction shall be given unless the company has first been afforded an opportunity of making a representation and of being heard;

(c)   the Commission or a person authorised by the Commission in that behalf shall not be entitled to present a petition for the winding up of a company unless an investigation into the affairs of the company has revealed that it was formed for any fraudulent or unlawful purpose or that it is carrying on a business not authorised by its memorandum or that its business is being conducted in a

[1] 2002 CLD 575
[2] 2019 CLD 301; 2019 CLD 72; 2018 CLD 1237; 2018 SCMR 1860; 2017 CLD 1039; 2012 CLD 1525; 2006 CLD 852; 2005 CLD 49; 2003 CLD 515; 2002 CLD 1781; 2002 CLD 602; 2001 CLC 1267; 2000 PLD 78; 1988 CLC 866; 1986 MLD 2983; 1986 PLD 409; 1986 CLC 2933; 1986 MLD 2762; 1985 PLD 193; 1982 PLD 94; 1977 PLD 787; 1967 PLD 44; 1967 PLD 44; 1965 PLD 221
[3] 2019 SCMR 365; 2019 CLD 294

(d)   manner oppressive to any of its members or persons concerned in the formation of the company or that its management has been guilty of fraud, mis-feasance or other misconduct towards the company or towards any of its members; and such petition shall not be presented or authorised to be presented by the Commission

(e)   unless the company has been afforded an opportunity of making a representation and of being heard[1]:

Provided that if sole business of the company is the licensed activity and that licence is revoked, no investigation into the affairs of the company shall be required to present the petition for winding up of the company;

(d)   the Court shall not give a hearing to a petition for winding up a company by a contingent or prospective creditor until such security for costs has been given as the Court thinks reasonable and until a *prima facie* case for winding up has been established to the satisfaction of the Court[2];

(e)   the Court shall not give a hearing to a petition for winding up a company by the company until the company has furnished with its petition, in the prescribed manner, the particulars of its assets and liabilities and business operations and the suits or proceedings pending against it.

305.   **Right to present winding up petition where company is being wound up voluntarily or subject to Court's supervision.--** (1) Where a company is being wound up voluntarily or subject to the supervision of the Court, a petition for its winding up by the Court may be presented by any person authorised to do so under section 304 and subject to the provisions of that section.

(2) The Court shall not make a winding up order on a petition presented to it under sub-section (1) unless it is satisfied that the voluntary winding up or winding up subject to the supervision of the Court cannot be continued with due regard to the interests of the creditors or contributories or both or it is in the public interest so to do[3].

306.   **Commencement of winding up by Court.--** A winding up of a company by the Court shall be deemed to commence at the time of the presentation of the petition for the winding up[4].

---

[1] 2019 SCMR 365; 2019 CLD 294
[2] 2017 LHC 2616
[3] 2019 CLD 72
[4] 1993 PLD 404; 1986 PLD 18; 1986 MLD 613; 1985 PLD 193; 1981 PLD 322

POWERS OF COURT HEARING APPLICATION

307. **Court may grant injunction.--** The Court may, at any time after presentation of the petition for winding up a company under this Act, and before making an order for its winding up, upon the application of the company itself or of any its creditors or contributories, restrain further proceedings in any suit or proceeding against the company, upon such terms as the Court thinks fit[1].

308. **Powers of Court on hearing petition.--** (1) The Court may, on receipt of a petition for winding up under section 304 pass any of the following orders[2], namely--

(a)   dismiss it, with or without costs;

(b)   make any interim order as it thinks fit;

(c)   appoint a provisional manager of the company till the making of a winding up order;

(d)   make an order for the winding up of the company with or without costs; or

(e)   any other order as it thinks fit:

Provided that an order under this sub-section shall be made within ninety days from the date of presentation of the petition:

Provided further that before appointing a provisional manager under clause (c), the Court shall give notice to the company and afford a reasonable opportunity to it to make its representations, if any, unless for special reasons to be recorded in writing, the Court thinks fit to dispense with such notice:

Provided also that the Court shall not refuse to make a winding up order on the ground only that the assets of the company have been mortgaged for an amount equal to or in excess of those assets, or that the company has no assets.

(2) Where a petition is presented on the ground that it is just and equitable that the company should be wound up, the Court may refuse to make an order of winding up, if it is of the opinion that some other remedy is available to the petitioners and that they are acting unreasonably in seeking to have the company wound up instead of pursuing the other remedy.

(3) Where the Court makes an order for the winding up of a company, it shall forthwith cause intimation thereof to be sent to the official liquidator appointed by it and to the registrar.

309. **Copy of winding up order to be filed with registrar.--** (1) Within fifteen days from the date of the making of the winding up order, the

---

[1] 1993 PLD 404; 1986 PLD 18; 1985 PLD 193

[2] 2018 SCMR 1860; 1993 PLD 404; 1985 PLD 193; 1983 PLD 45; 1982 PLD 634; 1968 PLD 231

petitioner in the winding up proceedings and the company shall file a certified copy of the order with the registrar[1].

(2) If default is made in complying with the foregoing provision, the petitioner or, as the case may require, the company, and every officer of the company who is in default, shall be liable to a penalty of level 1 on the standard scale.

(3) On the filing of a certified copy of a winding up order, the registrar shall forthwith make a minute thereof in his books relating to the company, and shall simultaneously notify in the official Gazette that such an order has been made.

(4) Such order shall be deemed to be notice of discharge to the employees of the company, except when the business of the company is continued.

310. **Suits stayed on winding up order.--** (1) When a winding up order has been made or a provisional manager has been appointed, no suit or other legal proceeding shall be proceeded with or commenced against the company except by leave of the Court, and subject to such terms as the Court may impose[2].

(2) The Court which is winding up the company shall, notwithstanding anything contained in any other law for the time being in force, have jurisdiction to entertain, or dispose of, any suit or proceeding by or against the company[3].

(3) Any suit or proceeding by or against the company which is pending in any court other than that in which the winding up of the company is proceeding may, notwithstanding anything contained in any other law for the time being in force, be transferred to and disposed of by the Court.

311. **Court may require expeditious disposal of suits.**(1) Notwithstanding anything contained in any other law--

(a) If any suit or proceedings, including an appeal, by or against the company which is allowed to be proceeded with in any Court other than the Court in which winding up of the company is proceeding, the Court may issue directions to that other Court if that Court is subordinate to it and, in any other case, make a request to that other Court for expeditious disposal of the pending suit or proceedings by or against the company; and

---

[1] 1985 PLD 193; 1984 PLD 541

[2] 2016 SCMR 816; 1993 PLD 404; 1987 CLC 1876; 1986 PLD 18; 1985 PLD 193; 1983 CLC 460; 1982 PLD 810; 1982 CLC 2462; 1981 PLD 322; 1980 PLD 86; 1972 PLD 287; 1965 PLD 418; 1964 PLD 326

[3] 2009 CLD 609

(b)   If any proceedings, including proceedings for assessment or recovery of any tax, duty or levies or appeal or review petitions against any order is pending or is likely to be instituted, before any officer, authority or other body, the Court may issue directions to that officer, authority or other body for expeditious action and disposal of the said proceedings.

(2) Upon issue of a direction or making of a request as aforesaid, the Court, officer, authority or body to whom the same is addressed shall, notwithstanding anything contained in any other law, proceed to dispose of the said suit or other proceedings expeditiously by according it special priority and adopting such measures as may be necessary in this behalf, and shall inform the Court issuing the direction or making the request of the action taken.

312.   **Effect of winding up order.--**An order for winding up a company shall operate in favour of all the creditors and of all contributories of the company as if made on the joint petition of a creditor and of a contributory[1].

313.   **Power of Court to stay winding up.--**(1) The Court may at any time not later than three years after an order for winding up, on the application of any creditor or contributory or of the registrar or the Commission or a person authorised by it, and on proof to the satisfaction of the Court that all proceedings in relation to the winding up ought to be stayed, withdrawn, cancelled or revoked, make an order accordingly, on such terms and conditions as the Court thinks fit[2].

(2) On any application under sub-section (1), the Court may, before making an order, require the official liquidator to furnish to the Court a report with respect to any facts or matters which are in his opinion relevant to the application.

(3) A copy of every order made under sub-section (1) shall forthwith be forwarded by the Court to the registrar, who shall make a minute of the order in his books relating to the company.

314.   **Court may ascertain wishes of creditors or contributories.--** (1) In all matters relating to the winding up of a company, the Court may[3]--

(a)   have regard to the wishes of creditors or contributories of the company, as proved to it by any sufficient evidence in a manner as provided under this Act;

---

[1] 2011 CLC 1078; 1985 PLD 193

[2] 2013 CLD 34; 2006 CLD 852; 2005 CLD 713

[3] 1985 PLD 193; 1982 PLD 1; 1976 PLD 1538; 1970 PLD 229; 1957 PLD 844

(b) if it thinks fit for the purpose of ascertaining their wishes, order meetings of the creditors or contributories to be called, held and conducted in such manner as may be directed; and

(c) appoint a person to act as chairman of any such meeting and to submit a report in this regard.

(2) While ascertaining the wishes of creditors or contributories under sub-section (1), regard shall be had to the value of each debt of the creditor or the voting power exercised by each contributory, as the case may be.

OFFICIAL LIQUIDATORS

315. **Appointment of official liquidator.—** (1) For the purpose of the winding up of companies by the Court, the Commission shall maintain a panel of persons from whom the Court shall appoint a provisional manager or official liquidator of a company ordered to be wound up[1].

(2) A person shall not be appointed as provisional manager or official liquidator of more than three companies at one point of time.

(3) The panel for the purpose of sub-section (1) shall consist of persons having at least ten years experience in the field of accounting, finance or law and as may be specified by the Commission such other persons, having at least ten years professional experience.

(4) Where a provisional manager is appointed by the Court, the Court may limit and restrict his powers by the order appointing him or by a subsequent order, but otherwise he shall have the same powers as a liquidator.

(5) On appointment as provisional manager or official liquidator, as the case may be, such liquidator shall file a declaration within seven days from the date of appointment in the specified form disclosing conflict of interest or lack of independence in respect of his appointment, if any, with the Court and such obligation shall continue throughout the term of his appointment.

(6) While passing a winding up order, the Court may appoint a provisional manager, if any, under clause (c) of sub-section (1) of section 308, as the official liquidator for the conduct of the proceedings for the winding up of the company.

(7) If more persons than one are appointed to the office of official liquidator, the Court shall declare whether any act by this Act required or authorised to be done by the official liquidator is to be done by all or any one or more of such persons:

---

[1] 2019 CLD 72; 1985 CLC 2176; 1985 CLC 2778; 1985 SCMR 925; 1985 PLD 193; 1979 SCMR 10; 1976 PLD 1538; 1973 PLD 60; 1973 PLD 491; 1970 PLD 235; 1970 PLD 539; 1969 PLD 194; 1967 PLD 44; 1957 PLD 844

Provided that in case of any dispute or any varying stance amongst the liquidators, the matter shall be referred to the Court for an appropriate order in chambers in the presence of the parties concerned.

(8) The Court may determine whether any, and what, security is to be given by any official liquidator on his appointment.

(9) Notwithstanding anything contained in sub-section (1), the Court may, on the application of creditors to whom amounts not less than sixty percent of the issued share-capital of the company being wound up are due, after notice to the registrar, appoint a person whose name does not appear on the panel maintained for the purpose, to be the official liquidator.

(10) An official liquidator shall not resign or quit his office before conclusion of the liquidation proceedings except for reasons of personal disability to the satisfaction of the Court.

(11) Any casual vacancy in the office of an official liquidator occurred due to his death, removal or resignation, shall be filled up by the Court by the appointment of another person from the panel maintained under sub-section (1):

Provided that in case of resignation, the outgoing official liquidator shall, unless the Court directs otherwise, continue to act until the person appointed in his place takes charge.

(12) The Commission may of its own, remove the name of any person from the panel maintained under sub-section (1) on the grounds of misconduct, fraud, misfeasance, breach of duties or professional incompetence:

Provided that the Commission before removing him from the panel shall give him a reasonable opportunity of being heard.

(13) The person appointed on the panel under this section shall be subject to such code of conduct and comply with the requirement of any professional accreditation programs as may be specified by the Commission.

316. **Removal of official liquidator.--** (1) The Court may, on a reasonable cause being shown including but not limited to lack of independence or lack of impartiality, remove the provisional manager or the official liquidator[1], as the case may be, on any of the following grounds, namely:—

(a)   misconduct;

(b)   fraud or misfeasance;

(c)   professional incompetence or failure to exercise due care and diligence in performance of the powers and functions;

(d)   inability to act as provisional manager or official liquidator, as the case may be;

---

[1] 1986 MLD 823; 1985 SCMR 925; 1985 PLD 193

(e) conflict of interest during the term of his appointment that will justify removal.

(2) Where the Court is of the opinion that any liquidator is responsible for causing any loss or damage to the company due to fraud or misfeasance or failure to exercise due care and diligence in the performance of his powers and functions, the Court may recover or cause to be recovered such loss or damage from the provisional manager or official liquidator, as the case may be, and pass such other orders as it may think fit.

317. **Remuneration of official liquidator.--** (1) The terms and conditions of appointment of a provisional manager or official liquidator and the fee payable to him shall be fixed by the Court on the basis of task required to be performed, experience, qualification of such liquidator and size of the company.

(2) An official liquidator, shall also be entitled to such remuneration by way of percentage of the amount realised by him by disposal of assets as may be fixed by the Court having regard to the amount and nature of the work actually done and subject to such limits as may be prescribed:

Provided that different percentage rates may be fixed for different types of assets and items.

(3) In addition to the remuneration payable under sub-section (2), the Court may permit payment of a monthly allowance to the official liquidator for meeting the expenses of the winding up for a period not exceeding one year from the date of the winding up order.

(4) The remuneration fixed as aforesaid shall not be enhanced subsequently but may be reduced by the Court at any time.

(5) If the official liquidator resigns, is removed from office or otherwise ceases to hold office before conclusion of the winding up proceedings, he shall not be entitled to any remuneration and the remuneration already received by him, if any, shall be refunded by him to the company.

(6) No remuneration shall be payable to official liquidator who fails to complete the winding up proceedings within the prescribed period or such extended time as may be allowed by the Court.

318. **Style and title of official liquidator.--** The official liquidator shall be described by the style of "the official liquidator" of the particular company in respect of which he acts, and in no case he shall be described by his individual name.

319. **General provisions as to liquidators.--** (1) The official liquidator shall conduct the proceedings in winding up the company and perform such duties in reference thereto as the Court may impose.

(2) The acts of a liquidator shall be valid, notwithstanding any defect that may afterwards be discovered in his appointment or qualification:

Provided that nothing in this sub-section shall be deemed to give validity to acts done by a liquidator after his appointment has been shown to be invalid.

(3) The winding up proceedings shall be completed by the official liquidator within a period as determined by the Court under section 322.

(4) If an official liquidator is convicted of misfeasance, or breach of duty or other lapse or default in relation to winding up proceedings of a company, he shall cease to be the official liquidator of the company and shall also become disqualified, for a period of five years from such conviction, from being the liquidator or to hold any other office including that of a director, in any company and if he already holds any such office he shall forthwith be deemed to have ceased to hold such office.

(5) The registrar or the Commission shall take cognizance of any lapse, delay or other irregularity on the part of the official liquidator and may, without prejudice to any other action under the law, report the same to the Court.

320. **Statement of affairs to be made to official liquidator.--** (1) Where the Court has appointed a provisional manager or made a winding up order and appointed an official liquidator, there shall be made out and submitted to the provisional manager or official liquidator, a statement as to the affairs of the company in the prescribed form, verified by an affidavit, and containing the following particulars, namely--

(a)   particulars of the company's assets, debts and liabilities;

(b)   the detail of cash balance in hand and at the bank;

(c)   the names and addresses of the company's creditors stating separately the amount of secured debts and unsecured debts, and, in the case of secured debts, particulars of the securities given, their value and the dates when they were given.

(d)   the names, residential addresses and occupations of the persons from whom debts of the company are due and the amount likely to be realised therefrom;

(e)   where any property of the company is not in its custody or possession, the place where and the person in whose custody or possession such property is;

(f)   full address of the places where the business of the company was conducted during the one hundred and eighty days preceding the relevant date and the names and particulars of the persons incharge of the same;

(g)   details of any pending suits or proceedings in which the company is a party; and

(h)   such other particulars as may be prescribed or as the Court may order or the provisional manager or official liquidator may require in writing, including any information relating to secret reserves and personal assets of directors.

(2) The statement shall be submitted and verified by persons who are at the relevant date the directors, chief executive, chief financial officer and secretary of the company.

(3) The provisional manager or official liquidator, subject to the direction of the Court, may also require to make out and submit to him a

(4) statement in the prescribed form as to the affairs of the company by some or all of the persons--

(a)   who have been directors, chief executives, chief financial officer, secretary or other officers of the company within one year from the relevant date;

(b)   who have taken part in the formation of the company at any time within one year before the relevant date;

(c)   who are in the employment of the company, or have been in the employment of the company within the said year, and are in the opinion of the official liquidator or provisional manager capable of giving the information required and to whom the statement relates;

(5) The statement shall be submitted within fifteen days from the relevant date, or within such extended time not exceeding forty-five days from that date as the official liquidator or provisional manager or the Court may, for special reasons, appoint.

(6) Any person making the statement required by this section shall be entitled to and be paid by the official liquidator or the provisional manager, as the case may be, the reasonable expenses incurred in preparation of such statement.

(7) Any contravention or default in complying with requirements of this section shall be an offence liable to a daily penalty of level 2 on the standard scale.

(8) Without prejudice to the operation of any provisions imposing penalties in respect of any such default as aforesaid, the Court which makes the winding up order or appoints a provisional manager may take cognizance of an offence under sub-section (6) and try the offence itself in accordance with the procedure laid down in the Code of Criminal Procedure, 1898 (Act V of 1898), for the trial of cases by Magistrates and further direct the persons concerned to

comply with the provisions of this section within such times as may be specified by it.

(9) Any person stating himself in writing to be a creditor or contributory of the company shall be entitled, by himself or by his agent, at all reasonable times, on payment of the prescribed fee, to inspect the statement submitted in pursuance of this section, and to a copy thereof or extract therefrom.

(10) Any person untruthfully so stating himself to be a creditor or contributory shall be guilty of an offence under section 182 of the Pakistan Penal Code, 1860 (Act XLV of 1860), and shall, on the application of the official liquidator or provisional manager, be punishable accordingly.

(11) In this section, the expression "**the relevant date**" means, in a case where a provisional manager is appointed, the date of his appointment, and, in a case where no such appointment is made, the date of the winding up order.

321. **Report by official liquidator.**-- (1) Where the Court has made a winding up order and appointed an official liquidator, such liquidator shall, as soon as practicable after receipt of the statement to be submitted under section 320 and not later than sixty days, from the date of the winding up order submit a report to the Court, containing the following particulars, namely.—

(a) the nature and details of the assets of the company including their location and current value duly ascertained by a registered valuer;

(b) the cash balance in hand and in the bank, if any, and the negotiable securities, if any, held by the company;

(c) the amount of authorised and paid up capital;

(d) the existing and contingent liabilities of the company indicating particulars of the creditors, stating separately the amount of secured and unsecured debts, and in the case of secured debts, particulars of the securities given;

(e) the debts due to the company and the names, addresses and occupations of the persons from whom they are due and the amount likely to be realised on account thereof;

(f) debts due from contributories;

(g) details of trademarks and intellectual properties, if any, owned by the company;

(h) details of subsisting contracts, joint ventures and collaborations, if any;

(i) details of holding and subsidiary companies, if any;

(j) details of legal cases filed by or against the company;

(k)   any other information which the Court may direct or the official liquidator may consider necessary to include.

(2)   The official liquidator shall also include in his report the manner in which the company was promoted or formed and whether in his opinion any fraud has been committed by any person in its promotion or formation, or by any director or other officer of the company in relation to the company since its formation.

(3) The official liquidator shall also make a report on the viability of the business of the company or the steps which, in his opinion, are necessary for maximising the value of the assets of the company.

(4) The official liquidator may also, if he thinks fit or upon directions of the Court, make any further report or reports.

(5)   A certified copy of the reports aforesaid shall also be sent to the registrar simultaneously with their submission to the Court .

322.   **Court directions on report of official liquidator**.-- (1) The Court shall, on consideration of the report of the official liquidator, fix a time limit within which the entire proceedings shall be completed and the company be dissolved:

Provided that the Court may, if it is of the opinion, at any stage of the proceedings, or on examination of the reports submitted to it by the official liquidator and after hearing the official liquidator, creditors or contributories or any other interested person, that it will not be advantageous or economical to continue the proceedings, revise the time limit within which the entire proceedings shall be completed and the company be dissolved.

(2) The Court may, on examination of the reports submitted to it by the official liquidator and after hearing the official liquidator, creditors or contributories or any other interested person, order sale of the company as a going concern or its assets or part thereof:

Provided that the Court may where it considers fit, appoint a sale committee comprising such creditors, promoters and officers of the company as the Court may decide to assist the official liquidator in sale under this sub-section.

(3) Where a report is received from the official liquidator or the Commission or any person that a fraud has been committed in respect of the company, the Court shall, without prejudice to the process of winding up, order for investigation under section 257, and on consideration of the report of such investigation it may pass order and give directions under sections 391 or 392 or direct the official liquidator to file a criminal complaint against persons who were involved in the commission of fraud.

(4) The Court may order for taking such steps and measures, as may be necessary, to protect, preserve or enhance the value of the assets of the company.

(5) The Court may pass such other order or give such other directions as it considers fit.

323. **Settlement of list of contributories and application of assets.--** (1) As soon as may be after making a winding up order, the Court shall settle a list of contributories, with power to rectify the register of members and shall cause the assets of the company to be collected and applied in discharge of its liabilities[1]:

Provided that, where it appears to the Court that it will not be necessary to make calls on or adjust the rights of contributories, the Court may dispense with the settlement of a list of contributories.

(2) In settling the list of contributories, the Court shall distinguish between persons who are contributories in their own right and persons who are contributories as being representatives of, or liable for the debts of, others.

324. **Custody of company's properties.--** (1) Where a winding up order has been made or where a provisional manager has been appointed, the official liquidator or the provisional manager, as the case may be, shall, on the order of the Court, forthwith take into his custody or control all the property, effects and actionable claims to which the company is or appears to be entitled to and take such steps and measures, as may be necessary, to protect and preserve the properties of the company[2].

(2) On an application by the official liquidator or otherwise, the Court may, at any time after the making of a winding up order, require any contributory for the time being on the list of contributories, and any trustee, receiver, banker, agent, officer or other employee of the company, to pay, deliver, surrender or transfer forthwith, or within such time as the Court directs, to the official liquidator, any money, property or books and papers in his custody or under his control to which the company is or appears to be entitled.

(3) The promoters, directors, officers and employees, who are or have been in employment of the company or acting or associated with the company shall extend full cooperation to the official liquidator in discharge of his functions and duties.

(4) Notwithstanding anything contained in sub-section (1), all the property and effects of the company shall be deemed to be in the custody of the Court from the date of the appointment of the Provisional manager or the passing of order for the winding up of the company as the case may be.

---

[1] 1985 PLD 193
[2] 1985 PLD 193; 1984 PLD 415; 1982 PLD 810

(5) Where any person, without reasonable cause, fails to discharge his obligations under sub-sections (2) or (3), he shall be punishable with imprisonment which may extend to two years or with fine which may extend to five hundred thousand rupees, or with both.

325. **Power to require delivery of property.--** Without prejudice to the obligation imposed under any other provisions, the Court may, at any time after making a winding up order, require any contributory for the time being on the list of contributories and any trustee, receiver, banker, agent, officer or employee or past officer or employee or auditor of the company to pay, deliver, convey, surrender or transfer forthwith, or within, such time as the Court directs, to the official liquidator any money, property or books and papers including documents in his hands to which the company is *prima facie* entitled[1].

326. **Power to summon persons suspected of having property of company.--** (1) The Court may, at any time after the appointment of a provisional manager or the making of winding up order, summon before it any officer of the company or person known or suspected to have in his possession any property or books or papers of the company, or known or suspected to be indebted to the company, or any person whom the Court deems capable of giving information concerning the promotion, formation, trade, dealings, books or papers, affairs or property of the company[2].

(2) The Court may examine a person summoned under sub-section (1) on oath concerning the matters aforesaid, either by word of mouth or on written interrogatories, and may reduce his answers to writing and require him to sign them.

(3) The Court may require a person summoned under sub-section (1) to produce any books and papers in his custody or power relating to the company, but, where he claims any lien on books or papers produced by him, the production shall be without prejudice to that lien, and the Court shall have jurisdiction in the winding up to determine all questions relating to that lien.

(4) If any person so summoned, after being paid or tendered a reasonable sum for his expenses, fails to come before the Court at the time appointed, not having a lawful impediment made known to the Court at the time of its sitting and allowed by it, the Court may cause him to be apprehended and brought before the Court for examination.

(5) If, on his examination, any officer or person so summoned admits that he is indebted to the company, the Court may order him to pay to the provisional manager or, as the case may be, the liquidator, at such time and in such manner as the Court may direct, the amount in which he is indebted, or any

---

[1] 1985 PLD 193; 1972 PLD 41; 1964 PLD 639; 1953 PLD 375
[2] 1985 PLD 193

part thereof, either in full discharge of the whole amount or not, as the Court thinks fit, with or without costs of the examination.

(6) If, on his examination, any such officer or person admits that he has in his possession any property belonging to the company, the Court may order him to deliver to the provisional manager or, as the case may be, the liquidator that property or any part thereof, at such time, in such manner and on such terms as the Court may direct.

(7) Orders made under sub-sections (5) and (6) shall be executed in the same manner as decrees for the payment of money or for the delivery of property under the Code of Civil Procedure, 1908 (Act V of 1908), respectively.

(8) Any person making any payment or delivery in pursuance of an order made under sub-section (5) or sub-section (6) shall by such payment or delivery be, unless otherwise directed by such order, discharged from all liability whatsoever in respect of such debt or property.

327. **Power to order public examination of promoters, directors.--** (1) When an order has been made for winding up a company by the Court, and the official liquidator has made a report to the Court stating that in his opinion a fraud or other actionable irregularity has been committed by any person in the promotion or formation of the company or by any director or other officer of the company in relation to the company since its formation, the Court may, after consideration of the report, direct that such person, director or other officer shall attend before the Court on a day appointed by the Court for that purpose, and be publicly examined as to the promotion or formation or the conduct of the business of the company, or as to his conduct and dealings as director, manager or other officer thereof[1].

(2) The official liquidator shall take part in the examination, and for that purpose may, if specially authorised by the Court in that behalf, employ such legal assistance as may be sanctioned by the Court.

(3) Any creditor or contributory may also take part in the examination either personally or by any person entitled to appear before the Court.

(4) The Court may put such questions to the person examined as the Court thinks fit.

(5) The person examined shall be examined on oath, and shall answer all such questions as the Court may put or allow to be put to him.

(6) A person ordered to be examined under this section--

(a)   shall, before his examination, be furnished at his own cost with a copy of the official liquidator's report; and

---

[1] 1987 PLD 618; 1985 PLD 193

(b)   may at his own cost employ any person entitled to appear before the Court, who shall be at liberty to put to him such questions as the Court may deem just for the purpose of enabling him to explain or qualify any answer given by him:

Provided that if he is, in the opinion of the Court, exculpated from any charges made or suggested against him, the Court may allow him such costs as in its discretion it may think fit.

(7) If any such person applies to the Court to be exculpated from any charges made or suggested against him, it shall be the duty of the official liquidator to appear on the hearing of the application and call the attention of the Court to any matters which appear to the official liquidator to be relevant, and if the Court, after hearing any evidence given or witnesses called by the official liquidator, grants the application, the Court may allow the applicant such costs as it may think fit.

(8) Notes of the examination shall be taken down in writing and shall be read over to or by, and signed by, the person examined, and may thereafter be used in evidence against him and shall be open to the inspection of any creditor or contributory at all reasonable times.

(9) The Court may, if it thinks fit, adjourn the examination from time to time.

(10) An examination under this section may, if the Court so directs, and subject to any rules in this behalf, be held before any officer of the Court, being an official referee, registrar, additional registrar or deputy registrar.

(11) The powers of the Court under this section as to the conduct of the examination, but not as to costs may be exercised by the person before whom the examination is held by virtue of a direction under sub-section (10).

328. **Power to arrest absconding contributory.--** The Court, at any time either before or after making a winding up order, on proof of probable cause for believing that a contributory is about to quit Pakistan or otherwise to abscond, or to remove or conceal any of his property, for the purpose of evading payment of calls or of avoiding examination respecting the affairs of the company, may cause the contributory to be arrested and his books and papers and movable property to be seized, and kept safely until such time as the Court may order[1].

329. **Power to order payment of debts by contributory.--** (1) The Court may, at any time after making a winding up order, make an order on any contributory for the time being settled on the list of contributories to pay, in a manner directed by the order, any money due from him or from the estate of the

---

[1] 1986 PCrLJ 335; 1985 PLD 193

person whom he represents to the company, exclusive of any money payable by him or the estate by virtue of any call in pursuance of this Act[1].

(2) The Court in making such an order may--

(a) in the case of an unlimited company, allow the contributory by way of set-off, any money due to him or to the estate which he represents from the company on any independent dealing or contract with the company, but not any money due to him as a member of the company in respect of any dividend or profit; and

(b) in the case of a limited company, make to any director whose liability is unlimited or to his estate the like allowance.

(3) In the case of any company, whether limited or unlimited, when all the creditors are paid in full, any money due on any account whatever to a contributory from the company may be allowed to him by way of set-off against any subsequent call.

330. **Power of Court to make calls.--** (1) The Court may, at any time after making a winding up order, and either before or after it has ascertained the sufficiency of the assets of the company, make calls on and order payment thereof by all or any of the contributories for the time being settled on the list of the contributories to the extent of their liability, for payment of any money which the Court considers necessary to satisfy the debts and liabilities of the company, and the costs, charges and expenses of winding up, and for the adjustment of the rights of the contributories among themselves[2].

(2) In making the call the Court may take into consideration the probability that some of the contributories may partly or wholly fail to pay the call.

331. **Power to order payment into bank.--** (1) The Court may order any contributory, purchaser or other person from whom any money is due to the company to pay the same into the account of the official liquidator in a scheduled bank instead of to the official liquidator, and any such order may be enforced in the same manner as if it had directed payment to the official liquidator[3].

(2) Information about the amount deposited shall be sent by the person paying it to the official liquidator within three days of the date of payment.

332. **Regulation of account with Court.--** All moneys, bills, notes and other securities paid and delivered into the scheduled bank where the official liquidator of the company may have his account, in the event of a company

---

[1] 1985 PLD 193; 1977 PLD 217; 1972 PLD 552
[2] 1985 PLD 193
[3] 1985 PLD 193

being wound up by the Court, shall be subject in all respect to the orders of the Court[1].

333. **Order on contributory conclusive evidence.--** (1) An order made by the Court on a contributory shall, subject to any right of appeal, be conclusive evidence that the money, if any, thereby appearing to be due or ordered to be paid is due.

(2) All other pertinent matters stated in the order shall be taken to be truly stated as against all persons, and in all proceedings whatsoever.

334. **Power to exclude creditors not proving in time.--** The Court may fix a time or times within which creditors are to prove their debts or claims, or to be excluded from the benefit of any distribution made before those debts are proved[2].

335. **Adjustment of rights of contributories.--** The Court shall adjust the rights of the contributories among themselves, and distribute any surplus among the persons entitled thereto[3].

336. **Power to order costs.--** The Court may, in the event of the assets being insufficient to satisfy the liabilities, make an order as to the payment out of the assets of the costs, charges and expenses incurred in the winding up in such order of priority as the Court thinks just[4].

337. **Powers and duties of official liquidator.--** (1) Subject to directions by the Court, if any, in this regard, the official liquidator, in a winding up of a company, shall have the power[5]—

    (a)   to carry on the business of the company so far as may be necessary for the beneficial winding up of the company;

    (b)   to do all acts and to execute, in the name and on behalf of the company, all deeds, receipts and other documents, and for that purpose, to use, when necessary, the company's seal;

    (c)   to sell the immovable and movable property and actionable claims of the company by public auction or private contract, with power to transfer such property to any person or body corporate;

    (d)   to sell whole of the undertaking of the company as a going concern;

---

[1] 1985 PLD 193

[2] 1985 PLD 193; 1983 PTD 93; 1977 PLD 1218

[3] 1987 CLC 1408; 1985 PLD 193

[4] 1985 PLD 193; 1964 PLD 742

[5] 2002 CLD 1781; 2000 PLD 391; 1996 SCMR 88; 1988 CLC 2147; 1988 SCMR 1717; 1985 PLD 193; 1982 CLC 1689; 1982 CLC 1749; 1982 PLD 810

(e)   to institute or defend any suit, prosecution or other legal proceeding, civil or criminal, in the name and on behalf of the company;

(f)   to invite and settle claim of creditors, employees or any other claimant and distribute sale proceeds in accordance with priorities established under this Act;

(g)   to draw, accept, make and endorse any negotiable instruments in the name and on behalf of the company, with the same effect with respect to the liability of the company as if such instruments had been drawn, accepted, made or endorsed by or on behalf of the company in the course of its business;

(h)   to obtain any professional assistance from any person or appoint any professional, in discharge of his duties, obligations and responsibilities and for protection of the assets of the company, appoint an agent to do any business which the official liquidator is unable to do himself;

(i)   to appoint an Advocate entitled to appear before the Court or such person as may be prescribed to assist him in the performance of his duties;

(j)   to take all such actions, steps, or to sign, execute and verify any paper, deed, document, application, petition, affidavit, bond or instrument as may be necessary-

      (i)   for winding up of the company;

      (ii)   for distribution of assets;

      (iii)   in discharge of his duties and obligations and functions as official liquidator; and

(k)   to apply to the Court for such orders or directions as may be necessary for the winding up of the company.

(2) The exercise of powers by the official liquidator under sub-section (1) shall be subject to the overall control of the Court, and any creditor or contributory or the registrar may apply to the Court with respect to any exercise or proposed exercise of any of the said powers.

(3) Notwithstanding the provisions of sub-section (1), the official liquidator shall perform such other duties as the Court may specify in this behalf.

338.   **Liquidator to keep books containing proceedings of meetings.-** The official liquidator of a company which is being wound up by the Court shall, in order to reflect a correct and fair view of the administration of the

company's affairs, maintain proper books of accounts[1] and also keep the following books--

(a) register showing the dates at which notices were issued to the creditors and contributories;

(b) minutes book of all proceedings and resolutions passed at any meeting of the contributories or the creditors;

(c) register containing particulars of all transactions and negotiations made by him in relation to the winding up of the company and the connected matters.

339. **Liquidator's account.--** (1) The official liquidator shall--

(a) maintain proper and regular books of accounts including accounts of receipts and payments made by him in such form and manner as may be prescribed;

(b) at the end of one hundred and eighty days from the date of winding up order, prepare a report consisting of account of his receipts and payments and dealings as liquidator, together with such further information as may be prescribed, which shall be subjected to a limited scope review by the company's auditor;

(c) present to the Court and file with the registrar a certified copy of such accounts within thirty days from the close of half year. Such copies shall be open to the inspection of any person on payment of prescribed fee;

(d) where the winding up is not concluded within one year from the date of winding up order, within sixty days after the close of each year, prepare a statement of financial position and the receipt and payment accounts, get it audited by the company's auditor and lay before the contributories in the general meeting in the same manner as the annual accounts of a company are laid before the annual general meeting, in terms of section 223 of this Act.

(2) The account and information as aforesaid shall be in the prescribed form, shall be made in duplicate, and shall be verified by a declaration in the prescribed form.

(3) When the account and the books and papers have been audited, one copy thereof along with the auditor's report shall be filed and kept by the Court, and the other copy along with the auditor's report shall be delivered to the registrar for filing; and each copy shall be open to the inspection of any person on payment of prescribed fee.

---

[1] 1985 PLD 193

(4) The official liquidator shall cause a copy of the account to be sent by post to every creditor and contributory:

(a)   within thirty days in case of half yearly accounts, referred in clause (b) of sub-section (1); and

(b)   at least fifty days before the date of general meeting in case of clause (d) of sub-section (1).

(5) The concerned Minister-in-Charge of the Federal Government may, by notification in the official Gazette require that the accounts and information referred to in sub-section (1) shall be furnished to an officer to be designated by it for the purpose and that such officer shall cause the accounts to be audited; and, upon the publication of such notification, reference to "Court" in the preceding provisions of this section shall be construed as a reference to such officer.

340. **Exercise and control of liquidator's powers.--** (1) Subject to the provisions of this Act, the official liquidator of a company which is being wound up by the Court shall, in the administration of the assets of the company and in the distribution thereof among its creditors, have regard to any directions that may be given by resolution of the creditors or contributories at any general meeting[1].

(2) The official liquidator may summon general meetings of the creditors or contributories for the purpose of ascertaining their wishes, and it shall be his duty to summon meetings at such times as the creditors or contributories, by resolution, may direct, or whenever requested in writing to do so by one-tenth in value of the creditors or contributories, as the case may be.

(3) Subject to the provisions of this Act, the official liquidator shall use his own discretion in the administration of the assets of the company and in the distribution thereof among the creditors.

(4) If any person is aggrieved by any act or decision of the official liquidator, that person may apply to the Court, and the Court may confirm, reverse or modify the act or decision complained of, and make such order as it thinks just in the circumstances.

341. **Distribution by official liquidator.--** Subject to any directions given by the Court, the official liquidator shall, within thirty days of the coming into his hands of funds sufficient to distribute among the creditors or contributories after providing for expenses of the winding up or for other preferential payments as provided in this Act, distribute in accordance with the provisions of this Act:

---

[1] 1990 SCMR 394; 1988 CLC 2147; 1985 PLD 193

Provided that in case of company licenced under section 42 of this Act, if on a winding up, there remains after the satisfaction of all debts and liabilities, any assets, those shall be transferred to another company licenced under section 42 of this Act, preferably having similar or identical objects to those of the company in the manner as may be specified and subject to such conditions as the Court may impose:

Provided further that such portion of the funds as may be required for meeting any claim against the company which may be *subjudice* or subject matter of adjudication or assessment shall not be distributed till the claim is finally settled:

Provided also that any amounts retained as aforesaid shall be invested by the official liquidator in Special Saving Certificates and the same shall be deposited by him with the Court and the distribution thereof shall be made by him after the pending claims are settled:

Provided also that in case of company licenced under section 42, if any of the assets is not transferred in the manner provided in first proviso due to any reason, all such assets shall be sold and proceeds thereof credited to the Investor Education and Awareness Fund formed under section 245.

342. **Dissolution of company**.-- (1) When the affairs of a company have been completely wound up, or when the Court is of the opinion that the official liquidator cannot proceed with the winding up of the company for want of funds and assets or any other reason whatsoever and it is just and reasonable in the circumstances of the case that an order of dissolution of the company be made, the Court shall make an order that the company be dissolved from the date of the order, and the company shall be dissolved accordingly[1]:

Provided that such dissolution of the company shall not extinguish and right of, or debt due to the company against or from any person.

(2) A copy of the order shall, within fifteen days of the making thereof, be forwarded by the official liquidator to the registrar, who shall make in his books a minute of the dissolution of the company and shall publish a notice in the official Gazette that the company is dissolved.

(3) If the official liquidator makes default in complying with the requirements of this section, he shall be liable to a daily penalty of level 1 on the standard scale.

343. **Saving of other proceedings.--** Any powers conferred on the Court by this Act shall be in addition to, and not in derogation of, any existing power of instituting proceedings against any contributory or debtor of the

---

[1] 2010 CLD 180; 2005 PLD 399; 2005 CLD 840; 1987 MLD 347; 1986 CLC 2408; 1985 PLD 193; 1985 PLD 404

company, or the estate of any contributory or debtor, for the recovery of any call or other sums[1].

ENFORCEMENT OF ORDERS

344. **Power to enforce orders.--** All orders made by a Court under this Act may be enforced in the same manner in which decrees of such Court made in any suit may be enforced[2].

345. **Order made by any Court to be enforced by other Courts.--** Any order made by a Court for, or in the course of, winding up of a company shall be enforceable in any place in Pakistan, and in the same manner in all respects as in such order had been made by a Court having jurisdiction in respect of that company or a Court to whom the Court refers the order for enforcement[3].

346. **Mode of Dealing with Orders to be enforced by other Courts.--** Where any order made by one Court is to be enforced by another Court, a certified copy of the order so made shall be produced to the proper officer of the Court required to enforce the same, and the production of such certified copy shall be sufficient evidence of such order having been made; and thereupon the last mentioned Court shall take the requisite steps in the matter for enforcing the order, in the same manner as if it were the order of the Court enforcing the same.

347. **Circumstances in which company may be wound up voluntarily.--** A company may be wound up voluntarily[4]--

(a)   if the company in general meeting passes a resolution requiring the company to be wound up voluntarily as a result of the expiry of the period for its duration, if any, fixed by its articles or on the occurrence of any event in respect of which the articles provide that the company should be dissolved; or

(b)   if the company passes a special resolution that the company be wound up voluntarily;

and, in the subsequent provisions of this Part, the expression "**resolution for voluntary winding up**" means a resolution passed under clause (a) or clause (b).

348. **Commencement of voluntary winding up.--** A voluntary winding up shall be deemed to commence at the time of the passing of the resolution for voluntary winding up[5].

---

[1] 1985 PLD 193

[2] 2000 PLD 391; 1985 PLD 193

[3] 1999 PLD 456

[4] 2016 CLD 1638; 2009 CLD 1713; 1999 PLD 456; 1985 PLD 193; 1952 PLD 148

[5] 2005 CLD 1802; 2005 CLD 1657; 2005 CLD 1802; 2005 CLD 1657; 1999 PLD 456; 1985 PLD 193

349. **Effect of voluntary winding up on status of company.--** In the case of voluntary winding up, the company shall, from the commencement of the winding up, cease to carry on its business, except so far as may be required for the beneficial winding up thereof[1]:

Provided that the corporate state and corporate powers of the company shall, notwithstanding anything to the contrary in its articles, continue until it is dissolved.

350. **Notice of resolution to wind up voluntarily.**(1) Notice of any resolution for winding up a company voluntarily shall be given by the company within ten days of the passing of the same by advertisement in a newspaper in English and Urdu languages at least in one issue each of a daily newspaper of respective language having wide circulation and a copy thereof shall be sent to the registrar immediately thereafter[2].

(2) Any contravention or default in complying with requirement of this section shall be an offence liable to a daily penalty of level 1 on the standard scale.

(3) For the purpose of this section, a liquidator of a company shall be deemed to be an officer of the company.

351. **Declaration of solvency in case of proposal to wind up voluntarily.--** (1) Where it is proposed to wind up a company voluntarily, its directors, or in case the company has more than three directors, the majority of the directors, including the chief executive, may, at a meeting of the board make a declaration verified by an affidavit to the effect that they have made a full inquiry into the affairs of the company, and that having done so, they have formed the opinion that the company has no debts, or that it will be able to pay all its debts in full from the proceeds of assets within such period not exceeding one year from the commencement of the winding up, as may be specified in the declaration[3].

(2) A declaration made as aforesaid shall have no effect for the purposes of this Act, Unless--

(a) it is made within the five weeks immediately preceding the date of the passing of the resolution for winding up the company and is delivered to the registrar for registration before that date;

(b) it contains a declaration that the company is not being wound up to defraud any person or persons; and

---

[1] 1985 PLD 193
[2] 1985 PLD 193
[3] 1985 PLD 193; 1952 PLD 148

(c)   it is accompanied by a copy of the report of the auditors of the company, prepared, so far as the circumstances admit, in accordance with the provisions of this Act, on the statement of financial position and profit and loss account of the company for the period commencing from the date up to which the last such accounts were prepared and ending with the latest practicable date immediately before the making of the declaration.

(3) Where the company is wound up in pursuance of a resolution passed within the period of five weeks after the making of the declaration, but its debts are not paid or provided for in full within the period specified in the declaration; it shall be presumed, until the contrary is shown, that the director did not have reasonable grounds for his opinion.

(4) Any director of a company making a declaration under this section without having reasonable grounds for the opinion that the company will be able to pay its debts in full from the proceeds of assets within the period specified in the declaration shall be liable to penalty of level 3 on the standard scale.

352. **Distinction between members and creditors voluntary winding up.**--A winding up in the case of which a declaration under section 351 has been made is a members' voluntary winding up and a winding up in the case of which such a declaration has not been made is a creditors' voluntary winding up[1].

353. **Appointment of liquidator.--** (1) In a members' voluntary winding up, the company in general meeting shall appoint one or more liquidators, whose written consent to act as such has been obtained in advance, for the purpose of winding up the company's affairs and distributing its assets.

(2) On the appointment of a liquidator all the powers of the board shall cease, except for the purpose of giving notice of resolution to wind up the company and appointment of liquidator and filing of consent of liquidator in pursuance of sections 351 and 363 or in so far as the company in general meeting, or the liquidator sanctions the continuance thereof.

(3) The liquidator shall subject to the specified limits be entitled to such remuneration by way of percentage of the amount realised by him by disposal of assets or otherwise, as the company in general meeting may fix having regard to the nature of the work done, experience, qualification of such liquidator and size of the company:

Provided that different percentage rates may be fixed for different types of assets and items.

(4) In addition to the remuneration payable under sub-section (3), the company in general meeting may authorise payment of a monthly allowance to

---

[1] 1985 PLD 193; 1952 PLD 148

the liquidator for meeting the expenses of the winding up for a period not exceeding one year from the date of the commencement of winding up.

(5) The remuneration fixed as aforesaid shall not be enhanced subsequently but may be reduced by the Court at any time.

(6) If the liquidator resigns, is removed from office or otherwise ceases to hold office before conclusion of winding up, he shall not be entitled to any remuneration and remuneration already received by him, if any, shall be refunded by him to the company.

(7) The liquidator shall not resign or quit his office as liquidator before conclusion of the winding up proceedings except for reasons of personal disability to the satisfaction of the members and also be removed by a resolution in general meeting.

(8) No remuneration shall be payable to liquidator who fails to complete the winding up proceedings within the prescribed period.

354. **Power to fill vacancy in office of liquidator.--** (1) If a vacancy occurs by death, resignation or otherwise in the office of any liquidator appointed by the company, the company in general meeting may fill the vacancy by appointing a person who has given his written consent to act as liquidator.

(2) For that purpose a general meeting shall be convened by the out-going liquidator before he ceases to act as liquidator except where the vacancy occurs by death, or where there were more liquidators than one, by the continuing liquidator, and failing that may be convened by any contributory, or by the Commission on the application of any person interested in the winding up of the company.

(3) The meeting shall be held in the manner provided by this Act or in such manner as may, on application by any contributory or by the continuing liquidator, or any person interested in the winding up be determined by the Commission.

(4) If default is made in complying with the provisions of this section, every person, including the outgoing liquidator, who is in default, shall be liable to a daily penalty of level 1 on the standard scale.

355. **Notice by liquidator of his appointment.--** (1) The liquidator shall, within ten days after his appointment, file with the registrar for registration a notice of his appointment in the specified form.

(2) If the liquidator fails to comply with this section, he shall be liable to a daily penalty of level 1 on the standard scale.

356. **Power of liquidator to accept shares as consideration for sale of property of company.--** (1) Where—

(a)   a company (in this section called the "transferor company") is proposed to be, or is in the course of being, wound up altogether voluntarily; and

(b)   the whole or a part of its business or property is proposed to be transferred or sold to another body corporate, whether a company within the meaning of this Act or not (in this section called "the transferee company"),

the liquidator of the transferor company may, with the sanction of a special resolution of that company conferring on the liquidator either a general authority or an authority in respect of any particular arrangement--

(i)   receive, by way of compensation or part compensation for the transfer or sale, shares, policies, or other like interests in the transferee company, for distribution among the members of the transferor company; or

(ii)   enter into any other arrangement whereby the members of the transferor company may, in lieu of receiving cash, shares, policies, or other like interests or in addition thereto,

(iii) participate in the profits of, or receive any other benefit from, the transferee company.

(2) Any sale or arrangement in pursuance of this section shall be binding on the members of the transferor company.

(3) If any member of the transferor company who did not vote in favour of the special resolution expresses his dissent therefrom in writing addressed to the liquidator and left at the registered office of the company within seven days after the passing of the special resolution, he may require the liquidator either-

(a)   to abstain from carrying the resolution into effect; or

(b)   to purchase his interest at a price to be determined by agreement or by arbitration in the manner hereafter provided.

(4) If the liquidator elects to purchase the member's interest, the purchase money shall be paid before the company is dissolved, and be raised by the liquidator in such manner as may be determined by special resolution.

(5) A special resolution shall not be invalid for the purpose of this section by reason only that it is passed before or concurrently with a resolution for voluntary winding up or for appointing liquidators; but if an order is made within a year for winding up the company by or subject to the supervision of the Court, the special resolution shall not be valid unless it is sanctioned by the Court.

(6) The provisions of the Arbitration Act, 1940 (X of 1940), other than those restricting the application of this Act in respect of the subject-matter of the arbitration, shall apply to all arbitrations in pursuance of this section.

357. **Duty of liquidator where company turns out to be insolvent.--** (1) Where the liquidator is of the opinion that the company will be unable to pay its debts in full within the period stated in the directors' declaration under section 351, he shall forthwith summon a meeting of the creditors and shall lay before the meeting a statement of the assets and liabilities of the company and such other particulars as may be specified.

(2) Where sub-section (1) becomes applicable, the creditors may in their meeting held as aforesaid decide to continue with the existing liquidator or appoint a different person as liquidator who has consented to act as such and in that case the person so appointed shall be the liquidator.

(3) In the case of a different person being nominated, any director, member of the company may, within fifteen days after the date on which the nomination was made by the creditors, apply to the Court for an order either—

(a)   directing that the person nominated as liquidator by the company shall be liquidator instead of or jointly with the person nominated by the creditors, or

(b)   appointing some other person to be liquidator instead of the person nominated by the creditors.

(4) A return of convening the creditors meeting as aforesaid along with a copy of the notice thereof and a statement of assets and liabilities of the company and the minutes of the meeting shall be filed with the registrar within ten days of the date of the meeting.

(5) If the liquidator fails to comply with any of the requirements of this section, he shall be liable to a penalty of level 1 on the standard scale.

358.   **Duty of liquidator to call general meetings.--** (1) The liquidator shall--

(a)   summon and hold annual general meeting of the company within a period of sixty days from the close of first year after the commencement of winding up, in the manner provided under section 132;

(b)   lay before the meeting audited accounts consisting of statement of financial position and the receipt and payment accounts, auditors' report and the liquidator's report on the acts, dealings and the conduct of the company's winding up during the preceding period from the date of winding up; and

(c)   forward by post to every contributory a copy of the accounts and the reports, as referred to in clause (b).

(2) A return of convening of each general meeting together with a copy of the notice, accounts and the reports as aforesaid, the list of contributories as on the date of the meeting and the minutes of the meeting shall be filed by the liquidator with the registrar within fifteen days of the date of the meeting.

(3) If the liquidator fails to comply with this section, he shall be liable, in respect of each failure, to a penalty of level 1 on the standard scale.

359. **Final meeting and dissolution.--** (1) As soon as the affairs of a company are fully wound up, the liquidator shall-

(a)   prepare final accounts of the company, get the same audited; and also prepare a report of the winding up, showing that the property and assets of the company have been disposed of and its debts fully discharged and such other particulars; as may be specified; and

(b)   call a general meeting of the company for the purpose of laying the report and accounts before it, and giving any explanation therefor.

(2) A copy of the report and accounts together with a copy of the auditor's report and notice of meeting shall be sent by post or courier or through electronic mode to each contributory of the company at least twenty-one days before the meeting required to be held under this section.

(3) The notice of the meeting specifying the time, place and object of the meeting shall also be published at least twenty-one days before the date of the meeting in the manner specified in section 350.

(4) Within one week after the meeting, the liquidator shall file with the registrar his final report in the specified form.

(5) If a quorum is not present at the meeting, the liquidator shall in lieu of the return referred to in sub-section (4), make a return that the meeting was duly summoned and that no quorum was present threat, and upon such a return being made within one week after the date fixed for the meeting along with a copy of his report and account in the specified manner, the provision of sub-section (4) as to the making of the return shall be deemed to have been complied with.

(6) The registrar, on receiving the report and account and either the return mentioned in sub-section (4) or the return mentioned in sub-section (5), shall, after such scrutiny as he may deem fit, register them, and on the expiration of ninety days from such registration, the company shall be deemed to be dissolved:

Provided that, if on his scrutiny the registrar considers that the affairs of the company or the liquidation proceedings have been conducted in a manner prejudicial to its interest or the interests of its creditors and members or that any actionable irregularity has been committed, he may take action in accordance with the provisions of this Act:

Provided further that the Court may on the application of the liquidator or of any other person who appears to the Court to be interested, make an order deferring the date at which the dissolution of the company is to take effect, for such time as the Court thinks fit.

(7) It shall be the duty of the person on whose application an order of the Court under the foregoing proviso is made, within fourteen days after the making of the order, to deliver to the registrar a certified copy of the order for registration, and, if that person fails so to do, he shall be liable to a daily penalty of level 1 on the standard scale.

(8) If the liquidator fails to comply with any requirements of this section, he shall be liable to a penalty of level 1 on the standard scale.

360. **Alternative provisions as to annual and final meetings in case of insolvency.--** Where section 357 has effect, sections 368 and 369 shall apply to the winding up, to the exclusion of sections 358 and 359 as if the winding up were creditors' voluntary winding up and not a members' voluntary winding up[1]:

Provided that the liquidator shall not be required to summon a meeting of creditors under section 368 at the end of the first year from the commencement of the winding up, unless the meeting held under section 362 has been held more than ninety days before the end of the year.

PROVISIONS APPLICABLE TO CREDITORS'
VOLUNTARY WINDING UP

361. **Provisions applicable to creditors' voluntary winding up.--** The provisions contained in sections 355 to 369, both inclusive, shall apply in relation to creditors' voluntary winding up[2].

362. **Meeting of creditors.**—(1) The company shall--

(a)   cause a meeting of its creditors to be summoned for a day not later than the fourteenth day after the day on which there is to be held the company meeting at which the resolution for voluntary winding up is to be proposed;

(b)   cause the notices of the creditors' meeting to be sent by post to the creditors not less than seven days before the day on which that meeting is to be held; and

---

[1] 2016 LHC 666
[2] 2016 CLD 1638; 1985 PLD 193

(c) cause notice of the creditors' meeting to be advertised in a newspaper in English and Urdu languages at least in one issue each of respective language having wide circulation and a copy thereof shall simultaneously be sent to the registrar.

(2) The directors of the company shall--

(a) make out a statement of the position of the company's affairs and assets and liabilities together with a list of the creditors of the company, details of securities held by them respectively along with the dates when such securities were held, the estimated amount of their claims to be laid before the meeting of creditors and such other information as may be specified; and

(b) appoint one of their members to preside at the said meeting.

(3) It shall be the duty of the director appointed to preside at the meeting of creditors to attend the meeting and preside thereat.

(4) Any contravention or default in complying with requirements of this section shall be an offence liable to a penalty of level 1 on the standard scale.

363. **Appointment of liquidator.--** (1) The creditors and the company at their respective meetings mentioned in sections 357 and 362 may nominate a person, who has given his written consent to act as such, to be liquidator for the purpose of winding up the affairs and distributing the assets of the company.

(2) If the creditors and company nominate different persons, the persons nominated by the creditors shall be liquidator:

Provided that any director, member or creditor of the company may, within fifteen days after the date on which the nomination was made by the creditors, apply to the Court for an order either directing that the person nominated as liquidator by the company shall be liquidator instead of or jointly with the person nominated by the creditors or appointing some other person to be liquidator instead of the person appointed by the creditors.

(3) If no person is nominated by the creditors, the person, if any, nominated by the company shall be liquidator.

(4) If no person is nominated by the company, the person, if any, nominated by the creditors shall be the liquidator.

(5) The liquidator shall not resign or quit his office as liquidator before conclusion of the winding up proceedings except for reasons of personal disability to the satisfaction of the Court and may also be removed by the Court for reasons to be recorded.

(6) Notice of appointment of liquidator as well as the resolution passed at a creditors' meeting in pursuance of section 362 shall be given by the

company to the registrar, along with the consent of the liquidator to act as such, within ten days of the passing thereof.

364. **Fixing of liquidator's remuneration.--** (1) The liquidator shall subject to the specified limits be entitled to such remuneration by way of percentage of the amount realised by him by disposal of assets or otherwise, as the creditors in their meeting or the Court in terms of proviso to sub-section (2) of section 317 as the case may be, may fix having regard to the nature of the work done, experience, qualification of such liquidator and size of the company[1]:

Provided that different percentage rates may be fixed for different types of assets and items.

(2) In addition to the remuneration payable under sub-section (1), the creditors in their meeting or the Court may authorise payment of a monthly allowance to the liquidator for meeting the expenses of the winding up for a period not exceeding one year from the date of the commencement of winding up.

(3) The remuneration fixed as aforesaid shall not be enhanced subsequently but may be reduced by the Court at any time.

(4) If the liquidator resigns, is removed from office or otherwise ceases to hold office before conclusion of winding up, he shall not be entitled to any remuneration and the remuneration already received by him, if any, shall be refunded by him to the company.

365. **Cessation of boards' powers.--** On the appointment of a liquidator, all the powers of the board, chief executive and other officers shall cease, except for the purpose of giving notice of resolution to wind up and appointment of the liquidator and filing of consent of the liquidator as required under this Act, the creditors, in general meeting may sanction the continuance thereof.

366. **Power to fill vacancy in office of liquidator.--** If a vacancy occurs, by death, resignation or otherwise, in the office of a liquidator, other than a liquidator appointed by or by the direction of, the Court, the creditors in their meeting may fill the vacancy by appointing a person who has given his written consent to act as liquidator, and for this purpose the provisions of section 354 shall *mutatis mutandis* apply.

367. **Application of section 356 to a creditors voluntary winding up.-** The provisions of section 356 shall apply in the case of a creditors voluntary winding up as in the case of member's voluntary winding up with the modification that the powers of the liquidator under the said section shall not be exercised except with the sanction of the Court.

---

[1] 1994 PCrLJ 1986

368. **Duty of liquidator to call meeting of company and of creditors.-** (1) The liquidator shall--

(a)   summon and hold annual general meeting of the company and a meeting of the creditors within a period of sixty days from the close of its financial year in the manner provided under section 132;

(b)   lay before the meetings mentioned in clause (a), audited accounts consisting of statement of financial position and the receipt and payment accounts, auditors' report and the liquidator's report on the acts, dealings and the conduct of the company's winding up during the preceding period from the date of winding up; and

(c)   forward by post to every contributory a copy of the accounts and the reports, as referred to in clause (b).

(2) A return of convening of each general meeting together with a copy of the notice, accounts and the reports as aforesaid, the list of contributories as on the date of the meeting and the minutes of the meeting shall be filed by the liquidator with the registrar within fifteen days of the date of the meeting.

(3) If the liquidator fails to comply with this section, he shall be liable to a penalty of level 1 on the standard scale.

369. **Final meeting and dissolution.--** (1) As soon as the affairs of a company are fully wound up, the liquidator shall--

(a)   prepare final accounts of the company, get the same audited; and also prepare a report of the winding up, showing that the property and assets of the company have been disposed of and its debts fully discharged and such other particulars; as may be specified;

(b)   summon and hold general meeting of the company and a meeting of the creditors within a period of sixty days from the close of its financial year in the manner provided under section 132; and

(c)   lay before the meetings mentioned in clause (a), audited accounts consisting of statement of financial position and the receipt and payment accounts, auditors' report and the liquidator's report on the acts, dealings and the conduct of the company's winding up during the preceding period from the date of winding up.

(2) A copy of the report and accounts together with a copy of the auditor's report and notice of meeting shall be sent by post or courier or through electronic mode to each contributory of the company at least twenty-one days before the meeting required to be held under this section.

(3) The notice of the meeting specifying the time, place and object of the meeting shall also be published at least twenty-one days before the date of the meeting in the manner specified in section 350.

(4) Within one week after the meeting, the liquidator shall file with the registrar his final report in the specified form.

(5) If a quorum (which for the purpose of this section shall be two persons) is not present at either of such meetings, the liquidator shall in lieu of the return referred to in sub-section (4), make a return that the meeting was duly summoned and that no quorum was present thereat, and upon such a return being made within one week after the date fixed for the meeting along with a copy of his report and account in the specified manner, the provision of sub-section (4) as to the making of the return shall be deemed to have been complied with.

(6) The registrar, on receiving the report and account and either the return mentioned in sub-section (4) or the return mentioned in sub-section (5), shall, after such scrutiny as he may deem fit, register them, and on the expiration of ninety days from such registration, the company shall be deemed to be dissolved:

Provided that, if on his scrutiny the registrar considers that the affairs of the company or the liquidation proceedings have been conducted in a manner prejudicial to its interest or the interests of its creditors and members or that any actionable irregularity has been committed, he may take action in accordance with the provisions of this Act:

Provided further that the Court may on the application of the liquidator or of any other person who appears to the Court to be interested, make an order deferring the date at which the dissolution of the company is to take effect, for such time as the Court thinks fit.

(7) It shall be the duty of the person on whose application an order of the Court under the foregoing proviso is made, within fourteen days after the making of the order, to deliver to the registrar a certified copy of the order for registration, and, if that person fails so to do, he shall be liable to a daily penalty of level 1 on the standard scale.

(8) If the liquidator fails to comply with any requirements of this section, he shall be liable to a penalty of level 1 on the standard scale.

PROVISIONS APPLICABLE TO EVERY VOLUNTARY WINDING UP

370. **Distribution of property of company.--** Subject to the provisions of this Act as to preferential payments, the property of a company shall, on its winding up, be applied in satisfaction of its liabilities *pari passu* and, subject to such application shall, unless the articles otherwise provide be distributed

among the members according to their rights and interests in the company[1].

371. **Application of sections 320 and 321 to voluntary winding up.--** The provisions of sections 320 and 321 shall, so far as may be, apply to every voluntary winding up as they apply to winding up by the Court except that references to—

(a)   "the Court" shall be omitted;

(b)   the "official liquidator" or the "provisional manager" shall be construed as references to the liquidator; and

(c)   the "relevant date" shall be construed as reference to the date of commencement of the winding up; and

the report referred to in section 321 shall be submitted to the registrar instead of the Court.

372. **Powers and duties of liquidator in voluntary winding up.--** (1) The liquidator may[2]--

(a)   in the case of a members' voluntary winding up, with the sanction of a special resolution of the company, and, in the case of a creditors' voluntary winding up, of a meeting of the creditors, exercise any of the powers given by sub-section (1) of section 337 to a liquidator in a winding up by the Court;

(b)   without the sanction referred to in clause (a), exercise any of the other powers given by this Act to the liquidator in a winding up by the Court;

(c)   exercise the power of the Court under this Act of settling a list of contributories, which shall be *prima facie* evidence of the liabilities of the persons named therein to be contributories;

(d)   exercise the powers of the Court of making calls;

(e)   summon general meeting of the company and creditors for the purpose of obtaining the sanction of the company by special resolution or for any other purpose he may think fit.

(2) The exercise by the liquidator of the powers given by clause (a) of sub-section (1) shall be subject to the control of the Court; and any creditor or contributory may apply to the Court with respect to any exercise or proposed exercise of any of the power conferred by this section.

(3) The liquidator shall pay the debts of the company and shall adjust the rights of the contributories among themselves.

---

[1] 2009 CLD 1713; 1986 PLD 18; 1985 PLD 193
[2] 2010 CLD 460; 2005 CLD 1657; 2005 CLD 1802; 1994 PLD 125; 1985 PLD 193

(4) The liquidator shall within thirty days of the coming into his hands of any funds sufficient to distribute among the creditors or contributories after providing for expenses of the winding up or for other preferential payments as provided in this Act, distribute in accordance with the provisions of this Act:

Provided that in case of company licenced under section 42 of this Act, if on a winding up, there remains after the satisfaction of all debts and liabilities, any assets, those shall be transferred to another company licenced under section 42 of this Act, preferably having similar or identical objects to those of the company in the manner as may be specified:

Provided further that such portion of the funds as may be required for meeting any claim against the company which may be *subjudice* or subject matter of adjudication or assessment shall not be distributed till the claim is finally settled:

Provided also that any amounts retained as aforesaid shall be invested by the official liquidator in Special Saving Certificates or in such other securities or instruments as may be specified and the distribution thereof shall be made by him after the pending claims are settled:

Provided also that in case of company licenced under section 42, if any of the assets is not transferred in the manner provided in first proviso due to any reason, all such assets shall be sold and proceeds thereof credited to the Investor Education and Awareness Fund formed under section 245.

(5) The winding up proceedings shall be completed by the liquidator within a period of one year from the date of commencement of winding up:

Provided that the Court may, on the application of the liquidator, grant extension by thirty days at any time but such extension shall not exceed a period of one hundred and eighty days in all and shall be allowed only for the reason that any proceedings for or against the company are pending in a court and the Court shall also have the power to require expeditious disposal of such proceedings as it could under section 337 if the company was being wound up by the Court.

(6) If an official liquidator is convicted of misfeasance, or breach of duty or other lapse or default in relation to winding up proceedings of a company, he shall cease to be the official liquidator of the company and shall also become disqualified, for a period of five years from such conviction, from being the liquidator of, or to hold any other office including that of a director in any company and if he already holds any such office he shall forthwith be deemed to have ceased to hold such office.

(7) When several liquidators are appointed, any power given by this Act may be exercised by such one or more of them as may be determined at the

time, of their appointment, or in default of such determination, by any two or more of them.

373. **Power of Court to appoint and remove liquidator in voluntary winding up.--** (1) If from any cause whatever, there is no liquidator acting, the Court may appoint a liquidator in accordance with the provisions of section 315 who shall have the same powers, as are exercisable by an official liquidator under sub-section (1) of section 337[1].

(2) The Court may, on cause shown, replace a liquidator on the application of any creditor or contributory or the registrar or a person authorised by the Commission.

(3) The remuneration to be paid to the liquidator appointed under sub-section (1) or sub-section (2) shall be fixed by the Court subject to the provisions of section 364.

374. **Notice by liquidator of his appointment.--** (1) Every liquidator shall, within fourteen days after his appointment, publish in the official Gazette, and deliver to the registrar for registration, a notice of his appointment in the form specified[2].

(2) If the liquidator fails to comply with the requirements of sub-section (1), he shall be liable to a daily penalty of level 1 on the standard scale.

375. **Arrangement when binding on company and creditors.--** (1) Any arrangement other than the arrangement referred to in section 356 entered into between a company which is about to be, or is in the course of being wound up and its creditors shall be binding on the company and on the creditors, if it is sanctioned by a special resolution of the company and acceded to by the creditors who hold three-fourths in value of the total amount due to all the creditors of the company[3].

(2) Any creditor or contributory may, within twenty-one days from the completion of the arrangement, appeal to the Court against it, and the Court may thereupon, as it thinks just, amend, vary, confirm or set aside the arrangement.

376. **Power to apply to Court to have questions determined or powers exercised.--** (1) The liquidator or any contributory or creditor may apply to the Court[4]--

    (a)   to determine any question arising in the winding up of a company; or

---

[1] 1985 PLD 193; 1960 PLD 384; 1952 PLD 148

[2] 1985 PLD 193

[3] 1985 PLD 193

[4] 2016 LHC 666; 2016 CLD 1978; 2009 CLD 1713; 1987 PLD 520; 1985 PLD 193; 1984 PLD 541

(b)   to exercise as respects the enforcing of calls, the staying of proceedings or any other matter, all or any of the powers which the Court might exercise if the company were being wound up by the Court.

(2) The liquidator or any contributory may apply to the Court specified in sub-section (3) for an order setting aside any attachment, distress or execution put into force against the estate or effects of the company after the commencement of the winding up.

(3)   An application under sub-section (2) shall be made-

(a)   if the attachment, distress or execution is levied or put into force by a Court, to such Court; and

(b)   if the attachment, distress or execution is levied or put into force by any other court, to the court having jurisdiction to wind up the company.

(4) The Court, if it is satisfied that the determination of the question or the required exercise of power or the order applied for will be just and beneficial, may accede wholly or partially to the application on such terms and conditions as it thinks fit, or may make such other orders on the application as it thinks just.

(5) A copy of an order staying the proceedings in the winding up, made by virtue of this section, shall forthwith be forwarded by the company, or

(6) otherwise as may be prescribed, to the registrar, who shall make a minute of the order in his books relating to the company.

377. **Application of liquidator to Court for public examination of promoters, directors.--** The liquidator may make a report to the Court stating that in his opinion a fraud or any other actionable irregularity has been committed by any person in the promotion or formation of the company or by any officer of the company in relation to the company since its formation; and the Court may, after considering the report, direct that person or officer shall attend before the Court on a day appointed by it for that purpose, and be publicly examined as to the promotion or formation or the conduct of the business of the company, or as to his conduct and dealings as officer thereof, in the manner provided for such examination in the case of winding up of a company by the Court.

378. **Costs of voluntary winding up.--** All costs, charges and expenses properly incurred in the winding up, including the remuneration of the liquidator, shall subject to the rights of secured creditors, if any, be payable out of the assets of the company in priority to all other claims[1].

---

[1] 1985 PLD 193; 1984 PLD 541

379. **Saving for right of creditors and contributories.--** The voluntary winding up of a company shall not bar the right of any creditor or contributory to have it wound up by the Court, but in the case of an application by a contributory, the Court must be satisfied that the rights of the contributories will be prejudiced by a voluntary winding up[1].

380. **Power of Court to adopt proceedings of voluntary winding up.--** Where a company is being wound up voluntarily, and an order is made for winding up by the Court, the Court may, if it thinks fit by the same or any subsequent order, provide for the adoption of all or any of the proceedings in the voluntary winding up[2].

WINDING UP SUBJECT TO SUPERVISION OF COURT

381. **Power to order winding up subject to supervision.--** When a company has passed a resolution for voluntary winding up, the Court may of its own motion or on the application of any person entitled to apply to the Court for winding up a company, make an order that the voluntary winding up shall continue, but subject to such supervision of the Court, and with such liberty for creditors, contributories or others to apply to the Court, and generally on such terms and conditions, as the Court thinks just[3].

382. **Effect of petition for winding up subject to supervision.--** A petition for the continuance of a voluntary winding up subject to the supervision of the Court shall, for the purpose of giving jurisdiction to the Court over suits and another legal proceedings, be deemed to be a petition for winding up by the Court[4].

383. **Court may have regard to the wishes of creditors and contributories.--** The Court may, in deciding between a winding up by the Court and a winding up subject to supervision, in the appointment of liquidators, and in all other matters relating to the winding up subject to supervision, have regard to the wishes of the creditors or contributories as proved to it by any sufficient evidence, but subject to the provisions which would have been applicable had the company been wound up by the Court[5].

384. **Power to replace liquidator.--** Where an order is made for winding up subject to supervision, the Court may on an application by any creditor or contributory or the registrar or a person authorised by the Commission in this behalf, replace the liquidator who shall have the same

---

[1] 1985 PLD 193
[2] 1985 PLD 193
[3] 1985 PLD 193
[4] 1985 PLD 193
[5] 1985 PLD 193

powers, be subject to the same obligations and in all respects stand in the same position as if he had been appointed by the company[1].

385. **Effects of supervision order.--** (1) Where an order is made for a winding up subject to supervision, the liquidator may, subject to any restriction imposed by the Court, exercise all his powers, without the sanction or intervention of the Court, in the same manner as if the company were being wound up altogether voluntarily.

(2) Except as provided in sub-section (1), and save for the purposes of section 327 an order made by the Court for a winding up subject to the supervision of the Court shall for all purposes including the staying of suits and other proceedings, be deemed to be an order of the Court for winding up the company by the Court, and shall confer full authority on the Court to make call or to enforce calls made by the liquidator, and to exercise all other powers which it might have exercised if an order had been made for winding up the company altogether by the Court.

(3) In the construction of the provisions whereby the Court is empowered to direct any act or thing to be done to or in favour of the official liquidator, the expression "**official liquidator**" shall be deemed to mean the liquidator conducting the winding up subject to the supervision of the Court.

(4) Unless otherwise directed by the Court, an order for winding up subject to supervision shall not in any way affect the duties, obligations and liabilities of the liquidator as provided for in respect of voluntary winding up.

386. **Appointment of voluntary liquidator as official liquidator in certain cases.--**Where an order has been made for the winding up of a company subject to supervision, and an order is afterwards made for winding up by the Court, the Court shall by the last mentioned order, appoint the voluntary liquidator, either provisionally or permanently, and either with or without the addition of any other person, to be official liquidator in the winding up by the Court[2].

387. **Status of companies being wound up.--** A company being wound up shall continue to be a company for all purposes till its final dissolution in accordance with the provisions of this Act and, unless otherwise specified, all provisions and requirements of this Act relating to companies shall continue to apply *mutatis mutandis* in the case of companies being wound up:

Provided that, from the date of commencement of the winding up of a company, the official liquidator or the liquidator shall be deemed to have taken the place of the board and chief executive of the company, as the case may be[3].

---

[1] 1985 PLD 193

[2] 2001 CLC 307; 1985 PLD 193

[3] 2019 CLD 1; 2002 CLD 978

PROOF AND RANKING OF CLAIMS

388. **Debts of all description to be proved.--** In every winding up (subject, in the case of insolvent companies, to the application in accordance with the provisions of this Act or the law of insolvency) all debts payable on a contingency, and all claims against the company, present or future, certain or contingent, ascertained or sounding only in damages, shall be admissible to proof against the company, a just estimate being made, so far as possible, of the value of such debts or claims as may be subject to any contingency, or may sound only in damages, or for some other reason do not bear a certain value[1].

389. **Application of insolvency rules in winding up of insolvent companies.--** In the winding up of an insolvent company the same rules shall prevail and be observed with regard to the respective rights of secured and unsecured creditors and to debts provable and to the valuation of annuities and future and contingent liabilities as are in force for the time being under the law of insolvency with respect to the estates of persons adjudged insolvent; and all persons who in any such case will be entitled to prove for and receive dividend out of the assets of the company may come in under the winding up, and make such claims against the company as they respectively are entitled to by virtue of this section[2].

390. **Preferential payments.**(1) In a winding up, there shall be paid in priority to all other debts[3]--

    (a)   all revenues, taxes, cesses and rates due from the company to the Federal Government or a Provincial Government or to a local authority at the relevant date and having become due and payable within the one year next before that date on *pari passu* basis;

    (b)   all wages or salary (including wages payable for time or piece work and salary earned wholly or in part by way of commission) of any employee in respect of services rendered to the company;

    (c)   all accrued holiday remuneration becoming payable to any employee or in the case of his death to any other person in his right, on the termination of his employment before, or by the winding up order, or, as the case may be, the dissolution of the company;

---

[1] 1985 PLD 193; 1983 PTD 93; 1975 PLD 306; 1954 PLD 551

[2] 2014 CLD 1097; 2001 PTD 3146; 2001 CLC 307; 1993 PLD 671; 1992 SCMR 1731; 1989 MLD 3909; 1988 CLC 956; 1985 PLD 193; 1985 PLD 229; 1982 PLD 236; 1982 CLC 2462; 1982 CLC 2660; 1982 PLD 810; 1960 PLD 141

[3] 2014 CLD 1097; 2009 SCMR 585; 2009 CLD 741; 2006 CLC 415; 2002 CLD 286; 2002 CLD 1006; 2002 SCMR 1747; 2002 SCMR 1777; 2001 PTD 3146; 1992 SCMR 1731; 1989 CLC 1743; 1988 CLC 2183; 1988 MLD 1533; 1988 PLD 28; 1988 CLC 2183; 1987 PLD 520; 1986 PLD 18; 1985 PLD 193; 1982 PLD 810; 1981 PLD 322; 1977 PLD 787; 1977 PLD 1218; 1975 PLD 306

(d)   unless the company is being wound up voluntarily merely for the purposes of reconstruction or of amalgamation with another company, all amounts due, in respect of contributions towards insurance payable during the one year next before the relevant date, by the company as employer of any persons, under any other law for the time being in force;

(e)   unless the company has, at the commencement of the winding up, under such a contract with insurers as is mentioned in section 14 of the Workmen's Compensation Act, 1923 (VIII of 1923), rights capable of being transferred to and vested in the workman, all amounts due in respect of any compensation or liability for compensation under the said Act in respect of the death or disablement of any employee of the company:

Provided that where any compensation under the said Act is a weekly payment, the amount payable under this clause shall be taken to be the amount of the lump sum for which such weekly payment could, if redeemable, be redeemed, if the employer made for that purpose under the said Act;

(f)   all sums due to any employee from a provident fund, a pension fund, a gratuity fund or any other fund for the welfare of the employees maintained by the company; and

(g)   the expenses of any investigation held in pursuance of sections 256, 257 or 258, in so far as they are payable by the company.

(2)   Where any payment has been made

(a)   to an employee of a company on account of wages or salary; or

(b)   to an employee of a company or, in the case of his death, to any other person in his right, on account of accrued holiday remuneration,

out of money advanced by some person for that purpose, the person by whom the money was advanced shall, in a winding up, have a right of priority in respect of the money so advanced and paid, up to the amount by which the sum in respect of which the employee or other person in his right would have been entitled to priority in the winding up has been diminished by reason of the payment having been made.

(3)   The foregoing debts shall-

(a)   rank equally among themselves and be paid in full, unless the assets are insufficient to meet them, in which case they shall abate in equal proportion; and

(b)   so far as the assets of the company available for payment of general creditors are insufficient to meet them, have priority over the claims of holders of debentures under any floating charge created by the company, and be paid accordingly out of any property comprised in or subject to that charge.

(4) Subject to the retention of such sums as may be necessary for the costs and expenses of the winding up, the foregoing debts shall be discharged forthwith so far as the assets are sufficient to meet them and, in the case of the debts to which priority is given by clause (d) of sub-section (1), formal proof thereof shall not be required except in so far as may be otherwise prescribed.

(5) In the event of a landlord or other person distraining or having distrained on any goods or effects of the company within ninety days next before the date of winding up order, the debts to which priority is given by this section shall be a first charge on the goods or effects so distrained on, or the proceeds of the sale thereof:

Provided that, in respect of any money paid under any such charge, the landlord or other person shall have the same rights of priority as the person to whom the payment is made.

(6)   For the purposes of this section--

(a)   any remuneration in respect of a period of holiday or of absence from work on medical grounds or other good cause shall be deemed to be wages in respect of services rendered to the company during that period;

(b)   the expression "accrued holiday remuneration" includes, in relation to any person, all sums which by virtue either of his contract of employment or of any enactment (including any order made or direction given under any enactment), are payable on account of the remuneration which would, in the ordinary course, have become payable to him in respect of a period of holiday had his employment with the company continued until he became entitled to be allowed the holiday; and

(c)   the expression "the relevant date" means--

(i)   in the case of a company ordered to be wound up by the Court, the date of the appointment (or first appointment) of the provisional manager or, if no such appointment was made, the date of the winding up order, unless in either case the company had commenced to be wound up voluntarily before that date; and

(ii)   in any other case, the date of the passing of the resolution for the voluntary winding up of the company.

391. **Avoidance of transfers.--** Except when an order to the contrary is passed by the Court-

(a) every transfer of shares and alteration in the status of a member made after the commencement of winding up shall, unless approved by the liquidator, be void;

(b) any transfer or disposition of property, including actionable claims of the company, not being a transfer or delivery made in the ordinary course of its business or in favour of a purchaser or encumbrancer in good faith and for valuable consideration, if made within a period of one year before the presentation of a petition for winding up by the Court or the passing of a resolution for voluntary winding up of the company, shall be void[1].

392. **Disclaimer of onerous property.--** (1) Where any part of the property of a company which is being wound up consists of-

(a) land of any tenure, burdened with onerous covenants;

(b) shares or stocks in companies;

(c) any other property which is not saleable or is not readily saleable by reason of the possessor thereof being bound either to the performance of any onerous act or to the payment of any sum of money; or

(d) unprofitable contracts,

the liquidator may, notwithstanding that he has endeavoured to sell or has taken possession of the property or exercised any act of ownership in relation thereto or done anything in pursuance of the contract, with the leave of the Court and subject to the provisions of this section, by writing signed by him, at any time within one year after the commencement of the winding up or such extended period as may be allowed by the Court, disclaim the property:

Provided that, where any such property has not come to the knowledge of the liquidator within thirty days after the commencement of the winding up, the power under this section of disclaiming the property may be exercised at any time within one year after he has become aware thereof or such extended period as may be allowed by the Court.

(2) The disclaimer shall operate to determine, as from the date of disclaimer, the rights, interest and liabilities of the company in or in respect of the property disclaimed, but shall not, except so far as is necessary for the purpose of releasing the company and the property of the company from liability, affect the rights, interest or liabilities of any other person.

---

[1] 2012 CLD 710; 1993 PLD 404; 1986 PLD 18; 1985 PLD 193; 1982 PLD 810; 1957 PLD 832; 1953 PLD 375

(3) The Court, before or on granting leave to disclaim, may require such notices to be given to persons interested, and impose such terms as a condition of granting leave, and make such other order in the matter as the Court considers just and proper.

(4) The liquidator shall not be entitled to disclaim any property in any case where an application in writing has been made to him by any person interested in the property requiring him to decide whether he will or will not disclaim and the liquidator has not, within a period of twenty-eight days after the receipt of the application or such extended period as may be allowed by the Court, give notice to the applicant that he intends to apply to the Court for leave to disclaim, and in case the property is under a contract, if the liquidator after such an application as aforesaid does not within the said period or extended period disclaim the contract, he shall be deemed to have adopted it.

(5) The Court may, on the application of any person who is, as against the liquidator, entitled to the benefit or subject to the burden of a contract made with the company, make an order rescinding the contract on such terms as to payment by or to either party of damages for the non-performance of the contract, or otherwise as the Court considers just and proper, and any damages payable under the order to any such person may be proved by him as a debt in the winding up.

(6) The Court may, on an application by any person who either claims any interest in any disclaimed property or is under any liability not discharged under this Act in respect of any disclaimed property, and after hearing any such persons as it thinks fit, make an order for the vesting of the property in, or the delivery of the property to, any person entitled thereto or to whom it may seem just that the property should be delivered by way of compensation for such liability as aforesaid, or a trustee for him, and on such terms as the Court considers just and proper, and on any such vesting order being made, the property comprised therein shall vest accordingly in the person named therein in that behalf without any conveyance or assignment for the purpose:

Provided that where the property disclaimed is of a leasehold nature, the Court shall not make a vesting order in favour of any person claiming under the company, whether as under-lessee or as mortgagee or holder of a charge by way of demise, except upon the terms of making that person--

(a)   subject to the same liabilities and obligations as those to which the company was subject under the lease in respect of the property at the commencement of the winding up; or

(b)   if the Court thinks fit, subject only to the same liabilities and obligations as if the lease had been assigned to that person at that date, and in either event as if the lease had comprised only the property comprised in the vesting order, and any mortgagee or under-lessee declining to accept a vesting order upon such terms shall be excluded from all interest in, and security upon the property, and, if there is no person claiming under the company who is willing to accept an order upon such terms, the Court shall have power to vest the estate and interest of the company in the property in any person liable, either personally or in a representative character, and either alone or jointly with the company, to perform the covenants of the lessee in the lease, free and discharged from all estates, encumbrances and interests created therein by the company.

(7) Any person affected by the operation of a disclaimer under this section shall be deemed to be a creditor of the company to the amount of the compensation or damages payable in respect of such effect, and may accordingly prove the amount as a debt in the winding up.

EFFECT OF WINDING UP ON ANTECEDENT AND OTHER TRANSACTIONS

393. **Fraudulent preference.--** (1) Where a company has given preference to a person who is one of the creditors of the company or a surety or guarantor for any of the debts or other liabilities of the company, and the company does anything or suffers anything done which has the effect of putting that person into a position which, in the event of the company going into liquidation, will be better than the position he would have been in if that thing had not been done prior to one hundred and eighty days of commencement of winding up, the Court, if satisfied that, such transaction is a fraudulent preference may order as it may think fit for restoring the position to what it would have been if the company had not given that preference[1].

(2) If the Court is satisfied that there is a preference transfer of property, movable or immovable, or any delivery of goods, payment, execution made, taken or done by or against a company within one hundred and eighty days before the commencement of winding up, the Court may order as it may think fit and may declare such transaction invalid and restore the position.

394. **Liabilities and rights of certain fraudulently preferred persons.--** (1) Where, in the case of a company which is being wound up, anything made or done after the commencement of this Act, is invalid under section 393 as a fraudulent preference of a person interested in property mortgaged or charged to secure the company's debt, then (without prejudice to any rights or liabilities arising apart from this provision) the person preferred shall be subject to the same liabilities and shall have the same rights as if he had undertaken to be personally liable as surety for the debt to the extent of the charge on the property or the value of his interest, whichever is less.

---

[1] 1985 PLD 193

(2) The value of the said person's interest shall be determined as at the date of the transaction constituting the fraudulent preference, and shall be determined as if the interest were free of all encumbrances other than those to which the charge for the company's debt was then subject.

(3) On any application made to the Court with respect to any payment on the ground that the payment was a fraudulent preference of a surety or guarantor, the Court shall have jurisdiction to determine any questions with respect to the payment arising between the person to whom the payment was made and the surety or guarantor and to grant relief in respect thereof, notwithstanding that it is not necessary so to do for the purposes of the winding up, and for that purpose may give leave to bring in the surety or guarantor as a third party as in the case of a suit for the recovery of the sum paid.

(4) Sub-section (3) shall apply, with the necessary modifications, in relation to transactions other than the payment of money as it applied in relation to such payments.

395. Avoidance of certain attachments, executions.-- (1) Where any company is being wound up by or subject to the supervision of the Court, any attachment, distress or execution put in force without leave of the Court against the estate or effects or any sale held without leave of the Court of any of the properties of the company after the commencement of the winding up shall be void[1].

(2) Nothing in this section applies to proceedings by the Government.

396. Effect of floating charge.-- Where a company is being wound up, a floating charge on the undertaking or property of the company created within one year immediately preceding the commencement of the winding up shall, unless it is proved that the company immediately after the creation of the charge was solvent, be invalid except to the amount of any cash paid to the company at the time of, or subsequently to the creation of, and in consideration for, the charge, together with markup on that amount at the rate of five percent per annum or part thereof or such other rate as may be notified by the Commission in the official Gazette[2].

OFFENCES ANTECEDENT TO OR IN COURSE OF WINDING UP

397. Power of Court to assess damages against delinquent directors.-- If in the course of winding up a company it appears that any person who has taken part in the promotion or formation of the company or any past or present director, liquidator or officer of the company-

---

[1] 2015 CLD 1351; 1993 PLD 404; 1986 PLD 18; 1986 MLD 613; 1985 PLD 193; 1982 PLD 810; 1981 PLD 322; 1972 PLD 287

[2] 2002 CLD 188; 1994 CLC 403 ; 1985 PLD 193; 1961 PLD 630

(a) has misapplied or retained or become liable or accountable for any money or property of the company; or

(b) has been guilty of any misfeasance or breach of trust in relation to the company;

the Court may, on the application of the official liquidator or the liquidator or of any creditor or contributory, made within the time specified in that behalf in sub-section (2), examine into the conduct of the person, director, liquidator or officer aforesaid, and compel him to repay or restore the money or property or any part thereof respectively, with surcharge at such rate as the Court thinks just, or to contribute such sum to the assets of the company by way of compensation in respect of the misapplication, retainer, misfeasance or breach of trust as the Court thinks just[1].

(2) An application under sub-section (1) shall be made within five years from the date of the order for winding up, or of the first appointment of the liquidator in the winding up, or of the misapplication, retainer, misfeasance or breach of trust, as the case may be, whichever is longer.

(3) This section shall apply notwithstanding that the matter is one for which the person concerned may be criminally liable.

398. **Liability for fraudulent conduct of business.--** (1) If in the course of the winding up of a company it appears that any business of the company has been carried on with intent to defraud creditors of the company or any other person, or for any fraudulent purpose, the Court, on the application of the official liquidator or the liquidator or any creditor or contributory of the company, may, if it thinks fit, declare that any persons who were knowingly parties to the carrying on of the business in the manner aforesaid shall be personally responsible, without any limitation of liability, for all or any of the debts or other liabilities of the company as the Court may direct[2].

(2) On the hearing of an application under sub-section (1), the official liquidator or the liquidator, as the case may be, may himself give evidence or call witnesses.

(3) Where the Court makes any such declaration, it may give such further directions as it thinks proper for the purpose of giving effect to that declaration; and, in particular, may make provision for making that liability of any such person under the declaration a charge on any debt or obligation due from the company to him, or on any mortgage or charge or any interest in any mortgage or charge on any assets of the company held by or vested in him, or

---

[1] 2018 CLD 177; 2018 PLD 52; 2016 CLD 1164; 2002 CLD 188; 1994 CLC 403; 1993 CLC 1413; 1989 PLD 435; 1987 CLC 577; 1987 PLD 618; 1985 PLD 193; 1970 PLD 211; 1967 PLD 811; 1965 PLD 110

[2] 2018 CLD 177; 2018 PLD 52; 2016 CLD 1164; 2002 CLD 188; 1994 CLC 403; 1993 CLC 1413

any company or person on his behalf, or any person claiming as assignee from or though the person liable or any company or person acting on his behalf, and may, from time to time, make such further order as may be necessary for the purpose of enforcing any charge imposed under this sub-section.

Explanation.-- For the purpose of this sub-section, the expression "**assignee**" includes any person to whom or in whose favour, by the directions of the person liable, the debt, obligation, mortgage or charge was created, issued or transferred or the interest was created, but does not include an assignee for valuable consideration (not including consideration by way of marriage) given in good faith and without notice of any of the matters on the ground of which declaration is made.

(4) Where any business of a company is carried on with such intent or for such purpose as is mentioned in sub-section (1), every person who was a party to the carrying on of the business in the manner aforesaid shall be punishable with imprisonment for a term which may extend to three years, or with fine which may extend to one million rupees, or with both.

(5) This section shall apply, notwithstanding that the person concerned may be criminally liable in respect of the matters on the ground of which the declaration is to be made.

399. **Liability under sections 397 and 398 to extend to partners or directors in firm or body corporate**.-- Where an order under section 397 or a declaration under section 398 is or may be made in respect of a firm or body corporate, the Court shall also have power to pass an order under section 397 or make a declaration under section 398, as the case may be, in respect of any person who was at the relevant time a partner in that firm or a director of that body corporate[1].

400. **Penalty for fraud by officers of companies which have gone into liquidation.**-- (1) If any person, being at the time of the commission of the alleged offence an officer of a company which is subsequently ordered to be wound up by the Court or which subsequently passes a resolution for voluntary winding up--

(a)   has, by false pretenses or by means of any other fraud, induced any person to give credit to the company; or

(b)   with intent to defraud creditors of the company, has made or caused to be made any gift or transfer of or charge on, or has caused or connived at the levying of any execution against, the property of the company; or

(c)   with intent to defraud creditors of the company, has concealed or removed any part of the property of the company since, or within

---

[1] 2002 CLD 188; 2001 YLR 1954; 1994 CLC 403

sixty days before, the date of any unsatisfied judgment or order for payment of money obtained against the company;

he shall be punishable with imprisonment for a term which may extend to three years, and shall also be liable to a fine which may extend to one million rupees.[1]

(2)   Where the Court has passed an order of winding up of a company and *prima facie* concludes that any of the offence provided in sub-section (1) has been committed, the Court may send a reference for adjudication of offence under sub-section (1) to the court as provided under section 482.

401. **Liability where proper accounts not kept.--** (1) If, where a company is being wound up, it is shown that proper books of account were not kept by the company throughout the period of two years immediately preceding the commencement of the winding up, or the period between the incorporation of the company and the commencement of the winding up, whichever is the shorter, every officer of the company who is in default shall, unless he shows that he acted honestly and that in the circumstances in which the business of the company was carried on the default was excusable, be punishable with imprisonment for a term which may extend to three years or with fine which may extend to one hundred thousand rupees or with both.

(2) For the purpose of sub-section (1), proper books of account shall be deemed not to have been kept in the case of a company, if there have not been kept-

(a)   such books or accounts as are necessary to exhibit and explain the transactions and financial position of the trade or business of the company, including books containing entries from day to day in sufficient detail of all cash received and all cash paid; and

(b)   where the trade or business has involved dealings in goods, statement of the annual stock takings and (except in the case of goods sold by way of ordinary retail trade) of all goods sold and purchased, showing the goods and the buyers and sellers thereof in sufficient detail to enable those goods and those buyers and sellers to be identified.

402. **Penalty for falsification of books.--** If any director, manager, officer, auditor or contributory of any company being wound up destroys, mutilates, alters or falsifies or fraudulently secrets any books, papers or securities, or makes or is privy to the making of any false or fraudulent entry in any register, books or paper belonging to the company with intent to defraud or deceive any person, he shall be liable to imprisonment for a term which may

---

[1] 2002 CLD 188; 1994 CLC 403; 1993 CLC 1413

extend to three years, or with fine which may extend to one million rupees, or with both[1].

403. Prosecution of delinquent directors.-- (1) If it appears to the Court in the course of winding up by, or subject to the supervision of the Court that any past or present director, or other officer, or any member, of the company has been guilty of any offence in relation to the company for which he is criminally liable, the Court may, either on the application of any person interested in the winding up or of its own motion, direct the liquidator either himself to prosecute the offender or to refer the matter to the registrar[2].

(2) If it appears to the liquidator in the course of a voluntary winding up that any past or present director, manager or other officer, or any member, of the company has been guilty of any offence in relation to the company for which he is criminally liable, he shall forthwith report the matter to the registrar and shall furnish to him such information and give to him such access to and facilities for inspecting and taking copies of any documents, being information or documents in the possession or under the control of the liquidator relating to the matter in question, as he may require.

(3) Where any report is made under sub-section (1) or (2) to the registrar, he may, if he thinks fit, refer the matter to the Commission for further inquiry and the Commission may thereupon investigate the matter and may, if it thinks it expedient, appoint one or more competent inspectors to investigate the affairs of the company and to report thereon as if it were a case falling under clause (c) of section 256 and thereupon the provision contained in sections 259 to 273 shall *mutatis mutandis* apply in all respects.

(4) If on any report to the registrar under sub-section (2) it appears to him that the case is not one in which proceedings ought to be taken by him, he shall inform the liquidator accordingly, giving his reasons, and thereupon, subject to the previous sanction of the Court, the liquidator may himself take proceedings against the offender.

(5) If it appears to the Court in the course of a voluntary winding up that any past or present director, manager or other officer, or any member, of the company has been guilty as aforesaid, and that no report with respect to the matter has been made by the liquidator to the registrar, the Court may, on the application of any person interested in the winding up or of its own motion, direct the liquidator to make such a report and, on a report being made accordingly, the provisions of this section shall have effect as though the report has been made in pursuance of the provisions of sub-section (1) or (2).

(6) If, where any matter is reported or referred to the registrar under this section, he considers that the case is one in which a prosecution ought to be

---

[1] 1989 PLD 435; 1987 CLC 577; 1985 PLD 193; 1984 PLD 541
[2] 1987 CLC 577; 1987 PLD 618; 1985 PLD 193

instituted, he shall report the matter to the Commission, and the Commission may, after taking such legal advice as it thinks fit, direct the registrar to proceed in accordance with sections 477 and 486:

Provided that no report shall be made by the registrar under this sub-section without first giving the accused person an opportunity of making a statement in writing to the registrar and of being heard thereon.

(7) Notwithstanding anything contained in the Qanun-e-Shahadat Order, 1984 (P.O. No. Act X of 1984), when any proceedings are instituted under this section it shall be the duty of the liquidator and of every officer and agent of the company past and present (other than the defendant in the proceedings) to give all assistance in connection with the prosecution which he is reasonably able to give, and for the purposes of this sub-section the expression "**agent**" in relation to a company shall be deemed to include any banker or legal adviser of the company and any person employed by the company as auditor, whether that person is or is not an officer of the company.

(8) If any person fails or neglects to give assistance in manner required by sub-section (7), the Court may, on the application of the registrar or the prosecutor, as the case may be, direct that person to comply with the requirements of the said sub-section, and where any such application is made with respect to a liquidator, the Court may, unless it appears that the failure or neglect to comply was due to the liquidator not having in his hands sufficient assets of the company to enable him so to do, direct that the cost of the application shall be borne by the liquidator personally.

404. **Penalty for false evidence.--** If any person, upon any examination upon oath authorised under this Act, or in any affidavit, disposition or solemn affirmation, in or about the winding up of any company under this Act, or otherwise in or about any matter arising under this Act, intentionally gives false evidence, he shall be liable to imprisonment for a term which may extend to three years, and shall also be liable to a fine which may extend to one million rupees[1].

405. **Penal Provisions.--** (1) If any person, being a past or present director, chief executive, manager, auditor or other officer of a company which at the time of the commission of the alleged offence, is being wound up, whether by or under the supervision of the Court or voluntarily or is subsequently ordered to be wound up by the Court or subsequently passes a resolution for voluntary winding up--

    (a)   does not to the best of his knowledge and belief fully and truly discover to the liquidator all the property, real and personal, of the company, and how and to whom and for what consideration and when the company disposed of any part thereof, except such part as

---

[1] 1985 PLD 193

(b) has been disposed of in the ordinary way of the business of the company; or

(c) does not deliver up to the liquidator, or as he directs, all such part of the real and personal property of the company as is in his custody or under his control, and which he is required by law to deliver up; or

(d) does not deliver up to the liquidator, or as he directs, all books and papers in his custody or under his control belonging to the company which he is required by law to deliver up; or

(e) within one year next before the commencement of the winding up or at any time thereafter, conceals any part of the property of the company to the value of one thousand rupees or upwards or conceals any debt due to or from the company; or

(f) within one year next before the commencement of the winding up or at any time thereafter, fraudulently removes any part of the property of the company to the value of one thousand rupees or upward; or

(g) makes any material omission in any statement relating to the affairs of the company; or

(h) knowing or believing that a false debt has been proved by any person under the winding up, fails for the period of a month to inform the liquidator thereof; or

(i) after the commencement of the winding up, prevents the production of any books or papers affecting or relating to the property or affairs of the company; or

(j) within one year next before the commencement of the winding up or at any time thereafter, conceals, destroys, mutilates or falsifies, or is privy to the concealment, destruction, mutilation or falsification of, any book or paper affecting or relating to the property or affairs of the company; or

(k) within one year next before the commencement of the winding up or at any time thereafter, makes or is privy to the making of any false entry in any book or paper affecting or relating to the property or affairs of the company; or

(k) within one year next before the commencement of the winding up or at any time thereafter, fraudulently parts with, alters or makes any omission in, or is privy to the fraudulent parting with, altering or making any omission in, any document affecting or relating to the property or affairs of the company; or

(l) after the commencement of the winding up or at any meeting of the creditors of the company within one year next before the commencement of the winding up, attempts to account for any part of the property of the company by fictitious loses or expenses; or

(m) has within one year next before the commencement of the winding up or at any time thereafter, by any false representation or other fraud, obtained any property for or on behalf of the company on credit which the company does not subsequently pay for; or

(n) within one year next before the commencement of the winding up or at any time thereafter, under the false pretense that the company is carrying on its business, obtains on credit, for or on behalf of the company, any property which the company does not subsequently pay for; or

(o) within one year next before the commencement of the winding up or at any time thereafter, pawns, pledges or disposes of any property of the company which has been obtained on credit and has not been paid for, unless such pawning, pledging or disposing is in the ordinary way of the business of the company; or

(p) is guilty of any false representation or other fraud for the purpose of obtaining the consent of the creditors of the company or any of them to an agreement with reference to the affairs of the company or to the winding up;

he shall be punishable, in the case of the offences mentioned respectively in clauses (m), (n) and of this sub-section, with imprisonment for a term which may extend to five years, and, in the case of any other offence, with imprisonment for a term which may extend to three years and shall also be liable to fine which may extend to five million rupees in each case and the liquidator may, with the permission of the Court, file a complaint before the Court as provided under section 482 for adjudication of offence:

Provided that it shall be a good defence, to a charge under any of clauses (b), (c), (d), (f), and (o), if the accused proves that he had no intent to defraud, and to a charge under any of clauses (a), (h), (i) and (j), if he proves that he had no intent to conceal the state of affairs of the company or to defeat the law.

(2) Where any person pawns, pledges or disposes of any property in circumstances which amount to an offence under clause (o) of sub-section (1) every person who takes in pawn or pledge or otherwise receives the property knowing it to be pawned, pledged or disposed of in such circumstances as aforesaid shall be punishable with imprisonment for a term which may extend to three years, and shall also be liable to a fine which may extend to one million rupees.

SUPPLEMENTARY PROVISIONS AS TO WINDING UP

406. **Liquidator to exercise certain powers subject to sanction.--** (1) The liquidator may, with the sanction of the Court when the company is being wound up by the Court or subject to the supervision of the Court, and with the sanction of a special resolution of the company in the case of a voluntary winding up, do the following things or any of them[1]-

(a)   pay any classes of creditors in full;

(b)   make any compromise or arrangement with creditors or persons claiming to be creditors or having or alleging themselves to have any claim, present or future, whereby the company may be rendered liable;

(c)   compromise any calls and liabilities to calls, debts, and liabilities, capable of resulting in debts, and all claims, present or future, certain or contingent subsisting or supposed to subsist between the company and a contributory or alleged contributory or other debtor or person apprehending liability to the company, and all questions in any way relating to or affecting the assets or liabilities or the winding up of the company, on such terms as may be agreed, and take any security for the discharge of any such calls, debt, liability or claim, and give a complete discharge in respect thereof.

(2) The exercise by the liquidator of the powers under sub-section (1) shall be subject to the control of the Court, and any creditor or contributory may apply to the Court with respect to any exercise or proposed exercise of any of these powers.

407. **Meetings to ascertain wishes of creditors or contributories.--** (1) In all matter relating to the winding up of a company, the Court[2]--

(a)   shall have regard to the wishes of creditors or contributories of the company, as proved to it by any sufficient evidence;

(b)   may, if it thinks fit for the purpose of ascertaining those wishes, direct meetings of the creditors or contributories to be called, held and conducted in such manner as the Court directs; and

(c)   may appoint a person to act as chairman of any such meeting and to report the result thereof to the Court.

(2) When ascertaining the wishes of creditors, regard shall be had to the value of each Creditor's debt.

(3) When ascertaining the wishes of contributories, regard shall be had to the number of votes which may be cast by each contributory.

---

[1] 2005 CLD 713

[2] 2005 CLD 713; 1985 PLD 193; 1984 PLD 541; 1952 PLD 465

408. **Documents of company to be evidence.--** Where any company is being wound up, all books and papers of the company and of the liquidators, shall, as between the contributories of the company, be *prima facie* evidence of the truth of all matters purporting to be recorded therein[1].

409. **Summary disposal of certain suits by liquidators.--** Notwithstanding anything contained in the Code of Civil Procedure, 1908 (Act V of 1908), a liquidator desiring to recover any debt due to the company may apply to the Court in which the proceedings are pending that the same be determined summarily, and the Court may determine it on affidavits but when the Court deems it just and expedient, either on an application made to it in this behalf or of its own motion, it may set down any issue or issues for hearing on other evidence also and pass such orders for discovery of particulars as it may do in a suit.

410. **Limitation.--** Notwithstanding anything contained in the Limitation Act (IX of 1908), in computing the time within which a liquidator may file a suit for the recovery of any debt due to the company, the period which elapses between the making of the petition for liquidation and the assumption of charge by the liquidator, or a period of one year, whichever be greater, shall be excluded.

411. **Court fees.--** (1) Notwithstanding anything contained in the Court-fees Act, 1870 (VII of 1870), or in the Code of Civil Procedure, 1908 (Act V of 1908), where sufficient funds are not available with the liquidator and it is necessary to file a suit for the recovery of a debt due to the company, no court-fee stamp need be affixed on the plaint.

(2) If the liquidator succeeds in the suit, the Court shall calculate the amount of court-fee which would have been paid by the liquidator if he had not been permitted to sue under sub-section (1), and such amount shall be recoverable by the Court from any party ordered by the decree to pay the same.

(3) Where the liquidator does not succeed, the court-fee shall be payable by him out of other assets, if any, whenever realised.

412. **Inspection of documents.--** (1) After an order for a winding up by or subject to the supervision of the Court, the Court may make such order for inspection by creditors and contributories of the company of its documents as the Court thinks just, and any documents in the possession of the company may be inspected by creditors or contributories accordingly[2].

(2) The order as aforesaid may, in the case of voluntary winding up, be made by the Commission.

---

[1] 1985 PLD 193
[2] 1985 PLD 193

(3) Nothing in sub-section (1) shall be taken as excluding or restricting any rights conferred by any law for the time being in force--

(a)   on the Federal Government or a Provincial Government; or

(b)   on the Commission or any officer thereof; or

(c)   on any person acting under the authority of any such Government or the Commission or officer thereof; or

(d)   on the registrar.

413. **Disposal of books and papers of company.**—(1) Subject to any rules made under sub-section (3), when a company has been wound up and is about to be dissolved, the books and papers of the company and of the liquidators may be disposed of as follows[1], that is to say

(a)   in the case of a winding up by or subject to the supervision of the Court in such way as the Court directs;

(b)   in the case of a members voluntary winding up, in such way as the company by special resolution directs; and

(c)   in the case of a creditors' voluntary winding up, in such a way, as the creditors of the company may direct.

(2) After the expiry of three years from the dissolution of the company no responsibility shall rest on the company, or the liquidators, or any person to whom the custody of the books and papers has been committed, by reason of any book or paper not being forthcoming to any person claiming to be interested therein.

(3) The concerned Minister-in-Charge of the Federal Government, may by notification, prevent for such period (not exceeding three years from the dissolution of the company) as the concerned Minister-in-Charge of the Federal Government thinks proper, the destruction of the books and papers of a company which has been wound up, and enable any creditor or contributory of the company to make representations to the concerned Minister-in-Charge of the Federal Government.

(4) Any contravention or default in complying with requirements of this section shall be an offence liable to a penalty of level 2 on the standard scale.

414. **Power of Court to declare dissolution of company void.--** (1) Where a company has been dissolved, the Court may at any time within two years of the date of the dissolution, on an application being made for the purpose by the liquidator of the company or by any other person who appears to the Court to be interested, make an order, upon such terms as the Court thinks fit,

---

[1] 1985 PLD 193

declaring the dissolution to have been void, and thereupon such proceedings may be taken as might have been taken if the company had not been dissolved[1].

(2) It shall be the duty of the person on whose application the order was made, within fifteen days after the making of the order, to file with the registrar a certified copy of the order, and if that person fails so to do he shall be punishable a daily penalty specified in level 1 on the standard scale.

415. **Information as to pending liquidations.--** (1) Where a company is being wound up, if the winding up is not concluded within one year after its commencement, the liquidator shall, once in each half year and at intervals of not more than one hundred and eighty days, or such shorter period as may be prescribed, until the winding up is concluded, file in the Court or with the registrar, as the case may be, a statement in the prescribed form and containing the prescribed particulars with respect to the accounts, proceedings in and position of the liquidation along with the report of auditors[2].

(2) Any person stating himself in writing to be a creditor or contributory of the company shall be entitled, by himself or by his agent, at all reasonable times, on payment of the prescribed fee, to inspect the statement, and to receive a copy thereof or extract therefrom; but any person untruthfully so stating himself to be a creditor or contributory shall be deemed to be guilty of an offence under section 182 of the Pakistan Penal Code, 1860 (Act XLV of 1860), and shall be punishable accordingly on the application of the liquidator.

(3) When the statement is filed in the Court a copy shall simultaneously be filed by the liquidator with the registrar and shall be kept by him along with the other records of the company.

(4) If a liquidator fails to comply with the requirements of this section, he shall be liable to a penalty of level 1 on the standard scale.

416. **Payments by liquidator into bank.--** (1) Every liquidator of a company shall, in such manner as may be prescribed, pay and keep all moneys received by him or which become available with him or come under his control in his capacity as such in a special account opened by him in that behalf in a scheduled bank in the name of the company.

(2) If any such liquidator at any time retains or allows any money to be not so paid and kept as aforesaid or utilises otherwise for more than three days a sum exceeding ten thousand rupees or such other amount as the Court may on the application of the liquidator authorise him to retain then he shall pay surcharge on the amount so retained at the rate of two percent per month or part thereof and shall be liable to (a) disallowance of all or such part of his remuneration as the Court may think just; (b) to make good any loss suffered by

---

[1] 2005 CLD 713; 1987 CLC 1348; 1985 PLD 193
[2] 1985 PLD 193

the company personally and (c) be removed from the office by the Court of its own motion or on application of the registrar or a creditor or contributory of the company, and shall also be liable personally for any loss occasioned by the default.

(3) No liquidator shall pay into his personal account or any account other than the liquidation account of the particular company in liquidation any sums received by him as liquidator.

(4) Every liquidator who makes default in complying with the provisions of this section shall, in addition to his other liabilities, be punishable with imprisonment for a term which may extend to three years and with fine which may extend to the amount of loss caused to the company or wrongful gain or five hundred thousand rupees, whichever is higher.

417. **Unclaimed dividends and undistributed assets to be paid to the account maintained under section 244.--** (1) Without prejudice to the provision of section 244, where any company is being wound up, if the liquidator has in his hands or under his control any money of the company representing unclaimed dividends or undistributed assets payable to any contributory which have remained unclaimed or undistributed for one hundred and eighty days after the date on which they became payable the liquidator shall forthwith deposit the said money in the account to be maintained under section 244 of this Act and the liquidator shall, on the dissolution of the company, similarly pay into the said account any money representing unclaimed dividends or undistributed assets in his hands at the date of dissolution.

(2) The liquidator shall when making any payment referred to in sub-section (1) furnish to the Commission a statement in the specified form setting forth in respect of all sums included in such payment the nature of the sums, the names and last known addresses of the persons entitled to participate therein, the amount to which each is entitled and the nature of his claim thereto, and such other particulars as may be specified, along with the official receipt of the receipt of the State Bank of Pakistan or National Bank of Pakistan, as the case may be.

(3) The receipt of the State Bank of Pakistan or National Bank of Pakistan, as the case may be, for any money paid to it under sub-section (1) shall be an effectual discharge of the liquidator in respect thereof.

(4) The liquidator shall, when filing a statement in pursuance of sub-section (1) of section 415 indicate the sum of money which is payable to the State Bank of Pakistan or National Bank of Pakistan, as the case may be, under sub-section (1) which he has had in his hands or under his control during the one hundred and eighty days preceding the date to which the said statement is brought down and shall within fourteen days of the date of filing the said statement, pay that sum into the account maintained under section 244.

(5) Any person claiming to be entitled to any money paid into the account maintained under section 244 may apply to the Commission for payment thereof in the manner prescribed under said section.

(6) Any liquidator retaining any money which should have been paid by him into the account maintained under section 244 shall, in addition to such money, pay surcharge on the amount retained at the rate of two per cent per month or part thereof and shall also be liable to pay any expenses or losses occasioned by reason of his default and he shall also be liable to disallowance of all or such part of his remuneration as the Court may think just and to be removed from his office by the Court on an application by the Commission.

418. **Books of accounts and other proceedings to be kept by liquidators.--** (l) Every liquidator shall maintain at the registered office proper books of accounts in the manner required in the case of companies under section 220 and the provisions of that section shall apply *mutatis mutandis* to companies being wound up.

(2) Every liquidator shall also keep at the registered office proper books and papers in the manner required under section 338.

(3) Any creditor or contributory may, subject to the control of the Court, inspect any books and papers kept by the liquidator under sub-section (l) and (2).

(4) The concerned Minister-in-Charge of the Federal Government may alter or add to any requirements of this section by a general or special order in which case the provisions so altered or added shall apply.

(5) If any liquidator contravenes any provisions of this section, he shall be punishable with imprisonment for a term, which may extend to two years and with fine, which may extend to five hundred thousand rupees.

419. **Application of provisions relating to audit.--** The provisions of this Act relating to audit of accounts, rights, powers, duties, liabilities and report of auditors of companies and the duties of companies and their officers as applicable to companies shall apply *mutatis mutandis* to companies being wound up, books of account and books and papers kept by the liquidator and his statements of accounts subject as follows-

(a)   all reference therein to officers of the company shall include references to the liquidator;

(b)   the appointment of auditor shall be made by the Court, members or creditors, as the case may be, who appointed the liquidator, who

(c)   shall also fix his remuneration which shall be paid by the liquidator from the funds of the company:

Provided that if no appointment of auditor is made by the members or creditors, as the case may be, the liquidator shall apply to the Commission who shall make the appointment and fix his remuneration.

420. **Enforcement of duty of liquidator to make return.--** (1) If any liquidator who has made any default in complying with any provision of this Act or committed any other irregularity in the performance of his duties fails to make good the default or undo the irregularity, as the case may be, within thirty days after the service on him of a notice requiring him to do so, the Court may of its own motion or on an application made to it by any contributory or creditor of the company or by the registrar, make an order directing the liquidator and any other person involved to make good the default or undo the irregularity or otherwise make amends as the circumstances may require, within such time as may be specified in the order:

Provided that, where an application under this section is made by the registrar, the Court shall dispose of the same within fourteen days of the submission thereof.

(2) Any such order may provide that all costs of, and incidental to, the application shall be borne by the liquidator.

(3) Nothing in this section shall be taken to prejudice the operation of any enactment imposing penalty on a liquidator in respect of any such default or irregularity as aforesaid.

421. **Notification that a company is in liquidation.--** (1) Where a company is being wound up, whether by or under the supervision of the Court or voluntarily, every advertisement, notice, invoice, order for goods, business letter or other communication or document issued by or on behalf of the company or a liquidator of the company or a receiver or manager of the property of the company, being a document on or in which the name of the company appears, shall contain a statement that the company is being wound up and about the mode of its winding up.

(2) If default is made in complying with this section, the company and any of the following persons who authorises or permits the default, namely, any officer of the company, any liquidator of the company and any receiver or manager, shall be liable to a penalty of level 1 on the standard scale.

422. **Court or person before whom affidavit may be sworn.--** (1) Any affidavit required to be sworn under the provisions or for the purposes of this Part may be sworn[1]-

    (a)   in Pakistan, before any Court, judge, or person lawfully authorised to take and receive affidavits; and

---

[1] 1985 PLD 193

(b)   elsewhere before a Pakistan Consul or Vice-Consul.

(2) All courts, judges, justices, commissioners, and persons acting judicially in Pakistan shall take judicial notice of the seal or stamp or signature, as the case may be, of any such court, judge, person, Consul or Vice-Consul, attached, appended or subscribed to any such affidavit or to any other document to be used for the purposes of this Part.

423.   **Power to make rules.--** (1) The Supreme Court may, in consultation with the Courts or, where the Supreme Court advises the Federal Government to do so, the Federal Government may in consultation with the Courts, from time to time, make rules, consistent with this Act, concerning the mode of proceedings to be held for winding up a company in a Court and in the courts subordinate thereto, and for voluntary winding up (both members and creditors), for the holding of meetings of creditors and members in connection with proceedings under section 279 of this Act, and for giving effect to the provisions as to the reduction of the capital and the scheme of reorganisation of a company and generally for all applications to be made to the Court and all other proceedings or matters coming within the purview or powers or duties of the Court under the provisions of this Act and shall make rules providing for all matters relating to the winding up of companies which, by this Act, are to be prescribed[1].

(2) Without prejudice to the generality of the foregoing powers, such rules may enable or require all or any of the powers and duties conferred and imposed on the Court by this Act in respect of the matters following, to be exercised or performed by the official liquidator, and subject to control of the Court, that is to say, the powers and duties of the Court in respect of

(a)   holding and conducting meetings to ascertain the wishes of creditors and contributories;

(b)   settling lists of the contributories and rectifying the register of members where required, and collecting and applying the assets;

(c)   requiring delivery of property or documents to the liquidator;

(d)   making calls;

(e)   fixing a time within which debts and claims must by proved:

Provided that the official liquidator shall not, without the special leave of the Court, rectify the register of members, and shall not make any call without the special leave of the Court.

424.   **Inactive Company.--** (1) Where a company, other than a listed company, is formed for a future project or to hold an asset or intellectual property and has no significant accounting transaction, such a company or an

---

[1] 2013 CLD 1229; 1985 PLD 193; 1952 PLD 465

inactive company may make an application to the registrar in such manner as may be specified for obtaining the status of an inactive company.

Explanation.—For the purposes of this section-

(a) **"inactive company"** means a company, other than a listed company, which has not been carrying on any business or operation, or has not made any significant accounting transaction during the last two financial years;

(b) **"significant accounting transaction"** means any transaction other than-

      (i) payments made by it to fulfill the requirements of this Act or any other law;

      (ii) allotment of shares to fulfill the requirements of this Act; and

      (iii) payments for maintenance of its office and records.

(2) The registrar on consideration of the application shall allow the status of inactive company to the applicant and issue a certificate in such form as may be specified to that effect.

(3) The registrar shall maintain a register of inactive companies in such form as may be specified.

(4) In case of a company which has not filed financial statements or annual returns for two financial years consecutively, the registrar shall issue a notice to that company and enter the name of such company in the register maintained for inactive companies.

(5) An inactive company shall have such minimum number of directors, file such documents as may be specified by the Commission through regulations to the registrar to retain its inactive status in the register and pay such annual fee as prescribed in the Seventh Schedule and may become an active company on an application made in this behalf accompanied by such documents as may be specified by the Commission through regulations on payment of such fee as prescribed in the Seventh Schedule.

(6) The registrar shall strike off the name of an inactive company from the register of inactive companies, which has failed to comply with the requirements of this section.

(7) Any contravention or default in complying with requirements of this section shall be an offence liable to a penalty of level 2 on the standard scale and in case false or misleading information has been given to obtain the status of an inactive company, the directors and other officers of the company in default shall be liable to imprisonment for a term which may extend to three years.

425. **Registrar may strike defunct company off register.**-- (1) Where the registrar has reasonable cause to believe that a company is not carrying on business or is not in operation, he may send to the company by post a letter inquiring whether the company is carrying on business or is in operation[1].

(2) If the registrar does not within fifteen days of sending the letter receive any answer thereto, he may send to the company by registered post another letter referring to the first letter, and stating that no answer thereto has been received and that, if an answer is not received to the second letter within thirty days from the date thereof, a notice will be published in the newspaper with a view to striking the name of the company off the register.

(3) If the registrar either receives an answer from the company to the effect that it is not carrying on business or is not in operation, or does not within fifteen days after sending the second letter receive any answer, he may publish in the newspaper having wide circulation, and send to the company by post a notice that, at the expiration of thirty days from the date of that notice, the name of the company mentioned therein will, unless cause is shown to the contrary, be struck off the register and the company will be dissolved.

(4) Without prejudice to any other provisions, if, in any case where a company is being wound up, the registrar has reasonable cause to believe either that no liquidator is acting or that the affairs of the company are fully wound up, and the returns required to be made by the liquidator have not been made for a period of three consecutive months after notice by the registrar demanding the returns has been sent by post to the company, or to the liquidator at his last known place of business, the registrar may publish in the newspaper having wide circulation and send to the company a like notice as is provided in the last preceding sub-section.

(5) At the expiration of the time mentioned in the notice the registrar may, unless cause to the contrary is previously shown by the company or the liquidator, as the case may be, strike its name off the register, and shall publish notice thereof in the official Gazette, and, on the publication in the official Gazette of this notice, the company shall be dissolved:

Provided that the liability criminal, civil or otherwise (if any) of every director, officer, liquidator and member of the company shall continue and may be enforced as if the company had not been dissolved:

Provided further that nothing in this section shall affect the powers of the Court to wind up a company the name of which has been struck off the register.

---

[1] 2017 CLD 1127; 2008 CLD 1312; 2007 CLD 1234; 2005 CLD 1177; 1992 MLD 1094; 1992 CLC 1099; 1991 CLC 1520; 1990 PTD 520; 1988 CLC 1538; 1985 PLD 193; 1981 PLD 447; 1974 SCMR 15

(6) If a company or any member or creditor thereof feels aggrieved by the company having been struck off the register, the Court, on the application of the company or a member or creditor made before the expiry of three years from the publication in the official Gazette of the notice aforesaid, may, if satisfied that the company was at the time of the striking off carrying on business or in operation, or otherwise that it is just that the company be restored to the register, order the name of the company to be restored to the register and, upon the filing of a certified copy of such order with the registrar, the company shall be deemed to have continued in existence as if its name had not been struck off, and the Court may by the order give such directions and make such provisions as seem just for placing the company and all other persons in the same position as nearly as may be as if the name of the company had not been struck off.

(7) A letter or notice under this section may be addressed to the company at its registered office, or if no office has been registered, to the care of some director, chief executive or other officer of the company whose name and address are known to the registrar or if no such address is known to the registrar, may be sent to each of the persons who subscribed the memorandum, addressed to him at the address mentioned in the memorandum.

(8) The provisions of this section shall not apply to a company which has any known assets and liabilities, and such company shall be proceeded against for winding up.

(9) If due to inadvertence or otherwise the name of any company which has any assets and liabilities or which has been in operation or carrying on business or about whose affairs any enquiry or investigation may be necessary has been struck off the register, the registrar may, after such enquiries as he may deem fit, move the Commission to have the name of the company restored to the register and thereupon the Commission may, if satisfied that it will be just and proper so to do, order the name of the company to be restored and shall exercise the powers of the Court in the manner provided in sub-section (6).

(10) The provisions of this section shall *mutatis mutandis* apply to a company established outside Pakistan but having a place of business in Pakistan as they apply to a company registered in Pakistan.

426. **Easy exit of a defunct company.--** (1) A company which ceases to operate and has no known assets and liabilities, may apply to the registrar in the specified manner, seeking to strike its name off the register of companies on payment of such fee mentioned in the Seventh Schedule.

(2) After examination of the application, the registrar on being satisfied, may publish a notice in terms of sub-section (3) of section 425 of this Act, in the Official Gazette stating that at the expiration of ninety days from the date of that notice, unless cause is shown to the contrary, the name of the applicant company

will be struck off the register of companies and the company will be dissolved. Such notice shall also be posted on the Commission's website.

(3) At the expiration of the time mentioned in the notice, the registrar may, unless any objection to the contrary is received by him, strike its name off the register, and shall publish a notice thereof in the official Gazette, and, on the publication of such notice, the company shall stand dissolved:

Provided that the liability criminal, civil or otherwise (if any) of every director, officer and member of the company shall continue and may be enforced as if the company had not been dissolved.

PART XI

WINDING UP OF UNREGISTERED COMPANIES

427. **Meaning of "unregistered company".--** For the purposes of this Part, the expression "**unregistered company**" shall not include a railway company incorporated by Act of Parliament of the United Kingdom or by a Pakistan law, nor a company registered under any previous Companies Act or under this Act, but save as aforesaid, shall include any partnership, association or company consisting of more than seven members[1].

428. **Winding up of unregistered companies.--** (1) Subject to the provisions of this Part, any unregistered company may be wound up under this Act, and all the provisions of this Act with respect to winding up shall apply to an unregistered company[2], with the following exceptions and additions--

(a) an unregistered company shall, for the purpose of determining the Court having jurisdiction in the matter of the winding up, be deemed to be registered in the Province where its principal place of business is situated or, if it has a principal place of business situate in more than one Province then in each Province where it has a principal place of business; and the principal place of business situate in the Province in which proceedings are being instituted shall, for all the purposes of the winding up, be deemed to be the registered office of the company;

(b) no unregistered company shall be wound up under this Act voluntarily or subject to supervision of the Court;

(c) the circumstances in which an unregistered company may be wound up are as follows (that is to say)-

---

[1] 1992 PLD 230; 1986 CLC 2933; 1951 PLD 293

[2] 2018 CLD 1205; 2005 CLD 879; 2002 CLD 746; 1998 CLC 1194; 1991 CLC 1148; 1986 CLC 2933; 1983 CLC 162; 1951 PLD 293

        (i)   if the company is dissolved, or has ceased to carry on business or is carrying on business only for the purpose of winding up its affairs;

        (ii)   if the company is unable to pay its debts;

        (iii)   if the Court is of opinion that it is just and equitable that the company should be wound up;

(d)   an unregistered company shall, for the purposes of this Act, be deemed to be unable to pay its debts-

        (i)   if a creditor, by assignment or otherwise, to whom the company is indebted in a sum exceeding fifty thousand rupees then due, has served on the company, by leaving at its principal place of business, or by delivering to the secretary, or some director, manager or principal officer of the company, or by otherwise serving in such manner as the Court may approve or direct, a demand under his hand requiring the company to pay the sum so due, and the company has for thirty days after the service of the demand neglected to pay the sum, or to secure or compound for it to the satisfaction of the creditor;

        (ii)   if any suit or other legal proceeding has been instituted against any member for any debt or demand due or claimed to be due, from the company or from him in his character of member, and notice in writing of the institution of the suit or other legal proceeding having been served on the company by leaving the same at its principal place of business or by delivering it to the secretary, or some director, manager or principal officer of the company or by otherwise serving the same in such manner as the Court may approve or direct, the company has not within fifteen days after service of the notice paid, secured or compounded for the debt or demand, or procured the suit or other legal proceeding to be stayed, or indemnified the defendant to his reasonable satisfaction against the suit or other legal proceeding, and against all costs, damages and expenses to be incurred by him by reason of the same;

        (iii)   if execution or other process issued on a decree or order obtained in any Court or other competent authority in favour of a creditor against the company, or any member thereof as such, or any person authorised to be sued as nominal defendant on behalf of the company, is returned unsatisfied in whole or in part;

(iv) if it is otherwise proved to the satisfaction of the Court that the company is unable to pay its debts; and, in determining whether a company is unable to pay its debts, the Court shall take into account the contingent and prospective liabilities of the company and its solvency.

(2) Nothing in this Part shall affect the operation of any enactment which provides for any partnership, association or company being wound up, or being wound up as a company or as an unregistered company, under any previous Companies Act:

Provided that references in any such enactment to any provision contained in any previous Companies Act shall be read as references to the corresponding provision (if any) of this Act.

(3) Where a company incorporated outside Pakistan which has been carrying on business in Pakistan ceases to carry on business in Pakistan, it may be wound up as an unregistered company under this Part, notwithstanding that it has been dissolved or otherwise ceased to exist as a company under or by virtue of the laws of the country under which it was incorporated.

429. Contributories in winding up of unregistered companies.-- (1) In the event of an unregistered company being wound up, every person shall be deemed to be a contributory who is liable to pay or contribute to the payment of any debt or liability of the company or to pay or contribute to the payment of any sum for the adjustment of the rights of the members among themselves, or to pay or contribute to the payment of the cost and expenses of winding up the company, and every contributory shall be liable to contribute to the assets of the company all sums due from him in respect of any such liability as aforesaid[1].

(2) In the event of any contributory dying or being adjudged insolvent, the provisions of this Act with respect to the legal representatives and heirs of deceased contributories, and to the assignees of insolvent contributories, shall apply.

430. Power to stay or restrain proceedings.-- The provisions of this Act with respect to staying and restraining suits and legal proceedings against a company at any time after the presentation of a petition for winding up and before the making of a winding up order shall, in the case of an unregistered company where the application to stay or restrain is by a creditor; extend to suits and legal proceedings against any contributory of the company[2].

431. Suits stayed on winding up order.-- Where an order has been made for winding up an unregistered company, no suit or other legal proceedings shall be proceeded with or commenced against any contributory of

---

[1] 1986 CLC 2933
[2] 1986 CLC 2933

the company in respect of any debt of the company, except by leave of the Court, and subject to such terms as the Court may impose[1].

432. **Directions as to property in certain cases.--** If an unregistered company has no power to sue and be sued in a common name, or if for any reason it appears expedient, the Court may, by the winding up order, or by any subsequent order, direct that all or any part of the property, movable or immovable, including all interests and rights in, to and out of property, movable and immovable, and including obligations and actionable claims as may belong to the company or to trustees on its behalf, is to vest in the official liquidator by his official name and thereupon the property or any part thereof specified in the order shall vest accordingly; and the official liquidator may, after giving such indemnity (if any) as the Court may direct, bring or defend in his official name any suit or other legal proceeding relating to that property, or necessary to be brought or defended for the purposes of effectually winding up the company and recovering its property[2].

433. **Provisions of this part cumulative.--** The provisions of this Part with respect to unregistered companies shall be in addition to, and not in derogation of, any provisions hereinbefore, in this Act contained with respect to winding up of companies by the Court and the Court or official liquidator may exercise any powers or do any act in the cases of unregistered companies which might be exercised or done by it or him in winding up companies formed and registered under this Act; but an unregistered company shall not, except in the event of its being wound up, be deemed to be a company under this Act, and then only to the extent provided by this Part[3].

---

[1] 2018 CLD 1205; 1986 CLC 2933
[2] 1986 CLC 2933
[3] 1986 CLC 2933

PART XII

COMPANIES ESTABLISHED OUTSIDE PAKISTAN

PROVISIONS AS TO ESTABLISHMENT OF PLACES OF BUSINESS IN PAKISTAN

434. **Application of this Part to foreign companies.--** This Part shall apply to all foreign companies, that is to say, companies incorporated or formed outside Pakistan which, after the commencement of this Act, establish a place of business within Pakistan or which have, before the commencement of this Act, established a place of business in Pakistan and continue to have an established either a place of business within Pakistan or conduct business in Pakistan through an agent or any other means at the commencement of this Act[1].

435. **Documents to be delivered to registrar by foreign companies.--** (1) Every foreign company which, after the commencement of this Act, establishes a place of business in Pakistan shall, within thirty days of the establishment of the place of business or conduct of business activity, deliver to the registrar[2]—

(a) a certified copy of the charter, statute or memorandum and articles of the company, or other instrument constituting or defining the constitution of the company, and if the instrument is not written in the English or Urdu language, a certified translation thereof in the English or Urdu language;

(b) the full address of the registered or principal office of the company;

(c) a list of the directors, chief executive and secretary (if any) of the company;

(d) a return showing the full present and former names and surnames, father's name or, in the case of a married woman or widow, the name of her husband or deceased husband, present and former nationality, designation and full address in Pakistan of the principal officer of the company in Pakistan by whatever name called;

(e) the full present and former names and surnames, father's name, or, in case of a married woman or widow, the name of her husband or deceased husband, present and former nationality, occupation and full addresses of some one or more persons resident in Pakistan authorised to accept on behalf of the company service of process and any notice or other document required to be served on the company together with his consent to do so; and

---

[1] 2000 SCMR 950

[2] 2018 CLD 668; 2013 PLD 461; 2012 PLD 1; 2012 CLD 675; 2007 CLD 248; 2004 CLD 399; 2003 YLR 2150; 2003 YLR 2843; 2003 CLD 211; 2002 SCMR 450; 2001 SCMR 1877; 2000 SCMR 950

(f)   the full address of that office of the company in Pakistan which is to be deemed its principal place of business in Pakistan of the company.

Explanation.—For the purposes of this section the term "conduct of business activity" includes any business to be undertaken by a foreign company by virtue of its memorandum and articles of association or as licensed or authorized by any law.

(2) The list referred to in clause (c) of sub-section (1) shall contain the following particulars, that is to say--

(a)   with respect to each director--

    (i)   in the case of an individual, his present and former name and surname in full, his usual residential address, his nationality, and if that nationality is not the nationality of origin, his

    (ii)   nationality of origin, and his business occupation, if any, and any other directorship which he holds;

    (iii)   in the case of a body corporate, its corporate name and registered or principal office; and the full name, address, nationality and nationality of origin, if different from that nationality, of each of its director;

(b)   with respect to the secretary, or where there are joint secretaries, with respect to each of them—

    (i)   in the case of an individual, his present and former name and surname, and his usual residential address;

    (ii)   in the case of a body corporate, its corporate name and registered or principal office:

Provided that, where all the partner in a firm are joint secretaries of the company, the name and principal office of the firm may be stated instead of the particulars mentioned in clause (b).

(3) Every foreign company, other than a company mentioned in sub-section (1) shall, if it has not delivered to the registrar before the commencement of this Act the documents and particulars specified in section 451 of the Companies Ordinance, 1984 (XLVII of 1984), shall continue to be subject to the obligation to deliver those documents and particulars and be liable to penalties in accordance with the provisions of that Ordinance.

436. **Return to be delivered to registrar by foreign companies whose documents altered.** If any alteration is made or occurs in—

(a)   the charter, statute or memorandum and articles of a foreign company or any such instrument as is referred to in section 435;

(b)   the address of the registered or principal office of the company

(c)   the directors, chief executive or secretary or in the particulars contained in the list referred to in section 435;

(d)   the principal officer referred to in section 435;

(e)   the name or addresses or other particulars of the persons authorised to accept service of process, notices and other documents on behalf of the company as referred to in the preceding section 435, or

(f)   the principal place of business of the company in Pakistan;

the company shall, within thirty days of the alteration, deliver to the registrar for registration a return containing the specified particulars of the alteration and in the case of change in persons authorised to accept service of process, notices and other documents on behalf of the company, also his consent to do so[1].

437. **Accounts of foreign companies.--** (1) Every foreign company shall in every year make out and file with the registrar, together with a list of Pakistani members and debenture-holders and of the places of business of the company in Pakistan[2]--

(a)   such number of copies of financial statements, not being less than three, as may be specified, in such form, audited by such person, containing such particulars and including or having annexed or attached thereto such documents (including, in particular documents relating to every subsidiary of the company) as nearly as may be as under the provisions of this Act it would, if it were a company formed and registered under this Act, be required to file in accordance with the provisions of this Act, in respect of the company's operations in Pakistan as if such operations had been conducted by a separate public company formed and registered in Pakistan under this Act; and

(b)   in a case where, by the law for the time being in force of the country in which the company is incorporated, such company is required to file with the public authority an annual statement of financial position and profit and loss accounts, also such number of copies of that statement of financial position and profit and loss account together with any documents annexed thereto as may be specified, and if the same is not in the English language a certified translation thereof in the English language; or

---

[1] 2018 CLD 668; 2013 PLD 461; 2012 CLD 675; 2012 PLD 1; 2007 CLD 248; 2004 CLD 399; 2003 CLD 211; 2003 CLD 1075; 2003 YLR 2843; 2002 CLD 1487; 2002 SCMR 450; 2001 SCMR 1877; 2000 SCMR 950
[2] 2011 CLD 1546; 2000 SCMR 950

(c)   in a case where a company is not required to file with the public authority of the country in which the company is incorporated an annual statement of financial position and profit and loss account as referred to in clause (b), the specified number of copies, not being less than three, of the statement of financial position and profit and loss account and the report of auditors and other documents annexed thereto, in such form and manner as under the provisions of this Act it would, if it had been a public company within the meaning of this Act, be required to make out and lay before the company in general meeting.

(2) The period within which the documents, returns or reports referred to in sub-section are to be filed with the registrar shall be a period of forty five days from the date of submission of such documents or returns to the public authority of the country of incorporation or within one hundred and eighty days of the date up to which the relevant accounts are made up, whichever is earlier.

438.   **Certain obligations of foreign companies.--** Every foreign company shall[1]–

(a)   maintain at its principal place of business in Pakistan, or, if it has only one place of business in Pakistan, in that place of business, a register of Pakistani members and debenture-holders, directors and officers, which shall be open to inspection and copies thereof supplied as in the case of similar registers maintained by a company under this Act;

(b)   in every prospectus inviting subscriptions for its shares or debentures in Pakistan, state the country in which the company is incorporated;

(c)   conspicuously exhibit on the outside of every place where it carries on business in Pakistan the name of the company and the country in which the company is incorporated in letter easily legible in English or Urdu characters and also, if any place where it carries on business is beyond the local limits of the ordinary original civil jurisdiction of a Court, in the characters of one of the vernacular language used in that place;

(d)   cause the name of the company and of the country in which the company is incorporated mentioned in legible English or Urdu characters in all bill-heads and letter papers, and in all notices, advertisements, documents and other official publications of the company; and

---

[1] 2000 SCMR 950

(e) if the liability of the members of the company is limited, cause notice of that fact to be stated in legible English or Urdu characters in every prospectus inviting subscriptions for its shares, and in all bill-heads and letter papers, notices, advertisements and other official publications of the company in Pakistan, and to be exhibited on the outside of every place where it carries on business in Pakistan.

439. Power of the Commission to require information from foreign companies.-- (1) The Commission may, at any time, call upon a foreign company to furnish information of shareholding including beneficial ownership or such other information or document, as may be required for the purposes of this Act or in connection with any inspection, inquiry or investigation and it shall be the duty of the company and its officers to furnish such information or document within specified time.

(2) Any person who fails to provide any information or document required under sub-section (1) shall commit an offence liable to a penalty of level 3 on standard scale.

440. Service on foreign company.-- Any process, notice or other document required to be served on such company as is referred to in this Part shall be deemed to be sufficiently served if addressed to any person whose name has been so filed with the registrar as aforesaid and left at or sent by post to the address which has been so filed[1]:

Provided that--

(a) where any such company makes default in delivering to the registrar the name and address of a person resident in Pakistan who is authorised to accept on behalf of the company service of process, notices or other documents; or

(b) if at any time all the persons whose names and addresses have been so filed are dead or have ceased to so reside, or refuse to accept service on behalf of the company or for any reason cannot be served;

a document may be served on the company against an acknowledgement or by post or courier service to, any place of business established by the company in Pakistan or through electronic means or in any other manner as may be specified.

441. Company's failure to comply with this part not to affect its liability under contracts.-- Any failure by a foreign company to comply with any of the requirement or section 435 or section 436 shall not affect the validity of any contract, dealing or transaction entered into by the company or its

---

[1] 2000 SCMR 950

liability to be sued in respect thereof; but the company shall not be entitled to bring any suit, claim any set-off, make any counter-claim or institute any legal proceeding in respect of any such contract, dealing or transaction, until it has complied with the provisions of section 435 and section 436[1].

442. **Provisions relating to names, inquiries to apply to foreign companies.--** The provisions of sections 10 to 13 relating to names and changes in the names of companies shall, as far as applicable, also apply to companies to which this Part applies; and the power of inspection, inquiries and investigation conferred by this Act on the registrar and the Commission in respect of companies shall likewise extend to such companies[2].

443. **Intimation of ceasing to have place of business to be given.--** (1) Any company to which this Part applies shall at least thirty days before it intends to cease to have any place of business in Pakistan, –

(a) give a notice of such intention to the registrar; and

(b) publish a notice of such intention at least in two daily newspapers circulating in the Province or Provinces in which such place or places of business are situate[3].

(2) As from the date of intention to cease to have any place of business in Pakistan stated in the notice referred to in sub-section (1), unless the said date is by a similar notice altered, the obligation of the company to delivery any document to the registrar shall cease, provided it has no other place of business in Pakistan.

444. **Penalties.--** (1)If any foreign company fails to comply with any of the provisions of this Part, except section 439, the company, and every officer or agent of the company who authorises or permits the default, shall be liable to a penalty of level 1 on the standard scale[4].

(2) If a foreign company or any of its directors or other persons as referred in section 439 fails to comply with the provisions of said section, shall be liable to a penalty of level 2 on the standard scale.

445. **Interpretation of provisions of this Part.--** For the purposes of this Part[5]--

(a) the expression "certified" means certified in the specified manner to be a true copy or a correct translation;

---

[1] 2018 CLD 668; 2013 PLD 461; 2007 CLD 248; 2004 CLD 399; 2003 CLD 211; 2003 YLR 2843; 2002 SCMR 450; 2002 CLD 1487; 2001 SCMR 1877; 2000 SCMR 950

[2] 2000 SCMR 950

[3] 2000 SCMR 950

[4] 2003 CLD 211; 2000 SCMR 950

[5] 2000 SCMR 950

(b)   the expression "director", in relation to a company includes any person in accordance with whose directives or instructions the directors of the company are accustomed to act;

(c)   the expression "place of business" includes a branch, management, share transfer or registration office, factory, mine or other fixed place of business, but does not include an agency unless the agent has, and habitually exercise, a general authority to negotiate and conclude contracts on behalf of the company or maintains a stock of merchandise belonging to the company from which he regularly fills orders on its behalf:

Provided that:

(i)   a company shall not be deemed to have an established place of business in Pakistan merely because it carries on business

(ii)   dealings in Pakistan through a bona fide broker or general commission agent acting in the ordinary course of his business as such;

(iii)   the fact that a company has a subsidiary which is incorporated, resident, or carrying on business in Pakistan (whether through an established place of business or otherwise) shall not of itself constitute the place of business of that subsidiary an established place of business of the company; and

(d)   the expression "secretary" includes any person occupying the position of secretary, by whatever name called.

PROSPECTUS

446.   **Issue of prospectus.--** No person shall issue, circulate or distribute in Pakistan any prospectus offering for subscription securities of a foreign company or soliciting deposits of money, whether the company has or has not established, or when formed will or will not establish, a place of business in Pakistan unless authorised to do so by the Commission under the relevant law or as may be specified[1].

447.   **Restriction on canvassing for sale of securities.--** (1) No person shall go from house to house offering securities of a foreign company for subscription or purchase to the public or any member of the public.

Explanation.-- In this sub-section, "**house**" shall not include an office used for business purposes.

---

[1] 1965 PLD 110

(2) Any contravention or default in complying with requirement of this section shall be an offence liable to a penalty of level 3 on the standard scale.

448. **Registration of charges.--** (1) The provision of sections 100 to 112 both inclusive, shall extend to charges on properties in Pakistan which are created, and to charges on property in Pakistan which is acquired, by a foreign company which has an established place of business in Pakistan:

Provided that references in the said sections to the registered office of the company shall be deemed to be reference to the principal place of business in Pakistan of the company:

Provided further that, where a charge is created outside Pakistan or the completion of the acquisition of property takes place outside Pakistan, clause (a) of the proviso to sub-section (1) and sub-section (4) of section 100 shall apply as if the property wherever situated were situated outside Pakistan.

(2) Where a company to which this section applies creates, or has created at any time before establishing a place of business in Pakistan, a charge

(3) on any property otherwise registerable under this Act it shall register the same with the registrar in accordance with the provisions of this Act-

(a)   within thirty days of the establishment of a place of business in Pakistan; or

(b)   if the charge was created before the commencement of this Act and subsisted immediately before such commencements, within ninety days thereof.

449. **Notice of appointment of receiver.--** The provisions of section 113 and 114 shall *mutatis mutandis* apply to the case of all foreign companies having an established place of business in Pakistan and the provisions of section 220 shall apply to such companies to the extent of requiring them to keep at their principal place of business in Pakistan the books of account required by that section with respect to money received and expended, sales and purchases made, and assets and liabilities in relation to its business in Pakistan:

Provided that references in the said section to the registered office of the company shall be deemed to be reference to the principal place of business in Pakistan of the company.

450. **Notice of liquidation.--** (1) If a foreign company having an established place of business in Pakistan goes into liquidation in the country of its incorporation, it shall–

(a)   within thirty days give notice thereof to the registrar, and simultaneously publish a notice at least in two daily newspapers circulating in the Province or Provinces or the part of Pakistan not forming part of a Province, as the case may be, in which its place or places of business are situated and furnish to the registrar within thirty days of the conclusion of the liquidation proceedings all returns relating to the liquidation and the liquidation account in respect of such portion of the company's affairs as relates to its business in Pakistan; and

(b)   cause in legible letters, a statement to appear, on every invoice, order, bill-head, letter paper, notice of other publication in Pakistan, to the effect that the company is being wound up in the country of its incorporation.

(2)   Where a company to which this section applies has been dissolved, or has otherwise ceased to exist, no person shall, after the date of such dissolution or cessation, carry on, or purport to carry on, any business in Pakistan in the name or on behalf of such company.

(3) Nothing in this section shall be construed as preventing a company to which this section applies from being wound up in Pakistan in accordance with the provisions of this Act, notwithstanding that it has neither been dissolved nor otherwise ceased to exist in the country of its incorporation.

PART XIII

GENERAL

451. **Certification of *Shariah* compliant companies and *Shariah* compliant securities.--** (1) No company shall claim that it is a *Shariah* compliant company unless it has been declared *Shariah* compliant in such form and manner as may be specified.

(2) No person shall claim that a security, whether listed or not, is *Shariah* compliant unless it has been declared *Shariah* compliant in such form and manner as may be specified.

(3) For the purposes of sub-section (1) and (2), no company shall appoint or engage any person for *Shariah* compliance, *Shariah* advisory, or *Shariah* audit unless that person meets the fit and proper criteria and fulfills such terms and conditions as may be specified:

Provided that the person already appointed or engaged by a company for the purpose of sub-section 3 shall have 180 days to meet the fit and proper criteria and fulfill such terms and conditions as may be specified.

(4) Every person who is responsible for contravention of this section shall without prejudice to other liabilities be liable to a penalty not exceeding level 3 on the standard scale.

(5)   Nothing in sub-section (1) and (3) shall apply to a banking company or any other company which is required to follow the *Shariah* governance framework prescribed by the State Bank of Pakistan.

452. **Companies' Global Register of Beneficial Ownership.**(1) Every substantial shareholder or officer of a company incorporated under the Company law, who is citizen of Pakistan within the meaning of the Citizenship Act, 1951 (II of 1951), including dual citizenship holder whether residing in Pakistan or not having shareholding in a foreign company or body corporate shall report to the company his shareholding or any other interest as may be notified by the Commission, on a specified form within thirty days of holding such position or interest.

Explanation.-- For the purposes of this section the expression "foreign company" means a company or body corporate incorporated or registered in any form, outside Pakistan regardless of the fact that it has a place of business or conducts any business activity or has a liaison office in Pakistan or not.

(2) The company shall submit all the aforesaid information received by it during the year to the registrar along with the annual return.

(3) Any investment in securities or other interest as may be notified in sub-section (1) by a company incorporated under this Act, in a foreign company or body corporate or any other interest shall also be reported to the registrar along with the annual return.

(4) All the above information shall be reported to the registrar through a special return on a specified form within sixty days from the commencement of this Act and thereafter in accordance with the sub-section (2).

(5) Any contravention or default in complying with requirements of this section shall be an offence liable to a fine of level 1 on the standard scale and the registrar shall make an order specifying time to provide information under sub-section (1) and (3).

(6) Any person who fails to comply with the direction given under sub-section (5) by the registrar shall be punishable with imprisonment which may extend to three years and with fine up to five hundred thousand rupees or both.

(7) The Commission shall keep record of the information in the Companies' Global Register of Beneficial Ownership.

(8) The Commission shall provide the information maintained under sub-section (7) to the Federal Board of Revenue or to any other agency, authority and court.

453. **Prevention of offences relating to fraud, money laundering and terrorist financing.--** (1)Every officer of a company shall endeavor to prevent the commission of any fraud, offences of money laundering including predicated offences as provided in the Anti-Money Laundering Act, 2010 (VII of 2010) with respect to affairs of the company and shall take adequate measures for the purpose.

(2) Whosoever fails to comply with the provisions of this section shall be liable to punishment of imprisonment for a term which may extend to three years and with fine which may extend to one hundred million rupees:

Provided that where any such officer has taken all reasonable measures available under the applicable laws within his capacity to prevent commission of such offence, shall not be liable under this section.

Provided further that the punishment provided under this section shall be in addition to any punishment attracted due to active involvement of such officer in commission of an offence of money laundering under Anti-Money Laundering Act, 2010 (VII of 2010).

454. **Free Zone Company.--** (1) A company incorporated for the purpose of carrying on business in the export processing zone or an area notified by the Federal Government as free zone, shall be eligible to such exemptions from the requirements of this Act as may be notified in terms of section 459.

(2) The Commission may, for the protection of foreign investors and to secure foreign investment, restrict the disclosure of information maintained by the registrar regarding promoters, shareholders and directors of the company incorporated under sub-section (1), who are foreign nationals unless such disclosure of information is authorized by the company in writing:

Provided that the restriction of non-disclosure contained in this section shall not apply to the revenue authorities collecting tax, duties and levies or requirement or obligation under international law, treaty or commitment of the Government.

(3) A company formed for the purposes stated in sub-section (1) may be dispensed with the words "Private Limited" or "Limited" as the case may be, and called as the "Free Zone Company" having the parenthesis and alphabets "FZC" at the end of its name.

(4) A Free Zone Company shall pay thc annual renewal fee as specified in the Seventh Schedule.

455. **Filing of documents through intermediaries**.-- (1) A person may, for the purpose of filing of documents under this Act, avail services of intermediary as may be specified.

(2) An intermediary intending to provide services in terms of sub-section (1) must possess the requisite qualification and be registered with the Commission in the manner as may be specified.

(3) The registration as intermediary under this section shall be liable to be cancelled by the Commission on such grounds and in such manner as may be specified after providing an opportunity of being heard.

456.   **Acceptance of advances by real estate companies engaged in real estate projects.--** (1) Notwithstanding anything contained in this Act or any other law, any company which invites advances from public for real estate project shall comply with the provisions of this section in addition to those provided in the other provisions of this Act.

(2)   A company engaged in real estate project shall--

(a)   not announce any real estate project, unless it has obtained the approval of the Commission and all necessary approvals, permissions, NOCs of the concerned authorities required as per applicable general, special and local laws, having jurisdiction over area under which the real estate project is being developed or undertaken to the satisfaction of the Commission and subject to such additional disclosure requirements as may be notified;

(b)   not make any publication or advertisement of real estate projects, unless it has obtained the approval of the Commission and all necessary approvals, permissions, NOCs of the concerned authorities required as per applicable general, special and local laws, having jurisdiction over area under which the real estate project is being developed or undertaken to the satisfaction of the Commission and subject to such additional disclosure requirements as may be notified;

(c)   not accept any advances or deposits in any form whatsoever against any booking to sell or offer for sale or invite persons to purchase any land, apartment or building, as the case may be, in any real estate project or part of it, unless it has obtained the approval of the Commission and all necessary approvals, permissions, NOCs, of the concerned authorities required as per applicable general, special and local laws, having jurisdiction over area under which the real estate project is being developed or undertaken to the satisfaction of the Commission and subject to such additional disclosure requirements as may be notified;

(d)   not accept a sum against purchase of the apartment, plot or building, as the case may be, as an advance payment from a person without first entering into a written agreement for sale with such person except nominal fee for application;

(e)   maintain and preserve such books of account, records and documents in the manner as may be specified;

(f)   deposit any sum obtained from the allottees, from time to time, in a separate escrow account opened in the name of the project as may be specified;

(g) comply with any directions notified by the Commission and accounting framework as may be notified; and

(h) do or not to do any act or activity as may be specified.

(3) For the purposes of this section the escrow accounts shall be dedicated exclusively for carrying out the project and no attachment shall be imposed on the payment of such escrow accounts for the benefit of creditors of the real estate company except for the purpose of project and the real estate company shall recognize its income in accordance with International Financial Reporting Standards notified by the Commission.

(4) The Commission shall provide copy of any returns or information submitted by real estate company free of cost to the concerned authority, on their request, to enable such authority to regulate real estate project under its jurisdiction in accordance with the applicable laws.

(5) The conditions laid down under this section shall be in addition to and not in derogation of requirement of law and concerned authority under whose jurisdiction the project is being undertaken by the real estate company shall continue to exercise its authority in a manner provided in the relevant law.

(6) Any person who contravenes the provisions of this section shall be guilty of an offence which is liable to a penalty of level 3 on the standard scale.

Explanations.-- For the purposes of this section the-

(i) expression "**real estate project**" shall include projects for the development and construction of residential or commercial buildings or compounds and shall not include other construction project;

(ii) expression "**authority**" shall include authority created or prescribed under any law which has powers to give permission for planning and development of real estate project in specific area.

457. **Agriculture Promotion Companies.--** (1) Notwithstanding anything contained in this Act or any other law for the time being in force, any person, having its Principal line of business related to produce for agriculture promotion or managing produce as collateral or engaged in any activity connected with or related to any Produce or other related activities may establish Agriculture Promotion Company under this section in such form and manner and subject to such terms, conditions and limitations as may be specified.

Explanation.-- For the purpose of this section:

(a) "**Agriculture Promotion Company**" includes a Producer Company or a Collateral Management Company involved in Produce or any other company or class of companies or corporate body or any other entity as the concerned Minister-in-Charge of the

Federal Government may, by notification in the official Gazette specify as Agriculture Promotion Company under this section;

(b)   **"Produce"** means-

(i)   produce of farmers, arising from agriculture (including animal husbandry, forest products, re-vegetation, bee raising and farming plantation products), or from any other activity or service which promotes the farming business; or

(ii)   any product resulting from any of the above activities, including by-products of such products;

(iii)   any activity which is intended to increase the production of anything referred to in above sub-clauses or improve the quality thereof;

(2) Producer Company means any company, with or without share capital, formed under this section by farmers and engaged in any activity connected with or related to any Produce including the following matters-

(a)   production, harvesting, procurement, grading, pooling, handling, marketing, selling, export of produce of the members or import of goods or services for their benefit;

(b)   processing including preserving, drying, distilling, brewing, canning and packaging of produce of its members;

(c)   rendering technical services, consultancy services, training research; and development and all other activities for the promotion of the interests of its Members;

(d)   arranging insurance of produce; and

(e)   financing of procurement, processing, marketing, extending of credit facilities including microfinance subject to such terms and conditions as may be specified, or any other financial services to its members;

(3) Every Producer Company shall deal primarily with the produce of its members for carrying out any of its activities.

(4) For the purposes of this section, member of a Producer Company means farmers as promoters and sponsors of a Producer Company and farmers admitted to membership after registration in accordance with requirements as specified in the regulations.

(5) Collateral Management Company means any company formed under this section to engage in the activity of managing produce as collateral, including but not limited to the following matters:

(a)   warehousing, *i.e.* provision of quality storage and preservation services for a range of agricultural commodities;

(b)   issuance of credible warehouse receipts for agricultural commodity financing; and

(c)   stock audit and verification services;

(6) If an Agriculture Promotion Company or Collateral Management Company or Producer Company or their members indulges in any activity which is prejudicial to the interests of farmers, members, lending institutions, commodity exchange, consumers, or other stakeholders, shall be liable to a penalty of level 3 on the standard scale.

(7) Any dues outstanding against agriculture promotion company under this section shall be recoverable as arrears of land revenue.

(8) Notwithstanding any provision of this section, the Government or any institution or authority owned and controlled by the Government may form an Agriculture Promotion Company.

458.   **Power to give exemptions by the Federal Government.--** Notwithstanding anything contained in this Act or any other law, the concerned Minister-in-Charge of the Federal Government may, by notification in the official Gazette exempt companies under sections 454, 456 and 457 from any provisions of law for the time being in force.

459.   **Quota for persons with disabilities in the public interest companies.—**Every Public interest company, employing one hundred or more employees shall ensure special quota for employment of persons with disabilities two percent or such higher percentage as may be specified or required under the applicable Federal and Provincial law:

Provided that in case of any conflict between this Act and any other Federal or Provincial law for persons with disabilities, the latter shall apply.

460. **Valuation by registered valuers.--** (1) Where a valuation is required to be made in respect of any property, stocks, shares, debentures, securities or goodwill or any other assets (herein referred to as the assets) or net worth of a company or its liabilities under the provisions of this Act, it shall be valued by a person having such qualifications and experience and registered as a valuer in such manner, on such terms and conditions as may be specified.

(2) The valuer appointed under sub-section (1) shall

(a)   make an impartial, true and fair valuation of any assets which may be required to be valued;

(b)   exercise due diligence while performing the functions as valuer; and

(c)   not undertake valuation of any assets in which he has a direct or indirect interest or becomes so interested at any time before submission of the report.

(3) The valuer shall prepare his report in such manner and applying such approaches, as may be specified.

(4) If a valuer contravenes the provisions of this section or the regulations made thereunder, the valuer shall be liable to a penalty of level 2 on the standard scale:

Provided that if the valuer has contravened such provisions with the intention to defraud the company, its members or creditors, he shall be punishable with imprisonment for a term which may extend to one year and with fine which may extend to five hundred thousand rupees.

(5)   Where a valuer has been convicted under sub-section (4), he shall be liable to--

(a)   refund the remuneration received by him to the company; and

(b)   pay for damages to the company or to any other person for loss arising out of incorrect or misleading statements of particulars made in his report.

(6) The registration as valuer under this section shall be liable to be cancelled by the Commission on such grounds and in such manner as may be specified after providing an opportunity of being heard.

461. **Security clearance of shareholder and director.--** The Commission may require the security clearance of any shareholder or director or other office bearer of a company or class of companies as may be notified by the concerned Minister-in-charge of the Federal Government.

REGISTRATION OFFICES AND FEES

462. **Registration offices.--** (1) For the purposes of the registration of companies and other work under this Act, there shall be offices at such places as the Commission thinks fit.

(2) The Commission may appoint such registrars as it thinks necessary for the registration of companies and performing other duties under this Act, and may make regulations with respect to their duties.

(3) While performing their functions and duties under this Act, all registrars shall observe and follow the order and instructions of the Commission.

(4) The Commission may direct a seal or seals to be prepared for the authentication of documents required for or connected with the registration of companies.

(5) Any person may, in the manner as may be specified, inspect the documents kept by the registrar and may require a certified copy of certificate of incorporation or any other certificate of any company, or a copy or extract of any other document or register maintained by the registrar or any part thereof on payment of the fees specified in the Seventh Schedule.

(6) A copy of or an extract from any document filed or lodged, whether in electronic or physical form, with the Commission or the registrar under this Act or the rules or regulations made thereunder or supplied or issued by the Commission or the registrar and certified to be a true copy thereof or extract therefrom under the hand and seal of an officer of the Commission or the registrar, shall be admissible in evidence in any proceedings as of equal validity as the original document.

(7) Where a document is filed or lodged, whether in electronic or physical form, with the Commission or the registrar, the Commission or the registrar shall not be liable for any loss or damage suffered by any person by reason of any error or omission of whatever nature arising or appearing in any document obtained by any person under the e-service or in physical form under this Act or the rules or regulations made thereunder, if such error or omission was made in good faith and in the ordinary course of the discharge of the duties of the Commission or the registrar or occurred or arose as a result of any defect or breakdown in the service or in the equipment used for the provision of the e-service.

(8) Wherever any act is by this Act directed to be done to or by the registrar it shall, until the Commission otherwise directs, be done to or by the existing Registrar of Companies or in his absence to or by such person as the

(9) Commission may for the time being authorise; but, in the event of the Commission altering the constitution of the existing registration offices or any of them, any such act shall be done to or by such officer and at such place with reference to the local situation of the registered offices of the companies to be registered as the Commission may appoint.

463. **Production of documents kept by registrar.--** (1) No process for compelling the production of any document or register kept by the registrar shall issue from any court except with the special leave of that court for reasons to be recorded; and any such process, if issued, shall bear thereon a statement that it is issued with the special leave of the court so granted and state the reasons for grant of such leave.

(2) A copy of, or extract from, any document or register kept and registered at any of the offices for the registration of companies under this Act, certified to be a true copy under the hand of the registrar (whose official position it shall not be necessary to prove) shall, in all legal proceedings, be admissible in evidence as of equal validity with the original document.

(3) Notwithstanding anything contained in any other law, no one shall, without the permission of the Commission in writing, take over or remove any original document or register from the custody of the registrar.

464. **Registrar not to accept defective documents.--** (1) Where, in the opinion of the registrar, any document required or authorised by or under this Act to be filed or registered with the registrar--

(a) contains any matter contrary to law, or does not otherwise comply with the requirements of law;

(b) is not complete owing to any defect, error or omission;

(c) is insufficiently legible or is written upon paper which is not durable; or

(d) is not properly authenticated;

the registrar may require the company to file a revised document in the form and within the period to be specified by him[1].

(2) If the company fails to submit the revised document within the specified period, the registrar may refuse to accept or register the document and communicate his decision in writing to the company.

(3) Subject to the provisions of sub-sections (4) and (5), if the registrar refuses to accept any document for any of the reasons aforesaid, the same shall not be deemed to have been delivered to him in accordance with the provisions of this Act unless a revised document in the form acceptable to the registrar is duly delivered within such time, or such extended time, as the registrar may specify in this behalf.

(4) If registration of any document is refused, the company may either supply the deficiency and remove the defect pointed out or, within thirty days of the order of refusal, prefer an appeal-

(a) where the order of refusal has been passed by an additional registrar, a joint registrar, a deputy registrar or an assistant registrar or such officer as may be designated by the Commission, to the registrar; and

(b) where the order of refusal has been passed, or upheld in appeal, by the registrar, to the Commission.

(5) An order of the Commission under sub-section (4) shall be final and shall not be called in question before any court or other authority.

(6) If a document has been accepted for record and its data or any of the information contained therein or any of the supporting documents subsequently found to be defective or incorrect or false or forged, the registrar concerned may

---

[1] 2018 CLD 383; 2017 CLD 636; 2017 CLD 1477; 2016 CLD 581; 2016 CLD 1638; 2010 CLD 1234

for special reasons to be recorded in writing, after obtaining such evidence as he may deem appropriate, allow the rectification in such document or allow the filing of a revised document in lieu thereof.

(7) If a document has been accepted for record and its data or any of the information contained therein or any of the supporting documents subsequently found to be defective or incorrect which is not possible of rectification or false or forged or it was accepted by mistake, the registrar concerned may for special reasons to be recorded in writing, after obtaining such evidence as he may deem appropriate cancel the recording thereof.

465. **Special return to rectify the data**.-- (1) The Commission or the registrar may at any time, by a general or specific order, require a company or class of companies or all the companies to file a special return signed by all the directors to rectify the record.

(2) The information provided in the special return filed under this section shall be a conclusive evidence of all the relevant facts and shall not be called in question by any of the person who has signed it.

(3) The persons who have signed the special return shall be responsible for the loss caused to any person on account of incorrect information provided in the return filed under this section.

(4) A company shall inform the registrar about any change of more than twenty five percent in its shareholding or membership or voting rights in a manner as may be specified by the Commission.

466. **Jurisdiction in the disputes relating to shareholding and directorship.--** The registrar shall have no jurisdiction to determine the rights of the parties relating to shareholding and directorship.

467. **Approval of transfer of shares by the agents licenced by the Commission**.-- (1) In case of companies to be notified for the purpose, before making any application for registration of the transfer of shares to the board the transferor and the transferee shall appear before the agent licenced by the Commission under this section; who shall record the statement of both the parties and forward a certified copy of the statement so recorded to the company for further necessary action in such form and manner and subject to such conditions as may be specified:

Provided that the provision of this sub-section shall not apply to transfer or transmission of shares by operation of law.

(2) The agent licenced under this section shall maintain complete record of all the statements recorded by him including the documents submitted by the parties, for a period of ten years.

(3) The licence under this section may be granted by the Commission in the manner and subject to such conditions, and to the persons having such qualification and infrastructure, as may be specified.

(4) An agent licenced under this section shall be responsible for the loss caused to any person due to any fault on his part, as determined by the Court while deciding a case under section 126.

(5) The agent licenced under this section may charge the fee for the services rendered by him, not exceeding the limit notified by the Commission.

(6) The Commission may at any time revoke a licence granted under this section on being satisfied that the agent has failed to comply with any of the terms or conditions to which the licence is subject:

Provided that, before a licence is so revoked, the Commission shall give to the agent notice in writing of its intention to do so, and shall afford the association an opportunity to be heard.

468. **Acceptance of documents presented after prescribed time.--** (1) Notwithstanding anything contained in section 479, where any document required under this Act to be filed or registered with the registrar is presented after the expiry of the prescribed period, the registrar may accept the same, on payment of the fee as specified below

    (a)   within ninety days, a fee equivalent to two times;

    (b)   within one hundred and eighty days, a fee equivalent to three times;

    (c)   within one year, a fee equivalent to four times;

    (d)   within two years, a fee equivalent to five times;

of the prescribed fee payable in respect thereof:

Provided that nothing contained in this sub-section shall be applicable to the public interest company.

(2) No such document as aforesaid shall be deemed to have been filed with the registrar until the specified fee, has been paid in full.

(3) The acceptance of the document by the registrar under sub-section (1) shall not absolve the defaulting company or other person concerned of any other liability arising from the default in complying with the requirements of this Act:

Provided that no proceeding shall be initiated against the company or any of its officers on account of delay in filing of any document required under this Act to be filed or registered with the registrar which is presented by the company or other person concerned on the payment of fee as specified under sub-section (1) and within the period as specified therein.

469. **Fees.--** (1) There shall be paid in respect of the several matters mentioned in the Seventh Schedule the several fees therein, for the time being, specified fees as the Commission may direct:

Provided that, in the case of resolutions to which section 150 applies, not more than one fee shall be required for the filing of more resolutions than one passed in the same meeting if such resolutions are filed with the registrar at the same time.

(2) All fees paid in pursuance of this Act shall be accounted for to the Commission.

(3) Any document required or authorised by this Act to be filed by a company with the registrar shall not be deemed to have been so filed until the fee payable in respect thereof has been duly paid and either the original receipt or other proof acceptable to the registrar has been furnished to him.

470. **Power to specify fees chargeable by companies.--** The maximum limits of fees to be paid to or charged by companies and liquidators from members, creditors or other persons for supply of copies of documents, inspection of records and other services as are required to be provided under this Act shall be such as may be specified.

471. **Filing of documents electronically.--** (1) The Commission may provide any means or mode for filing, any document, return or application required to be filed, lodged or submitted with the Commission or the registrar under this Act or the rules or regulations made thereunder electronically.

(2) Any additional information or document required to be submitted along with any document to be filed under this Act shall also be submitted through electronic means including in a scanned form.

(3) Any document to be submitted electronically shall be authenticated by the companies by affixing electronic signature or advanced electronic signature, as required under the Electronic Transactions Ordinance, 2002, (LI of 2002).

(4) From the date appointed by the Commission through notification in the official Gazette any document, return or application required to be filed, lodged or submitted with the Commission or the registrar under this Act or the rules or regulations made thereunder, shall only be lodged, filed or submitted electronically through e-service or any other means or service provided by the Commission for this purpose:

Provided that the Commission may relax the requirement of this section for a company or class of companies, for such document, return or application and for such time as may be notified from time to time.

472. **Destruction of physical record.--** The record of the companies including the statutory returns and applications, maintained by the registrar and

the Commission under this Act or the company law shall be preserved for such period as the Commission may determine and may be destroyed in the manner as may be specified:

Provided further that the physical record converted into electronic form in terms of first proviso, shall be admissible as an evidence in all legal proceedings and for all purposes.

473. **Supply of documents, information, notices to the members electronically.--** (1) After a date notified by the Commission, the information, notices and accounts or any other document to be provided by the company to its members under this Act, shall only be provided electronically on the email address provided by the members.

(2) A member requiring the supply of any of the document mentioned in sub-section (1) in physical form shall bear the cost as fixed by the company.

474. **Enforcing compliance with provisions of Act.--** (1) If a company, having made default in complying with any provision of this Act or committed any other irregularity fails to make good the default or undo the irregularity, as the case may be, within thirty days after the service of a notice on the company requiring it to do so, the Commission may, of its own motion or on an application made to it by any member or creditor of the company or a reference by the registrar and, in the case of a listed company, besides other persons as aforesaid, on a reference by the securities exchange, make an order directing the company and any officer thereof, as the case may be, to make good the default or undo the irregularity or otherwise make amends, as the circumstances may require, within such time as may be specified in the order[1].

(2) Any such order may provide that all costs of and incidental to the application or reference shall be borne by the company or by an officer of the company responsible for the default.

(3) Nothing in this section shall be taken to prejudice the operation of any enactment imposing penalties on a company or its officers in respect of any such default as aforesaid.

475. **Power of Court trying offences under Act to direct compliance with the provisions.--** The Court, the Commission, the registrar or other officer trying an offence for a default in compliance with any provisions or requirements of this Act may, at any time during the pendency of the trial or at the time of passing final order, direct, without prejudice to any liability, any officer, auditor or employee of the company in respect of which the default has

---

[1] 2017 CLD 368; 2017 CLD 927; 2017 CLD 1395; 2016 CLD 1077; 2014 CLD 588; 2012 CLD 741; 2012 CLD 1394; 2011 CLD 383; 2011 CLD 1141; 2008 CLD 1300; 2006 CLD 295; 2006 CLD 326; 2006 CLD 347; 2006 CLD 454; 2006 CLD 533; 2006 CLD 542; 2006 CLD 627; 2006 CLD 635; 2006 CLD 667; 2006 CLD 1055; 2005 CLD 350

been committed to undo the irregularity including but not limited to unwinding the unlawful transaction or to comply with the said provisions or requirements within such time as may be specified in the order[1].

LEGAL PROCEEDINGS, OFFENCES, ETC.

476. **Offences to be cognizable.--** Notwithstanding anything contained in the Code of Criminal Procedure, 1898 (V of 1898) or any other law, save as expressly provided otherwise in this Act or in the Eighth Schedule, any offence in which punishment of imprisonment is provided under this Act shall be cognizable by the Commission only and shall be proceeded in accordance with section 38 of the Securities and Exchange Commission of Pakistan Act, 1997 (XLII of 1997) and this Act.

477. **Complaint to the court by the Commission, registrar, member or creditor in case of certain offences.--** (1) Offences provided in the Eighth Schedule under this Act which is alleged to have been committed by any company or any officer or auditor or any other person shall not be taken cognizance by the court, except on the complaint in writing of-

(a) the Commission through its authorised officer or the registrar; or

(b) in the case of a company having a share capital, by a member or members holding not less than five percent of the issued share capital of the company or a creditor or creditors of the company having interest equivalent in amount to not less than five percent of the issued share capital of the company; or

(c) in the case of a company not having a share capital, by any member or creditor entitled to present a petition for winding up of the company:

Provided that nothing in this sub-section shall apply to a prosecution by a company of any of its officers or employees:

Provided further that the complaint filed under this section shall not require formal procedure as provided under section 38 of the Securities and Exchange Commission of Pakistan Act, 1997 (XLII of 1997) and such complaint shall be taken cognizance by the court in accordance with Chapter XVI of Code of Criminal Procedure, 1898 (Act V of 1898)[2].

(2) Sub-section (1) shall not apply to any action taken by the liquidator of a company in respect of any offence alleged to have been committed in

---

[1] 2014 CLD 299; 2014 CLD 430; 2013 CLD 28; 2013 CLD 1385; 2013 CLD 1179; 2012 CLD 1408; 2012 CLD 1430; 2012 CLD 2019; 2011 CLD 614; 2010 CLD 415; 2010 CLD 1716; 2009 CLD 65; 2009 CLD 931 ; 2009 CLD 951; 2009 CLD 1106; 2008 CLD 17; 2008 CLD 331; 2006 CLD 350; 2006 CLD 684; 2005 CLD 350

[2] 2017 CLD 368; 1987 MLD 3039; 1969 PLD 251; 1959 PLD 32

respect of any of the matters included in Part-X or in any other provision of this Act relating to the winding up to companies.

(3) A liquidator of a company shall not be deemed to be an officer of the company within the meaning of sub-section (1).

478. **Penalty to be imposed by the Commission.--** Wherever a penalty is provided for any offence, contravention of or default in complying with, any of the provisions of this Act, rules or regulations made under this Act such penalty shall be imposed by the Commission after providing a reasonable opportunity of hearing to the party.

479. **Adjudication of offences and standard scale of penalty.--** (1) There shall be a standard scale of penalty for offences under this Act, which shall be known as "the **standard scale**"[1].

(2) The standard scale consists of

Level	Limit of penalty	Per day penalty during Which the default continues
1	Upto Rs.25,000	Upto Rs.500
2	Upto Rs.500,000	Upto Rs.1,000
3	Upto Rs.100 million	Upto Rs.500,000

(3) Where a penalty is provided for any offence, contravention of, or default in complying with, any of the provisions of this Act or a directive of the Commission or the registrar or other authority empowered to issue a directive under any provisions of this Act, it shall be adjudged and imposed--

(a) where any person shall be liable to a penalty of level 1, by the officer who is in charge of the company registration office in which the company is registered:

Provided that the Commission and the registrar shall have concurrent jurisdiction under this clause;

(b) where any person shall be liable to a penalty of level 2, by the registrar designated for the purpose:

Provided that the Commission shall have concurrent jurisdiction under this clause; and

---

[1] 2019 CLD 242; 2007 CLD 1439

(c)   where any person shall be liable to a penalty of level 3, by the Commission or an officer authorised by it.

(4) Notwithstanding anything contained in sub-section (2), the Commission may, by an order in writing empower any officer to exercise the powers conferred by the said sub-section in respect of any case or class of cases, either to the exclusion of, or concurrently with, any other officer.

(5) The penalty as aforesaid shall be imposed after giving the person concerned an opportunity to show cause why he should not be punished for the alleged offence, contravention, default or non-compliance and, if he so requests, after giving him an opportunity of being heard personally or through such person as may be specified.

(6) The penalty imposed under this section by the Commission, the registrar designated for the purpose or the officer in charge of the company registration office, shall be without prejudice to any other action for the violation or contravention as provided under the relevant provision of this Act.

480. **Appeal against order passed by officer of the Commission.--** Any person aggrieved by any order passed under this Act may, within thirty days of such order, except as otherwise provided in this Act, prefer an appeal to[1]—

(a)   the registrar designated by the Commission against the order passed by an additional registrar, a joint registrar, an additional joint registrar, a deputy registrar or an assistant registrar or such officer as may be designated by the Commission; and

(b)   officer authorized by the Commission where the order has been passed or upheld by the registrar designated under clause (a) by the Commission.

481. **Appeal before the Appellate Bench.**—Any person aggrieved by an order passed by the registrar or an officer authorized by the Commission under section 480, may prefer an appeal to the Appellate Bench of the Commission under section 33 of the Securities and Exchange Commission of Pakistan Act, 1997 (XLII of 1997)[2]:

Provided that no appeal shall lie against—

(a)   an administrative direction given by a Commissioner or an officer of the Commission;

---

[1] 2017 CLD 1411; 2016 CLD 1399; 2013 CLD 1466; 2013 CLD 1421; 2007 CLD 297; 2007 CLD 1019; 2006 CLD 298; 2006 CLD 334

[2] 1988 CLC 866; 1988 CLC 2147; 1986 MLD 823; 1985 PLD 193; 1982 PLD 1; 1980 PLD 69; 1980 PLD 86; 1976 PLD 85; 1970 PLD 648

(b) a sanction provided or decision made by a Commissioner or an officer of the Commission to commence legal proceedings; and

(c) an interim order which does not dispose of the entire matter.

482. **Adjudication of offences involving imprisonment.**— Notwithstanding anything contained in the Code of Criminal Procedure, 1898 (Act V of 1898), no court other than court of sessions or such other court as may be notified under section 37 of the Securities and Exchange Commission of Pakistan Act, 1997(XLII of 1997), shall take cognizance of any offence punishable with imprisonment or imprisonment in addition to fine under this Act[1].

483. **Powers of the Commission in relation to enquiries and proceedings.**—(1) The Commission, an authorised officer or the registrar, as the case may be, shall, for the purposes of a proceeding or enquiry in exercise of its or his powers and discharge of functions, have the same powers as are vested in a Court under the Code of Civil Procedure, 1908 (Act V of 1908), while trying a suit, in respect of the following matters, namely--

(a) summoning and enforcing the attendance of any witness and examining him on oath or affirmation;

(b) compelling the discovery or production of any document or other material object;

---

[1] 2018 CLD 44; 2018 CLD 952; 2018 CLD 1031 ; 2017 CLD 169; 2017 CLD 531; 2017 CLD 759; 2017 CLD 767; 2017 CLD 839; 2017 CLD 927; 2017 CLD 1019; 2017 CLD 1035; 2017 CLD 1049; 2017 CLD 1142; 2017 CLD 1191; 2017 CLD 1249; 2017 CLD 1715; 2016 CLD 76; 2016 CLD 1697; 2016 CLD 1734; 2016 CLD 1814; 2016 CLD 2077; 2016 CLD 2233; 2016 CLD 2265; 2016 CLD 2276; 2016 CLD 2318; 2015 CLD 299; 2015 CLD 385; 2015 CLD 491; 2015 CLD 406; 2015 CLD 1098; 2014 CLD 449; 2013 CLD 82; 2013 CLD 108; 2013 CLD 220; 2013 CLD 327; 2013 CLD 357; 2013 CLD 1179; 2013 CLD 1466; 2013 CLD 1478; 2012 CLD 691; 2012 CLD 923; 2012 CLD 1065; 2012 CLD 1430; 2012 CLD 2019; 2012 CLD 1423; 2011 CLD 383; 2011 CLD 599; 2011 CLD 614; 2011 CLD 624; 2011 CLD 645; 2011 CLD 1149; 2011 CLD 1228; 2011 CLD 1647; 2011 CLD 1783; 2010 CLD 34; 2010 CLD 36; 2010 CLD 49; 2010 CLD 60; 2010 CLD 66; 2010 CLD 75; 2010 CLD 415; 2010 CLD 1035; 2010 CLD 1071; 2010 CLD 1096; 2010 CLD 1110; 2010 CLD 1210; 2010 CLD 1237; 2010 CLD 1725; 2010 CLD 1729; 2009 CLD 56; 2009 CLD 61; 2009 CLD 65; 2009 CLD 76; 2009 CLD 90; 2009 CLD 541; 2009 CLD 548; 2009 CLD 564; 2009 CLD 931; 2009 CLD 951; 2009 CLD 1106; 2009 CLD 1191; 2009 CLD 1197; 2009 CLD 1636; 2009 CLD 1609; 2008 CLD 17; 2008 CLD 126; 2008 CLD 252; 2008 CLD 266; 2008 CLD 305; 2008 CLD 331; 2008 CLD 436; 2008 CLD 825; 2008 CLD 627; 2008 CLD 731; 2008 CLD 746; 2008 CLD 786; 2008 CLD 796; 2008 CLD 803; 2008 CLD 809; 2008 CLD 861; 2007 CLD 57; 2007 CLD 93; 2007 CLD 566; 2007 CLD 574; 2007 CLD 599; 2007 CLD 605; 2007 CLD 621; 2007 CLD 630; 2007 CLD 1023; 2007 CLD 1038; 2007 CLD 1060; 2007 CLD 1116; 2007 CLD 1125; 2007 CLD 1251; 2007 CLD 1256; 2007 CLD 1271; 2007 CLD 1291; 2007 CLD 1439; 2007 CLD 1491; 2007 CLD 1498; 2006 CLD 347; 2006 CLD 350; 2006 CLD 378; 2006 CLD 381; 2006 CLD 399; 2006 CLD 418; 2006 CLD 431; 2006 CLD 480; 2006 CLD 556; 2006 CLD 660; 2006 CLD 756; 2006 CLD 997; 2006 CLD 1092; 2006 CLD 729; 2006 CLD 1034; 2006 CLD 1063; 2006 CLD 1150; 2006 CLD 1157; 2006 CLD 1295; 2006 CLD 1334; 2006 CLD 1357; 2006 CLD 1376; 2006 CLD 1386; 2006 CLD 1440; 2006 CLD 1455

      (c)   receiving evidence on affidavit; and

      (d)   issuing commissions for the examination of witnesses and documents.

(2) Any proceeding before the Commission, an authorised officer or registrar, as the case may be, shall be deemed to be a judicial proceeding within the meaning of section 193 and section 228 of the Pakistan Penal Code, 1860 (Act XLV of 1860), and the Commission, an authorised officer or registrar shall be deemed to be a civil court for the purposes of section 195 and Chapter XXXV of the Code of Criminal Procedure, 1898 (Act V of 1898).

484. Procedure for trial of a corporate body.-- (1) In any proceedings against a body corporate for an offence against any provisions of this Act a notice to show cause or appear may be sent to or served on the body corporate by registered post or in any other manner laid down for the service of summons issued by a court under the Code of Civil Procedure, 1908 (Act V of 1908), at its registered office, or if there is no registered office at its principal place of business in Pakistan and where no such office is known to exist or is not functioning, at the address of the chief executive or any director or officer of the body corporate[1].

(2) On service of the notice referred to in sub-section (1), it shall be the duty of the chief executive and other officers of the company to show cause or appear before the Court, Commission, registrar, other officer or authority himself or by a counsel or by an officer or other authorised representative of the body corporate who may be in a position to answer the charge as may be specified in the notice.

(3) Where a body corporate does not appear in the manner aforesaid, the Court, Commission, registrar or officer trying the offence, as the case may be, may either issue a directive to the chief executive or other officer of the body corporate as is referred to in sub-section (2) to appear personally and answer the charge, or, at its or his direction, proceed to hear and decide the case in the absence of the body corporate.

485. Recovery of penalty.— Any sum adjudged, penalty imposed by the Commission or the registrar in exercise of powers under this Act or any rules or any regulations made thereunder or directed to be paid, shall be recovered in accordance with section 42B of the Securities and Exchange Commission of Pakistan Act, 1997(XLII of 1997).

486. Prosecution of offences by the Commission.—All prosecution conducted by the Commission under this Act shall be made in the manner as provided in section 38 of Securities and Exchange Commission of Pakistan Act, 1997(XLII of 1997).

---

[1] 2000 PLD 391

487. **Appeal against acquittal.**—Notwithstanding anything contained in the Code of Criminal Procedure, 1898 (Act V of 1898), the Commission may, in any case arising out of this Act, direct any officer of the Commission or authorise any other person, either by name or by virtue of his office, to present an appeal from an order of acquittal passed by the court other than a Court and an appeal presented by such prosecutor or other person shall be deemed to have been validly presented to the appellate court[1].

488. **Payment of compensation in cases of frivolous or vexatious prosecution.**—(1) In respect of any case instituted upon the complaint of a member or creditor against the company or any officer thereof under section 477, the following provisions shall apply instead of the provisions of section 250 of the Code of Criminal Procedure, 1898 (Act V of 1898).

(2) If the Court, officer, Commission or registrar by whom any such case is heard discharges or acquits all or any of the accused, and is of opinion that the accusation against them or any of them was false and either frivolous or vexatious, the Court, officer, Commission or registrar, as the case may be, may by its or his order of discharge or acquittal, if the member or creditor upon whose complaint the accusation was made is present, call upon him forthwith to show cause why he should not pay compensation to such accused, or to each or any of such accused when there is more than one, or if such member or creditor is not present, direct the issue of a summons to him to appear and show cause as aforesaid.

(3) The Court, officer, Commission or registrar, as the case may be, shall record and consider any cause which such member or creditor may show; and if it or he is satisfied that the accusation was false and either frivolous or vexatious, it or he may, for reasons to be recorded, direct that compensation to such amount as it may determine be paid by such member or creditor, as the case may be, to the accused or to each or any of them not exceeding one million rupees in all.

(4) In default of payment of the compensation ordered under sub-section (3), the member or creditor ordered to pay such compensation shall suffer simple imprisonment for a term not exceeding one year, and shall also be liable to a fine not exceeding one hundred thousand rupees.

(5) When any person is imprisoned under sub-section (4), the provisions of sections 68 and 69 of the Pakistan Penal Code, 1860 (Act XLV of 1860) shall, so far as may be, apply.

(6) No person who has been directed to pay compensation under this section shall, by reason of such order, be exempted from any civil or criminal liability in respect of the complaint made by him:

---

[1] 2019 CLD 235; 2019 CLD 242; 2019 PCrLJ 504

Provided that any amount paid to an accused person under this section shall be taken into account in awarding compensation to such person in any subsequent civil suit relating to the same matter.

(7) A complainant who has been ordered to pay compensation under sub-section (3) may appeal from the order, in so far as it relates to the payment of compensation, as if such complainant had been convicted on a trial.

(8) Where an order for payment of compensation to an accused person is made, the amount of compensation recovered shall not be paid to him before the period allowed for the presentation of the appeal under sub-section (7) has elapsed; or, if an appeal is presented, before the appeal has been decided.

(9) Nothing contained in the Code of Criminal Procedure, 1898 (Act V of 1898) or anything contained in this section shall be applicable to the authorized officer of the Commission or the registrar and all actions by such officer or registrar shall deemed to be validly done in good faith and no compensation or suit for damages shall lie, whatsoever.

489. Application of fines or penalties.—(1) The Court, officer, Commission or registrar imposing any fine or penalty under this Act may direct that the whole or any part thereof shall be applied in or towards-

(a) payment of costs of the proceedings;

(b) rewarding the person on whose information the fine or penalty is recovered; and

(c) payment to an aggrieved party of compensation for any loss caused by the offence.

(2) Any amount recovered as fine or penalty which is not applied as aforesaid shall be accounted for in accordance with section 40AA of the Securities and Exchange Commission of Pakistan Act, 1997 (XLII of 1997).

490. Production and inspection of books where offence suspected.— (1) Without prejudice to the powers otherwise exercisable by the Commission or any of its authorised officers or registrar, or person under this Act, the Court in Chambers may, on an application made by a public prosecutor or the Attorney-General for Pakistan or the Advocate-General of the Province or an officer authorised by the Commission in this behalf or by a special public prosecutor appointed under section 38 of the Securities and Exchange Commission of Pakistan Act, 1997 (XLII of 1997) or by the registrar, if it is shown that there is reasonable cause to believe that any person has, while he was an officer of a company, committed an offence in connection with the management of the company's affairs, and that evidence of the commission of the offence is to be found in any books or papers of or under the control of the company or any officer or agent of the company, make an order--

(a) authorising any person named therein to inspect the said books or papers or any of them for the purpose of investigating, and obtaining evidence of the commission of, the offence; or

(b) requiring the chief executive of the company or such other officer thereof or person as may be named in the order, to produce the said books or papers or any of them to a person, and at a place and time, named in the order.

(2) Sub-section (1) shall apply also in relation to any books or papers of a person carrying on the business of banking so far as they relate to the company's affairs, as it applies to any books or papers of or under the control of the company, except that no such order as is referred to in clause (b) thereof shall be made by virtue of this sub-section.

(3) No appeal shall lie from a decision under this section.

491. Power to require limited company to give security for costs.— Where a limited company is plaintiff or petitioner in any suit or other legal proceeding, the Court having jurisdiction in the matter may, if it appears that there is reason to believe that the company will be unable to pay the costs of the defendant if successful in his defence, require sufficient security to be given for those costs, and may stay all proceedings until the security is given.

492. Power of Court to grant relief in certain cases.—(1) If in any criminal proceeding for negligence, default, breach of duty or breach of trust against a person to whom this section applies, it appears to the Court, hearing the case that that person is or may be liable in respect of the negligence, default, breach of duty or breach of trust, but that he has acted honestly and reasonably, and that having regard to all the circumstances of the case, including those connected with his appointment, he ought fairly to be excused for the negligence, default, breach of duty or breach of trust, the Court, may relieve him, either wholly or partly, from his liability on such terms as the Court may think fit[1].

(2) Where any person to whom this section applies has reason to apprehend that any claim will or might be made against him in respect of any negligence, default, breach of duty, or breach of trust, he may apply to the Court for relief, and the Court on any such application shall have the same power to relieve him as if proceedings against that person for negligence, default, breach of duty or breach of trust had been brought before the Court.

(3) The persons to whom this section applies are the following namely--

(a) directors of a company;

---

[1] 2003 CLD 131; 1997 CLD 1347; 1983 CLC 129; 1981 CLC 1051; 1977 PLD 1367; 1959 PLD 32; 1959 PLD 48; 1958 PLD 378; 1958 PLD 418

(b)   chief executive of a company;

(c)   officers of a company;

(d)   persons employed by a company as auditors, whether they are or are not officers of the company;

(e)   liquidator of a company.

(4)   The Court shall not grant any relief to any person under sub-section (1) or sub-section (2) unless it by notice served in the manner specified by it requires the Commission or the registrar and such other person, if any, as it thinks necessary to show cause why such relief should not be granted.

493. **Enforcement of orders of Court.**—Any order made by the Court under this Act may be enforced in the same manner as a decree made by a Court in a suit[1].

494. **Enforcement of orders of Court by other courts.**—(1) Where any order made by the Court is required to be enforced by another Court, a certified copy of the order shall be produced to the proper officer of the Court required to enforce the order[2].

(2) The production of such certified copy shall be sufficient evidence of the order.

(3) Upon the production of such certified copy, the Court shall take the requisite steps for enforcing the order, in the same manner as if it had been made by itself.

495. **Protection of acts done in good faith.**— No suit, prosecution or other legal proceeding shall lie against the Government or the Commission or any officer of Government or the Commission or the registrar or any other person in respect of anything which is in good faith done or intended to be done in pursuance of this Act or any rules or regulations or orders made thereunder or in respect of the publication by or under the authority of the Government, Commission or such officer of any report, paper or proceedings.

496. **Penalty for false statement, falsification, forgery, fraud, deception.**— (1) Notwithstanding anything contained in the Criminal Procedure Code, 1898, (V of 1898) or any other law, whoever in relations to affairs of the company or body corporate-

(a)   makes a statement or submit any document in any form, which is false or incorrect in any material particular, or omits any material fact, knowing it to be material, in any return, report, certificate, statement of financial position, profit and loss account, income and expenditure account, offer of shares, books of account, application,

[1] 2010 CLC 897
[2] 1985 PLD 193

information or explanation required by or for the purposes of any of the provisions of this Act or pursuant to an order or direction given under this Act with an intention to defraud, or cheat the Commission or to obtain incorporation or to avoid any penal action for an offence under this Act or administered legislation;

(b)   makes any false entry or omits or alter any material particular from books, paper or accounts with an intent to defraud, destroy, alter or falsifies any books of account belonging to or in his possession shall commit an offence of falsification of account;

(c)   submit, present or produce any forged or fabricated document, knowingly to be forged or fabricated, to the Commission for the purposes of cheating or cheating by personation or to obtain any wrongful gain or wrongful loss or to avoid any penal action for an offence under this Act or administered legislation; or

(d)   employ any scheme, artifice or practice in the course of business of the company to defraud or deceive general public;

shall be punishable with imprisonment which shall not be less than one year but which may extend to seven years and shall also be liable to fine which shall not be less than the amount involved in the fraud but may extend to three times the amount involved in the offence[1]:

Provided further that in case of offence involves public interest, the term of imprisonment under this section shall not be less than three years along with fine.

Explanation.-- For the purpose of this section-

(i)   "fraud" in relation to affairs of the company or body corporate shall mean doing a thing with an intent to defraud other person;

(ii)   "wrongful gain" means the gain by unlawful means of property to which the person gaining is not legally entitled;

(iii)   "wrongful loss" means the loss by unlawful means of property to which the person losing is legally entitled.

(iv)   "cheating, cheating by personation, falsification of accounts or forgery or forgery for the purposes of cheating" shall have the same meanings as assign to it in Pakistan Penal Code, 1860 (XLV of 1860).

---

[1] 2017 CLD 169; 2017 CLD 581; 2017 CLD 636; 2017 CLD 990; 2016 CLD 2233; 2016 CLD 2318; 2015 CLD 385; 2015 CLD 491; 2013 CLD 58; 2013 CLD 103

(2)　All offences under this section shall be non-bailable and non-compoundable.

497. **Penalty for wrongful withholding of property.**—(1) Any director, chief executive or other officer or employee or agent of a company who wrongfully obtains possession of any property of the company, or having any such property in his possession wrongfully withholds it or wilfully applies it to purposes other than those expressed or directed in the articles and authorised by this Act shall, on the complaint of the company or any creditor or contributory thereof or a memorandum placed on record by the registrar or an officer subordinate to him, be punishable with a fine not exceeding one million rupees and may be ordered by the Court, or officer, Commission or registrar or the concerned Minister-in-Charge of the Federal Government trying the offence, to deliver up or refund within a time to be fixed by the said Court, officer, Commission or registrar or the concerned Minister-in-Charge of the Federal Government any such property improperly obtained or wrongfully withheld or wilfully misapplied and any gain or benefit derived therefrom[1].

(2) Whoever fails to comply with an order under sub-section (1), shall be punishable with imprisonment for a term which may extend to three years and shall also be liable to a fine which may extend to five hundred thousand rupees.

498. **Liability of directors for allotment of shares for inadequate consideration.**—(1) Any director, creditor or member of a company may apply to the Court for a declaration that any shares of the company specified in the application have been allotted for inadequate consideration[2].

(2) Every director of the company who is a party to making the allotment of such shares shall be liable, jointly and severally with his co-directors, to make good to the company the amount by which the consideration actually received by the company for the shares is found by the Court, after full inquiry into the circumstances of the transaction, to be less than the consideration that the company ought to have received for such shares, if it is proved, as to any such first mentioned director, that such director-

(a)　had knowledge that the consideration so received by the company was inadequate; or

(b)　failed to take reasonable steps to ascertain whether such consideration so received by the company was in fact adequate.

499. **Punishment for non-compliance of directive of Court, etc.**—(1) Where any directive is given or order is issued by the Court, the officer, the Commission, the registrar or the concerned Minister-in-Charge of the Federal Government under any provision of this Act, non-compliance thereof within the

---

[1] 2015 CLD 1691; 1999 CLC 1984; 1987 MLD 413; 1987 CLC 577
[2] 2015 CLD 1978; 2008 CLD 879

period specified in such direction or order shall render every officer of the company or other person responsible for non-compliance thereof punishable, in addition to any other liability, shall be liable to a penalty of level 3 on the standard scale[1].

(2) If non-compliance or failure continues after conviction under sub-section (1), the officer or other person who is a party to such non-compliance or failure shall be liable to punishment with imprisonment which may extend to one year and fine not exceeding ten thousand rupees for every day after the first during which such non-compliance continues, and shall further cease to hold office in the company and be disqualified from holding any office in any company for a period of five years.

500. **Penalty for carrying on *ultra vires* business.**—If any business or part of business carried on or any transaction made, by a company is *ultra vires* of the company shall be an offence and every person who acted as a director or officer of the company and is responsible for carrying on such business shall be liable to a penalty of level 3 on the standard scale, and shall also be personally liable for the liabilities and obligations arising out of such business or transaction[2].

501. **Penalty for improper use of word "Limited".**—If any person or persons trade or carry on business under, or otherwise use or display, any name or title of which the word "Limited" or the words "(Private) Limited" or "(Guarantee) Limited" or "(SMC-Private) Limited" or any contraction or imitation thereof is or are the last word or words, that person or each of those persons shall, unless duly incorporated with limited liability or as a private limited company or with the liability of members limited by guarantee, as the case may be, be liable to a penalty of level 3 on the standard scale[3].

502. **Penalty where no specific penalty is provided.** If a company or any other person contravenes or fails to comply with any provision of this Act or any condition, limitation or restriction subject to which any approval, sanction, consent, confirmation, recognition, direction or exemption in relation to any matter has been accorded, given or granted, for which no punishment is provided elsewhere in this Act, the company and every officer of the company who is in default or such other person shall be liable to a penalty of level 3 on the standard scale[4].

---

[1] 2017 CLD 1395; 2014 CLD 588; 2010 CLD 60; 2010 CLD 1716; 2009 CLD 61; 2009 CLD 951; 2009 CLD 931; 2008 CLD 331; 2007 CLD 1491; 2006 CLD 542

[2] 2017 CLD 927; 2016 CLD 76; 2016 CLD 1668; 2010 CLD 193

[3] 2002 CLD 1390; 1975 SCMR 230

[4] 2016 CLD 2155; 2015 CLD 621; 2013 CLD 273; 2010 CLD 79; 2009 CLD 1593; 2009 CLD 1589; 2007 CLD 1498; 1975 SCMR 230

503. **Power to accord approval subject to conditions.**(1) Where the Commission or registrar is required or authorised by any provision of this Act--

    (a)   to accord approval, sanction, consent, confirmation or recognition to or in relation to any matter;

    (b)   to give any direction in relation to any matter; or

    (c)   to grant any exemption in relation to any matter,

then, in the absence of anything to the contrary contained in such or any other provision of this Act, the Commission or registrar may accord, give or grant such approval, sanction, consent, confirmation, recognition, direction or exemption subject to such conditions, limitations or restrictions as the Commission or registrar may think fit to impose and may, in the case of contravention of any such condition, limitation or restriction, rescind or withdraw such approval, sanction, consent, confirmation, recognition, direction or exemption.

(2) Save as otherwise expressly provided in this Act, every application which may be or is required to be made to the Commission or registrar under any provision of this Act

    (a)   in respect of any approval, sanction, consent, confirmation or recognition to be accorded by the Commission or registrar, or in relation to, any matter; or

    (b)   in respect of any direction or exemption to be given or granted by the Commission or registrar to or in relation to any other matter; or

    (c)   in respect of any other matter;

shall be accompanied by fee specified in the Seventh Schedule.

504. **Delegation of powers.--**The concerned Minister-in-Charge of the Federal Government may, by notification in the official Gazette, direct that all or any of his powers and functions under this Act may, subject to such limitations, restrictions or conditions, if any, as he may from time to time impose, be exercised or performed by the Commission or an officer specified for the purpose.

505. **Application of Act to companies governed by special enactments.**(1) The provisions of this Act shall apply[1]--

    (a)   to insurance companies, except in so far as the said provisions are inconsistent with the provisions of the Insurance Ordinance, 2000 (XXXIX of 2000);

---

[1] 2016 CLD 1668; 2015 CLD 659; 2015 CLD 569; 2002 CLD 1361; 2001 CLC 1833

    (b)   to banking companies, except in so far as the said provisions are inconsistent with the provisions of the Banking Companies Ordinance, 1962 (LVII of 1962)[1];

    (c)   to *modaraba* companies and *modarabas*, except in so far as the said provisions are inconsistent with the provisions of the Modaraba Companies and Modaraba (Floatation and Control) Ordinance, 1980 (XXXI of 1980)[2];

    (d)   to any other company governed by any special enactment for the time being in force, except in so far as the said provisions are inconsistent with the provisions of such special enactments.

(2) The provisions of sections 130, 132, 220 to 239, 247 to 267, 270 and 271 shall *mutatis mutandis* apply to listed companies or corporations established by any special enactment for the time being in force whose securities are listed and in the said sections the expression "**company**" shall include a listed company so established:

Provided that the Commission may, by notification in the official Gazette, direct that the provisions of any of the aforesaid sections specified in the notification shall, subject to such conditions, if any, as may be so specified, not apply to any listed company or securities so specified.

SCHEDULES, TABLES, FORMS AND GENERAL RULES

506. **Forms**.-- The forms in the schedules or forms as near thereto as circumstances admit and such other forms as may be prescribed in the rules or specified through regulations shall be used in all matters to which those forms refer.

507. **Power to alter schedules.--** (1) The concerned Minister-in-Charge of the Federal Government may, by notification, in the official Gazette, alter or add to, the Sixth and Eighth Schedules.

(2) The Commission may, by notification in the official Gazette, alter or add to any of the tables, regulations, requirements, forms and other provisions contained in any of the schedules except Sixth and Eighth Schedules, and such alterations or additions shall have effect as if enacted in this Act and shall come into force on the date of the notification, unless the notification otherwise directs.

508. **Power of the Federal Government to make rules.**— (1) In addition to the powers conferred by any other section, the Federal Government may, by notification in the official Gazette, make rules[3]-

---

[1] 1986 PLD 297; 1986 MLD 1317

[2] 2001 CLC 1890

[3] 2018 CLD 136; 2018 CLD 197; 2017 CLD 531; 2016 CLD 134; 2016 CLD 2155; 2011 CLD 1228; 2009 CLD 56

(a)   for the matters which by this Act are to be prescribed;

(b)   for establishment and regulating the activities of any company or class of companies; and

(2)   generally to carry out the purposes of this Act:

Provided that, before making any such rule, the draft thereof shall be published by the concerned Minister-in-Charge of the Federal Government in the official Gazette for eliciting public opinion thereon within a period of not less than fourteen days from the date of publication[1].

(2) Any rule made under sub-section (1) may provide that a contravention thereof shall be punishable with a penalty which may extend to five million rupees and, where the contravention is a continuing one, with a further penalty which may extend to one hundred thousand rupees for every day after the first during which such contravention continues[2].

509. **Repeal and savings**.—(1) The Companies Ordinance, 1984 (XLVII of 1984), hereinafter called as repealed Ordinance, shall stand repealed, except Part VIIIA consisting of sections 282A to 282N, from the date of coming into force of this Act and the provisions of the said Part VIIIA along with all related or connected provisions of the repealed Ordinance shall be applicable *mutatis mutandis* to Non-banking Finance Companies in a manner as if the repealed Ordinance has not been repealed[3]:

Provided that repeal of the repealed Ordinance shall not-

(a)   affect the incorporation of any company registered or saved under repealed Ordinance; or

(b)   revive anything not in force at the time at which the repeal take effect; or

(c)   affect the previous operation of the repealed Ordinance or anything duly done or suffered thereunder; or

(d)   affect any right, privilege, obligation or liability acquired, accrued or incurred under the said repealed Ordinance[4]; or

(e)   affect any penalty imposed, forfeiture made or punishment awarded in respect of any offence committed under the repealed Ordinance; or

(f)   affect any inspection, investigation, prosecution, legal proceeding or remedy in respect of any obligation, liability, penalty, forfeiture

---

[1] 2016 CLD 2155; 2016 CLD 134; 2009 CLD 56
[2] 2018 CLD 136; 2018 CLD 197; 2017 CLD 479; 2017 CLD 531; 2011 CLD 1228
[3] 2019 PLC(CS) 300; 1998 CLC 1194; 1989 CLC 2103
[4] 2019 PLC 300

(g)   or punishment as aforesaid, and any such inspection, investigation, prosecution, legal proceedings or remedy may be made, continued or enforced and any such penalty, forfeiture or punishment may be imposed, as if this Act has not been passed.

(2)   Notwithstanding the repeal of the repealed Ordinance[1]--

(a)   any document referring to any provision of the repealed Ordinance shall be construed as referring, as far as may be, to this Act, or to the corresponding provision of this Act;

(b)   all rules, regulations, notification, guideline, circular, directive, order (special or general) or exemption issued, made or granted under the repealed Ordinance shall have effect as if it had been issued, made or granted under the corresponding provision of this Act unless repealed, amended or substituted under this Act;

(c)   any official appointed and anybody elected or constituted under repealed Ordinance shall continue and shall be deemed to have been appointed, elected or constituted, as the case may be, under the corresponding provision of this Act;

(d)   all funds and accounts constituted or maintained under the repealed Ordinance shall be deemed to be in continuation of the corresponding funds and accounts constituted or maintained under this Act;

(e)   every mortgage and charge recorded in any register or book maintained at any office under the repealed Ordinance shall be deemed to have be recorded in the register or book maintained under the corresponding provisions of this Act;

(f)   any licence, certificate or document issued, made or granted under the repealed Ordinance shall be deemed to have been issued, made or granted under this Act and shall, unless cancelled, in pursuance of any provisions of this Act, continue to be in force until the date specified in the licence, certificate or documents.

(3) The mention of particular matters in this section or in any other section of this Act shall not prejudice the general application of section 6 of the General Clauses Act, 1897 (X of 1897), with regard to the effect of repeals.

(4) After the commencement of this Act, the expression Companies Ordinance, 1984(XLVII of 1984) and any referring sections thereof, used in any law for the time being in force including all administered legislation and rules,

---

[1] 1988 CLC 866; 1986 CLC 2933

regulations and guidelines made thereunder, shall be read as Companies Act, 2017 along with corresponding provisions of Companies Act, 2017 unless the context requires otherwise.

510. **Power to issue directives, circulars, guidelines.**—(1) The Commission may issue such directives, prudential requirements, codes, guidelines, circulars or notifications as are necessary to carry out the purposes of this Act and the rules and regulations made under this Act.

(2) Any person, who obstructs or contravenes or does not comply with any directive, prudential requirements, codes, circulars or notifications, given under this section shall be liable to a penalty of level 3 on the standard scale.

511. **Power of the Commission to permit use of Urdu words of abbreviations.**—The Commission may, by notification in the official Gazette, permit use of an Urdu equivalent of any English word or term required to be used pursuant to or for the purposes of this Act or an abbreviation of any such word or term instead of such word or term.

512. **Power to make regulations.**— (1) The Commission may, by notification in the official Gazette, make such regulations as may be necessary to carry out the purposes of this Act:

Provided that the power to make regulations conferred by this section shall be subject to the condition of previous publication and before making any regulations the draft thereof shall be published in the manner considered most appropriate by the Commission for eliciting public opinion thereon within a period of not less than fourteen days from the date of publication.

(2) Any regulation made under sub-section (1) may provide that a contravention thereof shall be punishable with a penalty which may extend to five million rupees and, where the contravention is a continuing one, with a further penalty which may extend to one hundred thousand rupees for every day after the first during which such contravention continues.

513. **Validation of laws.** (1) All amendments made to the Companies Ordinance, 1984 (XLVII of 1984) or any administered legislation through various Finance Acts shall be deemed to have been validly made from the date of commencement of such Acts.

(2) Notwithstanding anything contained in any other law, all orders made, proceedings taken and acts done, rules, regulations, instructions, notifications and other legal instruments made at any time before the promulgation of companies Ordinance, 1984 (XLVII of 1984) or any administered legislation, including appeals decided by the Appellate Bench of the Commission or authorization of investigation, enquiry and inspection by the Federal Government, the Commission or any officer of the Commission under delegated authority, the registrar or any other officer having authority under the

law in exercise or purported exercise of powers under amendments made to Companies Ordinance, 1984 (XLVII of 1984) or any administered legislation through various Finance Acts, and that have now been promulgated as well as affirmed in terms of sub-section (1) of this section, are declared and affirmed to have been and shall be deemed to have always been, validly made, decided, taken or done.

514. **Former registration offices and registers continued**. (1) The offices existing at the commencement of this Act for registration of companies shall be continued as if they had been established under this Act.

(2) Any books of account, book or paper, register or document kept under the provisions of any previous law relating to companies shall be deemed part of the books of accounts, book or paper, register or document to be kept under this Act.

515. **Removal of difficulty.**—If any difficulty arises in giving effect to any provision of this Act, the concerned Minister-in-Charge of the Federal Government may, by notification in the official Gazette make such provisions as may appear to it to be necessary for the purpose of removing the difficulty.

FIRST SCHEDULE

TABLE A

(See sections 2 and 36)

PART I

REGULATIONS FOR MANAGEMENT OF A COMPANY LIMITED BY SHARES

PRELIMINARY

1. (1)   In these regulations

(a)   "section" means section of the Act;

(b)   "the Act" means the Companies Act, 2017; and

(c)   "the seal" means the common seal or official seal of the company as the case may be.

(2)   Unless the context otherwise requires, words or expressions contained in these regulations shall have the same meaning as in this Act; and words importing the singular shall include the plural, and *vice versa*, and words importing the masculine gender shall include feminine, and words importing persons shall include bodies corporate.

BUSINESS

2. The directors shall have regard to the restrictions on the commencement of business imposed by section 19 if, and so far as, those restrictions are binding upon the company.

SHARES

3. In case of shares in the physical form, every person whose name is entered as a member in the register of members shall, without payment, be entitled to receive, within thirty days after allotment or within fifteen days of the application for registration of transfer, a certificate under the seal specifying the share or shares held by him and the amount paid up thereon:

Provided that if the shares are in book entry form or in case of conversion of physical shares and other transferable securities into book-entry form, the company shall, within ten days after an application is made for the registration of the transfer of any shares or other securities to a central depository, register such transfer in the name of the central depository.

4. The company shall not be bound to issue more than one certificate in respect of a share or shares in the physical form, held jointly by several persons and delivery of a certificate for a share to one of several joint holders shall be sufficient delivery to all.

5. If a share certificate in physical form is defaced, lost or destroyed, it may be renewed on payment of such fee, if any, not exceeding one hundred rupees, and on such terms, if any, as to evidence and indemnity and payment of expenses incurred by the company in investigating title as the directors think fit.

6. Except to the extent and in the manner allowed by section 86, no part of the funds of the company shall be employed in the purchase of, or in loans upon the security of, the company's shares.

TRANSFER AND TRANSMISSION OF SHARES

7. The instrument of transfer of any share in physical form in the company shall be executed both by the transferor and transferee, and the transferor shall be deemed to remain holder of the share until the name of the transferee is entered in the register of members in respect thereof.

8. Shares in physical form in the company shall be transferred in the following form, or in any usual or common form which the directors shall approve: -

Form for Transfer of Shares

(First Schedule to the Companies Act, 2017)

I ....s/o ....r/o ....(hereinafter called "the transferor") in consideration of the sum of rupees .... paid to me by .... s/o ....r/o ....(hereinafter called "the transferee"), do hereby transfer to the said transferee................................. the share (or shares) with distinctive numbers from ....to ....inclusive, in the ....Limited, to hold unto the said transferee, his executors, administrators and assigns, subject to the several conditions on which I held the same at the time of the execution hereof, and I, the said transferee, do hereby agree to take the said share (or shares) subject to the conditions aforesaid.

As witness our hands this.................. day of..........................., 20.....

Transferor	Transferee
Signature	Signature ....
Full Name, Father's / Husband's Name	Full Name, Father's / Husband's Name
CNIC Number (in case of foreigner, Passport Number)	CNIC Number (in case of foreigner, Passport Number)
Nationality	Nationality
Occupation and usual Residential Address	Occupation and usual Residential Address
	Cell number
	Landline number, if any
	Email address

Witness 1:   **Witness 2:**

Signature............date ......   Signature..........date .....

Name, CNIC Number and Full Address   Name, CNIC Number and Full
Address   Address

Bank Account Details of Transferee for Payment of Cash Dividend

(Mandatory in case of a listed company or optional for any other company)

It is requested that all my cash dividend amounts declared by the company, may be credited into the following bank account:

Title of Bank Account	
Bank Account Number	
Bank's Name	
Branch Name and Address	

It is stated that the above mentioned information is correct and that I will intimate the changes in the above-mentioned information to the company and the concerned Share Registrar as soon as these occur.

....

Signature of the Transferee(s)

9. (1) Subject to the restrictions contained in regulation 10 and 11, the directors shall not refuse to transfer any share unless the transfer deed is defective or invalid. The directors may also suspend the registration of transfers during the ten days immediately preceding a general meeting or prior to the determination of entitlement or rights of the shareholders by giving seven days' previous notice in the manner provided in the Act. The directors may, in case of shares in physical form, decline to recognise any instrument of transfer unless—

   a) a fee not exceeding fifty rupees as may be determined by the directors is paid to the company in respect thereof; and

   b) the duly stamped instrument of transfer is accompanied by the certificate of the shares to which it relates, and such other evidence as the directors may reasonably require to show the right of the transferor to make the transfer.

(2) If the directors refuse to register a transfer of shares, they shall within fifteen days after the date on which the transfer deed was lodged with the company send to the transferee and the transferor notice of the refusal indicating the defect or invalidity to the transferee, who shall, after removal of such defect or invalidity be entitled to re-lodge the transfer deed with the company.

Provided that the company shall, where the transferee is a central depository the refusal shall be conveyed within five days from the date on which the instrument of transfer was lodged with it notify the defect or invalidity to the transferee who shall, after the removal of such defect or invalidity, be entitled to re-lodge the transfer deed with the company.

TRANSMISSION OF SHARES

10. The executors, administrators, heirs, or nominees, as the case may be, of a deceased sole holder of a share shall be the only persons recognised by the company to deal with the share in accordance with the law. In the case of a share registered in the names of two or more holders, the survivors or survivor, or the executors or administrators of the deceased survivor, shall be the only persons recognised by the company to deal with the share in accordance with the law.

11. The shares or other securities of a deceased member shall be transferred on application duly supported by succession certificate or by lawful award, as the case may be, in favour of the successors to the extent of their interests and their names shall be entered to the register of members.

12. A person may on acquiring interest in a company as member, represented by shares, at any time after acquisition of such interest deposit with the company a nomination conferring on a person, being the relatives of the member, namely, a spouse, father, mother, brother, sister and son or daughter, the right to protect the interest of the legal heirs in the shares of the deceased in the event of his death, as a trustee and to facilitate the transfer of shares to the legal heirs of the deceased subject to succession to be determined under the Islamic law of inheritance and in case of non-*Muslim* members, as per their respective law.

13. The person nominated under regulation 12 shall, after the death of the member, be deemed as a member of company till the shares are transferred to the legal heirs and if the deceased was a director of the company, not being a listed company, the nominee shall also act as director of the company to protect the interest of the legal heirs.

14. A person to be deemed as a member under regulation 11, 12 and 13 to a share by reason of the death or insolvency of the holder shall be entitled to the same dividends and other advantages to which he would be entitled if he were the registered holder of the share and exercise any right conferred by membership in relation to meetings of the company.

ALTERATION OF CAPITAL

15. The company may, by special resolution--

   (a) increase its authorised capital by such amount as it thinks expedient;

   (b) consolidate and divide the whole or any part of its share capital into shares of larger amount than its existing shares;

(c) sub-divide its shares, or any of them, into shares of smaller amount than is fixed by the memorandum;

(d) cancel shares which, at the date of the passing of the resolution in that behalf, have not been taken or agreed to be taken by any person, and diminish the amount of its share capital by the amount of the share so cancelled.

16. Subject to the provisions of the Act, all new shares shall at the first instance be offered to such persons as at the date of the offer are entitled to such issue in proportion, as nearly as the circumstances admit, to the amount of the existing shares to which they are entitled. The offer shall be made by letter of offer specifying the number of shares offered, and limiting a time within which the offer, if not accepted, will deem to be declined, and after the expiration of that time, or on the receipt of an intimation from the person to whom the offer is made that he declines to accept the shares offered, the directors may dispose of the same in such manner as they think most beneficial to the company. The directors may likewise so dispose of any new shares which (by reason of the ratio which the new shares bear to shares held by persons entitled to an offer of new shares) cannot, in the opinion of the directors, be conveniently offered under this regulation.

17. The new shares shall be subject to the same provisions with reference to transfer, transmission and otherwise as the shares in the original share capital.

18. The company may, by special resolution--

(a) consolidate and divide its share capital into shares of larger amount than its existing shares;

(b) sub-divide its existing shares or any of them into shares of smaller amount than is fixed by the memorandum of association, subject, nevertheless, to the provisions of section 85;

(c) cancel any shares which, at the date of the passing of the resolution, have not been taken or agreed to be taken by any person.

19. The company may, by special resolution, reduce its share capital in any manner and with, and subject to confirmation by the Court and any incident authorised and consent required, by law.

GENERAL MEETINGS

20. The statutory general meeting of the company shall be held within the period required by section 131.

21. A general meeting, to be called annual general meeting, shall be held, in accordance with the provisions of section 132, within sixteen months from the date of incorporation of the company and thereafter once at least in every year

within a period of one hundred and twenty days following the close of its financial year.

22. All general meetings of a company other than the statutory meeting or an annual general meeting mentioned in sections 131 and 132 respectively shall be called extraordinary general meetings.

23. The directors may, whenever they think fit, call an extra-ordinary general meeting, and extra-ordinary general meetings shall also be called on such requisition, or in default, may be called by such requisitionists, as provided by section 133. If at any time there are not within Pakistan sufficient directors capable of acting to form a quorum, any director of the company may call an extra-ordinary general meeting in the same manner as nearly as possible as that in which meetings may be called by the directors.

24. The company may provide video-link facility to its members for attending general meeting at places other than the town in which general meeting is taking place after considering the geographical dispersal of its members:

Provided that in case of listed companies if the members holding ten percent of the total paid up capital or such other percentage of the paid up capital as may be specified, are resident in any other city, the company shall provide the facility of video-link to such members for attending annual general meeting of the company, if so required by such members in writing to the company at least seven days before the date of the meeting.

NOTICE AND PROCEEDINGS OF GENERAL MEETINGS

25. Twenty-one days' notice at the least (exclusive of the day on which the notice is served or deemed to be served, but inclusive of the day for which notice is given) specifying the place, the day and the hour of meeting and, in case of special business, the general nature of that business, shall be given in manner provided by the Act for the general meeting, to such persons as are, under the Act or the regulations of the company, entitled to receive such notice from the company; but the accidental omission to give notice to, or the non-receipt of notice by, any member shall not invalidate the proceedings at any general meeting.

26. All the business transacted at a general meeting shall be deemed special other than the business stated in sub-section (2) of section 134 namely; the consideration of financial statements and the reports of the board and auditors, the declaration of any dividend, the election and appointment of directors in place of those retiring, and the appointment of the auditors and fixing of their remuneration.

27. No business shall be transacted at any general meeting unless a quorum of members is present at that time when the meeting proceeds to business. The quorum of the general meeting shall be--

(a) in the case of a public listed company, not less than ten members present personally, or through video-link who represent not less than twenty-five percent of the total voting power, either of their own account or as proxies;

(b) in the case of any other company having share capital, two members present personally, or through video-link who represent not less than twenty-five percent of the total voting power, either of their own account or as proxies.

28. If within half an hour from the time appointed for the meeting a quorum is not present, the meeting, if called upon the requisition of members, shall be dissolved; in any other case, it shall stand adjourned to the same day in the next week at the same time and place, and, if at the adjourned meeting a quorum is not present within half an hour from the time appointed for the meeting, the members present, being not less than two, shall be a quorum.

29. The chairman of the board of directors, if any, shall preside as chairman at every general meeting of the company, but if there is no such chairman, or if at any meeting he is not present within fifteen minutes after the time appointed for the meeting, or is unwilling to act as chairman, any one of the directors present may be elected to be chairman, and if none of the directors is present, or willing to act as chairman, the members present shall choose one of their number to be chairman.

30. The chairman may, with the consent of any meeting at which a quorum is present (and shall if so directed by the meeting), adjourn the meeting from time to time but no business shall be transacted at any adjourned meeting other than the business left unfinished at the meeting from which the adjournment took place. When a meeting is adjourned for fifteen days or more, notice of the adjourned meeting shall be given as in the case of an original meeting. Save as aforesaid, it shall not be necessary to give any notice of an adjournment or of the business to be transacted at an adjourned meeting.

31. (1) At any general meeting a resolution put to the vote of the meeting shall be decided on a show of hands unless a poll is (before or on the declaration of the result of the show of hands) demanded. Unless a poll is so demanded, a declaration by the chairman that a resolution has, on a show of hands, been carried, or carried unanimously, or by a particular majority, or lost, and an entry to that effect in the book of the proceedings of the company shall be conclusive evidence of the fact, without proof of the number or proportion of the votes recorded in favour of, or against, that resolution.

(2)   At any general meeting, the company shall transact such businesses as may be notified by the Commission, only through postal ballot.

32.   A poll may be demanded only in accordance with the provisions of section 143.

33. If a poll is duly demanded, it shall be taken in accordance with the manner laid down in sections 144 and 145 and the result of the poll shall be deemed to be the resolution of the meeting at which the poll was demanded.

34. A poll demanded on the election of chairman or on a question of adjournment shall be taken at once.

35. In the case of an equality of votes, whether on a show of hands or on a poll, the chairman of the meeting at which the show of hands takes place, or at which the poll is demanded, shall have and exercise a second or casting vote.

36. Except for the businesses specified under sub-section (2) of section 134 to be conducted in the annual general meeting, the members of a private company or a public unlisted company (having not more than fifty members), may pass a resolution (ordinary or special) by circulation signed by all the members for the time being entitled to receive notice of a meeting. The resolution by circulation shall be deemed to be passed on the date of signing by the last of the signatory member to such resolution.

VOTES OF MEMBERS

37. Subject to any rights or restrictions for the time being attached to any class or classes of shares, on a show of hands every member present in person shall have one vote except for election of directors in which case the provisions of section 159 shall apply. On a poll every member shall have voting rights as laid down in section 134.

38. In case of joint-holders, the vote of the senior who tenders a vote, whether in person or by proxy or through video-link shall be accepted to the exclusion of the votes of the other joint-holders; and for this purpose seniority shall be determined by the order in which the names stand in the register of members.

39. A member of unsound mind, or in respect of whom an order has been made by any court having jurisdiction in lunacy, may vote, whether on show of hands or on a poll or through video link, by his committee or other legal guardian, and any such committee or guardian may, on a poll, vote by proxy.

40. On a poll votes may be given either personally or through video-link, by proxy or through postal ballot:

Provided that nobody corporate shall vote by proxy as long as a resolution of its directors in accordance with the provisions of section 138 is in force.

41. (1) The instrument appointing a proxy shall be in writing under the hand of the appointer or of his attorney duly authorised in writing.

(2) The instrument appointing a proxy and the power-of-attorney or other authority (if any) under which it is signed, or a notarially certified copy of that power or authority, shall be deposited at the registered office of the company not

less than forty-eight hours before the time for holding the meeting at which the person named in the instrument proposes to vote and in default the instrument of proxy shall not be treated as valid.

42. An instrument appointing a proxy may be in the following form, or a form as near thereto as may be:

INSTRUMENT OF PROXY

…………………..……………………… Limited

"I……………………………..s/o...r/o ....being a member of the…………………………………………….. Limited, hereby appoint…………………………s/o.............................r/o........................... ...as my proxy to attend and vote on my behalf at the (statutory, annual, extra-ordinary, as the case may be) general meeting of the company to be held on the …………….. day of ……………….., 20…… and at any adjournment thereof."

43. A vote given in accordance with the terms of an instrument of proxy shall be valid notwithstanding the previous death or insanity of the principal or revocation of the proxy or of the authority under which the proxy was executed, or the transfer of the share in respect of which the proxy is given, provided that no intimation in writing of such death, insanity, revocation or transfer as aforesaid shall have been received by the company at the office before the commencement of the meeting or adjourned meeting at which the proxy is used.

DIRECTORS

44. The following subscribers of the memorandum of association shall be the first directors of the company, so, however, that the number of directors shall not in any case be less than that specified in section 154 and they shall hold office until the election of directors in the first annual general meeting:

1.   ab

2.   cd

3.   ef

4.   gh

45. The remuneration of the directors shall from time to time be determined by the company in general meeting subject to the provisions of the Act.

46. Save as provided in section 153, no person shall be appointed as a director unless he is a member of the company.

POWERS AND DUTIES OF DIRECTORS

47. The business of the company shall be managed by the directors, who may pay all expenses incurred in promoting and registering the company, and may

exercise all such powers of the company as are not by the Act or any statutory modification thereof for the time being in force, or by these regulations, required to be exercised by the company in general meeting, subject nevertheless to the provisions of the Act or to any of these regulations, and such regulations being not inconsistent with the aforesaid provisions, as may be prescribed by the company in general meeting but no regulation made by the company in general meeting shall invalidate any prior act of the directors which would have been valid if that regulation had not been made.

48. The directors shall appoint a chief executive in accordance with the provisions of sections 186 and 187.

49. The amount for the time being remaining undischarged of moneys borrowed or raised by the directors for the purposes of the company (otherwise than by the issue of share capital) shall not at any time, without the sanction of the company in general meeting, exceed the issued share capital of the company.

50. The directors shall duly comply with the provisions of the Act, or any statutory modification thereof for the time being in force, and in particular with the provisions in regard to the registration of the particulars of mortgages, charges and pledge affecting the property of the company or created by it, to the keeping of a register of the directors, and to the sending to the registrar of an annual list of members, and a summary of particulars relating thereto and notice of any consolidation or increase of share capital, or sub-division of shares, and copies of special resolutions and a copy of the register of directors and notifications of any changes therein.

MINUTE BOOKS

51. The directors shall cause records to be kept and minutes to be made in book or books with regard to--

(a) all resolutions and proceedings of general meeting(s) and the meeting(s) of directors and Committee(s) of directors, and every member present at any general meeting and every director present at any meeting of directors or Committee of directors shall put his signature in a book to be kept for that purpose;

(b) recording the names of the persons present at each meeting of the directors and of any committee of the directors, and the general meeting; and

(c) all orders made by the directors and Committee(s) of directors:

Provided that all records related to proceedings through video-link shall be maintained in accordance with the relevant regulations specified by the Commission which shall be appropriately rendered into writing as part of the minute books according to the said regulations.

THE SEAL

52. The directors shall provide for the safe custody of the seal and the seal shall not be affixed to any instrument except by the authority of a resolution of the board of directors or by a committee of directors authorized in that behalf by the directors and in the presence of at least two directors and of the secretary or such other person as the directors may appoint for the purpose; and those two directors and secretary or other person as aforesaid shall sign every instrument to which the seal of the company is so affixed in their presence.

DISQUALIFICATION OF DIRECTORS

53. No person shall become the director of a company if he suffers from any of the disabilities or disqualifications mentioned in section 153 or disqualified or debarred from holding such office under any of the provisions of the Act as the case may be and, if already a director, shall cease to hold such office from the date he so becomes disqualified or disabled:

Provided, however, that no director shall vacate his office by reason only of his being a member of any company which has entered into contracts with, or done any work for, the company of which he is director, but such director shall not vote in respect of any such contract or work, and if he does so vote, his vote shall not be counted.

PROCEEDINGS OF DIRECTORS

54. The directors may meet together for the dispatch of business, adjourn and otherwise regulate their meetings, as they think fit. A director may, and the secretary on the requisition of a director shall, at any time, summon a meeting of directors. Notice sent to a director through email whether such director is in Pakistan or outside Pakistan shall be a valid notice.

55. The directors may elect a chairman of their meetings and determine the period for which he is to hold office; but, if no such chairman is elected, or if at any meeting the chairman is not present within ten minutes after the time appointed for holding the same or is unwilling to act as chairman, the directors present may choose one of their number to be chairman of the meeting.

56. At least one-third ($1/3^{rd}$) of the total number of directors or two (2) directors whichever is higher, for the time being of the company, present personally or through video-link, shall constitute a quorum.

57. Save as otherwise expressly provided in the Act, every question at meetings of the board shall be determined by a majority of votes of the directors present in person or through video-link, each director having one vote. In case of an equality of votes or tie, the chairman shall have a casting vote in addition to his original vote as a director.

58. The directors may delegate any of their powers not required to be exercised in their meeting to committees consisting of such member or members of their body as they think fit; any committee so formed shall, in the exercise of the

powers so delegated, conform to any restrictions that may be imposed on them by the directors.

59. (1) A committee may elect a chairman of its meetings; but, if no such chairman is elected, or if at any meeting the chairman is not present within ten minutes after the time appointed for holding the same or is unwilling to act as chairman, the members present may choose one of their number to be chairman of the meeting.

(2) A committee may meet and adjourn as it thinks proper. Questions arising at any meeting shall be determined by a majority of votes of the members present. In case of an equality of votes, the chairman shall have and exercise a second or casting vote.

60. All acts done by any meeting of the directors or of a committee of directors, or by any person acting as a director, shall, notwithstanding that it be afterwards discovered that there was some defect in the appointment of any such directors or persons acting as aforesaid, or that they or any of them were disqualified, be as valid as if every such person had been duly appointed and was qualified to be a director.

61. A copy of the draft minutes of meeting of the board of directors shall be furnished to every director within seven working days of the date of meeting.

62. A resolution in writing signed by all the directors for the time being entitled to receive notice of a meeting of the directors shall be as valid and effectual as if it had been passed at a meeting of the directors duly convened and held.

FILLING OF VACANCIES

63. At the first annual general meeting of the company, all the directors shall stand retired from office, and directors shall be elected in their place in accordance with section 159 for a term of three years.

64. A retiring director shall be eligible for re-election.

65. The directors shall comply with the provisions of sections 154 to 159 and sections 161, 162 and 167 relating to the election of directors and matters ancillary thereto.

66. Any casual vacancy occurring on the board of directors may be filled up by the directors, but the person so chosen shall be subject to retirement at the same time as if he had become a director on the day on which the director in whose place he is chosen was last elected as director.

67. The company may remove a director but only in accordance with the provisions of the Act.

DIVIDENDS AND RESERVE

68. The company in general meeting may declare dividends but no dividend shall exceed the amount recommended by the directors.

69. The directors may from time to time pay to the members such interim dividends as appear to the directors to be justified by the profits of the company.

70. Any dividend may be paid by a company either in cash or in kind only out of its profits. The payment of dividend in kind shall only be in the shape of shares of listed company held by the distributing company.

71. Dividend shall not be paid out of unrealized gain on investment property credited to profit and loss account.

72. Subject to the rights of persons (if any) entitled to shares with special rights as to dividends, all dividends shall be declared and paid according to the amounts paid on the shares.

73. (1) The directors may, before recommending any dividend, set aside out of the profits of the company such sums as they think proper as a reserve or reserves which shall, at the discretion of the directors, be applicable for meeting contingencies, or for equalizing dividends, or for any other purpose to which the profits of the company may be properly applied, and pending such application may, at the like discretion, either be employed in the business of company or be invested in such investments (other than shares of the company) as the directors may, subject to the provisions of the Act, from time to time think fit.

(2)   The directors may carry forward any profits which they may think prudent not to distribute, without setting them aside as a reserve.

74. If several persons are registered as joint-holders of any share, any one of them may give effectual receipt for any dividend payable on the share.

75. (1) Notice of any dividend that may have been declared shall be given in manner hereinafter mentioned to the persons entitled to share therein but, in the case of a public company, the company may give such notice by advertisement in a newspaper circulating in the Province in which the registered office of the company is situate.

(2)   Any dividend declared by the company shall be paid to its registered shareholders or to their order. The dividend payable in cash may be paid by cheque or warrant or in any electronic mode to the shareholders entitled to the payment of the dividend, as per their direction.

(3)   In case of a listed company, any dividend payable in cash shall only be paid through electronic mode directly into the bank account designated by the entitled shareholders.

76. The dividend shall be paid within the period laid down under the Act.

ACCOUNTS

77. The directors shall cause to be kept proper books of account as required under section 220.

78. The books of account shall be kept at the registered office of the company or at such other place as the directors shall think fit and shall be open to inspection by the directors during business hours.

79. The directors shall from time to time determine whether and to what extent and at what time and places and under what conditions or regulations the accounts and books or papers of the company or any of them shall be open to the inspection of members not being directors, and no member (not being a director) shall have any right of inspecting any account and book or papers of the company except as conferred by law or authorised by the directors or by the company in general meeting.

80. The directors shall as required by sections 223 and 226 cause to be prepared and to be laid before the company in general meeting the financial statements duly audited and reports as are referred to in those sections.

81. The financial statements and other reports referred to in regulation 80 shall be made out in every year and laid before the company in the annual general meeting in accordance with sections 132 and 223.

82. A copy of the financial statements and reports of directors and auditors shall, at least twenty-one days preceding the meeting, be sent to the persons entitled to receive notices of general meetings in the manner in which notices are to be given hereunder.

83. The directors shall in all respect comply with the provisions of sections 220 to 227.

84. Auditors shall be appointed and their duties regulated in accordance with sections 246 to 249.

NOTICES

85. (1) A notice may be given by the company to any member to his registered address or if he has no registered address in Pakistan to the address, if any, supplied by him to the company for the giving of notices to him against an acknowledgement or by post or courier service or through electronic means or in any other manner as may be specified by the Commission.

(2)   Where a notice is sent by post, service of the notice shall be deemed to be effected by properly addressing, prepaying and posting a letter containing the notice and, unless the contrary is proved, to have been effected at the time at which the letter will be delivered in the ordinary course of post.

86. A notice may be given by the company to the joint-holders of a share by giving the notice to the joint-holder named first in the register in respect of the share.

87. A notice may be given by the company to the person entitled to a share in consequence of the death or insolvency of a member in the manner provided under regulation 85 addressed to them by name, or by the title or representatives of the deceased, or assignees of the insolvent, or by any like description, at the address, supplied for the purpose by the person claiming to be so entitled.

88. Notice of every general meeting shall be given in the manner hereinbefore authorised to (a) every member of the company and also to (b) every person entitled to a share in consequence of the death or insolvency of a member, who but for his death or insolvency would be entitled to receive notice of the meeting, and (c) to the auditors of the company for the time being and every person who is entitled to receive notice of general meetings.

WINDING UP

89. (1) In the case of members' voluntary winding up, with the sanction of a special resolution of the company, and, in the case of creditors' voluntary winding up, of a meeting of the creditors, the liquidator shall exercise any of the powers given by sub-section (1) of section 337 of the Act to a liquidator in a winding up by the Court including *inter-alia* divide amongst the members, in specie or kind, the whole or any part of the assets of the company, whether they consist of property of the same kind or not.

(2) For the purpose aforesaid, the liquidator may set such value as he deems fair upon any property to be divided as aforesaid and may determine how such division shall be carried out as between the members or different classes of members.

(3) The liquidator may, with the like sanction, vest the whole or any part of such assets in trustees upon such trusts for the benefit of the contributories as the liquidator, with the like sanction, thinks fit, but so that no member shall be compelled to accept any shares or other securities whereon there is any liability.

INDEMNITY

90. Every officer or agent for the time being of the company may be indemnified out of the assets of the company against any liability incurred by him in defending any proceedings, whether civil or criminal, arising out of his dealings in relation to the affairs of the company, except those brought by the company against him, in which judgment is given in his favour or in which he is acquitted, or in connection with any application under section 492 in which relief is granted to him by the Court.

We, the several persons whose names and addresses are subscribed below, are desirous of being formed into a company, in pursuance of these articles of association, and we respectively agree to take the number of shares in the capital of the company set opposite our respective names:

Name and surname (present & former) in full(in Block letters	NIC No. (in case of foreigner, Passport No.)	Father's/ Husband's Name in full	Nationality (ies) with former Nationality	Occupation	Usual residential address in full or the registered/principal office address for a subscribe other than natural person	Number of shares taken by each subscriber (in figures and words)	Signature
Total number of shares taken (in figures and words)							

Dated the_____ day of_____, 20_____

Witness to above signatures: *(For the documents submitted in physical form)*

Signature	
Full Name (in Block Letters)	
Father's/Husband's name	
Nationality	
Occupation	
NIC No.	
Usual residential address	

Witness to above signatures: *(For the documents submitted electronically)*

(Digital Signature Certificate Provider)

Name:

Address:

PART II

REGULATIONS FOR MANAGEMENT OF A SINGLE MEMBER PRIVATE COMPANY LIMITED BY SHARES

INTERPRETATION

1. In the interpretation of these articles the following expressions shall have the following meanings unless repugnant to or inconsistent with the subject articles

    (a)   "company" or "this company" means _____ (SMC-Private) Limited;

(b) "directors" or "board of directors" means board of directors consist of only the sole director or more than one directors if so appointed under the relevant provisions of the Act;

(c) "member director" means a director who is a member of the company;

(d) "non-member director" means an individual who is not a member, but has been nominated under the provisions of the Act;

(e) "private company" means a private company having two more members;

(f) "sole member" means the single member of the company; and

(g) "sole director" means the director of the company who is for the time being the only director and includes a non-member director of the company.

2. Unless the context otherwise requires, words or expressions contained in these regulations shall have the same meaning as in the Act; and words importing the singular shall include the plural, and *vice versa*, and words importing the masculine gender shall include feminine, and words importing persons shall include bodies corporate.

PRELIMINARY

3. Any provision of the Act or rules and regulations made thereunder which apply in relation to a private company limited by shares incorporated under the Act shall, in the absence of any express provision to the contrary, apply in relation to a single member company as it applies in relation to such a company which is formed by two or more persons or which has two or more persons as members and the provisions contained in part I of Table A of First Schedule in the Act shall be deemed part of these articles of association in so far as these are not inconsistent with or repugnant to the provisions contained herein below.

SINGLE MEMBER COMPANY

4. The company is a single member company and as such being a private company limited by shares—

(a) it shall not invite the public to subscribe for any shares of the company;

(b) the company shall not register any share(s) in the name of two or more persons to hold one or more shares jointly; and

(c) number of the members of the company shall be limited to one.

SHARES

5. The company may alter its share capital in accordance with section 85.

6. Share certificate shall be issued under the seal of the Company and shall be signed by the member director or the non-member director, as the case may be.

TRANSFER AND TRANSMISSION OF SHARES

7. The company shall not transfer all of the shares of a single member to two or more persons or part of shares of single member to other person(s) or allot further shares to any person other than the single member or, at any time, allow transfer of shares or allotment of shares or both resulting in number of members to become two or more, except for change of status from single member company to private company and to alter its articles accordingly.

8. The single member may transfer all of his shares to a single person whereby the company shall remain a single member company as it was before such transfer.

9. The sole member shall nominate a person who, in the event of death of the sole member, shall be responsible to.

   (a)   transfer the shares to the legal heirs of the deceased subject to succession to be determined under the Islamic law of inheritance and in case of a non-Muslim members, as per their respective law; and

   (b)   manage the affairs of the company as a trustee, till such time the title of shares are transferred:

   Provided that where the transfer by virtue of the above provision is made to more than one legal heir, the company shall cease to be a single member company and comply with the provisions of section 47 of the Act.

CHANGE OF STATUS

10. The company may convert itself from single member private company to a private company in accordance with the provisions of section 47.

MEETINGS, VOTES AND ELECTION OF DIRECTORS

11. All the requirements of the Act regarding calling of, holding and approval in general meeting, board meeting and election of directors in case of a single member company, shall be deemed complied with; if the decision is recorded in the relevant minutes book and signed by the sole member or sole director as the case may be.

DIRECTOR(S)

12. The company shall always have the sole member or in case it is not a natural person its nominee, as a director but it may have such number of other director(s) who fulfill the conditions as specified in section 153.

13. The board shall not have the power to remove the member director provided that where the sole member is not a natural person, it may change its nominee.

14. The sole member shall have the power to remove any director, chief executive or secretary through a resolution.

15. The director(s) shall appoint a chief executive in accordance with the provisions of sections 186 and 187.

16. The directors may hold their meetings through tele or video link provided that the minutes of such meeting are approved and signed subsequently by all the directors.

17. The directors shall cause records to be kept and minutes to be made in book or books with regard to--

(a)   all resolutions and proceedings of the meeting(s) of directors and Committee(s) of directors, and every director present at any meeting of directors or Committee of directors shall put his signatures in a book to be kept for that purpose;

(b)   recording the names of the persons present at each meeting of the directors and of any committee of the directors, and the general meeting; and

(c)   all orders made by the directors and Committee(s) of directors:

Provided that all records related to proceedings through video-link shall be maintained in accordance with the relevant regulations specified by the Commission which shall be appropriately rendered into writing as part of the minute books according to the said regulations.

SECRETARY

18. The company may appoint a secretary who shall be responsible for discharge of duties and functions normally discharged by a secretary under the corporate laws and secretarial practice.

CONTRACTS WITH THE SINGLE MEMBER

19. Where a single member company enters into a contract with the single member of the company, the single member company shall, unless the contract is in writing, ensure that the terms of the contract are forthwith set out in a written memorandum or are recorded in the minutes of the first meeting of the directors of the company following the making of the contract.

DIVIDENDS AND RESERVES

20. The company may declare dividends and pay in accordance with the provisions of the Act.

ACCOUNTS

21. The director(s) shall cause to keep proper books of account in accordance with the provisions of section 220.

22. Auditors shall be appointed and their duties regulated in accordance with the provisions of sections 246 to 249.

THE SEAL

23.   The director shall provide for safe custody of the seal and the seal shall not be affixed to any instrument except by the authority of a resolution of the board of directors or by a committee of directors authorized in that behalf by the member director or the non-member director and in the presence of at least member director or the non-member director and of the secretary or such other person as the directors may appoint for the purpose and the member director or the non-member director and the secretary or other person as aforesaid shall sign every instrument to which the seal of the company is affixed in their presence.

WINDING UP

24. The company shall follow, in case of its winding up, the relevant provisions of the Act.

INDEMNITY

25. Every officer or agent for the time being of the company may be indemnified out of the assets of the company against any liability incurred by him in defending any proceedings, whether civil or criminal arising out of his dealings in relation to the affairs of the company, except those brought by the company against him, in which judgment is given in his favour or in which he is acquitted, or in connection with any application under section 487 in which relief is granted to him by the Court.

I, whose name and address is subscribed below, am desirous of forming a company in pursuance of these articles of association and agree to take the number of shares in the capital of the company as set opposite my name:

Name and surname (present & former) in full(in Block letters	NIC No. (in case of foreigner, Passport No.)	Father's/ Husband's Name in full	Nationality (ies) with former Nationality	Occupation	Usual residential address in full or the registered/principal office address for a subscribe other than natural person	Number of shares taken by each subscriber (in figures and words)	Signature
Total number of shares taken (in figures and words)							

Dated the_____ day of_____, 20_____

Witness to above signatures: *(For the documents submitted in physical form)*

Signature	
Full Name (in Block Letters)	
Father's/Husband's name	
Nationality	
Occupation	
NIC No.	
Usual residential address	

Witness to above signatures: *(For the documents submitted online)*

(Digital Signature Certificate Provider)

Name:

Address:

TABLE B

(See section 41)

MEMORANDUM OF ASSOCIATION OF

COMPANY LIMITED BY SHARES

1.   The name of the company is "ABC Textile Limited/(Private) Limited/(SMC-Private) Limited".

2.   The registered office of the company will be situated in the Province of Sindh.

3.(i) The principal line of business of the company shall be to carry-out the manufacturing, sale, import and export of textiles.

  (ii) Except for the businesses mentioned in sub-clause (iii) hereunder, the company shall engage in all the lawful businesses and shall be authorized to take all necessary steps and actions in connection therewith and ancillary thereto.

  (iii) Notwithstanding anything contained in the foregoing sub-clauses of this clause nothing contained herein shall be construed as empowering the Company to undertake or indulge, directly or indirectly in the business of a Banking Company, Non-banking Finance Company (Mutual Fund, Leasing, Investment Company, Investment Advisor, Real Estate Investment Trust management company, Housing Finance Company, Venture Capital Company, Discounting Services, Microfinance or Microcredit business), Insurance Business, *Modaraba* management company, Stock Brokerage business, forex, real estate business, managing agency, business of providing the services of security guards or any other business restricted under any law for the time being in force or as may be specified by the Commission.

(iv)   It is hereby undertaken that the company shall not:

    (a)   engage in any of the business mentioned in sub-clause (iii) above or any unlawful operation;

    (b)   launch multi-level marketing (MLM), Pyramid and Ponzi Schemes, or other related activities/businesses or any lottery business;

    (c)   engage in any of the permissible business unless the requisite approval, permission, consent or licence is obtained from competent authority as may be required under any law for the time being in force.

4.   The liability of the members is limited.

5.   The authorized capital of the company is Rs.1,000,000/- (Rupees one Million only) divided into 100,000 (one hundred thousand) ordinary shares of Rs.10/- (Rupees ten only) each.

We, the several persons whose names and addresses are subscribed below, are desirous of being formed into a company, in pursuance of this memorandum of association, and we respectively agree to take the number of shares in the capital of the company as set opposite our respective names:

Name and surname (present & former) in full(in Block letters	NIC No. (in case of foreigner, Passport No.)	Father's/ Husband's Name in full	Nationality (ies) with former Nationality	Occupation	Usual residential address in full or the registered/principal office address for a subscribe other than natural person	Number of shares taken by each subscriber (in figures and words)	Signature
Total number of shares taken (in figures and words)							

Dated the_____ day of_____, 20____

Witness to above signatures: *(For the documents submitted in physical form)*

Signature	
Full Name (in Block Letters)	
Father's/Husband's name	
Nationality	
Occupation	
NIC No.	
Usual residential address	

Witness to above signatures: *(For the documents submitted online)*

(Digital Signature Certificate Provider)

Name:

Address:

(Applicable in case of single member company)

I, whose name and address is subscribed below, am desirous of forming a company in pursuance of this memorandum of association and agree to take the number of shares in the capital of the company as set opposite my name:

Name and surname (present & former) in full(in Block letters	NIC No. (in case of foreigner, Passport No.)	Father's/ Husband's Name in full	Nationality (ies) with former Nationality	Occupation	Usual residential address in full or the registered/principal office address for a subscribe other than natural person	Number of shares taken by each subscriber (in figures and words)	Signature
Total number of shares taken (in figures and words)							

Dated the_____ day of_____, 20____

Witness to above signatures: *(For the documents submitted in physical form)*

Signature	
Full Name (in Block Letters)	
Father's/Husband's name	
Nationality	
Occupation	
NIC No.	
Usual residential address	

Witness to above signatures: *(For the documents submitted online)*

(Digital Signature Certificate Provider)

Name:

Address:

TABLE C

(See section 41)

MEMORANDUM AND ARTICLES OF ASSOCIATION OF A COMPANY LIMITED BY GUARANTEE AND NOT HAVING A SHARE CAPITAL

MEMORANDUM OF ASSOCIATION

1. The name of the company is "The ABC Hospital (Guarantee) Limited."

2. The registered office of the company will be situated in the Province of Baluchistan.

3.(i) The principal line of business of the company shall be to establish, run and manage hospitals.

  (ii) Except for the businesses mentioned in sub-clause (iii) hereunder, the company shall engage in all the lawful businesses and shall be authorized to take all necessary steps and actions in connection therewith and ancillary thereto.

(iii) Notwithstanding anything contained in the foregoing sub-clauses of this clause nothing contained herein shall be construed as empowering the Company to undertake or indulge, directly or indirectly in the business of a Banking Company, Non-banking Finance Company (Mutual Fund, Leasing, Investment Company, Investment Advisor, Real Estate Investment Trust management company, Housing Finance Company, Venture Capital Company, Discounting Services, Microfinance or Microcredit business), Insurance Business, *Modaraba* management company, Stock Brokerage business, forex, real estate business, managing agency, business of providing the services of security guards or any other business restricted under any law for the time being in force or as may be specified by the Commission.

(iv) It is hereby undertaken that the company shall not:

  (a) engage in any of the business mentioned in sub-clause (iii) above or any unlawful operation;

  (b) launch multi-level marketing (MLM), Pyramid and Ponzi Schemes, or other related activities/businesses or any lottery business;

  (c) engage in any of the permissible business unless the requisite approval, permission, consent or licence is obtained from competent authority as may be required under any law for the time being in force.

4. The liability of the members is limited.

5. Every member of the company undertakes to contribute to the assets of the company in the event of its being wound up while he is a member, or within one year afterwards, for payment of the debts and liabilities of the company contracted before he ceases to be a member, and the costs, charges and expenses of winding up and for the adjustment of the rights of the contributories among themselves, such amount as may be required not exceeding .... rupees.

We, the several persons whose names and addresses are subscribed below, are desirous of being formed into a company, in pursuance of this memorandum of association:

Name and surname (present & former) in full(in Block letters	NIC No. (in case of foreigner, Passport No.)	Father's/ Husband's Name in full	Nationality (ies) with former Nationality	Occupation	Usual residential address in full or the registered/principal office address for a subscribe other than natural person	Number of shares taken by each subscriber (in figures and words)	Signature
Total number of shares taken (in figures and words)							

Dated the_____ day of_____, 20____

Witness to above signatures: *(For the documents submitted in physical form)*

Signature	
Full Name (in Block Letters)	
Father's/Husband's name	
Nationality	
Occupation	
NIC No.	
Usual residential address	

Witness to above signatures: *(For the documents submitted online)*

(Digital Signature Certificate Provider)

Name:

Address:

(Applicable in case of single member company)

I, whose name and address is subscribed below, am desirous of forming a company in pursuance of this memorandum of association:

Name and surname (present & former) in full(in Block letters	NIC No. (in case of foreigner, Passport No.)	Father's/ Husband's Name in full	Nationality (ies) with former Nationality	Occupation	Usual residential address in full or the registered/principal office address for a subscribe other than natural person	Number of shares taken by each subscriber (in figures and words)	Signature
Total number of shares taken (in figures and words)							

Dated the_____ day of_____, 20_____

Witness to above signatures: *(For the documents submitted in physical form)*

Signature	
Full Name (in Block Letters)	
Father's/Husband's name	
Nationality	
Occupation	
NIC No.	
Usual residential address	

Witness to above signatures: *(For the documents submitted online)*

(Digital Signature Certificate Provider)

Name:

Address:

ARTICLES OF ASSOCIATION OF A COMPANY LIMITED BY GUARANTEE AND NOT HAVING A SHARE CAPITAL

INTERPRETATION

1. (1) In these articles —

> (a) "section" means section of the Act;
>
> (b) "the Act" means the Companies Act, 2017.
>
> (c) "the seal" means the common seal or official seal of the company as the case may be.

(2) Unless the context otherwise requires, words or expressions contained in these articles shall bear the same meaning as in the Act or any statutory modification thereof in force at the date at which these regulations become binding on the company.

MEMBERS

2. The number of members with which the company proposes to be registered is 200, but the directors may, from time to time, whenever the company or the business of the company requires it, register an increase of members.

3. The subscribers to the memorandum and such other persons as the directors shall admit to membership shall be members of the company.

GENERAL MEETINGS

4. A general meeting, to be called annual general meeting, shall be held within sixteen months from the date of incorporation of the company and thereafter once at least in every year within a period of one hundred and twenty days following the close of its financial year as may be determined by the directors.

5. All general meetings other than annual general meetings shall be called extraordinary general meetings.

6. The directors may, whenever they think fit, call an extraordinary general meeting.

PROCEEDINGS AT GENERAL MEETINGS

7. All business shall except the businesses stated in sub-section (2) of section 134 shall be deemed special that is transacted at a general meeting.

8. (1) No business shall be transacted at any general meeting unless a quorum of members is present at the time when the meeting proceeds to business.

(2) Save as otherwise provided, three members present in person or through video-link who represent not less than twenty five per cent of the total voting power either of their own account or as proxies in person, shall be a quorum.

9. (1) If within half an hour from the time appointed for a meeting a quorum is not present, the meeting, if called upon the requisition of members shall be dissolved.

(2) In any other case, the meeting shall stand adjourned to the same day in the next week, at the same time and place, or to such other day and such other time and place as the directors may determine.

(3) If at the adjourned meeting a quorum is not present within half an hour from the time appointed for the meeting the members present shall be a quorum.

10. (1) The Chairman, if any, of the board of directors shall preside as chairman at every general meeting of the company.

(2) If there is no such chairman, or if he is not present within fifteen minutes after the time appointed for the meeting or is unwilling to act as chairman of the meeting, the directors present shall choose one of their number to be chairman of the meeting.

(3) If at any meeting no director is willing to act as chairman or if no director is present within fifteen minutes after the time appointed for the meeting, the members present shall choose one of their number to be the chairman of the meeting.

11. (1) The chairman may, with the consent of any meeting at which a quorum is present (and shall if so directed by the meeting) adjourn the meeting from time to time and from place to place.

(2) No business shall be transacted at any adjourned meeting other than the business left unfinished at the meeting from which the adjournment took place.

(3) When a meeting is adjourned for thirty days or more, notice of the adjourned meeting shall be given as in the case of an original meeting.

(4) Save as aforesaid, it shall not be necessary to give any notice of an adjournment or of the business to be transacted at an adjourned meeting.

12. At any general meeting a resolution put to the vote to the meeting shall be decided on a show of hands and a declaration by the chairman that a resolution has been carried or carried unanimously, or by a particular majority, or lost and an entry to that effect in the minutes of proceedings shall be conclusive evidence of the fact without proof of the number of votes recorded in favour or against the resolution.

13. In the case of an equality of votes, the chairman of the meeting shall have and exercise a second or casting vote.

VOTES OF MEMBERS

14. Every member shall have one vote.

15. A member of unsound mind, or in respect of whom an order has been made by any court having jurisdiction in lunacy, may vote, by his committee or other legal guardian, and any such committee or guardian may, vote by proxy.

16. No member shall be entitled to vote at any general meeting unless all moneys presently payable by him to the company have been paid.

17. (1) Votes may be given on any matter by the members either personally or through video-link or by proxy or by means of postal ballot.

(2) At any general meeting, the company shall transact such businesses only through postal ballot as may be notified by the Commission.

18. (1) No objection shall be raised to the qualification of any voter except at a meeting or adjourned meeting at which the vote objected to is given or tendered, and every vote not disallowed at such meeting shall be valid for all purposes.

(2) Any such objection made in due time shall be referred to the chairman of the meeting, whose decision shall be final and conclusive.

19. A vote given in accordance with the terms of an instrument of proxy shall be valid, notwithstanding the previous death or insanity of the principal or the revocation of the proxy or of the authority under which the proxy was executed:

Provided that no intimation in writing of such death, insanity or revocation shall have been received by the company at its office before the commencement of the meeting or adjourned meeting at which the proxy is used.

20. An instrument appointing a proxy shall be in writing and shall be deposited at the office of the company or the place of meeting at least forty-eight hours before the meeting at which it is to be used.

DIRECTORS

21. The following subscribers of the memorandum of association shall be the first directors of the company, so, however, that the number of directors shall not in any case be less than that specified in section 154 and they shall hold office until the election of directors in the annual general meeting:

1.   ab

2.   cd

3.   ef

4.   gh

ELECTION OF DIRECTORS

22. (i)   The directors of the company shall be elected in accordance with provisions of sub-sections (1) to (4) of section 159 of the Act, in the following manner:

(a) the directors of the company shall be elected by the members of the company in general meeting;

(b) each member shall have votes equal to the number of directors to be elected;

(c) a member may give all his votes to a single candidate or divide them, not being in fractions, between more than one of the candidates in such manner as he may choose; and

(d) the candidate who gets the highest number of votes shall be declared elected as director and then the candidate who gets the next highest number of votes shall be so declared and so on until the total number of directors to be elected has been so elected.

(ii) If the number of persons who offer themselves to be elected is not more than the number of directors fixed by the directors under sub-section (1) of section 159, all persons who offered themselves shall be deemed to have been elected as directors.

POWER AND DUTIES OF DIRECTORS

22. The business of the company shall be managed by the directors, who may exercise all such powers of the company as are not by the Act required to be exercised by the company in general meeting.

PROCEEDINGS OF DIRECTORS

23. (1) The Directors may meet for the dispatch of business, adjourn and otherwise regulate their meetings, as they think fit.

(2) A director may, and the chief executive or secretary on the requisition of a director shall, at any time, summon a meeting of the directors.

24 (1) Save as otherwise expressly provided in the Act, questions arising at any meeting of the directors shall be decided by a majority of votes.

(2) In case of any equality of votes, the chairman shall have and exercise a second or casting vote.

25. The continuing directors may act notwithstanding any vacancy but, if and so long as their number is reduced below the minimum fixed by the Act, the continuing directors or director may act for the purpose of increasing the number of directors to that minimum or for summoning a general meeting of the company, but for no other purpose.

26. (1) The directors may elect a chairman and determine the period for which he is to hold office within the limits prescribed by the Act.

(2) If no such chairman is elected, or if at any meeting the Chairman is not present within fifteen minutes after the time appointed for the meeting or is

unwilling to act as chairman, the directors present may choose one of their number to be chairman of the meeting.

27. All acts done by any meeting of the directors or by any person acting as director, shall, notwithstanding that it may afterwards be discovered that there was some defect in the appointment of any such director or of any person acting as aforesaid, or that they or any of them were disqualified, be as valid as if every such director or such person had been duly appointed and was qualified to be a director.

28. At least one-third $(1/3^{rd})$ of the total number of directors or two (2) directors whichever is higher, for the time being of the company, present personally or through video-link, shall constitute a quorum.

28. A resolution in writing, signed by all the directors for the time being entitled to receive notice of a meeting, shall be as valid and effectual as if it had been passed at a meeting of the directors duly convened and held.

MINUTE BOOKS

29. The directors shall cause records to be kept and minutes to be made in book or books with regard to—

(a) all resolutions and proceedings of general meeting(s) and the meeting(s) of directors and committee(s) of directors, and every member present at any general meeting and every director present at any meeting of directors or committee of directors shall put his signature in a book to be kept for that purpose;

(b) recording the names of the persons present at each meeting of the directors and of any committee of the directors, and the general meeting; and

(c) all orders made by the directors and committee(s) of directors:

Provided that all records related to proceedings through video-link shall be maintained in accordance with the relevant regulations specified by the Commission which shall be appropriately rendered into writing as part of the minute books according to the said regulations.

CHIEF EXECUTIVE

30. Subject to the provisions of the Act, a chief executive shall be appointed by the directors for such term, at such remuneration and upon such conditions as they may think fit.

THE SEAL

31. The directors shall provide for the safe custody of the seal and the seal shall not be affixed to any instrument except by the authority of a resolution of the board of directors or by a committee of directors authorized in that behalf by the

directors and in the presence of at least two directors and of the secretary or such other person as the directors may appoint for the purpose; and those two directors and secretary or other person as aforesaid shall sign every instrument to which the seal of the company is so affixed in their presence.

We, the several persons whose names and addresses are subscribed below, are desirous of being formed into a company, in pursuance of this memorandum of association:

Name and surname (present & former) in full(in Block letters	NIC No. (in case of foreigner, Passport No.)	Father's/ Husband's Name in full	Nationality (ies) with former Nationality	Occupation	Usual residential address in full or the registered/principal office address for a subscribe other than natural person	Number of shares taken by each subscriber (in figures and words)	Signature
Total number of shares taken (in figures and words)							

Dated the_____ day of_____, 20____

Witness to above signatures: *(For the documents submitted in physical form)*

Signature	
Full Name (in Block Letters)	
Father's/Husband's name	
Nationality	
Occupation	
NIC No.	
Usual residential address	

Witness to above signatures: *(For the documents submitted online)*

(Digital Signature Certificate Provider)

Name:

Address:

(Applicable in case of single member company)

I, whose name and address is subscribed below, am desirous of forming a company in pursuance of these articles of association:

Name and surname (present & former) in full(in Block letters	NIC No. (in case of foreigner, Passport No.)	Father's/ Husband's Name in full	Nationality (ies) with former Nationality	Occupation	Usual residential address in full or the registered/principal office address for a subscribe other than natural person	Number of shares taken by each subscriber (in figures and words)	Signature
Total number of shares taken (in figures and words)							

Dated the_____ day of_____, 20____

Witness to above signatures: *(For the documents submitted in physical form)*

Signature	
Full Name (in Block Letters)	
Father's/Husband's name	
Nationality	
Occupation	
NIC No.	
Usual residential address	

Witness to above signatures: *(For the documents submitted online)*

(Digital Signature Certificate Provider)

Name:

Address:

TABLE D

[See section 41]

MEMORANDUM AND ARTICLES OF ASSOCIATION OF A COMPANY LIMITED BY GUARANTEE AND HAVING A SHARE CAPITAL

MEMORANDUM OF ASSOCIATION

1. The name of the company is "The ABC Hospital (Guarantee) Limited."

2. The registered office of the company will be situated in the Province of Baluchistan.

3. (i) The principal business of the company shall be to establish, run and manage hospitals.

    (ii) Except for the businesses mentioned in sub-clause (iii) hereunder, the company shall engage in all the lawful businesses and shall be authorized to take all necessary steps and actions in connection therewith and ancillary thereto.

    (iii) Notwithstanding anything contained in the foregoing sub-clauses of this clause nothing contained herein shall be construed as empowering the Company to undertake or indulge, directly or indirectly in the business of a Banking Company, Non-banking Finance Company (Mutual Fund, Leasing, Investment Company, Investment Advisor, Real Estate Investment Trust management company, Housing Finance Company, Venture Capital Company, Discounting Services, Microfinance or Microcredit business), Insurance Business, *Modaraba* management company, Stock Brokerage business, forex, real estate business, managing agency, business of providing the services of security guards or any other business restricted under any law for the time being in force or as may be specified by the Commission.

    (iv) It is hereby undertaken that the company shall not:

    a. engage in any of the business mentioned in sub-clause (iii) above or any unlawful operation;

    b. launch multi-level marketing (MLM), Pyramid and Ponzi Schemes, or other related activities/businesses or any lottery business;

    c. engage in any of the permissible business unless the requisite approval, permission, consent or licence is obtained from competent authority as may be required under any law for the time being in force.

4. The liability of the members is limited.

5. Every member of the company undertakes to contribute to the assets of the company in the event of its being wound up while he is a member, or within one year afterwards, for payment of the debts and liabilities of the company contracted before he ceases to be a member, and the costs, charges and expenses of winding up and for the adjustment of the rights of the contributories among themselves, such amount as may be required not exceeding _____rupees.

6. The authorized capital of the company is Rs.1,000,000/- (Rupees one Million only) divided into 100,000 (one hundred thousand) ordinary shares of Rs.10/- (Rupees ten only) each.

We, the several persons whose names and addresses are subscribed below, are desirous of being formed into a company, in pursuance of this memorandum of association, and we respectively agree to take the number of shares in the capital of the company as set opposite our respective names:

Name and surname (present & former) in full(in Block letters	NIC No. (in case of foreigner, Passport No.)	Father's/ Husband's Name in full	Nationality (ies) with former Nationality	Occupation	Usual residential address in full or the registered/principal office address for a subscribe other than natural person	Number of shares taken by each subscriber (in figures and words)	Signature
Total number of shares taken (in figures and words)							

Dated the_____ day of_____, 20____

Witness to above signatures: *(For the documents submitted in physical form)*

Signature	
Full Name (in Block Letters)	
Father's/Husband's name	
Nationality	
Occupation	
NIC No.	
Usual residential address	

Witness to above signatures: *(For the documents submitted online)*

(Digital Signature Certificate Provider)

Name:

Address:

(Applicable in case of single member company)

I, whose name and address is subscribed below, am desirous of forming a company in pursuance of this memorandum of association and agree to take the number of shares in the capital of the company as set opposite my name:

Name and surname (present & former) in full(in Block letters	NIC No. (in case of foreigner, Passport No.)	Father's/ Husband's Name in full	Nationality (ies) with former Nationality	Occupation	Usual residential address in full or the registered/principal office address for a subscribe other than natural person	Number of shares taken by each subscriber (in figures and words)	Signature
Total number of shares taken (in figures and words)							

Dated the_____ day of_____, 20____

Witness to above signatures: *(For the documents submitted in physical form)*

Signature	
Full Name (in Block Letters)	
Father's/Husband's name	
Nationality	
Occupation	
NIC No.	
Usual residential address	

Witness to above signatures: *(For the documents submitted online)*

(Digital Signature Certificate Provider)

Name:

Address:

ARTICLES OF ASSOCIATION OF A COMPANY LIMITED BY GUARANTEE AND HAVING A SHARE CAPITAL

PRELIMINARY

1. (1)   In these regulations--

    (a)   "section" means section of the Act;

    (b)   "the Act" means the Companies Act, 2017; and

    (c)   "the seal" means the common seal or official seal of the company as the case may be.

(2)   Unless the context otherwise requires, words or expressions contained in these regulations shall have the same meaning as in the Act; and words importing the singular shall include the plural, and *vice versa*, and words importing the masculine gender shall include feminine, and words importing persons shall include bodies corporate.

2. The number of members with which the company proposes to be registered is 100, but the directors may from time to time register an increase of members.

3. All the regulations in Table A of this Schedule shall be deemed to be incorporated with these articles and shall apply to the company.

We, the several persons whose names and addresses are subscribed below, are desirous of being formed into a company, in pursuance of these articles of association, and we respectively agree to take the number of shares in the capital of the company as set opposite our respective names:

Name and surname (present & former) in full(in Block letters	NIC No. (in case of foreigner, Passport No.)	Father's/ Husband's Name in full	Nationality (ies) with former Nationality	Occupation	Usual residential address in full or the registered/principal office address for a subscribe other than natural person	Number of shares taken by each subscriber (in figures and words)	Signature
Total number of shares taken (in figures and words)							

Dated the_____ day of_____, 20____

Witness to above signatures: *(For the documents submitted in physical form)*

Signature	
Full Name (in Block Letters)	
Father's/Husband's name	
Nationality	
Occupation	
NIC No.	
Usual residential address	

Witness to above signatures: *(For the documents submitted online)*

(Digital Signature Certificate Provider)

Name:

Address:

TABLE E

(See section 41)

MEMORANDUM AND ARTICLES OF ASSOCIATION OF AN UNLIMITED COMPANY HAVING A SHARE CAPITAL

MEMORANDUM OF ASSOCIATION

1. The name of the company is "Khyber Fruit Products Company Unlimited".

2. The registered office of the company will be situated in the Province of Sindh.

3.   (i)   The principal line of business of the company shall be preservation,   canning and marketing of fruit and fruit products.

  (ii) Except for the businesses mentioned in sub-clause (iii) hereunder, the company shall engage in all the lawful businesses and shall be authorized to take all necessary steps and actions in connection therewith and ancillary thereto.

  (iii) Notwithstanding anything contained in the foregoing sub-clauses of this clause nothing contained herein shall be construed as empowering the Company to undertake or indulge, directly or indirectly in the business of a Banking Company, Non-banking Finance Company (Mutual Fund, Leasing, Investment Company, Investment Advisor, Real Estate Investment Trust management company, Housing Finance Company, Venture Capital Company, Discounting Services, Microfinance or Microcredit business), Insurance Business, *Modaraba* management company, Stock Brokerage business, forex, real estate business, managing agency, business of providing the services of security guards or any other business restricted under any law for the time being in force or as may be specified by the Commission.

(iv) It is hereby undertaken that the company shall not:

(a) engage in any of the business mentioned in sub-clause (iii) above or any unlawful operation;

(b) launch multi-level marketing (MLM), Pyramid and Ponzi Schemes, or other related activities/businesses or any lottery business;

(c) engage in any of the permissible business unless the requisite approval, permission, consent or licence is obtained from competent authority as may be required under any law for the time being in force.

4. The liability of the members is unlimited.

5. The authorized capital of the company is Rs.1,000,000/- (Rupees one Million only) divided into 100,000 (one hundred thousand) ordinary shares of Rs.10/- (Rupees ten only) each.

We, the several persons whose names and addresses are subscribed below, are desirous of being formed into a company, in pursuance of this memorandum of association, and we respectively agree to take the number of shares in the capital of the company as set opposite our respective names:

Name and surname (present & former) in full(in Block letters	NIC No. (in case of foreigner, Passport No.)	Father's/ Husband's Name in full	Nationality (ies) with former Nationality	Occupation	Usual residential address in full or the registered/principal office address for a subscribe other than natural person	Number of shares taken by each subscriber (in figures and words)	Signature
Total number of shares taken (in figures and words)							

Dated the_____ day of_____, 20_____

Witness to above signatures: *(For the documents submitted in physical form)*

Signature	
Full Name (in Block Letters)	
Father's/Husband's name	
Nationality	
Occupation	
NIC No.	
Usual residential address	

Witness to above signatures: *(For the documents submitted online)*

(Digital Signature Certificate Provider)

Name:

Address:

(Applicable in case of single member company)

I, whose name and address is subscribed below, am desirous of forming a company in pursuance of this memorandum of association and agree to take the number of shares in the capital of the company as set opposite my name:

Name and surname (present & former) in full(in Block letters	NIC No. (in case of foreigner, Passport No.)	Father's/ Husband's Name in full	Nationality (ies) with former Nationality	Occupation	Usual residential address in full or the registered/principal office address for a subscribe other than natural person	Number of shares taken by each subscriber (in figures and words)	Signature
Total number of shares taken (in figures and words)							

Dated the_____ day of_____, 20_____

Witness to above signatures: *(For the documents submitted in physical form)*

Signature	
Full Name (in Block Letters)	
Father's/Husband's name	
Nationality	
Occupation	
NIC No.	
Usual residential address	

Witness to above signatures: *(For the documents submitted online)*

(Digital Signature Certificate Provider)

Name:

Address:

ARTICLES OF ASSOCIATION OF AN UNLIMITED COMPANY
PRELIMINARY

1.(1) In these regulations

(a) "section" means section of the Act;

(b) "the Act" means the Companies Act, 2017; and

(c) "the seal" means the common seal or official seal of the company as the case may be.

(2) Unless the context otherwise requires, words or expressions contained in these regulations shall have the same meaning as in the Act; and words importing the singular shall include the plural, and *vice versa*, and words importing the masculine gender shall include feminine, and words importing persons shall include bodies corporate.

2.   All the regulations in Table A of this Schedule shall be deemed to be incorporated with these articles and shall apply to the company.

We, the several persons whose names and addresses are subscribed below, are desirous of being formed into a company, in pursuance of these articles of association, and we respectively agree to take the number of shares in the capital of the company as set opposite our respective names:

Name and surname (present & former) in full(in Block letters	NIC No. (in case of foreigner, Passport No.)	Father's/ Husband's Name in full	Nationality (ies) with former Nationality	Occupation	Usual residential address in full or the registered/principal office address for a subscribe other than natural person	Number of shares taken by each subscriber (in figures and words)	Signature
Total number of shares taken (in figures and words)							

Dated the_____ day of_____, 20_____

Witness to above signatures: *(For the documents submitted in physical form)*

Signature	
Full Name (in Block Letters)	
Father's/Husband's name	
Nationality	
Occupation	
NIC No.	
Usual residential address	

Witness to above signatures: *(For the documents submitted online)*

(Digital Signature Certificate Provider)

Name:

Address:

(Applicable in case of single member company)

I, whose name and address is subscribed below, am desirous of forming a company in pursuance of these articles of association and agree to take the number of shares in the capital of the company as set opposite my name:

Name and surname (present & former) in full(in Block letters	NIC No. (in case of foreigner, Passport No.)	Father's/ Husband's Name in full	Nationality (ies) with former Nationality	Occupation	Usual residential address in full or the registered/principal office address for a subscribe other than natural person	Number of shares taken by each subscriber (in figures and words)	Signature
Total number of shares taken (in figures and words)							

Dated the_____ day of_____, 20____

Witness to above signatures: *(For the documents submitted in physical form)*

Signature	
Full Name (in Block Letters)	
Father's/Husband's name	
Nationality	
Occupation	
NIC No.	
Usual residential address	

Witness to above signatures: *(For the documents submitted online)*

(Digital Signature Certificate Provider)

Name:

Address:

TABLE F

(See section 42)

MEMORANDUM AND ARTICLES OF ASSOCIATION OF
A COMPANY LICENCED UNDER SECTION 42

[A company set up under Section 42 of the Companies Act, 2017]

MEMORANDUM OF ASSOCIATION

I.   The name of the company is "XYZ Association".

II.   The registered office of the company will be situated in the Province of Baluchistan.

III.   The object for which the company is established, are as follows:

   (1) To promote education in the country by establishing, maintaining, assisting, running and managing schools and colleges for the low income segment in society in rural and urban areas.

   (2) To ……………

   (3) To ……………

IV.   In order to achieve its object, the company shall exercise the following powers:

   (1) To appeal, solicit or accept contributions, donations, grants and gifts, in cash or in kind, from lawful sources and to apply the same or income thereof for the objects of the company.

   (2) To open and operate bank accounts in the name of the company and to draw, make, accept, endorse, execute and issue promissory notes, bills, cheques and other instruments.

   (3) To acquire, alter, improve, charge, take on lease, exchange, hire, sell, let or otherwise dispose of any movable or immovable property and any rights and privileges whatsoever for any of the objects or purposes specified herein above. Provided that the company shall not undertake the business of real estate or housing schemes.

(4) To borrow or raise money, with or without security, required for the purposes of the company upon such terms and in such manner as may be determined by the company for the promotion of its objects.

(5) To mortgage the assets of the company and / or render guarantee for the performance of any contract made, discharge of any obligation incurred or repayment of any moneys borrowed by the company.

(6) To purchase, sell, exchange, take on lease, hire or otherwise acquire lands, construct, maintain or alter any building and any other moveable or immovable properties or any right or privileges necessary or convenient for the use and purposes of the company.

(7) To nominate delegates and advisors to represent the company at conferences, government bodies and other gatherings.

(8) To co-operate with other charitable trusts, societies, associations, institutions or companies formed for all or any of these objects and statutory authorities operating for similar purposes and to exchange information and advice with them.

(9) To pay out of the funds of the company the costs, charges and expenses of and incidental to the formation and registration of the company.

(10) To invest the surplus moneys of the company not immediately required, in such a manner as may from time to time be determined by the company.

(11) To create, establish, administer and manage funds including endowment fund conducive for the promotion of the objects of the company.

(12) To enter into agreements, contracts and arrangements with organizations, institutions, bodies and individuals for the purpose of carrying out the functions and activities of the company.

(13) To take such actions as are considered necessary to raise the status or to promote the efficiency of the company.

(14) To conduct, hold and arrange symposia, seminars, conferences, lectures, workshops and dialogue and to print, publish and prepare journals, magazines, books, circulars, reports, catalogues and other works relating to any of the objects of or to the work done by the company, subject to the permission, if required of the relevant authorities.

(15) To do all other such lawful acts and things as are incidental or conducive to the attainment of the above objects or any one of them.

V.   The company shall achieve the above said objects subject to the following conditions:-

(1)   The company is formed as a public company limited by guarantee.

(2)   Payment of remuneration by the company or its subsidiary entity for services or otherwise to members of the company or to their family members whether holding an office in the company or its subsidiary or not, shall be prohibited provided that the prohibition shall continue to apply for a period of five years after a member quits from his membership of the company.

(3)   No change in the Memorandum and Articles of Association shall be made except with the prior approval of the Securities and Exchange Commission of Pakistan.

(4)   Patronage of any government or authority, express or implied, shall not be claimed unless such government or authority has signified its consent thereto in writing.

(5)   The company shall not itself set up or otherwise engage in industrial and commercial activities or in any manner function as a trade organization.

(6)   The company shall not exploit or offend the religious susceptibilities of the people.

(7)   The company shall not, directly or indirectly, participate in any political campaign for elective public office or other political activities akin to those of a political party or contribute any funds or resources to any political party or any individual or body for any political purpose.

(8)   The subscribers to the Memorandum and Articles of Association of the company shall continue to be the members of the company unless allowed by the Commission on application to quit as members.

(9)   The company shall not appoint any person as director or chief executive unless he meets the fit and proper criteria as specified by the Commission from time to time.

(10)   The company in all its letterheads, documents, sign boards, and other modes of communication, shall with its name, state the phrase "A company set up under section 42 of the Companies Act, 2017."

(11)   The income and any profits of the company, shall be applied solely towards the promotion of objects of the company and no portion thereof shall be distributed, paid or transferred directly or indirectly by way of dividend, bonus or otherwise by way of profit to the members of the company or their family members.

(12) The company shall not appeal, solicit, receive or accept funds, grants, contributions, donations or gifts, in cash or in kind, from foreign sources except with the prior permission, clearance or approval from the relevant public authorities as may be required under any relevant statutory regulations and laws. No funds shall be received otherwise than through proper banking channels i.e., through crossed cheque, pay-order, bank draft.

(13) The company shall close its accounts on 30th of June each year.

(14) The company shall make no investment, whatsoever, in its associated companies except with the prior approval of the Commission and subject to such conditions as it may deem fit to impose.

(15) The company shall not undertake any trading activities and shall conform to relevant statutory regulations and laws.

(16) Notwithstanding anything stated in any object clause, the company shall obtain such other licences, permissions, or approvals of the relevant public authorities as may be required under any relevant statutory regulations and laws for the time being in force, to carry out its specific object.

(17) The company shall comply with such conditions as may be imposed by the Securities and Exchange Commission of Pakistan from time to time.

VI. The territories to which the object of the company shall extend are declared to include whole of Pakistan.

VII. The liability of the members is limited.

VIII. Every member of the company undertakes that he shall contribute to the assets of the company in the event of its being wound up while he is a member or within one year afterwards, for payment of the debts or liabilities of the company contracted before he ceases to be a member and the costs, charges and expenses of winding up and for adjustment of the rights of the contributories among themselves such amount as may be required but not exceeding Rs.100,000/- (Rupees One Hundred Thousand Only).

IX. On the revocation of licence of a company under section 42 of the Companies Act, 2017, by the Commission:

(a) the company shall stop all its activities except the recovery of money owed to it, if any;

(b) the company shall not solicit or receive donations from any source; and

(c) all the assets of the company after the satisfaction of all debts and liabilities, shall be transferred to another company licenced under section 42 of the Companies Act, 2017, preferably having similar or identical objects to those of the company, within ninety days from the revocation of the licence or such extended period as may be allowed by the Commission:

Provided that a reasonable amount to meet the expenses of voluntary winding up or making an application to the registrar for striking the name of the company off the register may be retained by the company.

X.   In the case of winding up or dissolution of the company, any surplus assets or property, after the satisfaction of all debts and liabilities, shall not be paid or disbursed among the members, but shall be given or transferred to some other company established under section 42 of the Companies Act, 2017, preferably having similar or identical objects to those of the company and with the approval required under the relevant provisions of the Income Tax Ordinance, 2001 and under intimation to the Securities and Exchange Commission of Pakistan.

We, the several, persons whose names and addresses are subscribed below are desirous of being formed into a company in pursuance of this memorandum of association:-

Name and surname (present & former) in full(in Block letters	NIC No. (in case of foreigner, Passport No.)	Father's/ Husband's Name in full	Nationality (ies) with former Nationality	Occupation	Usual residential address in full or the registered/principal office address for a subscribe other than natural person	Number of shares taken by each subscriber (in figures and words)	Signature
Total number of shares taken (in figures and words)							

Dated the_____ day of_____, 20____

Witness to above signatures: *(For the documents submitted in physical form)*

Signature	
Full Name (in Block Letters)	
Father's/Husband's name	
Nationality	
Occupation	
NIC No.	
Usual residential address	

Witness to above signatures: *(For the documents submitted online)*

(Digital Signature Certificate Provider)

Name:

Address:

[A company set up under Section 42 of the Companies Act, 2017]

ARTICLES OF ASSOCIATION

1.   In these Articles, unless the context or the subject matter otherwise requires:

   (a)   "the company" means XYZ Association'.

   (b)   "the office" means the registered office for the time being of the company.

   (c)   "the directors" mean the directors for the time being of the company.

   (d)   "the seal" means the common seal or official seal of the company as the case may be.

   (e)   "the Act" means the Companies Act, 2017.

   (f)   "the Commission" means the Securities and Exchange Commission of Pakistan.

   (g)   "the registrar" means the registrar of companies as defined in the Companies Act, 2017.

   (h)   "the register" means the register of the members to be kept in pursuant to section 119 of the Act.

   (i)   "chief executive" means the chief executive of the company.

   (j)   "secretary" means the company secretary of the company.

   (k)   "memorandum" means the memorandum of association of the company.

   (l)   "person" includes an individual, company, corporation and body corporate.

   (m) "articles" means the articles of association of the company.

   (n)   "board" means the board of directors of the company.

   (o)   "year" used in the context of financial matters shall mean financial year of the company.

   (p)   Expressions referring to writing shall be construed as including references to typewriting, printing, lithography, photography and other modes of representing or reproducing words in visible form.

(q) Words importing the singular number include the plural number and *vice versa* and words importing the masculine gender include the feminine gender.

(r) Unless the context otherwise requires words or expressions contained in these Articles shall be of the same meaning as in the Act or any statutory modification thereof in force at the date at which these Articles become binding on the company.

MEMBERSHIP

2.   The number of members with which the company proposes to be registered is ......, but the minimum number of members shall not be, at any time, less than three (3). However, the directors may, from time to time, whenever the company or the business of the company requires, increase the number of members.

3.   The company in general meeting may from time to time lay down the qualifications and conditions subject to which any person or class of persons shall be admitted to membership of the company.

4.   The rights and privileges of a member shall not be transferable and shall cease on his death or otherwise ceasing to be a member.

5.   The subscribers to the memorandum and such other persons as the directors shall admit to membership shall be members of the company.

6.   One person shall have the right to hold one membership.

ADMISSION TO MEMBERSHIP

7.   The application for seeking membership of the company shall be required to be seconded by an existing member whereupon the board of directors shall decide the matter of his admission as member or otherwise within ninety days of making of such application. No minor or lunatic shall be admitted as a member of the company.

8.   Every person, upon applying for admission to membership, shall submit to the company an undertaking on the stamp paper of appropriate value that:

(a) I have not been associated with any money laundering or terrorist financing activities and neither have approved receipt of nor received such monies and likewise neither have approved disbursement of nor disbursed such monies in any manner for money laundering or terrorist financing purposes; and

(b) I have not been associated with any illegal banking business, deposit taking or financial dealings or any other illegal activities.

9.   The board shall subject to the Articles, accept or reject any application for admission to membership. The board's decision shall be final and it shall not be liable to give any reasons thereof.

CESSATION / EXPULSION FROM MEMBERSHIP

10.   A member renders himself liable to expulsion or suspension by the board if:

(a) he refuses or neglects to give effect to any decision of the board; or

(b) he infringes any of the regulations of the articles; or

(c)   he is declared by a court of competent jurisdiction to have committed a fraud, or to be bankrupt, or to be insane or otherwise incompetent; or

(d)   he is held by the Committee of the company to have been guilty of any act discreditable to a member of the company; or

(e)   he is acting or is threatening to act in a manner prejudicial to the objects, interest or functioning of the company or any other institute, body corporate, society, association or institution in which the company has an interest.

11.   The company in general meeting may, on an appeal of the aggrieved member and after giving an opportunity of hearing, annul or modify the decision of the board with regard to expulsion of the member by resolution supported by two-thirds majority. The person expelled shall be reinstated as a member from the date of the resolution of the general meeting annulling the decision of the board.

12.   Termination of membership shall occur automatically:

(a)   in the event of the death of a member; and

(b)   in the event a member fails to pay any amount due by him to the company within three (3) months after such obligation has become due.

GENERAL MEETINGS AND PROCEEDINGS

ANNUAL GENERAL MEETING

13.   A general meeting to be called annual general meeting, shall be held, in accordance with the provisions of Section 132, within sixteen months (16) months from the date of incorporation of the company and thereafter once at least in every calendar year within a period of four (4) months following the close of its financial year as may be determined by the directors.

OTHER GENERAL MEETINGS

14.   All other meetings of the members of the company other than an annual general meeting shall be called "extraordinary general meetings".

EXTRAORDINARY GENERAL MEETINGS

15.   The directors may, whenever they think fit, call an extraordinary general meeting, and extraordinary general meeting shall also be called on such requisition(s), as is provided by section 133 of the Act.

NOTICE OF GENERAL MEETINGS

16.   Twenty-one (21) days' notice at least (exclusive of the day on which the notice is served or deemed to be served, but inclusive of the day for which notice is given) specifying the place, the day and the hour of meeting and, in case of special business, the general nature of that business, shall be given in the manner provided by the Act for the general meeting, to such persons as are, under the Act or the Articles of the company, entitled to receive such notices from the company but the accidental omission to give notice to or the non-receipt of notice by any member shall not invalidate the proceedings at any general meeting.

SPECIAL BUSINESS

17.   All business that is transacted at an extra ordinary general meeting and that is transacted at an annual general meeting with the exception of the consideration of the financial statements and the reports of the director and auditors, the election of directors, the appointment of and the fixing of remuneration of the auditors shall be deemed special business.

QUORUM

18.   No business shall be transacted at any general meeting unless a quorum of members representing not less than two (2) members or twenty-five percent of the total number of members of the company, whichever is greater, is present personally or through video-link at the time when the meeting proceeds to business--

   (a) in the case of a public listed company, unless the articles provide for a larger number, not less than ten members present personally, or through video-link who represent not less than twenty-five percent of the total voting power, either of their own account or as proxies;

   (b) in the case of any other company having share capital, unless the articles provide for a larger number, two members present personally, or through video-link who represent not less than twenty-five percent of the total voting power, either of their own account or as proxies.

EFFECT OF QUORUM NOT BEING PRESENT

19.   If within half an hour from the time appointed for the meeting a quorum is not present, the meeting, if called upon the requisition of members, shall be dissolved and in any other case, it shall stand adjourned to the same day in the next week at the same time and place and if at the adjourned meeting a quorum

is not present within half an hour from the time appointed for the meeting, the members present in person or through video-link, being not less than two, shall be a quorum.

CHAIRMAN OF MEETING

20.   The chairman of the board of directors, shall preside as chairman at every general meeting of the company, but if he is not present within fifteen minutes after the time appointed for the meeting, or is unwilling to act as chairman, any of the directors present may be elected to be the chairman and if none of the directors present is willing to act as chairman, the members present shall choose one of their number to be the chairman.

ADJOURNMENT

21.   The chairman may, with the consent of any meeting at which a quorum is present (and shall if so directed by the meeting), adjourn the meeting from time to time but no business shall be transacted at any adjourned meeting other than the business left unfinished at the meeting from which the adjournment took place. When a meeting is adjourned for fifteen (15) days or more, notice of the adjourned meeting shall be given as in the case of an original meeting. Save as aforesaid, it shall not be necessary to give any notice of an adjournment or of the business to be transacted at an adjourned meeting.

VOTING

22.   At any general meeting a resolution put to the vote to the meeting shall be decided on a show of hands and a declaration by the chairman that a resolution has been carried, or carried unanimously, or by a particular majority, or lost, and an entry to that effect in the book of the proceedings of the company shall be conclusive evidence of the fact, without proof of the number or proportion of the votes recorded in favour of or against that resolution.

CASTING VOTE

23.   In the case of an equality of votes, the chairman of the meeting shall have and exercise a second or casting vote.

VOTES OF MEMBERS

24. (1) Votes may be given on any matter by the members either personally or through video-link or by proxy or by means of postal ballot.

(2)   At any general meeting, the company shall transact such businesses only through postal ballot as may be notified by the Commission.

OBJECTION TO VOTE

25.   No objection shall be raised to the qualification of any voter except at the meeting or adjourned meeting at which the vote objected to is given and tendered, and every vote not disallowed at such meeting shall be valid for all

purposes. Any such objection made in due time shall be referred to the chairman of the meeting, whose decision shall be final and conclusive.

MANAGEMENT AND ADMINISTRATION

26.   There shall be, for the overall management of the company's affairs, a board of directors, which will be elected from amongst the members.

27.   One term of the board of directors would be for three years.

28.   No person shall be appointed as a director if he is ineligible to hold office of director of a company under section 153 of the Act.

29.   No member / person shall hold more than one office in the company, such as those of Chief Executive / director or company secretary simultaneously.

FIRST DIRECTORS

30.   The following subscribers of the memorandum of association shall be the first directors of the company, so, however, that the number of directors shall not in any case be less than that specified in section 154 and they shall hold office until the election of directors in the annual general meeting:

1.   ab

2.   cd

3.   ef

4.   gh

NUMBER OF DIRECTORS

31.   The number of directors shall not be less than three (3) and not more than nine (9). The directors of a company shall, subject to section 154, fix the number of elected directors of the company not later than thirty-five days before the convening of the general meeting at which directors are to be elected, and the number so fixed shall not be changed except with the prior approval of a general meeting of the company such that the minimum number of directors shall not be, at any time, less than three (3). A retiring director shall be eligible for re-election.

PROCEDURE FOR ELECTION OF DIRECTORS

32.   (i)The directors of the company shall be elected in accordance with provisions of sub-sections (1) to (4) of section 159 of the Act, in the following manner:

   (a)   the directors of the company shall be elected by the members of the company in general meeting;

(b) each member shall have votes equal to the number of directors to be elected;

(c) a member may give all his votes to a single candidate or divide them, not being in fractions, between more than one of the candidates in such manner as he may choose; and

(d) the candidate who gets the highest number of votes shall be declared elected as director and then the candidate who gets the next highest number of votes shall be so declared and so on until the total number of directors to be elected has been so elected.

(ii) If the number of persons who offer themselves to be elected is not more than the number of directors fixed by the directors under sub-section (1) of section 159, all persons who offered themselves shall be deemed to have been elected as directors.

CASUAL VACANCY AND ALTERNATE OR SUBSTITUTE DIRECTORS

33. (a) Any casual vacancy occurring among the directors may be filled up by the directors within thirty days of the vacancy and the person so appointed shall hold office for the remainder of the term of director in whose place he is appointed.

(b) An existing director may, with the approval of the board of directors, appoint an alternate director to act for him during his absence from Pakistan of not less than ninety days. The alternate director so appointed shall *ipso facto* vacate office if and when the director appointing him returns to Pakistan.

(c) A person shall be eligible for appointment against casual vacancy or to act as alternate director only if he is a member and is not already a director of the company.

REMOVAL OF DIRECTOR

34. The company may remove a director through a resolution passed in a general meeting of members in accordance with section 163 of the Act.

CHAIRMAN OF THE BOARD

35. The directors may elect one of their members as the Chairman of the board. The Chairman of the board shall preside at all meetings of the board but, if at any meeting the chairman is not present within ten minutes after the time appointed for holding the same or is unwilling to act as chairman, the directors present in person or through video-link may choose one of their member to be chairman of the meeting.

DUTIES AND POWERS OF THE BOARD

36.　The board shall conduct and manage all the business affairs of the company, exercise all the powers, authorities and discretion of the company, obtain or oppose the application by others for all concessions, grants, charters and legislative acts and authorization from any government or authority, enter into such contracts and do all such other things as may be necessary for carrying on the business of the company, except only such of them as under the statutes and Articles are expressly directed to be exercised by general meetings and (without in any way prejudicing or limiting the extent of such general powers) shall have the following special powers and duties:

(a) To present to the general meeting of the company any matters which the directors feel are material to the company, its objects or interests or affecting the interests of members and make suitable recommendations regarding such matters.

(b) To regulate, through articles, the admission of members.

(c) To appoint, remove or suspend the legal advisors, bankers, or other officers on such terms and conditions as they shall think fit and as may be agreed upon.

(d) To determine the remuneration, terms and conditions and powers of such appointees and from time to time, revoke such appointments and name another person of similar status to such office except for the auditor in which case the relevant provisions of the Act shall be followed.

(e) To delegate, from time to time, to any such appointee all or any of the powers and authority of the board and to reconstitute, restrict or vary such delegations.

(f) To appoint any qualified person as a first auditor(s) subject to provisions of the Act;

(g) To agree upon and pay any expenses in connection with the company's objects and undertakings and pay all the expenses incidental to the formation and regulation of the company.

(h) To constitute from time to time committee(s) from among themselves or co-opt other persons for the purpose and delegate to them such functions and powers as the board may deem fit to carry out the objects of the company.

(i) Subject to the provisions of section 183 of the Act, the directors may exercise all the powers of the company to borrow and mortgage or charge its undertaking, property and assets (both present and future) or issue securities, whether outright security for any debt, liability or obligation of the company.

PROCEEDINGS OF THE BOARD

37.   The board shall meet at least once in each quarter of every year, subject thereto meetings of the board shall be held at such time as the directors shall think fit. All meetings of the board shall be held at the registered office of the company or at such other place as the board shall from time to time determine. The meetings of the board shall be called by the chairman on his own accord or at the request of the chief executive (or any three directors) by giving at least seven (7) days' notice to the members of the board.

38.   At least one-third $(1/3^{rd})$ of the total number of directors or two (2) directors whichever is higher, for the time being of the company, present personally or through video-link, shall constitute a quorum.

39.   Save as otherwise expressly provided in the Act, every question at meetings of the board shall be determined by a majority of votes of the directors present in person or through video-link, each director having one vote. In case of an equality of votes or tie, the chairman shall have a casting vote in addition to his original vote as a director.

40.   The directors shall cause records to be kept and minutes to be made in book or books with regard to--

(a)   all resolutions and proceedings of general meeting(s) and the meeting(s) of directors and committee(s) of directors, and every member present at any general meeting and every director present at any meeting of directors or committee of directors shall put his signature in a book to be kept for that purpose;

(b)   recording the names of the persons present at each meeting of the directors and of any committee of the directors, and the general meeting; and

(c)   all orders made by the directors and committee(s) of directors:

     Provided that all records related to proceedings through video-link shall be maintained in accordance with the relevant regulations specified by the Commission which shall be appropriately rendered into writing as part of the minute books according to the said regulations.

RESOLUTION THROUGH CIRCULATION

41.   A resolution in writing signed by all directors for the time being entitled to receive notice of the meeting of directors or affirmed by them in writing shall be as valid and effectual as if it had been passed at a meeting of the directors duly convened and held.

CHIEF EXECUTIVE

42.   The directors may appoint a person to be the Chief Executive of the company and vest in him such powers and functions as they deem fit in relation to the management and administration of the affairs of the company subject to

their general supervision and control. The Chief Executive, if not already a director, shall be deemed to be a director of the company and be entitled to all the rights and privileges and subject to all the liabilities of that office.

QUALIFICATION OF THE CHIEF EXECUTIVE

43.   No person who is not eligible to become a director of the company under section 153 of the Act, shall be appointed or continue as the Chief Executive of the company.

REMOVAL OF CHIEF EXECUTIVE

44.   The directors by passing resolution by not less than three-fourths of the total number of directors for the time being or the company may by a special resolution passed in a general meeting remove a chief executive before the expiry of his term in office.

MINUTE BOOKS

45.   The directors shall cause records to be kept and minutes to be made in book or books with regard to--

(a)   all resolutions and proceedings of general meeting(s) and the meeting(s) of directors and committee(s) of directors, and every member present at any general meeting and every director present at any meeting of directors or committee of directors shall put his signature in a book to be kept for that purpose;

(b)   recording the names of the persons present at each meeting of the directors and of any committee of the directors, and the general meeting; and

(c)   all orders made by the directors and committee(s) of directors:

Provided that all records related to proceedings through video-link shall be maintained in accordance with the relevant regulations specified by the Commission which shall be appropriately recorded into writing and made part of the minute books according to the said regulations.

SECRETARY

46.   The Secretary shall be appointed (or removed) by the chairman of the company with the approval of the board.

47.   The Secretary shall be responsible for all secretarial functions and shall ensure compliance with respect to requirements of the Act concerning the meetings and record of proceedings of the board, committees and the general meeting of members, review the applications for admission to membership and the recommendations accompanying the same to ensure that they are in the form prescribed, ensure that all notices required by these Articles or under the Act are

duly sent and that all returns required under the Act are duly filed with concerned Company Registration Office.

COMMITTEES

48.   The directors may delegate any of their powers to committees consisting of such member or members of their body as they think fit and they may from time to time revoke such delegation. Any committee so formed shall, in the exercise of the powers so delegated, conform to any regulations that may from time to time be imposed on it by the directors.

CHAIRMAN OF COMMITTEE MEETINGS

49.   A committee may elect a chairman of its meetings, but, if no such chairman is elected, or if at any meeting the chairman is not present within fifteen (15) minutes after the time appointed for holding the same or is unwilling to act as chairman, the members present may choose one of them to be the chairman of the meeting.

PROCEEDINGS OF COMMITTEE MEMBERS

50.   A committee may meet and adjourn as it thinks proper. Questions arising at any meeting shall be determined by a majority of votes of the members present. In case of an equality of votes, the chairman shall have and exercise a second or casting vote.

VALIDITY OF DIRECTORS' ACTS

51.   All acts done by any meeting of the directors or of a committee of directors, or by any person acting as a director, shall, notwithstanding that it be afterwards discovered that there was some defect in the appointment of such directors or persons acting as aforesaid, or that they or any of them were disqualified, be as valid as if every such person had been duly appointed and was qualified to be a director.

THE SEAL

52.   The directors shall provide for the safe custody of the seal, which shall not be affixed to any instrument except by the authority of a resolution of the board or by a committee of directors authorized in that behalf by the directors, and two directors or one director and the Secretary of the company shall sign every instrument to which the seal shall be affixed.

FINANCES

53.   The funds of the company shall be applied in defraying the expenses and shall be applicable in or towards the acquisition by purchase, lease or otherwise and furnishing and maintenance of suitable premises and assets for the use of the company and shall be subject to the general control and direction of the board.

54.   No person, except persons duly authorized by the board and acting within the limits of the authority as conferred, shall have authority to sign any cheque or to enter into any contract so as thereby to impose any liability on the company or to pledge the assets of the company.

ACCOUNTS

BOOKS OF ACCOUNT

55.   The directors shall cause to be kept proper books of account as required under Section 220 of the Act so that such books of account shall be kept at the registered office or at such other place as the directors think fit as provided in the said section 220 and shall be open to inspection by the directors during business hours.

INSPECTION BY MEMBERS

56.   The directors shall from time to time determine the time and places for inspection of the accounts and books of the company by the members not being directors, and no member (not being a director) shall have any right to inspect any account and book or papers of the company except as conferred by law or authorized by the directors or by the company in general meeting.

ANNUAL ACCOUNTS

57.   The directors shall as required by section 223 of the Act cause to be prepared and to be laid before the company in annual general meeting such financial statements duly audited and reports of the auditors and the directors as are required under the Act.

COPY OF ACCOUNTS TO BE SENT TO MEMBERS

58.   A copy of financial statements along with the reports of directors and auditors of the company shall, at least twenty-one (21) clear days before the holding of the general meeting, be sent to all the members and the persons entitled to receive notices of general meetings, in the manner in which notices are to be given as provided in section 55 of the Act.

AUDIT

59.   Auditors shall be appointed and their duties regulated in accordance with Sections 246 to 249 of the Act.

NOTICE TO MEMBERS

60.   Notice shall be given by the company to members and auditors of the company and other persons entitled to receive notice in accordance with section 55 of the Act.

INDEMNITY

61. Every officer or agent for the time being of the company may be indemnified out of the assets of the company against any liability incurred by him in defending any proceedings, whether civil or criminal, arising out of his dealings in relation to the affairs of the company, except those brought by the company against him in which judgment is given in his favour or in which he is acquitted, or in connection with any application under section 492 in which relief is granted to him by the Court.

SECRECY

62. Every director, secretary, auditor, trustee, member of a committee, officer, servant, agent, accountant, or other person employed in the business of the company shall observe strict secrecy representing all transactions of the company, and the state of account with individuals and in matters relating thereto and shall not reveal any of the matters which may come to his knowledge in the discharge of his duties except when required so to do by the directors or the company in general meeting or by a court of law, and except so far as may be necessary in order to comply with any of the provisions herein contained.

WINDING UP

63. In the case of winding up or dissolution of the company, any surplus assets or property, after the satisfaction of all debts and liabilities, shall not be paid or disbursed among the members, but shall be given or transferred to some other company established under section 42 of the Act, preferably having similar or identical objects to those of the company and with the approval required under the relevant provisions of the Income Tax Ordinance, 2001 and under intimation to the Securities and Exchange Commission of Pakistan.

64. With regard to winding up, the company shall comply with the relevant provisions of the Act and the conditions of licence granted under section 42 of the Act or any directions contained in a revocation order passed by the Commission under the said section 42.

SUPPLEMENTARY PROVISIONS RELATING TO TAX

65. The company shall abide by and adhere to the following rules:

(i) The company shall get its annual accounts audited from a firm of Chartered Accountants.

(ii) The company shall, in the event of its dissolution, after meeting all liabilities, transfer all its assets to an Institution, fund, trust, society or organization, which is an approved non-profit organization, and intimation of such transfer will be given to Commissioner, Federal Board of Revenue, within ninety days of the dissolution.

(iii) The company shall utilize its money, property or income or any part thereof, solely for promoting its objects.

(iv) The company shall not pay or transfer any portion of its money, property or income, directly by way of dividend, bonus or profit, to any of its members(s) or the relative or relatives of member or members.

(v) The company shall maintain its banks accounts with a scheduled bank or in a post office or national saving organization, National Bank of Pakistan or national commercialized banks.

(vi) The company shall regularly maintain its books of accounts in accordance with generally accepted accounting principles and permit their inspection to the interested members of the public, without any hindrance, at all reasonable times.

(vii) Without prejudice to the powers conferred on the Commission under section 42 of the Act, the association shall not change its memorandum and articles of association without approval of Commissioner, Income Tax, if it has been approved by him as a non-profit organization.

(viii) The company shall restrict the surpluses or monies validly set apart, excluding restricted funds, up to twenty five percent (25%) of the total income of the year. Provided that such surpluses or monies set apart are invested in Government Securities, a collective investment scheme authorized or registered under the Non-Banking Finance Companies (Establishment and Regulation) Rules, 2003, mutual funds, a real estate investment trust approved and authorized under Real Estate Investment Trust Regulations, 2008 or scheduled banks.

We, the several, persons whose names and addresses are subscribed below are desirous of being formed into a company in pursuance of these articles of association:-

Name and surname (present & former) in full(in Block letters	NIC No. (in case of foreigner, Passport No.)	Father's/ Husband's Name in full	Nationality (ies) with former Nationality	Occupation	Usual residential address in full or the registered/principal office address for a subscribe other than natural person	Number of shares taken by each subscriber (in figures and words)	Signature
Total number of shares taken (in figures and words)							

Dated the_____ day of_____, 20____

Witness to above signatures: *(For the documents submitted in physical form)*

Signature	
Full Name (in Block Letters)	
Father's/Husband's name	
Nationality	
Occupation	
NIC No.	
Usual residential address	

Witness to above signatures: *(For the documents submitted online)*

(Digital Signature Certificate Provider)

Name:

Address:

SECOND SCHEDULE

FORM OF STATEMENT IN LIEU OF PROSPECTUS TO BE DELIVERED TO REGISTRAR BY A COMPANY WHICH DOES NOT ISSUE A PROSPECTUS

SECTION 1

FORM OF STATEMENT AND PARTICULARS TO BE

CONTAINED THEREIN

(Pursuant to section 19 of the Companies Act, 2017)

1.	Name of the company	
2.	Corporate Universal Identification No. (CUIN)	
3.	Registered Office:	
4.	Telephone No.	
5.	Fax No.	
6.	Website Address:	
7.	E-mail Address:	

8.   Authorized share capital of the company:-

S. No	Kind of shares	Class of shares	Face/nominal Value Rs.	Number of Shares	Total Amount (Rs)	Special rights in case of other than ordinary shares
1.						
2.						
3.						

9.   Description of the business to be actually undertaken:-

10.   Future prospects of the said business:-

11. Particulars of chief executive, directors, company secretary, chief accountant, chief financial officer, auditor, legal advisor and managing agent (if any) of the company:

Name*	Father's/ husband 's name	CNIC No.	Occupation and directorship in other company**	Tele. No.	Cell No	E-mail Address	Residen tial Address ***
(a) Chief Executive							
(b) Directors:-							
1.							
2.							
3.							
4.							
5.							
6.							
7.							
(c)Company Secretary:-							
(d)Chief Accountant/Chief Financial Officer:-							
(e)Auditor(s) of the company:-							
(f)Legal Advisor:-							
(g)Managing agent, if any:-							

12.   Remuneration payable to the persons referred to in 11 above:-

S. No.	Position in the Company	Remuneration payable	Relevant provision of article, if any	Relevant clause of agreement if any
(a)	Chief Executive			
(b)	Directors			
	(1)			
	(2)			
	(3)			
	(4)			
	(5)			
	(6)			
	(7)			
(c)	Company Secretary			
(d)	Chief Accountant/Chief Financial Officer			
(e)	Auditor			
(f)	Legal Advisor			
(g)	Managing Agent			

13. Number and amount of shares issued, including those agreed to be taken by virtue of Memorandum of Association for cash:-

S. No.	Kind of shares	Class of shares	Face / Nominal Value	Number of shares	Amount	Names of allottee

14. Number and amount of shares agreed to be issued for consideration otherwise than in cash:-

Number of shares	Face / nominal Value	Amount	Details of consideration otherwise than in cash	Date for exercising the option	To whom option offered

15. Commission agreed to be paid for arranging the subscribers of shares:-

Nature of the commission	Number of shares agreed to be subscribed against the commission	Rate of the commission	Amount of the commission paid	Amount of the commission payable	Direct or indirect interest if any, of the persons, stated in clause 11

16. Number and amount of debentures agreed to be issued for cash:-

Number of debentures	Face/ Nominal Value	Amount	Date for exercising the option	To whom option offered	Whether offer accepted Yes / No

17. Number and amount of debentures agreed to be issued for consideration otherwise than in cash:-

Number of debentures	Face Value	Amount	Details of consideration	Date for exercising the option

18. Commission agreed to be paid for arranging the subscribers of debentures:-

Nature of the commission	Number of debentures agreed to be subscribed against the commission	Rate of the commission	Amount of the commission paid	Amount of the commission payable	Direct or indirect interest if any, of the persons, stated in clause 11

19. Details of the every agreement entered into since the date of incorporation relating to property or other intangible assets of the value exceeding Rs.100,000/- :-

Name(s) & address(es) of the vendor/purchaser	Particulars of the property or other intangible assets intended to be purchased or sold	Amount intended to be paid or received in cash	Consideration	Direct or indirect interest if any, of the persons, stated in clause 11

20. Details of all other material contracts executed or intended to be executed by the company:-

S. No.	Nature of contract	Dates and places of execution of contracts	Time and place for inspection of contracts	Name of the parties to contracts	Important terms & conditions of contracts	Direct or indirect interest if any, of the persons, narrated in clause 11
1.						
2.						
3.						

(Copies of contracts to be enclosed. If a contract is not reduced in writing, a memorandum giving full particulars and if not in English, its translation in English or Urdu shall be enclosed)

21. In case it is proposed to acquire a running business, net profit / loss of that business as certified by the auditor for the last 5 years:-

Year ended	Amount of net profit / loss	Business carried on since (date)	Direct or indirect interest, if any, of the persons, stated in clause 11

22. Details of preliminary expenses:-

S. No.	Particulars of payment	Amount of preliminary expenses	Paid / Payable to	Paid by	Payable by	Consideration (in cash or kind to be specified)
1.						
2.						
3.						
4.						

22.   Minimum subscription and   its proposed utilization

Amount of minimum subscription	
Proposed utilization of minimum subscription:-	
(i)	Price of any property purchased or to be purchased	
(ii)	Preliminary expenses payable by the company	
(iii)	Commission payable to any person in consideration of his agreeing to subscribe or procure any shares in the company	
(iv)	Repayment of any moneys borrowed by the company in respect of any of the foregoing matters.	
(v)	Working capital	
(vi)	Other expenditures	

24.   Amount to be provided in respect of the matters aforesaid otherwise than out of the proceeds of minimum subscription and the sources out of which those amount to be provided.

S. No.	Amount	Source of funds

25. Signatures of the Directors or their agents authorized in writing.

S. No.	Name	Signature

Date: --------------

Note: * - In case of Auditor and Legal Advisor, being a firm the name of firm shall be mentioned.

** - The occupation of the individual and the name(s) of the company(s) in which he holds the office of Chief Executive/Director shall be mentioned.

*** - In case of Auditor and Legal Advisor, the address of his/its office shall be mentioned.

SECTION 2

REPORTS TO BE SET OUT

1. Where it is proposed to acquire a business, a report made by auditors (who are named in the statement) upon:-

    (a)   the profits or losses of the business in respect of each of the five financial years immediately preceding the delivery of the statement to the registrar; and

    (b)   the assets and liabilities of the business as at the last date to which the accounts of the business were made up.

2.   (1) where it is proposed to acquire shares in a body corporate, which by reason of the acquisition or anything to be done in consequence thereof or in connection therewith will become a subsidiary of the company, a report made by auditors (who shall be named in the statement) with respect to the profits and losses and assets and liabilities of the other body corporate in respect of each of the five financial years immediately preceding the delivery of the statement to the registrar;

(2) If the other body corporate has no subsidiaries, the report referred to in sub-clause (1) shall –

    (a) so far as regards profits and losses, deal with the profits or losses of the body corporate in respect of each of the five financial years immediately preceding the delivery of the statement to the registrar; and

    (b) so far as regards assets and liabilities, deal with the assets and liabilities of the body corporate as at the last date to which the accounts of the body corporate were made up.

(3) If the other body corporate has subsidiaries the report referred to in sub-clause(1) shall–

    (a) so far as regards profits and losses, deal separately with other body corporate's profits or losses as provided by sub-clause (2), and in addition either –

(i) as a whole with the combined profits or losses of its subsidiaries so far as they concern members of the other body corporate; or

(ii) individual with the profits or losses of each subsidiary, so far as they concern member of the other body corporate; or instead of dealing separately with the other body corporate's profits or losses, deal as a whole with the profits or losses of the other body corporate and, so far as they concern members of the other body corporate, with the combined profits or losses of its subsidiaries; and

(b) so far as regards assets and liabilities deal separately with the other body corporate's assets and liabilities as provided by sub-clause (2) and, in addition, deal either –

(i) as a whole with the combined assets and liabilities of its subsidiaries, with or without the other body corporate's assets and liabilities; or

(ii) individually with the assets and liabilities of each subsidiary; and shall indicate, as respects the assets and liabilities of the subsidiaries, the allowance to be made for persons other than members of the company.

SECTION 3

PROVISIONS APPLYING TO SECTIONS 1 AND 2 OF THIS STATEMENT

3.(1) Every person shall, for the purposes of the statement, be deemed to be a vendor who has entered into any contract, absolute or conditional, for the sale or purchase, or for any option of purchase, of any property to be acquired by the company, in any case where-

(a) the purchase money is not fully paid at the date of the issue of the statement;

(b) the purchase money is to be paid or satisfied, wholly or in part, out of the proceeds of the issue offered for subscription; or

(c) the contract depends for its validity or fulfillment on the result of that issue.

(2)   In case the company was incorporated or the body corporate referred above was established less than five years before the making of the statement, reference to five financial years in sections 1 and 2 shall be deemed replaced for the actual period.

4.   Any report required by section 2 of the statement shall either –

(a) indicate by way of note any adjustments as respects and figures of any profits or losses or assets and liabilities dealt with by the report which appears to the person making the report necessary; or

(b) make those adjustments and indicate that adjustments have been made.

5. Any report by auditors required by section 2 of the statement, shall be made by auditors qualified under the Act for appointment as auditors of a company.

THIRD SCHEDULE[1]
(Section 224 and 225 of the Act)
Classification of Companies

S. No	Classification Criteria of Company		Applicable Accounting Framework	Relevant schedule of companies
1	Public interest company (PIC)			
	Sub categories of PIC:			
	a)	Listed company	International Financial Reporting Standards	Fourth schedule
	b)	Non-listed company which is : (i) A public sector company as defined in the act; or (ii) A public utility or similar company carrying on the business of essential public service ; or (iii) Holding assets in a fiduciary capacity for a board group of outsiders, such as a bank, insurance company, securities broker/dealer , pension fund , mutual fund or investment banking entity. (iv) Having such number of members holding ordinary shares as may be notified ; or (v) Holding assets exceeding such value as may be notified.	International Financial Reporting Standards	Fifth Schedule
2	Large Sized company (LSC)			
	Sub categories of LSC			
	a)	Non-listed comp[any with : (i) paid up capitals of Rs. 200 million or more ; or (ii) turnover of Rs. 1 billion or more ; or (iii) employees 750 or more.	International Financial Reporting Standards	Fifth schedule
	b)	A foreign company with turnover of Rs. 1 billion or more.		

---

[1]Amended vide S.R.O 1169 (I) 2017 dated November 7th , 2017 and S.R.O 1092(I)/2018 dated September 3rd , 2017

	c)	Non-listed company licensed/formed under section 42 / section 45 of the act having annual gross revenue (grants/income/subsidies/donations) including other income/revenue of Rs. 200 million or more.	International Financial Reporting Standards and Accounting Standards for NPOs	Fifth schedule
3	Medium Sized company (MSC)			
	Sub categories of MSC			
	a)	Non-listed public company with : (i) Paid up capital less than Rs 200 million; (ii) Turnover less than Rs. 1 billion ; and (iii) Employees less than 750.	International Financial Reporting Standards for SMEs	Fifth schedule
	b)	Private company with: (i) paid up capital of greater than Rs. 10 million but less than Rs.200 million ; (ii) turnover greater than Rs . 100 million but less than Rs. 1 billion ; or (iii) employees more than 250 but less than 750.		
	c)	A foreign company which have turnover less than Rs. 1 billion .		
	d)	Non-listed company licensed / formed under section 42 or section 45 of the Act which has annual gross revenue(grants/income/subsidies/donations) including other income or revenue less than Rs 200 million .	International Financial Reporting Standards for SMEs and Accounting Standards for NPOs	Fifth Schedule
4.	Small Sized Company (SSC)			
		A private company having : (i) Paid up capital up to Rs 10 million ; (ii) Turnover not exceeded Rs 100 million; and (iii) Employees not more than 250.	Revised AFRS for SSEs	Fifth schedule

NOTE:

1. The classification of a company shall be based on the previous year's audited financial statement.

2. The classification of a company can be changed where it does not fall under the previous criteria for two consecutive years.

3. The number of employers means the average number of persons employed by a company in that financial year calculated on monthly basis.

4. Subsidiary companies of a listed company shall follow the requirements of the Fourth schedule.

5. The Medium Sized Company that are otherwise required to follow IFRS for SMEs and Accounting standards for NPOs, may opt to follow the IFRS notified by the Commission for the preparation of financial statements.

6. The small size companies that are otherwise required to follow revised AFRS for SSEs may opt to follow IFRS notified by the Commission or IFRS for SMEs.

FOURTH SCHEDULE[1]

(See Section 225)

DISCLOSURE REQUIREMENTS AS TO FINANCIAL STATEMENTS OF LISTED COMPANIES AND THEIR SUBSIDIARIES

PART I

GENERAL REQUIREMENTS

I.   All listed companies and their subsidiaries shall follow the International Financial Reporting Standards in regard to financial statements as are notified for the purpose in the official Gazette by the Commission, under section 225 of the Companies Act, 2017 (Act);

II.   The disclosure requirements, as provided in this schedule, are applicable to the annual financial statements and are in addition to the disclosure requirements prescribed in International Financial Reporting Standards and shall be made in the notes to the accounts unless specifically required otherwise;

III.   In addition to the information expressly required to be disclosed under the Act and this schedule, there shall be added such other information as may be considered necessary to ensure that required disclosure is not misleading.

IV.   In this schedule, unless there is anything repugnant in the subject or context-

A.   "capital reserve" includes:

    (i)   share premium account;

    (ii)   reserve created under any other law for the time being in force;

    (iii)   reserve arising as a consequences of scheme of arrangement;

    (iv)   profit prior to incorporation; and

    (v)   any other reserve not regarded free for distribution by way of dividend

B.   "executive" means an employee, other than the chief executive and directors, whose basic salary exceeds twelve hundred thousand rupees in a financial year;

C.   "revenue reserve" means reserve that is normally regarded as available for distribution through the profit and loss account, including general reserves and other specific reserves created out of profit and un-appropriated or accumulated profits of previous years;

V.   Any word or expression used herein but not defined in the Act shall have the same meaning as under the International Financial Reporting Standards;

---

[1] Amended vide S.R.O. 1169 (I)/2017 dated November 7th, 2017

VI.   The following shall be disclosed in the financial statements, namely:—

1.   General information about the company comprising the following:

   (i)   Geographical location and address of all business units including Mills/plant;

   (ii)   Particulars of company's immovable fixed assets, including location and area of land;

   (iii)   The capacity of an industrial unit, actual production and the reasons for shortfall;

   (iv)   Number of persons employed as on the date of financial statements and average number of employees during the year [1];

   (v)   Names of associated companies or related parties or undertakings, with whom the company had entered into transactions or had agreements and / or arrangements in place during the financial year, along with the basis of relationship describing common directorship and percentage of shareholding;

Explanation: Definition of related party as per International Financial Reporting Standards shall be considered for the disclosure requirements;

2. In respect of associated companies, subsidiaries, joint ventures or holding companies incorporated outside Pakistan, with whom the company had entered into transactions or had agreements and / or arrangements in place during the financial year, following shall be separately disclosed;

   (i)   Name of undertaking [2] and country of incorporation;

   (ii)   Basis of association; and[3]

   (iii) Aggregate Percentage of shareholding, including shareholding through other companies or entities;

   (iv) [Omitted[4]]

   (v)   [Omitted[5]]

   (vi) [Omitted[6]]

---

[1] Comma and words "separately disclosing factory employees" omitted by SRO 888 (I)/2019 dated 29th July, 2019.

[2] Comma and "registered address" omitted by SRO 888 (I)/2019 dated 29th July, 2019.

[3] The word 'and" added by SRO 888 (I)/2019 dated 29th July, 2019.

[4] Omitted by SRO 888 (I)/2019 dated 29th July, 2019.

[5] Ibid

[6] Ibid

3. General nature of any credit facilities available to the company under any contract, other than trade credit available in the ordinary course of business, and not availed of at the date of the statement of financial position;

4. [Omitted][1]

5. [Omitted][2]

6. In financial statements issued after initial or secondary public offering(s) of securities or issuance of debt instrument(s) implementation of plans as disclosed in the prospectus/offering document with regards to utilization of proceeds raised shall be disclosed till full implementation of such plans;

7. (*Clause deleted*).

8. In cases where company has given loans or advances or has made investments (both short term and long term) in foreign companies or undertakings following disclosures are required to be made:

    (i)   Name of the company or undertaking along with jurisdiction where it is located;

    (ii)   Name and address of beneficial owner of investee company, if any;

    (iii) Amount of loan/investment (both in local and foreign currency);

    (iv) Terms and conditions and period for which loans or advances or investments has been made;

    (v)   Amount of return received;

    (vi) Details of all litigations against the Investee company in the foreign jurisdictions;

    (vii) Any default/breach relating to foreign loan or investment; and

    (viii) Gain or loss in case of disposals of foreign investments.

9.   In cases where company has made export sales following disclosures are required to be made in respect of outstanding trade debts:

    (i)   [Omitted][3]

    (ii)   Name of company or undertaking in case of related party; and[4]

    (iii) Name of defaulting parties, relationship if any, and the default amount; []⁵and

    (iv) [Omitted][1]

---

[1] Omitted by SRO 888 (I)/2019 dated 29th July, 2019.

[2] Ibid.

[3] Ibid.

[4] The word "and" added by SRO 888 (I)/2019 dated 29th July, 2019.

[5] The word "and" omitted by SRO 888 (I)/2019 dated 29th July, 2019.

10.   Shariah compliant companies and the companies listed on Islamic index shall disclose:

(i)   Loans/advances obtained as per Islamic mode;

(ii)   Shariah compliant bank deposits/bank balances;

(iii)   Profit earned from shariah compliant bank deposits/bank balances;

(iv)   Revenue earned from a shariah compliant business segment;

(v)   Gain/loss or dividend earned from shariah compliant investments;

(vi)   Exchange gain earned;

(vii)   Mark up paid on Islamic mode of financing;

(viii)   Relationship with shariah compliant banks; and

(ix)   Profits earned or interest paid on any conventional loan or advance.

PART II

REQUIREMENTS AS TO STATEMENT OF FINANCIAL POSITION

11.   Following items shall be disclosed as separate line items on the face of the statement of financial position;

(i)   Revaluation surplus on property, plant and equipment;

(ii)   Long term deposits and prepayments;

(iii)   Unpaid dividend;

(iv)   Unclaimed dividend; and

(v)   Cash and bank balances.

Fixed Assets

12.   Where any property or asset acquired with the funds of the company and is not held in the name of the company or is not in the possession and control of the company, this fact along with reasons for the property or asset not being in the name of or possession or control of the company shall be stated; and the description and value of the property or asset, the person in whose name and possession or control it is held shall be disclosed;

13.   Land and building shall be distinguished between free-hold and leasehold;

14.   Forced sale value shall be disclosed separately in case of revaluation of Property, Plant and Equipment or investment property.

15.   In the case of sale of fixed assets, if the aggregate book value of assets exceeds [five million rupees, following particulars of each asset,

---

[1] Omitted by SRO 888 (I)/2019 dated 29th July, 2019.

which has book value of five hundred thousand rupees or more][1] shall be disclosed ,—

    (i)   cost or revalued amount, as the case may be;

    (ii)   the book value;

    (iii)   the sale price and the mode of disposal (e.g. by tender or negotiation);

    (iv)   the particulars of the purchaser;

    (v)   gain or loss; and

    (vi)   relationship, if any of purchaser with Company or any of its directors.

Long Term Investments

16.   [Omitted][2]

Long Term Loans And Advances

17.   With regards to loans and advances to directors following shall be disclosed:

    (i)   [Omitted][3]

    (ii)   the purposes for which loans or advances were made; and

    (iii)   reconciliation of the carrying amount at the beginning and end of the period, showing disbursements and repayments;

18.   In case of any loans or advances obtained/provided, at terms other than arm's length basis, reasons thereof shall be disclosed;

19.   In respect of loans and advances to associates and related parties there shall be disclosed,—

    (i)   the name of each associate and related party;

    (ii)   the terms of loans and advances;

    (iii)   the particulars of collateral security held, if any;

    (iv)   the maximum aggregate amount outstanding at any time during the year calculated by reference to month-end balances;

    (v)   provisions for doubtful loans and advances; and

    (vi)   loans and advances written off, if any.

Current Assets

---

[1] Substituted for "five hundred thousand rupees, following particulars of each asset" by SRO 888 (I)/2019 dated 29th July, 2019.

[2] Omitted by SRO 888 (I)/2019 dated 29th July, 2019.

[3] Ibid.

20.   In respect of debts/receivables from associates and related parties there shall be disclosed,—

(i)   the name of each associate and related party;

(ii)   the maximum aggregate amount outstanding at any time during the year calculated by reference to month-end balances;

(iii)   receivables, that are either past due or impaired, along with age analysis distinguishing between trade debts, loans, advances and other receivables;

(iv)   debts written off as irrecoverable, distinguishing between trade debts and other receivables;

(v)   provisions for doubtful or bad debts distinguishing between trade debts, loans, advances and other receivables; and

(vi)   justification for reversal of provisions of doubtful debts, if any;

21.   In respect of loans and advances, other than those to [employees as company's human resource policy or to][1] the suppliers of goods or services, the name of the borrower and terms of repayment if the loan or advance exceeds rupees one million, together with the particulars of collateral security, if any, shall be disclosed separately;

22.   Provision, if any, made for bad or doubtful loans and advances or for diminution in the value of or loss in respect of any asset shall be shown as a deduction from the gross amounts;

Share Capital And Reserves

23.   Capital and Revenue reserves shall be clearly distinguished. Any reserve required to be maintained under the Act shall be separately disclosed. Any legal or other restrictions, on the ability of the company to distribute or otherwise, shall be disclosed for all kind of reserves maintained by the company;

24.   In respect of issued share capital of a company following shall be disclosed separately:

(i)   shares allotted for consideration paid in cash;

(ii)   shares allotted for consideration other than cash, showing separately shares issued against property and others (to be specified);

(iii)   shares allotted as bonus shares; and

(iv)   treasury shares;

---

[1] Added by SRO 888 (I)/2019 dated 29th July, 2019.

24A.   Discount on issue of shares shall be shown separately as a deduction from share capital in the statement of financial position and the statement of changes in equity;

25.   Shareholder agreements for voting rights, board selection, rights of first refusal, and block voting shall be disclosed.

Non-Current Liabilities

26.   Amount due to associated companies and related parties shall be disclosed separately;

Current Liabilities

27.   Following items shall be disclosed as separate line items:

(i)   Payable to provident fund, contributory pension fund or any other contributory retirement fund;

(ii)   Deposits, accrued liabilities and advances;

(iii)   Loans from banking companies and other financial institutions, other than related parties;

(iv)   Loans and advances from related parties including sponsors and directors along with purpose and utilization of amounts; and

(v)   Loans and advances shall be classified as secured and unsecured.

28.   In the case of provident fund, contributory pension fund or any other contributory retirement fund, maintained by the company a statement that, investments in collective investment schemes, listed equity and listed debt securities out of aforementioned funds have been made in accordance with the provisions of section 218 of the Act and the conditions specified thereunder;

29.   In respect of security deposit payable, following shall be disclosed:

(i)   Bifurcation of amount received as security deposits for goods/services to be delivered/provided, into amounts utilizable for company business and others;

(ii)   Amount utilized for the purpose of the business from the security deposit in accordance with requirements of written agreements, in terms of section 217 of the Act; and

(iii)   Amount kept in separate bank account;

Contingencies And Commitments

30.   In describing legal proceedings, under any court, agency or government authority, whether local or foreign, include name of the court, agency or authority in which the proceedings are pending, the date instituted, the principal parties thereto, a description of the factual basis of the proceeding and the relief sought;

PART III

REQUIREMENTS AS TO [STATEMENT OF][1] PROFIT AND LOSS ACCOUNT

31.   Following items shall be disclosed as deduction from turnover as separate line items:

(i) trade discount; and

(ii) sales and other taxes directly attributed to sales.

32.   The aggregate amount of auditors' remuneration, showing separately fees, expenses and other remuneration for services rendered as auditors and for services rendered in any other capacity and stating the nature of such other services. In the case of joint auditors, the aforesaid information shall be shown separately for each of the joint auditors;

33.   In case, donation to a single party exceeds [10 per cent of company's total amount of donation or Rs. 1 million, whichever is higher][2], name of donee(s) shall be disclosed and where any director or his spouse has interest in the donee(s), irrespective of the amount, names of such directors along with their interest shall be disclosed;

34.   [Omitted][3]

35.   Complete particulars of the aggregate amount charged by the company shall be disclosed separately for the directors, chief executive and executives together with the number of such directors and executives such as:

(i)   fees;

(ii)   managerial remuneration;

(iii) commission or bonus, indicating the nature thereof;

(iv)   reimbursable expenses which are in the nature of a perquisite or benefit;

(v)   pension, gratuities, company's contribution to provident, superannuation and other staff funds, compensation for loss of office and in connection with retirement from office;

(vi)   other perquisites and benefits in cash or in kind stating their nature and, where practicable, their approximate money values; and

(vii) amount for any other services rendered.

---

[1] Substituted by SRO 888 (I)/2019 dated 29th July, 2019.

[2] Substituted for words "Rs. 500,000" by SRO 888 (I)/2019 dated 29th July, 2019.

[3] Omitted by SRO 888 (I)/2019 dated 29th July, 2019.

36.   In case of royalties paid to companies/entities/individuals, following shall be disclosed:

(i)   Name and registered address; and

(ii)   Relationship with company or directors, if any.

FIFTH SCHEDULE[1]

(See section 225)

DISCLOSURE REQUIREMENTS AS TO FINANCIAL STATEMENTS OF NON-LISTED COMPANIES AND THEIR SUBSIDIARIES

PART I

GENERAL REQUIREMENTS

I.   The companies other than listed companies and their subsidiaries shall follow the applicable Financial Reporting Framework as defined in Third Schedule, in regards to financial statements as are notified for the purpose in the official Gazette by the Commission, under Section 225 of the Companies Act, 2017;

II.   The disclosure requirements, as provided in this schedule, are in addition to the disclosure requirements prescribed in applicable Financial Reporting Framework and shall be made in the notes to the accounts unless specifically required otherwise;

III.   In addition to the information expressly required to be disclosed under the Act and this schedule, there shall be added such other information as may be necessary to ensure that required disclosure is not misleading;

IV. Any word or expression used herein but not defined in the Act and/or Fourth Schedule shall have the same meaning as under the applicable Accounting Framework.

V.   The following shall be disclosed in the financial statements namely:

1.   General information about the company comprising the following:

    (i)   geographical location of all business units including mills/plant;

    (ii)   the capacity of an industrial unit, actual production and the reasons for shortfall;

    (iii)   number of persons employed as on the date of financial statements and average number of employees during the year []^2; and

    (iv)   Names of associated companies or related parties or undertakings, with whom the company had entered into transactions or had agreements and / or arrangements in place during the financial year, along with the basis of relationship describing common directorship and percentage of shareholding;

---

[1] Amended vide S.R.O. 1169 (I)/2017 dated November 7th, 2017
[2] The words "separately disclosing factory employees" omitted by SRO 888 (I)/2019 dated 29th July, 2019.

Explanation: Definition of related party as per Financial Reporting Framework shall be considered for the disclosure requirements;

2.   In respect of associated companies, subsidiaries, joint ventures or holding companies incorporated outside Pakistan, with whom the company had entered into transactions or had agreements and / or arrangements in place during the financial year, name of undertaking, registered address and country of incorporation shall be disclosed;

3.   [Omitted][1]

4.   (*Clause deleted*)

5.   In cases, where company has given loans or advances or has made investments (both short term and long term) in foreign companies or undertakings, name of the company or undertaking along with jurisdiction where it is located shall be disclosed.

PART II

REQUIREMENTS AS TO STATEMENT OF FINANCIAL POSITION

6.   Following items shall be disclosed as separate line items on the face of the statement of financial position;

   (i)   revaluation surplus on property, plant & equipment;

   (ii)   long term deposits and prepayment;

   (iii) unpaid dividend;

   (iv)   unclaimed dividend; and

   (v)   cash and bank balances.

Fixed Assets

7.   Where any property or asset acquired with the funds of the company, is not held in the name of the company or is not in the possession and control of the company, this fact along with reasons for the property or asset not being in the name of or possession or control of the company shall be stated; and the description and value of the property or asset, the person in whose name and possession or control it is held shall be disclosed;

8.   Land and building shall be distinguished between freehold and leasehold.

9.   Forced sale value shall be disclosed separately in case of revaluation of property, plant and equipment or investment property;

10.   In the case of sale of fixed assets, if the aggregate book value of assets exceeds [five million rupees, following particulars of each asset,

---

[1] Omitted by SRO 888 (I)/2019 dated 29th July, 2019.

which has book value of five hundred thousand rupees or more]^1 shall be disclosed,—

    (i)   cost or revalued amount, as the case may be;

    (ii)   the book value;

    (iii) the sale price and the mode of disposal (e.g. by tender or negotiation);

    (iv) the particulars of the purchaser;

    (v)   gain or loss; and

    (vi) relationship, if any of purchaser with company or any of its directors.

Long Term Investments

11.   [Omitted]^2

Long Term Loans And Advances

12.   With regards to loans and advances to directors, following shall be disclosed:

    (i) the purposes for which loans or advances were made; and

    (ii) reconciliation of the carrying amount at the beginning and end of the period, showing disbursements and repayments;

13.   In case of any loans or advances obtained/provided, at terms other than arm's length basis, reasons thereof shall be disclosed;

14.   In respect of loans, advances to associates there shall be disclosed:

    (i)   the name of each associate and related parties;

    (ii)   the terms of loans and advances;

    (iii) the particulars of collateral security held, if any;

    (iv) the maximum aggregate amount outstanding at any time during the year calculated by reference to month-end balances;

    (v)   provisions for doubtful loans and advances; and

    (vi) loans or advances written off, if any.

Current Assets

15.   In respect of debts/receivables from associates there shall be disclosed:

---

^{1} Inserted for the words "five hundred thousand rupees, following particulars of each asset" by SRO 888 (I)/2019 dated 29th July, 2019.

^{2} Omitted by SRO 888 (I)/2019 dated 29th July, 2019.

(i)   the name of each associate and related party;

(ii)   the maximum aggregate amount outstanding at any time during the year calculated by reference to month-end balances;

(iv)   receivables, that are either past due or impaired, along with age analysis distinguishing between trade debts, loans, advances and other receivables;

(v)   debts written off as irrecoverable distinguishing between trade debts and other receivables;

(vi)   provisions for doubtful or bad debts distinguishing between trade debts, loans, advances and other receivables; and

(vii)   justification for reversal of provisions of doubtful debts, if any;

16.   Provision, if any, made for bad or doubtful loans and advances or for diminution in the value of or loss in respect of any asset shall be shown as a deduction from the gross amounts;

Share Capital And Reserves

17.   Capital and revenue reserves shall be clearly distinguished. Any reserve required to be maintained under the Act shall be separately disclosed. Any legal or other restrictions on the ability of the company to distribute or otherwise apply its reserves shall also be disclosed for all kind of reserves maintained by the company;

18.   In respect of issued share capital of a company following shall be disclosed separately;

(i)   shares allotted for consideration paid in cash;

(ii)   shares allotted for consideration other than cash, showing separately shares issued against property and others (to be specified);

(iii)   shares allotted as bonus shares; and

(iv)   treasury shares;

18A. Discount on issue of shares shall be shown separately as a deduction from share capital in the statement of financial position and the statement of changes in equity (if applicable);

19.   Shareholder agreements for voting rights, board selection, rights of first refusal, and block voting shall be disclosed.

Non-Current Liabilities

20.   Amount due to associated company shall be disclosed separately;

Current Liabilities

21.   Following items shall be disclosed as separate line items;

(i)   payable to provident fund, contributory pension fund or any other contributory retirement fund;

(ii)   deposits, accrued liabilities and advances;

(iii)   loans from banking companies and other financial institutions other than associated company;

(iv)   loans and advances from associated company, sponsors and directors along with purpose and utilization of amounts; and

(v)   loans and advances shall be classified as secured and unsecured.

22.   In the case of provident fund, contributory pension fund or any other contributory retirement fund, maintained by the company a statement that, investments in collective investment schemes, listed equity and listed debt securities out of aforementioned funds have been made in accordance with the provisions of section 218 of the Act and the conditions specified thereunder;

23.   In respect of security deposit payable, following shall be disclosed:

(i)   bifurcation of amount received as security deposits for goods/services to be delivered/provided, into amounts utilizable for company business and others;

(ii)   amount utilized for the purpose of the business from the security deposit in accordance with requirements of written agreements, in terms of section 217 of the Act; and

(iii)   amount kept in separate bank account;

Contingencies And Commitments

24.   In describing legal proceedings, under any court, agency or government authority, whether local or foreign include name of the court, agency or authority in which the proceedings are pending, the date instituted, the principal parties thereto, a description of the factual basis of the proceeding and the relief sought.

PART III

REQUIREMENTS AS TO [STATEMENT OF]¹ PROFIT AND LOSS

25.   Following items shall be disclosed as deduction from turnover as separate line items;

(i)   trade discount; and

---

¹ Inserted by SRO 888 (I)/2019 dated 29ᵗʰ July, 2019.

(ii)   sales and other taxes directly attributable to sales.

26.   The aggregate amount of auditors' remuneration, showing separately fees, expenses and other remuneration for services rendered as auditors and for services rendered in any other capacity and stating the nature of such other services. In the case of joint auditors, the aforesaid information shall be shown separately for each of the joint auditors;

27.   In case, donation to a single party exceeds [10 per cent of company's total amount of donation or Rs. 1 million, whichever is higher], [1]name of donee(s) shall be disclosed and where any director or his spouse has interest in the donee(s) irrespective of the amount, names of such directors along with their interest shall be disclosed;

28.   (*Clause deleted*)

29.   Complete particulars of the aggregate amount charged by the company shall be disclosed separately for the directors, chief executive and executives together with the number of such directors and executives such as:

(i)   fees;

(ii)   managerial remuneration;

(iii)   commission or bonus, indicating the nature thereof;

(iv)   reimbursable expenses which are in the nature of a perquisite or benefit;

(v)   pension, gratuities, company's contribution to provident, superannuation and other staff funds, compensation for loss of office and in connection with retirement from office;

(vi)   other perquisites and benefits stating their nature and, where practicable, their approximate money values; and

(vii)   amount for any other services rendered.

30.   In case of royalties paid to companies/entities/individuals following shall be disclosed:

(i)   Name and registered address; and

(ii)   Relationship with company or directors, if any.

---

[1] Substituted for the words "Rs. 500,000" by SRO 888 (I)/2019 dated 29th July, 2019.

SIXTH SCHEDULE
(See section 258)

OFFENCES PUNISHABLE UNDER SECTION 258
(SERIOUS FRAUD)

1. Offences punishable under section 496.

SEVENTH SCHEDULE
(See section 462 and 469)

TABLE OF FEES TO BE PAID TO THE REGISTRAR AND THE COMMISSION

Item	For submission of documents electronically Rs.	For submission of documents in physical form Rs.
I. By company having a share capital:		
(1) For registration of a company whose nominal share capital does not exceed 100,000 rupees a fee of …..	1,000	2,000
(2) For registration of a company whose nominal share capital does not exceed 100,000 rupees, the additional fee to be determined according to the amount of nominal share capital as follows, namely ____		
(i) For every 100,000 Rs of nominal share capital or part of 100,000 Rs , up to 10,000,000 rupees, a fees of …..	500	1000
(ii) For every 100,000 rupees of nominal share capital or part of 100,000, rupees , after the first 10,000,0000 rupees up to 5,000,000,000 a fees of ……..	400	750
(iii) For every 100,000 rupees of nominal share capital or part of 100,000 rupees after the first 5,000,000,000 Rs up to any amount of fee of …….. Provided that a company which is wholly owned by the Federal Government and has been notified by the Federal Government in the official gazette for exemption from paying fee shall be charged a fee of Rs. 10,000; Provided further that the fee payable at the time of registration of company shall not exceed forty million rupees in case of electronic submission and fifty million rupees in case of physical submission.	150	250

(3) For registration of an increase in the share capital made after the first registration of the company , an amount equal to the difference between the amount which would have been payable on registration of the company by reference to its capital as increased and the amount which would have been payable by reference to its capital immediately before the increase, calculated at the rates given under sub-item (2) : Provided that no such fee shall be applicable on registration of an increase in authorized share capital of a transferee company after merger consequent to sanction of application for compromises, arrangements or reconstruction for merger of companies by the commission pursuant to Section 279 to 282 or section 284 of the Act, to the extent of aggregate of authorized capital of the transferor and transferee companies. ***Explanation***:- For the purpose of calculation of fee for registration of an increase in the share capital of the company which has shifted from physical mode of filing to electronic mode of filing, the difference of fee shall be calculated on the basis of the rates applicable for electronic submission on the amount of capital before and after such increase: Provided further that where a company to be formed has been notified by the Federal Government in the official Gazette to be wholly owned by it, a fee of Rs.10,000/- shall be charged irrespective of amount of share capital.		
(4) For conversion of any existing company not having share capital into a company having a share capital, the same fee as is charged for registration of a new company having share capital.		
(5) For filing, registering or recording any document notifying particulars relating to a mortgage or charge or pledge or other interest created by a company, or any modification therein or satisfaction thereof, a fee of ...	5,000	7,500
(6) For filing, registering or recording the particulars relating to satisfaction of mortgage or charge or pledge beyond the period prescribed under section 109 but not exceeding one year, a fee of ...	10,000	15,000
(7) For filing, registering or recording the particulars relating to satisfaction of mortgage or charge or pledge beyond one year of the period prescribed under section 109, a fee of ...	15,000	22,500

(8) For filing, registering or recording any document other than that at sub-items (5), (6) and (7) above, required to be filed, registered or recorded under the Act or making a record of any fact under the Act, a fee to be determined according to the amount of nominal share capital as follows, namely-		
(i) For Company having a nominal share capital of up to 100,000 rupees, a fee of …..	250	500
(ii) For company having a nominal share capital of more than 100,000 rupees but not more than 1,000,000 rupees, a fee of….	300	600
(iii) For company having a nominal share capital of more than 1,000,000 rupees but not more than 10,000,000 rupees, a fee of….	400	800
(iv) For company having a nominal share capital of more than 10,000,000 rupees but not more than 100,000,000 rupees, a fee of….	500	1000
(v) For company having a nominal share capital of more than 100,000,000 rupees, a fee of….	600	1200
II. By a company limited by guarantee and not having a share capital, other than a company registered under a licence granted under section 42.		
(1) For registration of a new company, a fee of …. (2) For conversion of any existing company having a share capital into company limited by guarantee, the same fees as is charged for registration a new company in terms of sub-item (1). (3) Companies limited by guarantee and having share capital shall be charged registration fee as mentioned at item I above	20,000	30,000
(4) For Filing, registering or recording any document notifying particulars relating to a mortgage or charge or pledge or other interest created by a company, or any modification therein or satisfaction thereof , a fee of	5,000	7,500
(5) For Filing, registering or recording the particulars relating to satisfaction of mortgage or charge or pledge beyond the period prescribed under section 109 but not exceeding one year, a fee of…..	10,000	15,000
(6) For Filing, registering or recording the particulars relating to satisfaction of mortgage or charge or pledge beyond one year of the period prescribed under section 109, a fee of ……	15,000	22,500
(7) For Filing, registering or recording any document other than that at Sr. No. (4), (5) and (6) above,	600	1,200

required to be filed, registered or recorded under the act or making the record of any fact under the Act, a fee of…		
III. By a company registered under a licence granted under section 42 and not having a share capital:-		
(1) For an application seeking grant of licence [¹], a non-refundable processing fee of…	15,000	25,000
(2) Fee registration, a fee of….	25,000	50,000
(3) Companies limited by guarantee and having share capital shall be charged registration fee as mentioned at item I above.		
(4) For Filing, registering or recording any document notifying particulars relating to a mortgage or charge or pledge or other interest created by a company, or any modification therein or satisfaction thereof, a fee of….	5,000	7,500
(5) For Filing, registering or recording the particulars relating to satisfaction of mortgage or charge or pledge beyond the period prescribed under section 109 but not exceeding one year, a fee of…	10,000	15,000
(6) For Filing, registering or recording the particulars relating to satisfaction of mortgage or charge or pledge beyond one year of the period prescribed under section 109, a fee of …	15,000	22,500
(7) For Filing, registering or recording any document other than that at Sr.No. (4) ,(5) and (6) above, required to be filed, registered or recorded under the act or making a record of any fact under the Act, a fee of….	250	500
IV. By accompany established outside Pakistan which has a place of business in Pakistan:-		
(1) For Filing, registering or recording a document containing charter/statute/memorandum and articles for registration by a foreign company under the Act required or authorized to be filed, registered or recorded, a fee of…²	10,000	20,000
(2) For Filing, registering or recording any document notifying particulars relating to a mortgage or charge or pledge or other interest created by a company, or any modification therein or satisfaction thereof, a fee of….	5,000	7,500
(3) For Filing, registering or recording any document notifying particulars relating to satisfaction of mortgage or charge or pledge beyond the period prescribe under section 109 but not exceeding one year, a fee of….	10,000	15,000
(4) For Filing, registering or recording the particulars relating to satisfaction of mortgage or charge or pledge beyond one year of the period prescribed under section 109, a fee of….	15,000	22,500

---

¹ The words "or its renewal" omitted by SRO.812 (I)/2019 dated 11ᵗʰ July 2019.

² Figures 10,000 and 20,000 substituted for 25,000 and 50,000 respectively vide SRO.812 (I)/2019 dated 11ᵗʰ July 2019.

(5) For Filing, registering or recording any document other than that at Sr.No. (2) ,(3) and (4) above, required to be filed, registered or recorded under the act or making a record of any fact under the Act, a fee of….	600	1,200
V. For inspection of documents and register kept by the registrar in respect of a company, a fee of…..	200	500
VI. (1) For a certified copy of the certificate of incorporation or a certificate of commencement of business or a certificate of registration of mortgage or charge or any other certificate or licence issued under the Act, a fee of…..	100	200
(2) For a certified copy of the memorandum and articles of Association of private limited company, a fee of…..	250	500
(3) For a certified copy of the memorandum and articles of Association of other than a private limited company, a fee of…..	500	1,000
(4) For a certified copy of any return excepting financial statements, of a private limited company, a fee of…..	100	200
(5) For a certified copy of any return excepting financial statements, of other than a private limited company a fee of…..	200	300
(6) For a certified copy or extract of any other document, financial statements or register, calculated at the rate, per page or fractional part thereof required to be copied, subject to a minimum fee of one hundred rupees, a fee of….	20	20
Provided that fee prescribed under this item shall not be charged for certified copies of one set of incorporation documents consisting of Certificate of Incorporation, Memorandum and Articles of Association, and the relevant forms, to be issued one time only at the time of registration of company: Provided further that upon registration of any return (i.e. statutory forms) one certified copy of the said return shall be issued along with the acknowledgement of filing without charging any copying fee.		
VII. System generated reports:-		
(1) For providing a system generated list of companies registered with the commission, a fee calculated at the rate per data field, subject to a minimum fee of five hundred rupees, a fee of….	Rs. 2 per data field	Rs. 2 per data field
(2) For a system generated company profile, per company, a fee of…	200	200

VIII. Annual fee payable by an inactive company under section 424 of the Act, payable on 1ˢᵗ January each year after obtaining the status of an inactive company:-			
(1)	not having any capital	1,000	2,000
(2)	having an authorized share capital of –	1,000	2,000
(i)	up to Rs 5.0 million, a fee of.	2,000	4,000
(ii)	more than Rs 5.0, million and up to Rs 10.0 million, a fee of …		
(iii)	more than Rs 10.0 million, a fee of…..	5,000	10,000
IX. [Omitted][1]			
X. For seeking approval, sanction, permission, exemption, direction or confirmation of the commission or the registrar in the following matters , as the case may be , a non-refundable application processing fee in respect of application for-			
(1) Reservation of any proposed name for registration of a company from the registrar under section10, a fee of… Provided that no fee for reservation of proposed name shall be charged in case the same is applied for with three name choices in priority, along with submission of related incorporation of company's documents.		200	500
(2) approval for change of name of a company under section 11 and 12, a fee of….		2,500	5,000
(3) alteration in memorandum of association under section 32, a fee of…		5,000	10,000
(4) conversion of status of company from a public company to a private company under section 46, a fee of		2,500	5,000
(5) conversion of status of company from a public company to a single member company under section 47, a fee of		2,500	5,000
(6) conversion of status from an unlimited company to a limited under section 48, a fee of		2,500	5,000
(7) conversion of status of a company limited by guarantee to a company limited by shares under section 49, a fee of. ….		2,500	5,000

[1] Omitted by SRO.812 (I)/2019 dated 11ᵗʰ July 2019. Omitted item read as "Annual renewal fee for companies incorporated as free zone company under section 454 of the Act"

(8) Issuance of shares at discount under section 83, a fee of...	5,000	10,000
(9) (i) Issuance of further share capital, otherwise than right under section 83, a fee of....[1]	25,000	50,000
(ii) for approval of Employee Stock Option Scheme under section 83,a fee of...[2]	25,000	50,000
(iii) Issuance of shares with different rights and privileges, a fee of...[3] Provided that in case of a financial institution in which the Federal Government owns not less than 90% shares, only a fixed amount of Rs.25,000 in case of application submitted electronically and Rs.50,000 in case of physical submission shall be charged as application processing fee.	25,000	50,000
(10) rectification in the particulars of mortgages or charges or pledge or extension in time for filing the particulars of mortgages or charges or pledge under section 108, a fee of...	5,000	7,500
(11) extension in the prescribed period for holding annual general meeting under section 132, a fee of... (i) by a public company, a fee of.. (ii) by a private company, a fee of...	 10,000 3,000	 15,000 5,000
(12) direction for holding annual general meeting/ Extra Ordinary General Meeting under section 147- (i) by a public company, a fee of.. (ii) by a private company, a fee	 10,000 3,000	 15,000 5,000
(13) fresh election of directors by an unlisted Company under section 162, a fee of...	5,000	10,000
(14) approval of loan to director under section 182, a fee of	5,000	10,000
(15) approval for preparation of accounts of more than one year under section 223, a fee of.....	2,500	5,000
(16) seeking modification under section 225, in respect of requirements of the relevant schedule, a fee of...	2,500	5,000
(17) exemption under section 225 from the applicability of fourth schedule or fifth schedule, a fee of...	2,500	5,000
(18) exemption from the applicability of section 228, a fee of...	2,500	5,000

---

[1] Figures "25,000" substituted for "Rs.25,000 or 0.1% of the proposed further issue of share capital whichever is higher" and "50,000" for "Rs.50,000 or 0.1% of the proposed further issue of share capital whichever is higher" respectively by SRO.812 (I)/2019 dated 11th July 2019.
[2] Ibid
[3] Ibid

(19) appointment of auditor under section 246, a fee of…	2,500	5,000
(20) investigation into the affairs of a company under section 256, a fee of….	10,000	20,000
(21) approval of the commission to refer the matter to the Mediation and Conciliation Panel under section 276, a fee of….	5,000	10,000
(22) sanctioning compromise or arrangement including reconstruction, amalgamation or division under section 279 to 282, a fee of….	50,000	100,000
(23) appointment of administrator under section 291, a fee of….	10,000	20,000
(24) obtaining the status of an inactive company under section 424, a fee of…..	5,000	10,000
(25) for an application by an inactive company for obtaining the status of an active company under section 424, a fee of….	5,000	10,000
(26) restoration of name of a company , struck off by the registrar under section 425…	5,000	10,000
(27) easy exit of a company by striking its name off the register under section 426, a fee of….	5,000	10,000

(28) registration as intermediary under section 455, a fee of…
(i) [1]For Individuals:
      Registration Fee
      Correction/ Update Fee
      Filing Fee
(ii) For Firms/Companies/ Limited Liability Partnerships:
      Registration Fee
      Correction/ Update Fee
      Filing Fee
	
	10,000
	2,000
	500
	
	10,000
	5,000
	500
		
		10,000
		2,000
		500
		
		10,000
		5,000
		500

(29) approval by the commission sought by a real estate company under section 456, a fee of…	25,000	50,000
(30) registration as valuer under section 460, a fee of….	10,000	20,000
(31) licence as transfer agent under section 467, a fee of….	10,000	20,000
(32) issuance of duplicate of any certificate issued under the provisions of the Act or the rules or regulation framed thereunder, a fee of…	1,000	2,000
(33) for an application other than those specified in this item or an appeal submitted to the registrar or the commission under the Act by or on behalf of a company, a fee of….	500	1,000

---

[1] Sub items (i) and (ii) inserted by SRO.812 (I)/2019 dated 11th July 2019.

(34) for an application/appeal /complaint submitted to the registrar or the commission under the Act-		
(i) by a member of the company or any other person having dealing with the company, a fee of...	500	500
(ii) by any creditor of the company, a fee of	500	1,000
(35) for processing under Fast Track Registration Services (FTRS), the FTRS fee shall be in addition to normal fee and charged as given below:		
(i) for incorporation of a company...	Equal to normal fee but subject to maximum of Rs. 10,000	Equal to normal fee but subject to maximum of Rs. 20,000
(ii) for reservation of any proposed name for registration of company...	500	1,000
(iii) for seeking approval of change of name ...	2,500	5,000
(iv) for filing, registering or recording any documents notifying particulars relating to a mortgage or charge or pledge or other interest created by a company, or any modification therein or satisfaction thereof...	5,000	7,500

EIGHTH SCHEDULE
(See section 477)
DIRECT COMPLAINT TO THE COURT BY THE COMMISSION, REGISTRAR, MEMBER OR CREDITOR IN CASE OF CERTAIN OFFENCES

1. Sub-section (5) of section 73.

2. Section 95.

3. Section 177.

4. Sub-section (2) of section 243.

5. Sub-section (4) of section 351.

6. Section 404.

7. Sub-section (5) of section 418.

8. Proviso to sub-section (4) of section 460.

9. Sub-section (2) of section 497.

10. Sub-section (2) of section 499.

S.R.O. 905(1) 2023 dated 07/07/2023

S.R.O. 906 (1) 2023 " ———— "

S.R.O. 1313 (1) 2023 " 09/14/2023

S.R.O 1331/2023 " 09/18/2023

S.R.O. 1356 (1) 2023 " 09/21/2023

Amendments in Approved
by SCEP   09/19/23
               11/28/23

Made in the USA
Monee, IL
17 November 2023

46785396R00238